DIVERSITY, ANTI-RACISM & THE COLLEGE EXPERIENCE

THIRD EDITION

Aaron Thompson

Emeritus, Eastern Kentucky University

Joseph B. Cuseo

Professor Emeritus of Psychology, Marymount California University

Kendall Hunt
publishing company

Book Team

Chairman and Chief Executive Officer: Mark C. Falb
President and Chief Operating Officer: Chad M. Chandlee
Vice President, Higher Education: David L. Tart
Director of Publishing Partnerships: Paul B. Carty
Supervisor and Senior Developmental Editor: Lynnette M. Rogers
Vice President, Operations: Kevin Johnson
Senior Publishing Specialist: Noelle Henneman
Permissions Editor: Caroline Kieler
Cover Designer: Heather Richman

www.kendallhunt.com
Send all inquiries to:
4050 Westmark Drive
Dubuque, IA 52004-1840

Published in the United States of America

Brief Contents

Contents

 Preface

Preview of Content

Chapter 1. What Is Diversity, Equity, and Inclusion?

Defines "diversity," delineates its key forms or dimensions, and explains its relationship to individuality, humanity, equity, and inclusion. The chapter concludes by identifying the meaning and key components of "culture," how they are expressed through cultural diversity, and how they are appreciated when viewed through the lens of multiculturalism.

Chapter 2. Forms and Varieties of Diversity

Explores the spectrum of human diversity, which encompasses a wide variety of group differences, including differences in race, ethnicity, national citizenship, socioeconomic status, sexual orientation, gender identity, and religious affiliation. The chapter examines how these different dimensions of diversity shape an individual's personal identity and life experiences, and how the growing diversity in America and at American colleges campuses represents an unprecedented learning and development opportunity for today's college students.

Chapter 3. The Benefits of Diversity

Defines multicultural education and explains how it is a process that not only promotes acceptance and appreciation of minority groups, but also deepens learning and elevates the critical and creative thinking skills of all students. In addition to documenting the cognitive benefits of diversity, the chapter demonstrates how appreciating diversity serves to reduce societal prejudice, preserve democracy, enhance emotional intelligence and self-awareness, and cultivate intercultural competencies essential for career success in the twenty-first century.

Chapter 4. Barriers to Diversity Appreciation: Implicit Bias, Stereotypes, Prejudice, and Discrimination

Analyzes and synthesizes common forms of personal bias, stereotyping, prejudice, and discrimination. Examines the roots of prejudice—what causes its formation in the first place and what holds it in place once it has been formed. The chapter concludes by examining the underlying causes of bias—a form of critical thinking—an important objective of a college education and a key characteristic of a well-educated person.

Chapter 5. Overcoming Bias, Combating Prejudice, and Developing Cultural Competence

Supplies a systematic, four-step process for increasing awareness of implicit bias and engaging in effective intercultural interaction. The chapter concludes with a set of specific, research-based action strategies for increasing interpersonal contact, friendship formation, and constructive collaboration between members of diverse groups.

Chapter 6. Racism: Current Forms, Historical Roots, and Underlying Causes

Defines and describes the major forms of racism, identifies their historical roots, and examines their underlying psychological causes. It traces the development of racism to the various beliefs and ideologies that led to its initial formation and examines the factors that continue to preserve and perpetuate racism today.

Chapter 7. Understanding Systemic Racism, Part I: Housing, Education, and Employment

Explains how racism takes place on a scale wider than individual prejudice, extending to institutional racism exhibited by the practices of an organization or institution and systemic racism that pervades entire social systems. The chapter focuses on three particular forms of systemic racism: housing, schooling and employment, tracing their historical development and documenting their current impact on people of color.

Chapter 8. Understanding Systemic Racism, Part II: Health Care, Voting Rights, and Criminal Justice

Examines systemic racism in America's health care system, providing evidence of how people of color, compared to whites of equivalent socioeconomic status, receive lower-quality health care. The chapter also examines how America's electoral system has often restricted or denied the right of people of color to vote through the use of voter suppression tactics and policies. The chapter concludes with an analysis of historical and current racial inequities in the criminal justice system with respect to monitoring and arrest, pre-trial detention, conviction and sentencing, incarceration rates, and post-incarceration punishment.

Chapter 9. Engaging in Anti-Racism and Advocating for Social Justice

Describes the difference between being "non-racist"—someone who does not personally profess or practice racism and being "anti-racist"—someone who takes an active role in opposing racism displayed by other individuals and existing societal systems. The chapter identifies specific strategies for countering common racist beliefs with anti-racist arguments supported by sound logic and hard evidence, as well as strategies for taking collective action to change societal systems and political policies that work to preserve or perpetuate racial injustice.

Chapter Sequence

The chapters in this book are arranged in an order that asks and answers the following series of questions:

1. What are diversity, equity, and inclusion, and what are its benefits? (Chapters 1–3)
2. What biases and stereotypes interfere with diversity, equity, and inclusion, and how they can be overcome? (Chapters 4–5)
3. What are the root causes of personal and systemic racism, and what anti-racist strategies can be used to remedy them? (Chapters 6–9)

Content Presentation Style and Rationale

The educational impact of any book depends on both the quality of information it contains (its content) and on how that information is presented (its delivery). The information-delivery process used in this book is infused with effective learning features designed to: (a) stimulate motivation to read, (b) deepen understanding of what is being read, and (c) strengthen retention (memory) for what has been read. These learning features include the following:

Chapter Purpose and Preview

At the start of each chapter, a statement of the chapter's primary purpose and key goals is provided. This feature is designed to provide readers a reason (and motivation to) to read the chapter and supply them with a sense of direction. Educational research consistently shows that when learners see the reason or relevance of what they are expected to learn, it increases their motivation to learn and how much they do learn.

Reflections

Pauses for reflections are infused throughout each chapter to stimulate thinking about what is being read. These reflective pauses help ensure the reader remains mentally active during the reading process and breaks up reading time with thinking, serving to reduce the "attention drift" that typically takes place when the brain engages in the same mental task for a continuous period of time—such as continuous reading. The reflections also deepen understanding of the material by having the reader *write* in response to what's being read. Rather than simply (and passively) highlighting information, writing while reading keeps the reader more actively engaged in the reading process and deepens understanding of the content being read. It is recommended that students record their written reflections in a *reading journal.*

Personal Experiences

Appearing throughout the book are relevant stories drawn from the personal experiences of the authors and others. The stories shared in the chapters serve the dual purpose of "personalizing" the book and promoting learning. Studies show that comprehension and retention of concepts is strengthened when those concepts are illustrated by storytelling. Research also shows that storytelling is an effective way to reduce prejudice because it allows readers to gain insight into, and empathy for, people whose life experiences differ from their own.

Sidebar Quotes

Appearing in the book's side margins are quotes from scholars and famous figures that relate to and reinforce key ideas presented in the chapter. The words of wisdom shared in the sidebar quotes have been selected to serve as both a source of inspiration and a resource for learning.

Internet Resources

Each chapter contains recommended websites where additional information relating to the chapter's major ideas can be found. These current online resources can be used to take a deeper dive into the chapter's content.

Chapter Summary and Highlights

At the end of each chapter, an encapsulated version of the chapter's key content and main ideas is presented. This material could be read after reading the chapter—to help retain its essential points, or read before starting the chapter—to get a sneak preview and overview of what is to come.

Chapter Reflections and Applications

At the very end of each chapter are reflective exercises that call for "real-life" application of the chapter's key concepts. Acquiring knowledge is just the first step to appreciating diversity and combating racism. True wisdom is attained when knowledge acquisition is followed by knowledge *application*—taking knowledge acquired and putting it into practice.

We hope that the ideas contained in this book, and the manner in which they are presented, will help you gain a deeper appreciation of diversity, equity, and inclusion, and equip you with effective strategies for combating both individual and systemic racism.

Sincerely,
Aaron Thompson & Joe Cuseo

Acknowledgments

I would like to thank all of my former teachers and professors who gave me many breaks when I may not have deserved them and for believing in me and protecting me when I did deserve them. I would also like to thank my current and former employers for both giving and denying me opportunities which helped shape the person I am today. Diversity, as I know it, comes from many of these experiences. I also want to thank my forefathers and foremothers who paved the way for me, my children, and my grandchildren Andrew, Dominic, Layla, and Evan Szymkowiak. We live in a global society that is very diverse and our American society is becoming diverse at a pace that demographers are finding difficult to hard to track.

I would also like to thank Paul Carty and the editorial staff at Kendall Hunt who are truly author-centred professionals. Last but not least (only in height), I would like to thank my co-author Joe Cuseo. He knows how to take knowledge to a higher level and collaborate well with his co-author while doing it.

Aaron Thompson

I would like to thank the original members of the San Francisco Giants and the original blues musicians who enabled me to identify with (and advocate for) people of different colors and cultures. Thanks also to my college professors who awakened me to the value of diversity and the history of racism—starting with my first college history professor, Dr. Hughes, who assigned an eye-opening book in my U.S. history course, titled *The Peculiar Institution: Slavery in the Ante-Bellum South.*

I would also like to acknowledge an old childhood friend I grew up with in New York who recently reconnected with me for the first time since 1970. His text messages and e-mails helped remind me that rabid racism is still alive and well in the 21st century. Thank you, George, for motivating and energizing me (albeit unknowingly) to write this revised edition of the book.

Last, but not least (only in humility), thanks to my co-author, Aaron Thompson, for joining forces with me to form an interracial team characterized not only by racial diversity, but vertical diversity as well.

Joe Cuseo

About the Authors

© The Kentucky Council on Postsecondary Education

Aaron Thompson, PhD is the nationally recognized leader in higher education with a focus on policy, student success, and organizational leadership and design. He currently serves as the President of the Council on Postsecondary Education in Kentucky and holds the title of Professor Emeritus in Educational Leadership and Policy Studies at Eastern Kentucky University. He has served in many faculty and higher education administrative capacities, such as Interim President of Kentucky State University, Executive Vice-President and Chief Academic Officer, Vice President of Academic Affairs, Associate VP for University Programs, Associate VP for Enrollment Management, and Executive Director of the Student Success Institute, to mention several. Many of these roles were served at Eastern Kentucky University, where he also held the position of tenured full professor.

His leadership experience spans 29 years across higher education, business, and numerous nonprofit boards. Throughout his career, Thompson has researched, taught, and consulted in areas of diversity, leadership, ethics, teacher education, educational leadership, multicultural families, race and ethnic relations, student success, first-year students, retention, cultural competence, and organizational design.

As a highly sought-after national speaker, Thompson has presented more than 800 workshops, seminars, and invited lectures in areas of race and gender diversity, living an unbiased life, overcoming obstacles to gain success, creating a school environment for academic success, cultural competence, workplace interaction, leadership, organizational goal setting, building relationships, the first-year seminar, and a variety of other topics. He continues to serve as a consultant to educational institutions (elementary, secondary, and postsecondary), corporations, nonprofit organizations, police departments, and other governmental agencies. Dr. Thompson has accumulated many awards for his service, including being inducted into the Kentucky Civil Rights Hall of Fame.

Thompson has more than 30 publications and numerous research and peer-reviewed presentations. He has authored or co-authored the following books: *The Sociological Outlook, Infusing Diversity and Cultural Competence into Teacher Education,* and *Peer to Peer Leadership: Research-Based Strategies for Peer Mentors and Peer Educators.* He also co-authored *Thriving in College and Beyond: Research-Based Strategies for Academic Success, Thriving in the Community College and Beyond: Strategies for Academic Success and Personal Development, Thriving in High School & Beyond: Strategies for Academic Success and Personal Development Diversity and the College Experience, Focus on Success* and *Black Men and Divorce.*

Joe Cuseo is Professor Emeritus of Psychology, Marymount California University. He is a 14-time recipient of the "faculty member of the year award" on his home campus—a student-driven award based on effective teaching and academic advising, a recipient of the "Outstanding First-Year Student Advocate Award" from the National Resource Center for The First-Year Experience and Students in Transition, and a recipient of the "Diamond Honoree Award" from the American College Personnel Association (ACPA) for contributions made to the field of student development and the Student Affairs profession.

Joe has served as an educational advisor to *AVID for Higher Education*—a nonprofit organization whose mission is to promote the college access and success of underserved student populations, and an academic program advisor for *UThrive*—a psychoeducational program designed to integrate positive psychology, mindfulness, and self-compassion into the college curriculum. He has delivered hundreds of campus workshops, conference presentations and keynote addresses across North America, as well as Europe, Asia, Australia, Africa, and the Middle East. Joe has authored numerous articles and books for college students, the most recent of which are: *Infusing Equity & Cultural Competence into Teacher Development, Thriving in College and Beyond: Research-Based Strategies for Academic Success & Personal Development, Peer-to-Peer Leadership: Research-Based Strategies for Peer Mentors & Peer Educators,* and *Humanity, Diversity, & The Liberal Arts: The Foundation of a College Education.*

What Is Diversity, Equity, and Inclusion?

Chapter Purpose and Preview

This chapter defines "diversity," delineates its key forms or dimensions, and explains its relationship to individuality, humanity, equity, and inclusion. Also defined is "culture," how its various components are expressed through cultural diversity and how they are appreciated when viewed through the lens of multiculturalism, equity, and inclusion.

Reflection 1.1

When I hear the word "diversity," the first thought that comes to mind is …

Diversity: Definition and Description

The word *diversity* derives from the Latin *diversus*, meaning "various" or "variety." Thus, *human diversity* represents the various groups that comprise humanity (the human species). The relationship between diversity and humanity may be likened to the relationship between sunlight and the variety of colors that make up the visual spectrum. Similar to how sunlight passing through a prism gets dispersed into a variety of colors that make up the visual spectrum, the human species residing on planet Earth is dispersed into a variety of groups that make up the human spectrum (humanity). This metaphorical relationship between diversity and humanity is illustrated in **Figure 1.1**. As the figure illustrates, human diversity manifests itself in a variety of ways, including variations among human groups in terms of their national origins, cultural backgrounds, physical characteristics, sexual orientations, and sexual identities. Some of these dimensions of diversity are easily detectable, some are very subtle, and others are totally invisible.

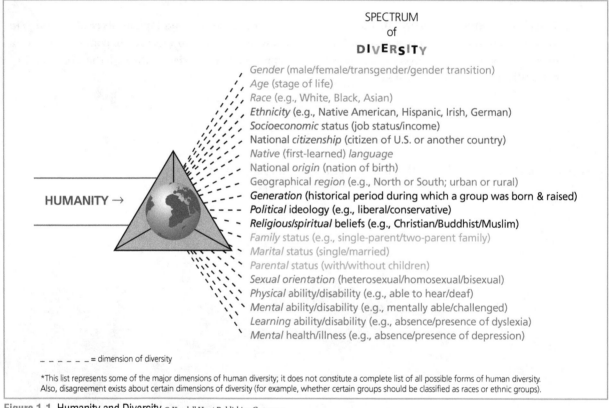

Figure 1.1 Humanity and Diversity © Kendall Hunt Publishing Company

Keep in mind that diversity is a human issue that embraces and benefits all people; it's not a code word for "some" people. Although a major goal of diversity is to promote appreciation and equitable treatment of particular groups of people who have experienced and continue to experience prejudice and discrimination, it is also an *educational* issue—an integral element of a well-rounded college education that strengthens the learning, development, and career preparation of *all* students (Banks, 2016; May, 2012). (Specific details about the multiple benefits of diversity are discussed in Chapter 3.)

Diversity and Culture

Culture refers to the distinctive pattern of customs, beliefs, and values learned by a group of people who share the same social heritage and traditions. In short, it is the whole way in which a group of people have learned to live (Peoples & Bailey, 2008). Cultural anthropologists draw a distinction between *surface* culture—which includes aspects of a culture that are externally visible and easy to detect (e.g., language, fashion, food, art, and music) and *deep* culture— which refer to internally held beliefs, values, and world views (Shaules, 2007) that are less obvious but often more important to understand and appreciate (National Council for the Social Sciences, 1991).

"A comparison of American cultural products, practices, and perspectives to those of another culture will lead to a more profound understanding of what it means to be an American."

—DAVID CONLEY, *COLLEGE KNOWLEDGE: WHAT IT REALLY TAKES FOR STUDENTS TO SUCCEED AND WHAT WE CAN DO TO GET THEM READY*

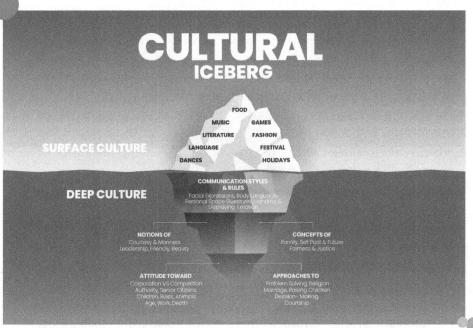

Differences between cultures can be easily detectable ("surface culture") as well as underlying beliefs and values ("deep culture") that require more knowledge and experience to appreciate. © Whale Design/Shutterstock.com

Although the terms "culture" and "society" are often used interchangeably, they are not synonymous. Each term refers to a different aspect of humanity. Society is a group of people organized under the same social system. For example, all members of American society are organized under the same system of government, justice, and education. In contrast, culture is what different groups of people share with respect to their past traditions and current ways of living, regardless of the particular society or social system in which they are living (Nicholas, 1991). Thus, cultural differences may be: (a) *multicultural*—cultural differences within the same nation (domestic diversity) or (b) *cross-cultural*—cultural differences between different nations (international diversity) (Mio et al., 2012).

Box 1.1 summarizes the key components of culture typically shared by members of the same cultural group.

Box 1.1   Key Components of Culture

Language: How members of the culture communicate through written or spoken words, including their particular dialect and distinctive style of nonverbal communication (body language).

Use of Physical Space: How cultural members arrange themselves with respect to social-spatial distance (e.g., how closely they position themselves when having a conversation).

Use of Time: How the culture conceives of, divides up, and uses time (e.g., the speed or pace at which cultural members conduct business).

Aesthetics: How cultural members express and appreciate artistic beauty and creativity (e.g., their style of visual art, culinary art, music, theater, literature, and dance).

Family: The culture's attitudes and habits with respect to family customs (e.g., customary styles of parenting children and caring for elderly parents).

Economics: How the culture meets its members' material needs and the ways in which wealth is acquired and distributed (e.g., its average wealth and the wealth gap between its wealthiest and poorest members).

Gender Roles: The culture's expectations for "appropriate" male and female behavior (e.g., how men and women are expected to dress and whether women are granted the same rights as men).

Politics: How the culture exercises its decision-making power (e.g., democratically or autocratically).

Science and Technology: The culture's attitude toward, and use of, science and technology (e.g., the degree to which the culture is technologically "advanced").

Philosophy: The culture's ideas and viewpoints on wisdom, goodness, truth, and social values (e.g., whether its members place greater value on individualism and competition or collective collaboration).

Spirituality and Religion: The culture's beliefs about the existence of a supreme being and an afterlife (e.g., its members' predominant faith system and views about the supernatural).

Consider This...

Fiorello La Guardia, mayor of New York City from 1933 to 1945 was fluent in English, Italian, and Yiddish. Researchers viewed films of his campaign speeches with the sound turned off and were able to detect which language he was speaking just by observing his nonverbal behavior. For instance, when speaking Italian he used the most body language; when speaking English, he used the least (Adler et al., 2004).

Reflection 1.3

Look back at the components of culture cited in **Box 1.1**. Do you see a component or characteristic of a culture missing from the list that should be added and considered?

Personal Experience

I was once watching a game between two professional basketball teams. A short scuffle broke out between two members of the opposing teams: Pau Gasol—who is from Spain and Chris Paul—who is African American. After the scuffle ended, Gasol tried to show Paul that there were no hard feelings by patting him on the head. Instead of interpreting Gasol's head pat as a peacemaking gesture, Paul took it as a putdown and returned the favor by slapping (rather than patting) Gasol in the head.

This head-patting, head-slapping misunderstanding stemmed from a basic difference in nonverbal communication between two players from two different cultures. Patting someone on the head in European cultures is a friendly gesture; for example, European soccer players often do it to an opposing player to express no ill will after a foul or collision. However, this same nonverbal message had a very different cultural meaning something to Chris Paul—an African American raised in the United States.

—Joe Cuseo

Culture serves the positive purpose of helping bind its members into a supportive, tight-knit community. Although culture helps bind its members, it can also blind them from taking the perspective of other cultures. Because culture shapes thought and perception, people from the same cultural (ethnic) group can become *ethnocentric*—so centered on their own culture that they perceive the world solely through one cultural lens and fail to consider or appreciate other cultural viewpoints (Colombo et al., 2013).

Optical illusions are a good example of how strongly our particular cultural perspective can limit our perspective and create misperceptions. Compare the lengths of the two lines depicted in **Figure 1.2**. Both lines are actually equal in length. (If you don't believe it, take out a ruler and measure them.) If you misperceived the line on the right to be longer than the line on the left, you experienced an optical illusion created by your cultural background. This optical illusion is experienced only by people from Western cultures

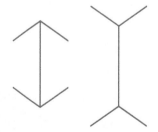

Figure 1.2

© Kendall Hunt Publishing Company

*People whose cultural experiences involve living and working in circular structures are not deceived by the optical illusion in **Figure 1.2**.*
© MattLphotography/Shutterstock.com

(e.g., Americans and Europeans) whose living spaces consist primarily of rectangular-shaped buildings and angled corners. The illusion is not experienced by people living in non-Western cultures whose living spaces are predominantly circular—e.g., huts or igloos (Segall et al., 1966).

This optical illusion is just one of many illusions experienced by people in certain cultures but not others (Shiraev & Levy, 2013). Cross-cultural differences in susceptibility to optical illusions illustrate how strongly our cultural experiences can influence and sometimes misinform our perception of reality. People think they are seeing things objectively (as they actually are), but their viewpoint is actually subjective (as shaped by their particular cultural background).

If our cultural experiences can shape our perception of the physical world, they can certainly shape our perception of the social world. Research reveals that the more familiar something is to them, they are more likely to perceive it positively and judge it favorably. This phenomenon is so prevalent and powerful that social psychologists have come to call it the "familiarity principle"—the more familiar something is, the more favorable or likeable it is perceived to be (Zajonc, 1968, 1970, 2001). One consequence of the familiarity principle is that familiar cultural experiences shared by the same cultural members can bias them to view their culture as better, more "normal," and more acceptable than others. By making an intentional effort to resist this tendency and remain open to the viewpoints of people from other cultures (who view the world from different vantage points than our own), we can uncover our cultural blind spots and expand our range of perception, enabling us to adopt a multicultural perspective that allows us to view other cultures with less ethnocentricity and more cultural sensitivity.

> "To say that a people have no culture is to say that they have no common history which has shaped and taught them . . . and to deny the history of people is to deny their humanity."
>
> —ANDREW BILLINGSLEY, SOCIOLOGIST, AND AUTHOR, *BLACK FAMILIES IN WHITE AMERICA*

A *multicultural* perspective takes the position that: (a) the experiences and contributions of different cultural groups should be recognized and valued, (b) the cultural identities of different groups should be preserved, and (c) no particular cultural group should be seen as superior or be privileged (Takaki, 1993; Taylor, 1994). A multicultural perspective differs sharply from the old "cultural deficit" model that believed minority cultures are deficient and should be replaced by America's mainstream (majority) culture. In contrast to this cultural *deficit* model, multiculturalism is a cultural *difference* model that involves acknowledging and appreciating minority cultures, not eliminating or marginalizing them (Banks, 2016).

Reflection 1.4

What cultural groups in America do you think are most underappreciated or devalued? Why?

However, cultural appreciation should not be confused with cultural *appropriation*, which takes place when the majority or dominant culture goes beyond appreciating a minority or marginalized culture to confiscating aspect of its culture and uses it for its own social or economic advantage (Oluo, 2019). One of the first forms of cultural appropriation in America occurred during the 1840s when whites who called themselves "Nigger Minstrels" wore black (burnt cork) face and sang tunes derived from those sung by black plantation workers, taking the music of black slaves and using it for entertainment purposes. Whites derisively titled one of these songs, "Jump Jim Crow," naming it after a handicapped black stable-hand in Louisville, Kentucky (Oakley, 1976). (The term "Jim Crow" was used later to refer to laws that segregated and discriminate against blacks.) Cultural appropriation of black music occurred again in the 1950s when white rock-and-roll recording artists (e.g., Elvis Presley) "borrowed" heavily from black rhythm-and-blues music, and again in the 1960s, when British bands recorded black blues music (e.g., Rolling Stones and Led Zeppelin). Currently, white vocalists are profiting from recording rap music—a genre originated by blacks living in America's inner cities.

A particularly interesting example of cultural appropriation took place in the late 1970s when a white movie actress (Bo Derek) wore her hair in cornrows with beads in a very popular movie titled "10." The movie's popularity led many white women to get their hair braided in the same way. White media raved about cornrows as the latest beauty craze, referring to the style as "Bo Braids." Yet at about the same time, American Airlines fired a black ticket agent (Renee Rogers) for violating a work appearance code by wearing her hair in cornrows, which had long been a natural style for black women. When Ms. Rogers sued the airlines for discriminating against her cultural heritage, the judge rejected her claim, citing "Bo Braids" as an example of how wearing cornrows was not unique to her cultural heritage and, therefore, could not qualify as cultural discrimination (Byrd & Tharps, 2014).

Diversity and Humanity

Diversity and humanity are interdependent, complementary concepts. *Humanity* is what all humans have in common; diversity represents variation among humans. Thus, understanding human diversity involves understanding both our differences and our similarities, and valuing human diversity involves both appreciating the unique experiences of different social groups while acknowledging that different groups also share universal experiences that are common to all human beings. For instance, members of different ethnic and racial groups may have distinctive cultural or physical characteristics, but members of all ethnic and racial groups live in communities, form intimate relationships, and undergo social experiences that shape their personal identity. Furthermore, all human groups have the same, basic human needs, such as those identified by psychologist Abraham Maslow in his famous hierarchy of human needs—depicted in **Figure 1.3**.

"Diversity is a value that is shown in mutual respect and appreciation of similarities and differences."
—PUBLIC SERVICE ENTERPRISE GROUP

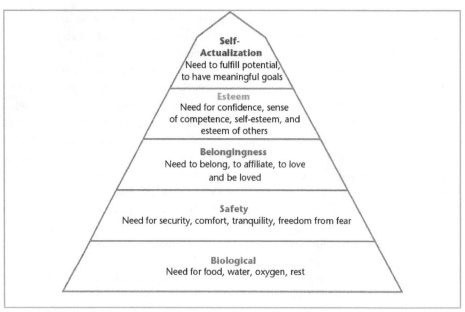

Figure 1.3 Maslow's Hierarchy of Human Needs © Kendall Hunt Publishing Company

Humans of all races and all cultures also experience similar emotions and typically express those emotions through similar facial expressions (see **Figure 1.4**).

Anthropologists have also found that all groups of humans in every corner of the world share the following characteristics: storytelling, dance, music, decorating, adorning the body, socialization of children by elders, moral codes of conduct, supernatural beliefs, and mourning the dead (Pinker, 2000). Different cultural groups may express these experiences in distinctive ways, but they are universal experiences shared by all cultural groups. Cultures may be apart from one another in terms of their particular group customs and traditions, but they are also a part of the same, larger group: humanity. You may have heard the question: "We're all human, aren't we?" The answer is "yes and no." Yes, all humans are the same, but not in the same way.

Reflection 1.5

In addition to the universal characteristics mentioned above, can you think of any other human characteristic or experience shared by all human groups, no matter what their race or culture may be?

© Olhy/Shutterstock.com
© kurhan/Shutterstock.com
© Marcos Mesa Sam Wordley/Shutterstock.com
© Diego Cervo/Shutterstock.com
© WAYHOME studio/Shutterstock.com
© IKO-studio/Shutterstock.com

Answers: The emotions expressed by the top-three faces (left to right): anger, fear, and sadness. The bottom-three faces (left to right) express the following emotions: disgust, happiness, and surprise.

Figure 1.4 Humans all over the world display similar facial expressions when they experience and express certain emotions. See if you can detect the universal emotions being expressed by the following faces of people from very different cultural backgrounds. (Answers appear below the second row of photos.)

A metaphor for making sense of the apparent contradiction of humans beings the same in different ways is to picture humanity as a quilt composed of different patches (representing different cultural groups) woven together by a common thread: their shared humanity. (See nearby picture below.) The quilt metaphor acknowledges the separate identity and beauty of all cultures; at the same time, it illustrates how different cultures interweave to create a larger, unified tapestry. Despite their differences, diverse cultures come together to form a seamless, integrated whole. This metaphor is reflected in the experiences of the earliest English immigrants in the United States who depended heavily on Native Americans for their survival (e.g., Native farming methods and tools) and integrated components of Native American culture with their English culture to begin the formation of American culture (Weatherford, 1991).

The quilt metaphor contrasts sharply with the "melting pot" metaphor, which viewed cultural differences in America as something to be melted away (eliminated) through assimilation (Cubberly, 1909); it also differs from the "salad bowl" metaphor that depicted

"We have become not a melting pot but a beautiful mosaic."

–JIMMY CARTER, 39TH PRESIDENT OF THE UNITED STATES AND WINNER OF THE NOBEL PEACE PRIZE

© steven r. hendricks/Shutterstock.com

America as a hodgepodge or mishmash of cultures thrown together without any common connection (Bourne, 1916; Drachsler, 1920). Instead, the quilt metaphor captures the idea that separate cultures can be preserved and recognized, yet remain unified.

This blending of diversity and unity is captured in the Latin expression *E pluribus unum* ("Out of many, one")—the motto of the United States. When students experience multicultural education grounded in the context of national unity, America's noble motto is put into actual practice (National Council for the Social Sciences, 1991).

Personal Experience

I was a 12-year-old boy, living in the New York metropolitan area, when I returned home after school one Friday. My mother asked me if anything interesting happened in class that day. I told her that the teacher went around the room asking students what they had for dinner the night before. At that moment, my mother stopped what she was doing and nervously asked me: "What did you tell your teacher?" I said: "I told her and the rest of the class that I had pasta last night because my family always eats pasta on Thursdays and Sundays." My mother became very agitated and fired the following question back at me in an annoyed tone: "Why didn't you tell her we had steak or roast beef?" I was surprised and confused because I didn't understand what I had done wrong, or why I should have hidden the fact that we had eaten pasta. Then it dawned on me: My mom wanted me to conceal our Italian heritage so that we would be viewed as being "American."

As I grew older, I understood why my mother felt the way she did. She was raised in America's "melting pot" generation—a time when different American ethnic groups were expected to melt down and melt away their ethnicity. That generation of Americans was more likely to view cultural diversity as something not to be celebrated, but eradicated.

—Joe Cuseo

"Unity without diversity results in cultural repression and hegemony. Diversity without unity leads to ethnic and cultural separatism and the fracturing of the nation-state."

—JAMES BANKS, FOUNDING DIRECTOR FOR THE CENTER OF MULTICULTURAL EDUCATION, UNIVERSITY OF WASHINGTON

 Consider This...

When different human groups are appreciated for both their diversity and their unity, their separate cultural streams converge and merge into a single river that harnesses the multicultural power of humanity.

Diversity and Individuality

"Most variation is within, not between, 'races.' That means two random Koreans may be as genetically different as a Korean and an Italian."

—CALIFORNIA NEWSREEL, *RACE—THE POWER OF AN ILLUSION*

Just as no two snowflakes are exactly alike and no two zebras have the same pattern of stripes, each human being is a unique individual. When viewing the diversity of a social group, it is important to keep in mind that differences among individuals within that group are greater than differences between groups. For instance, individual differences among members of the same racial group in terms of their physical characteristics (e.g., height and weight) and psychological characteristics (e.g., temperament and personality) are greater than any average differences that may between their racial group and other racial groups (Caplan & Caplan, 1994).

Although it is valuable to learn about group differences, the variation among *individuals* within the same group should neither be overlooked nor underestimated. It cannot be assumed that individuals who share the same race or same culture also share similar personal characteristics. This tendency to falsely assume that one member of a group shares the same general characteristics commonly associated with that person's cultural group is referred to by diversity scholars as "essentializing" (Smith, 2015).

As you encounter diversity in college and beyond, keep the following key distinctions in mind:

- **Humanity.** All humans are members of the *same group*—the human species.
- **Diversity.** All humans are members of *different groups* (e.g., cultural groups).
- **Individuality.** All humans are a *unique individuals* who differ from all other members of any group(s) to which they belong.

"I realize that I'm black, but I like to be viewed as a person, and this is everybody's wish."
—MICHAEL JORDAN, HALL OF FAME BASKETBALL PLAYER

"Every human is, at the same time, like all other humans, like some humans, and like no other human."
—CLYDE KLUCKHOLN, RENOWNED AMERICAN ANTHROPOLOGIST

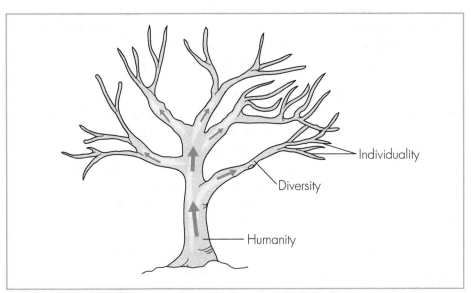

Figure 1.5 The Relationship between Humanity, Diversity, and Individuality

Reflection 1.6

Identify one way in which you are like:

(a) *all* other humans,

(b) *some* humans, and

(c) *no other* human?

What Is Inclusion? Equity?

Inclusion refers to a process in which members of all social groups are recognized and included, ensuring they feel welcomed and that their voices are heard—particularly if they are members of minority groups that have been previously excluded or marginalized as "out groups."

Equity refers to treating all groups *fairly* so they have equal opportunities to compete (e.g., starting a footrace at the same starting line). Equity is not synonymous with *equality*, which means treating everyone the *same*. Treating all groups the same after a race has begun doesn't ensure they are being treated equitably if some groups have begun the race with an unfair advantage, such as starting the race closer to the finish line or being provided with expert coaching that others are denied. For example, treating all racial groups equally today is not equity because minority racial groups have a long history of being treated in an unequal (discriminatory) manner, the consequences of which still affect them today. (See Chapters 7 and 8 for evidence and details.) To achieve equity and a level playing field, these unfairly treated groups now need to be treated unequally by giving them more opportunities to participate fairly with advantaged or privileged groups that have had a head start.

A good example of group inequity exists in America's public schools. Schools are funded by local property taxes, so the higher the value of the residential property where a school is located, the higher are the property taxes available for school funding. Consequently, the amount of financial support local schools receive for educating their children varies drastically from community to community, depending on the wealth of the surrounding area. The wealthier the community that surrounds the school, the more tax dollars are available to the school to educate its students (Orfield & Eaton, 1996). Students living in poorer communities are educated in lower-funded schools that have fewer educational resources and poorer physical facilities. A disproportionate number of students of color are from low-income families and attend racially segregated schools (Arum & Roska, 2011), thus inequalities in school-funding formulas disproportionately impact the quality of education received by students from minority racial and ethnic groups. To achieve equity, students in these schools need to be treated unequally (e.g., their schools need to receive more governmental funding than schools in wealthy communities) so its students have equal opportunity to participate fairly with students whose environmental circumstances have provided them with an unfair (and unearned) advantage.

> "It is obvious that if a man is entered at the starting line in a race three hundred years after another man, the first would have to perform some impossible feat in order to catch up with his fellow runner."
> —MARTIN LUTHER KING, JR. *WHY WE CAN'T WAIT*

> "The route to achieving *equity* will not be accomplished through treating everyone *equally*. It will be achieved by treating everyone justly according to their circumstances."
> —PAULA DRESSEL, PH.D., RACE MATTERS INSTITUTE

EQUALITY   VS   EQUITY

Figure 1.6 *Equality* involves treating people equally regardless of their competitive advantage or privilege. *Equity* involves treating people differently so they can have equal opportunity to compete.
© iam2mai/Shutterstock.com

Besides inequality in school funding, can you think of another inequality experienced by some groups in America that may now require that members of their group be treated differently so they can compete fairly and achieve equity?

Personal Experience

The example I use when I explain the difference between Diversity, Equity, and Inclusion (DEI) is a dance analogy. If you are having a dance, inviting people from all different backgrounds (race, ethnicity, sexual orientation, political ideology, etc.) would focus on diversity. If you invite all the diverse people at the dance to get up "off the wall" and dance (sometimes you will have to take them by the hand), that would be inclusion. Giving them all dance instructions to help them be the best dancers they can be is equity. Not all of them come to the dance of equal dance talent. My co-author Joe and I show our diversity in many ways (race, ethnicity, height) but both of us like to dance. However, Joe needs far more instruction in the "art and science" of dancing than I need.

—Aaron Thompson

Diversity and the College Experience

There are more than 3,000 public and private colleges in the United States. They vary in size (small, mid-sized, large), location (urban, suburban, and rural), and purpose or mission (research universities, comprehensive state universities, liberal arts colleges, and community colleges). This variety makes America's higher education system the most diverse and accessible system in the world (Association of American Colleges & Universities, 2002). The diversity and accessibility of educational opportunities provided by American colleges and universities embodies our nation's commitment to the democratic principle of equal opportunity (American Council on Education, 2008).

America's diverse higher education system is becoming increasingly more diverse with respect to the type of students enrolled. The ethnic and racial diversity of students in American colleges and universities today is rapidly rising. In 1960, students of color made up about 5% of the total college population; by 2016, it had grown to over 45% (Espinosa et al., 2019). National surveys indicate that the vast majority of Americans believe it is important for the country's colleges and universities to have a racially and ethnically diverse study body (Parker, 2019).

The rise in ethnic and racial diversity on American campuses is particularly noteworthy when viewed in light of the historical treatment of educating minority groups in the United States. In the early 19th century, education was not a right, but a privilege available only to those who could afford to attend private schools. Education was something experienced largely by Protestants of European descent. Later, white immigrants from other cultural backgrounds began migrating to America and public education was then made

"Of all the civil rights for which the world has struggled and fought for 5,000 years, the right to learn is undoubtedly the most fundamental."

—W.E.B. DUBOIS, BLACK SOCIOLOGIST, HISTORIAN, AND CIVIL RIGHTS ACTIVIST

The ethnic and racial diversity of students enrolled in American college and universities is on the rise.
© Prostock-studio/Shutterstock.com

mandatory—with the goal that education would "Americanize" these new immigrants (Luhman, 2007). Members of certain minority groups were left out of the educational process altogether or were forced to be educated in racially segregated settings, such as Americans of color who were taught in separate schools with inferior educational facilities.

My mother was a direct descendent of slaves and moved with her parents from the deep south at the age of seventeen. My father lived in an all-black coal mining camp, into which my mother and her family moved in 1938. My father remained illiterate because he was not allowed to attend public schools in eastern Kentucky.

In the early 1960s, I was integrated into the white public schools along with my brother and sister. Physical violence and constant verbal harassment caused many other blacks to quit school at an early age and opt for jobs in the coal mines. But my father remained constant in his advice to me: "It doesn't matter if they call you n_____; don't you ever let them beat you by walking out on your education." He'd say to me, "Son, you will have opportunities that I never had. Many people, white and black alike, will tell you that you are no good and that education can never help you. Don't listen to them because soon they will not be able to keep you from getting an education like they did me. Just remember, when you do get that education, you'll never have to go in those coal mines and have them break your back. You can choose what you want to do, and then you can be a free man."

Being poor, black, and Appalachian did not offer me great odds for success, but constant reminders from my parents that education was the key to my future freedom and happiness enabled me to beat the odds. My parents were not able to provide me with gifts of monetary wealth, but they did provide me with the gifts of self-worth, educational motivation, and aspiration for academic achievement.

—Aaron Thompson

Personal Experience

"The most important thing I got out of college was self-confidence. All my life, I heard subtle and not so subtle messages that I was inferior, and that I couldn't really succeed like a white person could. College taught me I could. Besides, going to college was the key to a good job—a one-way ticket out of the ghetto and the means to give something back to my community. Now I have a real reason to have black pride. I think the most important thing I learned in college was that we must fight for equality not just by demonstrating, but by showing the world that we can."

—AFRICAN AMERICAN COLLEGE GRADUATE

In addition to growing racial and ethnic diversity, American colleges have also grown more diverse with respect to *gender* and *age*. In 1955, only 25% of college students were female; in 2000, the percentage had jumped to almost 66% (Postsecondary Education Opportunity, 2001). From 1990 to 2009, the proportion of women in college increased at a rate that almost tripled that of males (Kim, 2011). The percentage of college students 24 years of age or older has also grown to 44% of the total student body (Chronicle of Higher Education, 2003), up from 28% in 1970 (U.S. Department of Education, 2002). By 2010, more than one-third of American students enrolled in college were over the age of 25 (Center for Postsecondary and Economic Success, 2011).

Adding further to student diversity on college campuses are *international* students. From 1990 to 2000, the number of international students attending American colleges and universities increased by over 140,000 (Institute of International Education, 2001). By the 2010–2011 academic year, a record-high number of nearly 820,000 international students were enrolled on American campuses (Institute of International Education, 2013). Currently, there are more than one million *international* students currently attending colleges and universities in the United States (Watanabe, 2021).

Consider This...

The degree of diversity on college campuses today represents an unprecedented educational opportunity. You may never again be a member of a community that includes so many people from such a rich variety of backgrounds who can expand your mind and broaden your perspective. Seize this opportunity! You're in the right place at the right time to experience a range of human diversity that will enrich the quality of your education, personal development, and career prepration.

Chapter Summary and Highlights

Human diversity refers to the variety of groups that comprise humanity (the human species). This variety manifests itself in multiple ways, including differences among human groups in terms of their national origins, cultural backgrounds, physical characteristics, sexual orientations, and sexual identities. Some these different dimensions of diversity are easily detectable, some are very subtle, and others are totally invisible.

> "One of the most compelling arguments for the importance of diversity has framed it as an educational opportunity for groups from different backgrounds to learn from and with one another."
>
> —DARYL G. SMITH, *DIVERSITY'S PROMISE FOR HIGHER EDUCATION*

Diversity is a human issue that embraces and benefits all people; it is not a code word for "some" people. Although a major goal of diversity is to promote appreciation and equitable treatment of particular groups of people who have experienced and continue to experience prejudice and discrimination, it is also an *educational* issue—an integral element of a well-rounded college education that strengthens the learning, development, and career preparation of *all* students.

Culture refers to the distinctive pattern of beliefs and values learned by a group of people who share the same social heritage and traditions. *Surface* culture refers to those aspects of a culture that are external and easily observable, such as language, fashion, food, art, and music. *Deep* culture refers to internally held beliefs, values, and world views, which are less obvious but often more important to understand and appreciate. Cultural differences may be classified into two major categories: (a) *multicultural*—cultural differences within the same nation (domestic diversity) and (b) *cross-cultural*—cultural differences between different nations (international diversity).

Culture serves the positive purpose of helping bind its members into a supportive, tight-knit community. While culture helps bind its members together, it can also blind them from taking the perspective of other cultures. Since culture shapes thought and perception, people from the same cultural (ethnic) group can become *ethnocentric*—so centered on their own culture that they perceive the world solely through one cultural lens and fail to consider or appreciate other cultural viewpoints.

Multiculturalism is an ideology that believes: (a) the experiences and contributions of different cultural groups should be recognized and valued, (b) the cultural identities of different groups should be preserved, and (c) no particular cultural group should be seen as superior or be unfairly privileged. This ideology differs dramatically from the old "cultural deficit" model that considered minority cultures to be deficient and were to be replaced or displaced by America's mainstream (majority) culture. In contrast to the cultural *deficit* model, multiculturalism is a cultural *difference* model that acknowledges and appreciates minority cultures instead of attempting to eliminate or marginalize them. However, cultural appreciation should not be confused with cultural *appropriation*, which is when the majority or dominant culture goes beyond appreciation of a minority or marginalized culture to confiscation of some aspect its culture and uses for its own social or economic advantage.

Diversity and humanity are interdependent, complementary concepts. *Humanity* is what unites all humans; diversity represents variation on this unifying theme. Thus, understanding human diversity involves understanding our differences *and* our similarities, and appreciating human diversity involves valuing the unique experiences of different cultural groups while, at the same time, acknowledging that different groups also share universal experiences that are common to all humans.

When acknowledging and appreciating diverse social groups, it is important to keep in mind that differences among *individuals* within the same group are greater than differences between groups. For instance, individual differences among members of the same racial group in terms of their physical characteristics (e.g., height and weight) and psychological characteristics (e.g., temperament and personality) are greater than any average differences that may exist between their racial group and other racial groups. Thus, it should not be assumed that individuals who share the same race or same culture also share similar personal characteristics. Making the false assumption that a particular person possesses the general characteristics associated with that person's cultural group is referred to by diversity scholars as "essentializing."

When experiencing diversity in college and beyond, keep the following key distinctions in mind: *humanity*: all humans are members of the *same group*—the human species; *diversity*: all humans are members of *different groups* (e.g., cultural groups); and *individuality*: all humans are *unique individuals* who differ from all other members of any group(s) in which they share membership.

Inclusion refers to a process in which members of all social groups are recognized and included, ensuring they feel welcomed and that their voices are heard, particularly if they are members of minority groups that have been previously excluded or marginalized "out groups."

Equity refers to treating everyone *fairly* so that they have equal opportunities to compete (e.g., starting a footrace at the same starting line). Equity is not synonymous with *equality*—which means treating everyone the *same*. For instance, treating all racial groups equally today will not result in equity because minority racial groups have a long history of being treated in an unequal (discriminatory) manner, the consequences of which still affect them today. To achieve equity and level the playing field, these unfairly treated groups now need to be treated unequally by giving them more opportunities to participate fairly with advantaged or privileged groups that have had a head start.

The ethnic and racial diversity of students in America has been rapidly rising. In 1960, students of color made up about 5% of the total college population; by 2016, it had grown to over 45%. National surveys indicate that the vast majority of Americans believe it is important for the country's colleges and universities to have a racially and ethnically diverse study body.

American colleges have also grown increasingly diverse with respect to *gender* and *age*. More female students and students 24 years of age or older are now enrolled in college. Adding further to student diversity on campuses are the more than one million *international* students currently attending college in the United States. The degree of diversity present on campuses today represents an unprecedented educational opportunity for college students to learn about and from the diverse groups of people that surround them.

Internet Resources

Dimensions of diversity: http://sgba-resource.ca/en/concepts/diversity/describe-the-various-dimensions-of-diversity/

Dimensions of culture: https://www.cleverism.com/understanding-cultures-people-hofstede-dimensions/http://changingminds.org/explanations/culture/hall_culture.htm

Cross-cultural communication: http//guide.culturecrossing.net/about.php

Difference between equity and equality: https://www.thoughtco.com/equity-vs-equality-4767021

Diversity, equity, and inclusion: https://dei.extension.org/

References

Adler, R. B., Rosenfield, L. B., & Proctor, R. G., II. (2004). *Interplay: The process of communication*. Oxford University Press.

American Council on Education. (2008). *Making the case for affirmative action.* http://www.acenet.edu/bookstore/descriptions/making_the_case/works/research.cfm

Arum, R., & Roska, J. (2011). *Academically adrift: Limited learning on college campuses.* University of Chicago Press.

Association of American Colleges & Universities. (2002). *Greater expectations: A new vision for learning as a nation goes to college.* Author.

Banks, J. A. (2016). *Cultural diversity and education: Foundations, curriculum, and teaching* (6th ed.). Routledge.

Bourne, R. S. (1916). Trans-national America. *Atlantic Monthly,* 118, 95.

Byrd, A. D., & Tharps, L. L. (2014). *Hair story: Untangling the roots of black hair in America* (2nd ed.). St. Martin's Press.

Caplan, P. J., & Caplan, J. B. (1994). *Thinking critically about research on sex and gender.* HarperCollins College Publishers.

Center for Postsecondary and Economic Success. (2011). *Yesterday's nontraditional student is today's traditional student.* www.clasp.org/admin/site/.../Nontraditional-Students-Facts-2011.pdf

Chronicle of Higher Education. (2003, August 30). Almanac 2003–4. *The Chronicle of Higher Education, 49*(1). Author.

Colombo, G., Cullen, R., & Lisle, B. (2013). *Rereading America: Cultural contexts for critical thinking and writing* (9th ed.). Bedford Books of St. Martin's Press.

Cubberly, E. P. (1909). *Changing conceptions of education.* Houghton Mifflin.

Drachsler, J. (1920). *Democracy and assimilation.* Macmillan.

Espinosa, L. L., Turk, J. M., Taylor, M., & Chessman, H. M. (2019). *Race and ethnicity in higher education: A status report.* American Council on Education.

Institute of International Education. (2013). *Open doors 2012.* http://www.iie.org/Research-and-Publications/Publications-and-Reports/IIE-Bookstore/Open-Doors-2012

Kim, Y. M. (2011). *Minorities in higher education: Twenty-fourth status report, 2011 supplement.* American Council on Education.

Luhman, R. (2007). *The sociological outlook.* Rowman & Littlefield.

May, S. (2012). Critical multiculturalism and education. In J. A. Banks (Ed.), *Encyclopedia of diversity in education* (vol. 1, pp. 472–478). Sage.

Mio, J. S., Barker, L., & Tumambing, J. (2012). *Multicultural psychology: Understanding our diverse communities.* Oxford.

National Council for the Social Sciences. (1991). *Curriculum guidelines for multicultural education.* Prepared by the NCSS Task Force on Ethnic Studies Curriculum Guidelines. www.socialstudies.org/positions/multicultural

Nicholas, R. W. (1991). Cultures in the curriculum. *Liberal Education, 77*(3), 16–21.

Oakley, G. (1976). *The devil's music: A history of the blues.* Taplinger.

Oluo, I. (2019). *So you want to talk about race.* Seal Press.

Orfield, G., & Eaton, S. E. (1996). *Dismantling desegregation: The quiet reversal of Brown v. Board of Education.* The New Press.

Parker, K. (2019, October 8). *The growing partisan divide in views of higher education.* Pew Research Center. http//www.latinopublicpolicy.org/2019/10/the-growing-partisan-divide-inviews-of-higher-education/

Peoples, J., & Bailey, G. (2008). *Humanity: An introduction to cultural anthropology* (8th ed.). Wadsworth.

Pinker, S. (2000). *The language instinct: The new science of language and mind.* Perennial.

Postsecondary Education Opportunity. (2001). *Enrollment rates for females 18 to 34years, 1950–2000.* Number 113 (November). Center for the Study of Opportunity in Higher Education.

Segall, M. H., Campbell, D. T., & Herskovits, M. J. (1966). *The influence of culture on visual perception.* Bobbs-Merrill.

Shaules, J. (2007). *Deep culture: The hidden challenges of global living.* Multilingual Matters.

Shiraev, E. D., & Levy, D. (2013). *Cross-cultural psychology: Critical thinking and contemporary applications* (5th ed.). Pearson Education.

Smith, D. (2015). *Diversity's promise for higher education: Making it work* (2nd ed.). Johns Hopkins University Press.

Takaki, R. T. (1993). *A different mirror: A history of multicultural America.* Little, Brown.

Taylor, C. (1994). *Multiculturalism and the "politics of recognition."* Princeton University Press.

Watanabe, T. (2021, May 21). Foreign students struggle to return. *Los Angeles Times,* pp. A1 & A9.

Weatherford, J. (1991). *Native roots: How the Indians enriched America.* Crown Publishers.

Zajonc, R. B. (1968). Attitudinal effects of mere exposure. *Journal of Personality and Social Psychology, 9,* Monograph Supplement, No. 2, part 2.

Zajonc, R. B. (1970). Brainwash: Familiarity breeds comfort. *Psychology Today* (February), 32–35, 60–62.

Zajonc, R. B. (2001). Mere exposure: A gateway to the subliminal. *Current Directions in Psychological Science, 10,* 224–228.

Reflections and Applications

Name

_____

Date

_____

1.1 Review the sidebar quotes contained in this chapter and select two that you think are particularly meaningful or inspirational. For each quote you selected, provide an explanation why you chose it.

1.2 Prepare a brief (30-second) elevator pitch that supports the following statement: Diversity is not just a "PC" issue pertaining to certain groups of students; it's an educational issue that enhances the learning experience and future success of *all* students.

1.3 Sudden Realization Scenario

You meet someone sitting at a party; after talking for several hours, you realize that you really like this person and you have a lot in common. The attraction is mutual, so you both exchange phone numbers. As you both leave the party, the other person gets into a motorized wheelchair (that you had not noticed previously) and drives away.

What thoughts and feelings do you think would immediately cross your mind after you discovered this person had a physical disability?

Would you still give the person a call? Why?

Source: University of New Hampshire, Office of Residential Life

20

1.4 Exercise: Gaining Awareness of Your Group Identities

Each of us is likely to be member of multiple groups at the same time and membership in these overlapping groups is likely to have a combined effect on our personal development and identity. In the figure below, consider the shaded center circle to be yourself and the six non-shaded circles to be six different groups of which you are a member. You can use the diversity spectrum on p. 2 to identify different group memberships that apply to you.

Fill in the non-shaded circles with the names of groups to which you belong that have had the most influence on your personal development and identity. Don't feel compelled to fill in all six circles; more important than filling in all the circles is identifying those groups you belong to that have had the most impact on your life.

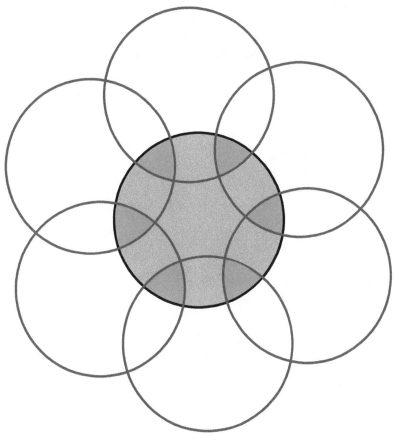

© Kendall Hunt Publishing Company

Self-Assessment Questions:

a)   Which one of your groups has had the *greatest influence* on your development or identity? Why?

b)   Have you ever felt *limited* or *disadvantaged* by being a member of any group(s) to which you belong? Why?

c)   Have you experienced *advantages* or *privileges* as a result of being a member of any group(s) to which you be-long? Why?

1.5 Cultural Differences Interview

Find a student, faculty member, or an administrator on campus whose cultural background differs from yours. Ask if you could interview that person about his or her culture. Use the following questions in your interview, and feel free to add any other questions that you think would be relevant.

a) How is "family" defined in your culture? What are the traditional roles and responsibilities of different family members?

b) What are the traditional gender (male/female) roles in your culture? Are they changing?

c) What is your culture's approach to time? For instance: Is there an emphasis on punctuality? Doing thinks quickly or deliberately? Is higher value placed on taking time to be present and experience the current moment, or forging ahead to accomplish other tasks?

d) What are your culture's staple foods and favorite beverages?

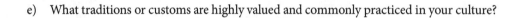

e) What traditions or customs are highly valued and commonly practiced in your culture?

f) What special holidays are celebrated by your culture?

Forms and Varieties of Diversity

Chapter Purpose and Preview

This chapter explores the spectrum of human diversity that encompasses a wide variety of group differences, including differences in race, ethnicity, national citizenship, socioeconomic status, sexual orientation, gender identity, and religious affiliation. The chapter examines how these different dimensions of diversity affect an individual's life experiences and likelihood of experiencing prejudice or discrimination.

Racial Diversity

A *racial group (race)* is a group of people that share distinctive physical traits, most notably, the color of their skin. Variations in skin color that exist among different human groups today are largely due to biological adaptations that took place over thousands of years, beginning when humans first started to migrate to different climatic regions of the world. Currently, the most widely accepted explanation for racial differences in skin color is the "Out of Africa" theory. Genetic studies and fossil evidence indicate that all *Homo sapiens* originally inhabited Africa for about their first 200,000 years of existence; over time, some migrated out of Africa to other parts of the world (Kolbert, 2018; Mendez et al., 2013; Meredith, 2011). Those who continued to live and reproduce in Africa or moved to regions of the world nearer the equator (e.g., Latin and South America) developed darker skin color because their bodies produced greater amounts of melanin—a chemical that provides protection against the harmful effects of ultraviolet radiation, thus enabling these groups to better adapt and survive in their warmer environment (Bridgeman, 2003; Reid & Hetherington, 2010). In contrast, lighter skin tones emerged over time among humans who moved to colder regions of the earth farther from the equator (e.g., Central and Northern Europe). The lighter skin color of these groups contributed to their survival by enabling them to absorb greater amounts of vitamin D from the more limited and less direct sunlight they experienced in their region of the world (Jablonksi & Chaplin, 2002).

Currently, the U.S. Census Bureau (2020) categorizes humans into five racial categories:

- **American Indian and Alaska Native:** people whose lineage may be traced to the original humans inhabiting North and South America (including Central America), and who continue to maintain their tribal affiliation or attachment.
- **Asian:** people whose lineage may be traced to the original humans inhabiting the Far East, Southeast Asia, or the Indian subcontinent, including Cambodia, China, India, Japan, Korea, Malaysia, Pakistan, the Philippine Islands, Thailand, and Vietnam.
- **Black or African American:** people whose lineage may be traced to the original humans inhabiting Africa.
- **Native Hawaiian and Other Pacific Islanders:** people whose lineage may be traced to the original humans inhabiting Hawaii, Guam, Samoa, and other Pacific Islands.
- **White:** people whose lineage may be traced to the original humans inhabiting Europe, the Middle East, or North Africa.

"The story of our current usage of Caucasian is one of myth living on in defiance of science. Using the term Caucasian is no more scientific than, say, calling people of short stature Hobbits—another fictional race with European origins."

—JOE DINERSTEIN, PROFESSOR, TULANE UNIVERSITY

Consider This…

The term "Caucasian" was coined by a German anthropologist who discovered a female human skull in the Caucasus Mountains, a region of Russia. The anthropologist thought that the skull he discovered was "handsome and becoming," and assumed it was associated with a white person. He then concluded (erroneously) that the Caucasus Mountains must be the birthplace of the white race.

Attempting to categorize people into distinct racial groups has always been a difficult process, but it is more difficult today than at any other time in history because of the growing number of interracial families. The number of Americans who identify themselves as being of two or more races is projected to be the fastest-growing racial group category in the United States; by 2050, the number of multiracial Americans is expected to more than triple, growing to 26.7 million (U.S. Census Bureau, 2013).

Personal Experience

As the child of a black man and a white woman, and as someone born in the racial melting pot of Hawaii, with a sister who's half Indonesian but who's usually mistaken for Mexican or Puerto Rican, and a brother-in-law and niece of Chinese descent, with some blood relatives who resemble Margaret Thatcher and others who could pass for Bernie Mac, family get-togethers over Christmas take on the appearance of a UN General Assembly meeting. I've never had the option of restricting my loyalties on the basis of race.

—Barrack Obama, 44th president of the United States

It is important to keep in mind that racial categories are social classifications that humans decided to create or construct; in other words, race is a *socially constructed* concept (Anderson & Fienberg, 2000). "Races" are merely categories that societies have elected to devise, based on how humans differ with respect to certain visible, physical characteristics, particularly the color or shade of their outer layer of skin (Jacobson, 1998). As Kendi (2019) notes, "For roughly two hundred thousand years, before race and racism were constructed in the fifteenth century, humans saw color but did not group the colors into races, nor did they attach negative or positive characteristics to those colors and rank the races to justify racial inequity" (p. 238). Although skin color has been used as the basis for creating social categories (and for treating people differently on the basis of these categories), humans could just as easily have been categorized by eye color (blue, brown, and green), hair color (brown, black, blonde, or red), or body size (tall, short, or mid-sized). Wilkerson (2020) notes that if height had been used to determine race, "The Dutch people of the Netherlands would be the same 'race' as the Nilote people of South Sudan or the Tutsis of Rwanda, as they are all among the tallest in our species . . . . On other end, the Pygmies and Sardinians would be their own separate 'race,' as they have historically been among the shortest humans" (p. 63). Even though "race" is merely an artificial, socially constructed category, it has very real social consequences in terms of their personal identity, and the privileges and prejudices they experience (Bonilla-Silva, 2018).

"Biologically, race is an illusion. Sociologically, it is a pervasive phenomenon."
—JANE FRIED, PROFESSOR, COUNSELING AND STUDENT DEVELOPMENT, CENTRAL CONNECTICUT STATE UNIVERSITY

Personal Experience

My father stood approximately six feet tall and had straight, light brown hair. His skin color was that of a Western European with a very slight suntan. My mother was from Alabama; she was dark in skin color with high cheekbones and had long curly black hair. In fact, if you didn't know that my father was of African American descent, you would not think he was black.

All my life, I've thought of myself as African American, and all people who know me think of me as being African American. I've lived more than half a century with that as my racial identity. Several years ago, I carefully reviewed records of births and deaths in my family history and discovered that I had less than 50% African lineage. Biologically, I can no longer call myself black; socially and emotionally, I still am. Clearly, my "race" has been socially constructed, not biologically determined.

—Aaron Thompson

It is also important to understand that there is no set of genes that distinguish one race from another. In fact, there is much disagreement among scholars about what groups of humans constitute a human "race" or whether distinctive races actually exist (Wheelright, 2005). No blood test or any other type of internal, biological exam can be conducted that will diagnose or determine a person's race. In fact, more than 98 percent of the genes found in all humans are exactly the same, regardless of what their particular racial category may be (Bronfenbrenner, 2005). This large amount of genetic overlap accounts for why humans can be identified and distinguished from members of all other animal species. The tremendous amount of internal genetic overlap among humans also explains why our internal body parts look the same and whatever the color of our outer layer of skin may be, when it's cut, we all bleed in the same color. Although differences between human races in their external appearance are superficial and easily detectable, commonalities across races in their internal biological makeup are less obvious but often more meaningful.

 ## Consider This…

After initially banning African American blood donations, the American Red Cross eventually admitted in 1942 that blood donated by blacks was acceptable for transfusion into white bodies. This change in policy enabled the Red Cross to overcome its blood shortage during World War II and save the lives of wounded white soldiers.

"The results of genome sequences prove my point [that] there are greater genetic differences between individuals of the same 'racial' group than between individuals of different groups. The concept of race has no genetic or scientific basis."

—JOHN CRAIG VENTER, GENETICIST AND LEAD RESEARCHER ON THE HUMAN GENOME PROJECT—AN INTERNATIONAL RESEARCH PROJECT THAT MAPPED THE ENTIRE SET OF HUMAN GENES

"There is no such thing as a set of genes that belongs exclusively to one [racial] group and not another. Race is not a biological category that is politically charged. It is a political category that has been disguised as a biological one."

—DOROTHY ROBERTS, AUTHOR, *FATAL INVENTION: HOW SCIENCE, POLITICS, AND BIG BUSINESS RE-CREATE RACE IN THE TWENTY-FIRST CENTURY*

Modern genetic sequencing techniques allow people to trace their racial ancestry and the results of these traces show that their racial background is more mixed than they realized. For instance, one black man learned that in addition to ancestors from Ghana, he had others from Scandinavia. Another man, who was biracial, was stunned to discover that his ancestors were almost all European (Kolbert, 2018). Genetic sequencing research has also shown that there is considerable genetic variation between members of the human species but this variation exists between different individuals, not between different racial groups. In fact, research has shown that there is often more genetic similarity between members of different racial groups than there is among members within the same racial group. For example, there is more genetic similarity between white Europeans and sub-Saharan Africans than there is between sub-Saharan Africans and Melanesians (inhabitants of islands northeast of Australia) who have similar dark skin, hair texture, and facial features (Templeton, 1998).

In fact, racial categories based on skin color were not even included in the U.S. Census until 1870; before then, American citizens were categorized and counted as either "slave" or "free" (Bowman et al., 2004). English settlers first used the term "white race" to distinguish themselves from Native Americans and African Americans whom they deemed to be "uncivilized" and "savages." At that time, the cotton industry was booming in the United States, creating a need for more land to grow cotton and a larger labor force to cultivate it. To meet these needs, whites devised and disseminated the idea of a politically privileged "white race" to justify their taking land occupied by Native Americans and their using African American slaves as a free source of labor (Berlin, 2004; Fogel, 1989).

The groups that have been categorized as "superior" and as "white" have also changed considerably over time. In the mid- to late-nineteenth century, it was widely believed there were different white races, each of which had had its own personality traits and temperaments. For instance, the Saxons (e.g., English and Germans) were believed to be a superior white race whose members were energetic, intelligent, and beautiful; in contrast, the Celts (Irish) were considered to be an inferior white race whose members were stupid, impulsive, and ugly (Painter, 2015). Eventually, in the early twentieth century, the Irish came to be viewed as also being members of the superior white race of northern Europeans, and the new wave of darker-skinned, white immigrants were coming to America from eastern and southern Europe (e.g., Hungarians, Jews, Greeks and Italians) were viewed as "non-white" by the western and northern European groups that were already settled the United States and had become socially dominant (Martin, 2011). Gradually, eastern and southern European immigrants who came to America did not define themselves as "white" when they were in Europe but began to refer to themselves as "white" as they moved up to higher levels of socioeconomic and political status in the United States (Roediger, in Feagin & Feagin, 2011). Pulitzer Prize-winning author, Isabel Wilkerson describes what happened to European immigrants after they came to America: "Somewhere in the journey, Europeans became something they had never been or needed to be before. They went from being Czech or Hungarian or Polish to white, a political designation that only has meaning when set against something not white. It was in becoming American that they became white" (Wilkerson, 2020, p. 49).

 ## Consider This…

In the 1920s, a Japanese immigrant named Takao Ozawa had been living in the United States for more than two decades and was denied citizenship because Asians were not considered to be white. He challenged this racially discriminatory practice and applied for citizenship, making the case that he should qualify as white because his skin was actually lighter than that of many white people. His case went all the way to the U.S. Supreme court, which ruled that he was not "Caucasian." Ironically, very few white Americans were Caucasian because Caucasians were people whose origin was from the Caucasus Mountains of Russia. Doubling the irony, no Russians living in the Caucasus region, or anywhere else in Russia, could legally immigrate to the United States at that time.

Reflection 2.1

What race(s) do you consider yourself to be? Would you say you identify strongly with your racial identity, or do you rarely think about it? How do you think other students would answer these questions?

Ethnic Diversity

Culture refers to habits, customs, and traditions shared by the same people (e.g., language, food, art); an *ethnic* group is a social group that shares the same cultural characteristics. In contrast to a racial group whose shared characteristics are inherited (e.g., skin color), an ethnic group's shared characteristics have been learned or acquired through shared social experiences. Members of different ethnic groups can be members of the same racial group. For example, white Americans constitute the same racial group but are members of different ethnic groups (e.g., French, German, Irish). Similarly, Asian Americans constitute the same racial group but are members of different ethnic groups (e.g., Japanese, Chinese, Korean). The major ethnic (cultural) groups in the United States include:

- **Native Americans (American Indians)**: Cherokee, Navaho, Hopi, Alaskan natives, Blackfoot, etc.
- **European Americans (Whites)**: Descendents from Western Europe (e.g., United Kingdom, Ireland, Netherlands), Eastern Europe (e.g., Hungary, Romania, Bulgaria), Southern Europe (e.g., Italy, Greece, Portugal), and Northern Europe or Scandinavia (e.g., Denmark, Sweden, Norway)
- **African Americans (Blacks)**: Americans whose cultural roots lie in the continent of Africa (e.g., Ethiopia, Kenya, Nigeria) and the Caribbean Islands (e.g., Bahamas, Cuba, Jamaica)
- **Hispanic Americans (Latino/Latina aka Latinx)**: Americans with cultural roots in Mexico, Puerto Rico, Central America (e.g., El Salvador, Guatemala, Nicaragua), and South America (e.g., Brazil, Columbia, Venezuela)
- **Asian Americans**: Americans who are cultural descendents of East Asia (e.g., Japan, China, Korea), Southeast Asia (e.g., Vietnam, Thailand, Cambodia), and South Asia (e.g., India, Pakistan, Bangladesh)
- **Middle Eastern Americans**: Americans with cultural roots in Iraq, Iran, Israel, etc.

Reflection 2.2

What ethnic group(s) do you belong to or identify with? What do you think are the key cultural values shared by your ethnic group(s)?

European Americans still represent the majority ethnic group in the United States; they account for more than 50% of the American population. Native Americans, African Americans, Hispanic Americans, and Asian Americans are referred to as ethnic *minority groups* because each of these groups represents less than 50% of the U.S. population. However, two of America's most populated states, California and Texas, are called "minority-majority" states because more than half of their population is now composed of people from minority groups; the same is true for Hawaii and New Mexico (U.S. Census Bureau, 2008).

Because the ethnicity of whites cannot be detected by the color of their skin, members of different white ethnic groups have had the option of choosing whether they want to identify with their ethnic group and reveal their ethnic identity to the dominant culture. As a result, ethnic minority groups of European ancestry (e.g., Armenians and Croatians) can more easily "blend into" and assimilate into the majority (dominant) culture because their skin color (white) is similar that of the majority group. In fact, many white immigrants of Eastern and Southern European ancestry attempted to further ease their assimilation into the dominant Anglo-Saxon American culture by changing their last names to appear to be Americans of Western European descent (as illustrated in the personal experience shared below). Also, the daughter of a white Eastern or Southern European could escape prejudice relating to her ethnic origin by marrying a Northern or Western European; the white children she gave birth to could then take on the identity of the more privileged ethnic group of their father (Wilkerson, 2020). In contrast, prejudice aimed at Native Americans, African Americans, Hispanic Americans, and Asian Americans could not be hidden because their distinctive physical features were immediately visible; they could not easily present themselves as members of an already-assimilated and favored majority group (National Council for the Social Sciences, 1991).

Personal Experience

My grandparents changed their last name from the very Italian-sounding "DeVigilio" to the more American-sounding "Vigilis," and my mother had her first name changed from the Italian-sounding Carmella to Mildred. Similarly, my father's first name was changed from Biaggio to Blase and he chose to list his first name (Blase), not his last name (Cuseo), on the sign outside his watch-repair cubicle in New York City because he thought it would conceal his Italian ethnicity and reduce discrimination against him from customers who would bring their business from elsewhere if they were away of his ethnic heritage.

Thus, my parents were able to minimize their risk of appearing "different" and encountering prejudice, while maximizing their chances of being accepted and assimilated into the dominant American culture. If my parents were members of a non-white ethnic group, they would not have been able to "hide" their ethnicity and reduce their risk of encountering prejudice or discrimination. I learned later that some Jewish Americans used the same name-changing strategies as did my parents and grandparents. For example, the parents of my favorite guitarist, Peter Green, changed their last name from Greenbaum to Green to avoid being victims of anti-Semitism.

—Joe Cuseo

Similar to categorizing people into racial groups, classifying people into ethnic groups often reflects subjective, socially constructed interpretations (or misinterpretations). Currently, the U.S. Census Bureau classifies Hispanics as an ethnic group and members of the white race. Listed under "white" on the U.S. Census form are two subcategories: "non-Hispanic" white and "Hispanic" white. From 1980 to 2020, when Hispanics completed national census surveys and saw the racial categories listed on the form, almost one-half of them checked the box "other" (Gómez, 2020). For example, in the 2000 national census, 97 percent of Americans who checked this box were Hispanic, which means that America's second-largest race describes itself as "other." These census survey results suggest that Hispanic Americans do not view themselves as an ethnic group, but as a racial group; in fact, some darker-skinned Latinos call themselves Afro-Dominicans or

"I'm the only person from my 'race' in class."

—HISPANIC STUDENT COMMENTING ON WHY HE FELT UNCOMFORTABLE BEING THE ONLY LATINO IN HIS CLASS ON RACE, ETHNICITY, & GENDER

Afro-Puerto Ricans (Bonilla-Silva, 2018), most likely because they feel their ethnicity is clearly visible to others and influences how others perceive and treat them (Cianciotto, 2005). Their feeling justified, as evidenced by the media's use of the term "racial profiling" to describe Arizona's controversial 2010 law that allowed police to target darker-skinned people who "look" like they may be illegal Hispanic immigrants.

This is another example of how race and ethnicity are subjective, socially constructed concepts that reflect how society arbitrarily decides to perceive and treat certain social groups which, in turn, affects how members of these groups perceive themselves. This subjectivity is reflected in America's history of changing (and self-serving) racial categorization of Mexican Americans—who were once declared by white judges to be members of the white race when it disqualified Mexican Americans from gaining access to benefits reserved for minority groups, yet ruled they were non-white to restrict their access to other rights and privileges that were reserved for whites only (Martinez, 1997).

Reflection 2.3

Prior to reading this chapter, did you think of Hispanics as a racial group or an ethnic (cultural) group?

Native Americans (American Indians)

Members of every ethnic or racial group in the United States are either immigrants themselves or descendants of immigrants, except for one group: Native Americans. There is only one ethnic or racial group who can legitimately call themselves U.S. "natives" and they are Native American Indians. When British colonists came to what is now the United States, Americans Indians became the targets of intense prejudice and discrimination. They were demonized as "uncivilized non-Christian savages" (Salisbury, 1982), were driven off their land, either by force or mass murder, and were also enslaved (Horn, 2018). In the 1850s, California budgeted 1.29 million dollars to wage a military war against Native Americans, which included the paying of bounties for Indian body parts (e.g., 25 cents for a scalp and as much as $5 for an entire head). In 1851, California's first elected governor, Peter Burnett, declared: "A war of extermination will continue to be waged between the two races until the Indian race becomes extinct" (Skelton, 2020). In 1866, when America's first Civil Rights Act was passed, it defined citizens as all persons born in the United States—except Native Americans (Anderson, 2016). Indian children were forcibly educated in American boarding schools, where the expression, "Kill the Indian, save the child" was commonly used to describe the teacher's role, which was to save Native American children from their "inferior" Indian culture (Barker, 1997).

Native Americans now comprise slightly less than 1% of the American population. They come from more than 550 different tribes that differ in terms of income, level of education, geographic locations, and traditional customs. A common misconception about

Native Americans is that they all speak the same language. The reality is that there were approximately 1,000 languages spoken by Native Americans prior to the arrival of Europeans, and the number today remains closer to 250. Nearly one-half of all state names in America originate from Indian languages, such as: Alabama, Alaska, Arizona, Arkansas, Connecticut, Hawaii, Illinois, Iowa, Kentucky, Massachusetts, Michigan, Minnesota, Mississippi, Missouri, Nebraska, New Mexico, North Dakota, Ohio, Oklahoma, South Dakota, Tennessee, Texas, Utah, Wisconsin, and Wyoming (NativeAmericans.com, 2008).

> "Everyone is a house with four rooms: a physical, a mental, an emotional, and a spiritual. Most of us tend to live in one room most of the time but unless we go into every room every day, even if only to keep it aired, we are not complete."
>
> —NATIVE AMERICAN PROVERB

Native Americans have contributed much to the United States we see today. They have a long tradition of respect for and connection with the natural world, which is an important element of today's conception of spirituality (National Wellness Institute, 2005). It could be said that they were the first ecology-minded Americans and the first group to appreciate the connection between humankind and nature. Native American culture reminds us to balance our desire to manipulate and control the physical environment with our responsibility to respect and protect the Earth. The need to strike this balance is strikingly relevant to the current concern about the dangers of human-induced climate change.

American Indian Heritage Month is celebrated annually in November
© Ruslana Iurchenko/Shutterstock.com

Reflection 2.4

When you think about the history of Native Americans in the United States, what thoughts immediately come to mind? As a group, what do you think Native Americans should be most proud of and most concerned about?

 ## Consider This…

Lacrosse—the oldest organized sport in North America—originated in a tribal game played by Native American in eastern parts of the United States and Canada. In 2018, the first Native American women were elected to the U.S. Congress.

Hispanic Americans (Latinos and Latinas or Latinx)

Hispanic Americans are people whose heritage lies in one of the many countries where Spanish is the primary language. *Latin* Americans are technically descendants from Mexico, the Caribbean, Central America, or South America. Because many Hispanics have Latin American origins, they are also referred to generally as *Latinos* (male Hispanics) and *Latinas* (female Hispanics), and more recently as *Latinx*—a term that can be used to refer to any person of Latin American descent. Latinx is a term that began to be used more frequently after a mass shooting took place in 2016 at an Orlando nightclub frequented by younger members of the LGBTQ community. LGBTQ members favor that term because it is more inclusive of people who have a non-binary gender identity than the gendered nouns Latino and Latina (Francis-Fallon, 2000). However, in a national survey of Hispanic Americans, only about one in four had heard of the term Latinx and just 3% of Hispanic adults who had heard of the term prefer to use it (Pew Research Center, 2020a).

Based on a national survey conducted by the U.S. Census Bureau, Hispanics in the United States have the following origins: Mexico (65.5%), Puerto Rico (8.6%), Central America (8.2%), South America (6%), Cuba (3.7%), and other origins (8%). There are now 48 million American citizens of Hispanic origin, including 3.8 million residents of Puerto Rico who were granted American citizenship in 1917. Currently, Hispanics constitute 15% of the U.S. population, making them the largest minority population in the United States; it has been projected that the Hispanic population in America will nearly triple between 2008 and 2050 and will account for one-third of the U.S. population by the middle of the 21st century (U.S. Census Bureau, 2008).

Although many people think that Hispanic presence in the United States is the result of recent immigration, Hispanic heritage in America is centuries old, predating the arrival of European immigrants by many years. Spanish settlements in the part of the United States that we now call the Southwest and the Florida peninsula existed before the Puritans landed at Plymouth Rock in 1620.

Like other minority groups, Hispanics have encountered significant prejudice and discrimination throughout their time in the United States. As important as the *Brown v. Board of Education* ruling was that outlawed racially segregated schools for blacks and whites, an often overlooked earlier development in the historical quest for equal educational opportunity in America took place in 1947 when a California judge ruled in the case of *Mendez v. Westminster* that segregation of Mexican American school children was unconstitutional. The *Mendez* case was critical to the legal arguments used in the *Brown* case and illustrates how the struggles of different minority groups to attain civil rights often intersect and work jointly to promote equal opportunity for Americans of all colors (Blanco, 2010).

Hispanics also have a long history of being targets of hate crimes. **Box 2.1** contains a chronological list of some of the most heinous hate crimes that have been committed against Latinos in the United States.

Box 2.1

History of Anti-Latino Violence in the United States

1849: Expulsion of Mexicans from mines during the California Gold Rush. When gold was first discovered in California, violent mobs of prospectors forced all Spanish speakers off mines and lands they inhabited near rivers where prospectors started panning for gold.

1857: Texas Cart War. White vigilantes close to the town of Collad, Texas attacked Mexican American ox cart drivers, stealing their cargo and murdering about 70 of them in the process. Others were hung from a tree that later came to be called the "Cart War Oak."

1877: A mob in Bakersfield, California abducted five Mexican men suspected of theft before they had a chance to defend themselves and hung them in a mock trial.

1915: The "La Matanza" massacre. In Cameron County, Texas, dozens of Mexicans were killed by Texas Rangers without questioning, based on the unconfirmed assumption that they were bandits.

1931: La Placita Raid. Immigrant agents stormed the La Placita section of Los Angeles, forcing hundreds of Mexicans (some of whom were American citizens) into vans where they were taken to trains for deportation to Mexico.

1943: Zoot Suit Riots. In the summer of 1943, American sailors and other servicemen in Los Angeles targeted young Mexican men dressed in zoot suits (a style of dress popular with Mexican Americans at the time), stripped them of their clothes and beat them.

2008: The Murdering of Marcelo Lucero. In New York, seven teenagers who considered attacking Latinos to be a sport they called "beaner hopping," told friends they were going to attack a Mexican. They came across Marcelo Lucero, an immigrant from Ecuador, cornered him, punched him repeatedly, and stabbed him to death.

2019: A gunman looking to kill Mexicans drove to El Paso, Texas, where he entered a Walmart and gunned down 22 people. Prior to doing so, he posted a comment on social media that he intended to do something about the "Hispanic invasion of Texas."

Sources: "A Long, Bloody History of Anti-Latino Violence in the U.S." (2019); Carrigan and Webb (2013); Martinez Muñoz (2018)

Today, when most Americans think and talk about immigrants, they typically focus on immigrants from Hispanic countries (Valentino et al., 2013), and white Americans are more likely to oppose Hispanic immigrants than immigrants from European nations (Brader et al., 2008). Undocumented Hispanic immigrants, in particular, face intense prejudicial attitudes—such as the belief that unauthorized immigrants of Hispanic descent commit more crimes—when in fact, evidence points to the contrary—their crime rate is actually lower than native-born citizens (Dingemann & Rumbaut, 2010). It is also commonly believed that illegal immigrants rely on free governmental social services and do not contribute to the American economy. In reality, these immigrants pay considerably more in taxes (through payroll withholdings) than they receive in governmental services (López, 2014). It should also be noted that about 3 of every 4 illegal immigrants in the United States are essential workers, many of whom kept the American economy going during the COVID-19 pandemic by working in low-paying service jobs that put them at high risk for infection. Hispanics were eight times more likely to live in a household with an essential worker and had significantly higher COVID-related deaths, including people dying at a younger age (Guerrero, 2012).

Prior to the September 11, 2001 attack on the United States, the Immigration and Naturalization Services (INS) policed the border for illegal immigrants but allowed illegal Mexican immigrants to enter whom the United States needed for labor in the agricultural industry. However, after the September 11th attack, America's immigration policy changed drastically and the INS was replaced by Homeland Security agencies such as ICE (Immigration Customs & Enforcement) whose new more militaristic mission was national security and the deportation of "criminal aliens." Suddenly, migrant agricultural workers who had been coming to America for decades were now viewed as criminal suspects. In 2018, ICE forcibly removed migrant children from their parents at the United States–Mexico border and housed them in cages until the United States courts ordered them to be reunited. Many of these reunited families, however, still remain separated or in detention (Nájera, 2015, 2020).

Ian Hanley López, Professor of Law, argues that America's increasingly intense resistance to Hispanic immigration may have less to do with whether these immigrants are here legally or illegally than it does with their race and ethnicity: "Scapegoating unauthorized immigrants carries a facade of neutrality insofar as it purports to refer to all persons present in the United States without proper authorization. Ostensibly, this would include the German citizen here on a tourist visa who takes a job, or the Canadian who enters as a visitor but decides to live in Aspen indefinitely. Yet these are not the faces that come to mind when the term [illegal immigrant] is bandied about" (López, 2014, p. 123).

 Consider This…

On March 25, 2006 in Los Angeles, approximately 750,000 protesters participated in "La Gran Marcha" (The Great March) to protest a bill that would treat undocumented immigrants as felons and punish any American who provided assistance to them. Two days after the march, more than 125,000 Hispanic middle school and high school students marched to Los Angeles City Hall. Two months after this march came a second, nationwide protest called the "Day Without an Immigrant" (a.k.a. "The Great American Boycott")—a day in which immigrants boycotted schools and businesses to oppose the proposed anti-immigrant bill and to show how important the labor of undocumented immigrants was to the nation's economy.

Reflection 2.5

As a group, what do you think Hispanic Americans should be most proud of and most concerned about?

Hispanic Heritage Month is celebrated annually in September © Monkey Business Images/Shutterstock.com

African Americans (Blacks)

Americans classified as black consist of people whose skin color ranges from ebony to a shade paler than many whites. Only a small percentage of black Americans actually have "black" colored skin; most are some shade of brown (Feagin & Feagin, 2003). In contrast to American immigrants who chose to come to the United States voluntarily, the original African Americans were brought to America against their will, sold as slaves, forced to perform unpaid labor, and denied all civil rights. Under slave law, blacks and their children were considered to be the "property" of slave owners who could break up families at any time by selling one or more family members for purchase (Andrews, 2019).

In 2021, the United States designated June 19th (a.k.a. "Juneteenth") as a national holiday commemorating the emancipation of black Americans on June 19, 1865. © Dmitriy NDM/Shutterstock.com

African Americans were enslaved from America's birth as a nation and continued to be enslaved for almost 100 years thereafter. Once slavery was abolished after the Civil War, blacks were then subjected to another 100 years of formal and informal laws that kept them segregated from whites, denied them the same civil rights as whites, and perpetuated the ideology that they were inferior to whites and should be subordinate to whites (Thompson, 2009). Anti-black prejudice has been the most and intense, extreme, and extensively documented form of racism in American history (Bobo & Huthcings, 1996; Jardina, 2019) and is manifested most prevalently today in the form of systemic racism (Feagin, 2006; Kendi, 2016). For these reasons, anti-black racism and systemic racism are covered comprehensively in Chapters 7–9.

When you see me, do not look at me with disgrace.

Know that I am an African-American birthed by a woman of style and grace.

Be proud To stand by my side.

Hold your head high Like me.

Be proud. To say you know me.

Just as I stand by you, proud to be me.

—POEM WRITTEN BY BRITTANY BEARD, A BLACK FIRST-YEAR COLLEGE STUDENT

In 2008, for the first time in U.S. history, an African American was elected President of the United States. As someone who grew up at a time when discussion of African Americans in history books focused almost exclusively on their role as slaves, this was truly a historic occasion. Being an African American and great grandson of slaves, I didn't think I would ever witness such an event in my lifetime. Although we have a long way to go before dismantling all the systemic barriers that keep us separated in this country, I'm an American who is very proud today to have seen a new chapter added to America's history books. All Americans should be proud that by electing its first black president, our country put its promise of equality into action and moved closer to fulfilling its democratic ideals.

—Aaron Thompson

Reflection 2.6

As a group, what do you think African Americans should be most proud of and most concerned about?

 ## Consider This…

African Americans were the originators of blues music, a musical genre that has influenced virtually every form of contemporary American music. The roots of the blues are grounded in the experiences of black slaves in the Deep South, particularly the Mississippi Delta. Most musicologists trace the origin of the blues to the work experiences of the first black slaves who while toiling in the hot plantation fields, uttered moans, shouts, and hollers to provide themselves with emotional release from the drudgery of slave labor and to communicate with other slaves working many yards away. Thus, the blues is an original American musical genre, distinguished from almost all other forms of music played in the United States that were imported wholesale, or in part, from European countries.

After World War I, when blacks migrated from the rural south to search for better jobs and a better life in the more industrialized northern cities, they brought the blues music with them. By the end of World War II, Chicago had replaced the Mississippi Delta as the home of the blues. The softer, slower, and gentler acoustic blues played in the country gave way to the new, urban blues that black musicians played louder with amplified instruments, and played faster—reflecting the faster tempo of city life. This cranked-up, sped-up style of urban blues influenced the later development of amplified "rock and roll" in the 50s, "acid rock" (psychedelic music) in the 60s, "heavy metal" in the 70s, and "hard rock" in the 80s. Internationally the blues enjoyed great popularity in western European countries, fueling the "British invasion" of bands to America, such as the Beatles and Rolling Stones—a band whose name derives from a blues song recorded by Muddy Waters—a famous blues musician. In fact, when the Beatles came to America, one of the first questions they asked American reporters was if they could see Muddy Waters (to which, American reporters naively replied: "Where's that?").

To think that this music, which now moves people all over the world and has influenced virtually all major forms of contemporary American music, was created by the original African Americans—imported slaves who were socially segregated, economically impoverished, educationally deprived, and functionally illiterate—whose musical skills were entirely self-taught and whose original instruments were entirely self-made—is an astonishing accomplishment. It is also a powerful tribute to their resiliency and creativity. Now permanently etched in America's musical memory and still continuing to influence the development of new musical genres, the blues represents a major artistic contribution of African American people to American culture that should never be overlooked or ever forgotten.

Black History Month is celebrated annually in February.
© Monkey Business Images/Shutterstock.com

Sources: Charter (1975), Jones (1963), Leadbitter (1971), and Palmer (1981).

Asian Americans

Although the U.S. Census Bureau defines Asians as a single "race," Asians come from a wide variety of origins. In addition to Chinese and Japanese Americans, Asian Americans include citizens who have immigrated to the United States from:

- East Asia (e.g., Hong Kong, Mongolia, North Korea, South Korea, and Taiwan),
- Southeast Asia (e.g., Cambodia, Malaysia, Philippines, and Vietnam),
- South Asia (e.g., India, Bangladesh, and Nepal),
- Central Asia (e.g., Afghanistan, Tajikistan, and Sri Lanka), and the
- Pacific Islands (e.g., Polynesia, Micronesia, and Melanesia).

Asians now represent America's fastest-growing racial group (Budiman & Ruiz, 2021); the Asian American population in the United States is expected to increase by 213% between 2000 and 2050—compared to a 49% for America's overall population. By 2050, 8% of the total U.S. population will identify themselves as Asians. Second to Spanish, the next most widely spoken non-English language in the United States is an Asian language—Chinese—which is spoken by 2.5 million Americans (AsianNation.org, 2008).

On the whole, Asian Americans have similar socioeconomic status as whites, but large differences exist among different Asian subgroups. For instance, compared with white Americans, Asian Americans from Cambodia, Laos, Thailand and Hmong (southern China) have significantly higher poverty rates (Wu, 2015) and Asian-American Pacific Islanders have substantially higher unemployment rates (Oluo, 2019). In fact, when all Asian subgroups are counted as part of the Asian American population, the income gap between the top 10% and bottom 10% of Asians is larger than any other racial or ethnic group in the United States (Kochhar & Cilluffo, 2018). The economic disparity among different Asian American groups may be traced to the time when, why they immigrated to the United States, and how they were treated once they arrived here. The first Asian American immigrants came to the United States from low-income backgrounds and were used to perform unskilled labor (e.g., Chinese railroad workers). In 1965, America changed its immigration laws to prioritize admission of highly educated and financially prosperous Asians from China and Japan, thus contributing to the stereotype that all Asians have been educationally and economically successful (Takaki, 2008). In the late 1980s, a new influx of Asian immigrants came to the United States from different South and East Asian countries, many of whom left their homeland to escape poverty and political unrest. These newer immigrants often had little formal education and economic resources, and once arriving here, they took on low-wage jobs (Lee, 2021). Today, these more recent immigrants from South and East Asia comprise more than 25% of America's foreign-born population (Jardina, 2019).

Similar to other minority groups, Asian immigrants have experienced prejudice and discrimination. The first immigration law ever passed in the United States that explicitly prohibited a particular ethnic or national group from entering the country was the Chinese Exclusion Act of 1882, which prohibited immigration of all Chinese laborers for ten years; it was renewed in 1892 for an additional ten years. When Chinese Americans were finally allowed to enter the United States, they were required to carry identification cards and were not permitted to marry whites, own homes, obtain an education, or live in certain geographical areas—which led them to develop their own residential communities known as "Chinatowns." These segregated Asian communities emerged not because of a desire of Asians to segregate themselves from other Americans but because they were excluded from the general population, which forced them to create their own businesses, housing areas, and eateries. Anti-Asian prejudice and discrimination took place again during World War II when the U.S. government interned over 110,000 Japanese Americans in "relocation camps" encircled by barbed wire.

Anti-Asian hate increased dramatically during the COVID-19 pandemic.
© Ringo Chiu/Shutterstock.com

Asian Americans also have been, and continue to be, the victims of hate crimes. In 1982, an Asian American was beaten to death by autoworkers who were angry about economic competition from Japan (AsianNation.org, 2008). In 2019, after the COVID pandemic began in China, racially motivated attacks against all Asian American groups increased dramatically. Between 2020 and 2021 alone, there were over 3,000 anti-Asian hate incidents, including verbal and online harassment, denial of services, and physical assault—for example, one man punched an Asian American woman, then followed her while fake-coughing and shouting, "Chinese b—" (Do, 2021).

Reflection 2.7

As a group, what do you think Asian Americans should be most proud of and most concerned about?

Asian Pacific American Heritage Month is celebrated annually in May. © Monkey Business Images/Shutterstock.com

 Consider This…

Tien Fuh Wu, a former Chinese-American slave, became a key figure in the fight against sex trafficking in the West. She was one of America's first anti-sex-trafficking activists; she campaigned publicly against the practice and advocated personally for sex-trafficked women in court. However, her story, like that of many other Chinese activists, was not covered in American mainstream history and her pioneering work never received national recognition.

Source: Siler (2019).

The Growth of Racial and Ethnic Diversity in America

In 2011, for the first time in history the majority of all children born in the United States were members of racial and ethnic minority groups. Racial and ethnic minorities now account for more than 45 percent of the total American population—an all-time high (Brookings Institution, 2019). By the middle of the 21st century, minority groups are projected to comprise 57% of the American population and more than 60% of American children (U.S. Census Bureau, 2015).

Diversity among America's native-born citizens is accompanied by its rich diversity of immigrants. The United States is home to more immigrants than any other nation in the world; about 1 in 4 people living in America today is foreign born or the child of immigrants ("Immigrants from 1776 Onward," 2019), and over 80% of U.S. immigrants are non-European and non-White (Camorata, 2012).

More diversity exists in America's school system today than at any other time in the nation's history and its diversity will continue to increase. By 2021, students of color are projected to comprise 52% of America's K–12 system (U.S. Department of Education,

2013). The growing diversity in America's K-12 is matched by growing diversity in its colleges and universities. In 1960, whites made up almost 95% of the total college population; in 2010, that percentage had decreased to 61.5%. Between 1976 and 2010, the percentage of ethnic minority students in higher education increased from 17% to 40% (National Center for Education Statistics, 2011). Today, a major goal of virtually all American colleges and universities is to ensure that students from diverse backgrounds have the opportunity to enter higher education, benefit from the college experience, and enrich the learning experience of their college classmates.

Socioeconomic Diversity

Diversity also exists among groups in terms of *socioeconomic status (SES)*—measured by the group's level of education, amount of income, and the occupational prestige of jobs they hold (American Psychological Association, 2019). Human societies are typically stratified into three different socioeconomic classes: upper, middle, and lower. With higher socioeconomic status comes greater privileges (Feagin & Feagin, 2011). *Privilege* may be defined as an advantage acquired without being earned, such as inheriting money or being admitted to a college because a family member was a previous graduate or has donated money to the college (Minnich, 2005). Higher SES families are privileged with two major forms of capital: (a) *economic* capital—*what* they have (e.g., homes, health benefits, and discretionary income for travel and other enriching experiences for their children), and (b) *social* capital—*who* they know (e.g., contacts with employers and access to people in powerful legal, political, and educational positions) (DiAngelo, 2018). Children born into higher-income families acquire these privileges without having earned them and benefit from them throughout their life. For instance, children with parents of higher socioeconomic status have greater social capital for getting into college (e.g., personal connections with private counselors and admissions officers) and greater economical capital to help them complete college (e.g., financial resources to pay for college tuition and participate in educatioally enriching college programs, such as study-abroad). As a result, children born into wealthier families are much more likely to attend and complete college than children from low-income families. This gap in college-completion rate between students from low- and high-come families is widening. Over a 3-year period starting in the 1970s, the percentage of children from families in the top 20% of income that earned a college degree grew from 41% to 81%; during the same time period, the percentage of children from families in the lowest 20% of income that earned a college degree only increased from 6% to 8% (Edsall, 2012).

Sharp socioeconomic differences exist across different racial and ethnic groups in America. For example, in 2018, the median household income for non-Hispanic white households was $70,642 compared with $51,450 for Hispanics and $41,361 for African Americans (Peter G. Peterson Foundation, 2019). The great housing and mortgage collapse after the turn of the 21st century had its most damaging impact on lower-income, ethnic minorities. Household wealth fell by 66% for Hispanics and 53% for Blacks compared to 16% for Whites (Kochhar et al., 2011). The 2019 COVID pandemic has also had more negative financial impact on low-income Americans of color than white Americans ("COVID's Financial Effects Varied," 2021).

The Widening Income Gap between the Rich and the Poor

The percentage of rich Americans (e.g., number of billionaires) is higher than any other democratic nation and the economic status of the poor Americans is lower than other major democratic countries (Diamond, 2019); this gap between America's rich and poor has been steadily widening (Stiglitz, 2012). In the 1970s, chief executives of major U.S. corporations earned about 40 times more than what the average worker made; by 2013, executives at the top 500 Americans earned an average income 354 times higher than the average worker, meaning that the typical executive earns in one day what the typical worker makes in a full year (López, 2014). The 400 wealthiest Americans now possess more wealth than the bottom 150 million; this represents the largest income-inequality gap in America since the 1920s (Bruenig, 2019). Today, the wealthiest 1% of U.S. Americans now hold about 40% of all our nation's wealth; the bottom 90% hold less than 25 percent. About one-quarter of American families have a total wealth of less than $10,000 wealth, putting them at a poverty level (Washington Center for Equitable Growth, 2019). The 2019 COVID pandemic further widened the income-inequality gap, so much so that nearly 40% of Americans reported that they would be unable to cover a $400 with cash, savings, or credit (Board of Governors of the Federal Reserve System, 2019).

Research shows that the higher the income inequality there is in a country, the lower is its citizens' feelings of well-being (Hagerty, 2000) and happiness (Hallowell et al., 2016). In contrast, citizens of nations with more equitable distribution of wealth and services have higher levels of health and happiness, higher levels of academic achievement, lower crime rates, and fewer teenage births (Wilkinson & Pickett, 2009).

Compared with other major democracies in the world, America is less likely to adopt policies that distribute money equitably across richer and poorer people (e.g., income tax policies). Jared Diamond, professor of geography and winner of the National Medal of Science, attributes America's much lower rate of income "redistribution" and higher rate of income inequality to two factors: (a) political campaign financing practices and restrictive voting policies that give disproportionate political power to the wealthy and make it more difficult for poor people to vote and elect politicians who would adopt policies that decrease income inequities; and (b) a belief more widely held in the United States than other countries that poor people are to blame for their economic condition because they are not working hard enough and providing them with governmental support is unfair to those who do work hard (Diamond, 2019).

Declining Socioeconomic Mobility

Socioeconomic mobility refers to the ability of people to move up the socioeconomic ladder (e.g., from poverty to the middle class). Since 1980, rates of intergenerational socioeconomic mobility in America have steadily declined. In 2019, the percentage of working adults earning as much or more than their parents was at its lowest point since 1940. The United States is now one of the hardest industrialized nations for children born into poverty to escape poverty by the time they reach adulthood (Corak, 2010). In America, a child born to parents in the lowest income quintile (bottom 20%) is more than ten times likely to end up in the lowest quintile than the highest quintile when they become an adult (Mitnik & Gruskey, 2015).

People of all racial and ethnic groups experience poverty; however, members of racial and ethnic minority groups experience it at a significantly higher rate. In 2018, poverty rates for different ethnic and racial groups were as follows: Whites (10.1%), Asians (10.1%), Hispanics (17.6%), Blacks (20.8%), and Native Americans (25.4%) (U.S. Department of Education, 2013). The fact that people of color are also more likely to be poorer illustrates the concept of *intersectionality*—membership in two or more disadvantaged social groups (e.g., race and socioeconomic status) often intersect to exert a combined effect that further disadvantages people who hold joint membership in the intersecting groups (Cho et al., 2013; Crenshaw, 1991).

Personal Experience

When I was a four-year-old boy living in the mountains of Kentucky, it was safe for a young lad to walk the roads and railroad tracks alone. Knowing this, my mother was comfortable sending me on long walks to the general store to buy a variety of small items we needed for our household. Since we had very little money, she made sure that whatever money we had would be spent on just the most basic necessities. I could only buy items from the general store that my mother strictly ordered me to purchase. In the early 1960s, most of these items cost less than a dollar and many times you could buy multiple items for a dollar. At the store's checkout counter, there were jars with different kinds of candy or gum. Since you could buy two pieces of candy for one cent, I didn't think there would be any harm in rewarding myself for the long walk to the grocery store with just two pieces of candy. I could even devour the evidence of my disobedience on my slow walk home.

When I returned from the store, my mother—the protector of the vault and the sergeant-of-arms in our household—would carefully check each item I bought to make sure I had been charged correctly. She never failed to notice if the total was off by a single cent. After discovering that I had spent an extra cent on something unessential, she scolded me and said in no uncertain terms: "Boy, you better learn how to count your money if you're ever going to be successful in life!"

Growing up in poverty wasn't fun, but we managed. What we ate had to be reasonable in price and bought in bulk. Every morning, my mother fixed rice or oatmeal for breakfast along with wonderful buttermilk biscuits. At night, she fixed pinto beans and cornbread for dinner. We also had fresh vegetables from the garden and apples, hickory nuts, and walnuts from surrounding trees. Meat was not readily available and was only eaten when we killed a chicken or hog we had raised.

—Aaron Thompson

One of America's deepest-held ideals is that all people are created equal and that the pursuit and achievement of socioeconomic prosperity can be achieved through individual initiative and personal merit, not by birthright or family heritage. To believe in the "*American Dream*" is to believe that all Americans, regardless of where they were born or what class they were born into, have the same opportunity to attain success in a country where anyone can change their circumstances and improve their quality of life through individual effort. According to Ginsberg and Wlodkowski (2009), the American Dream is "rooted in cultural mythology that overlooks the social, political, and economic forces that favor certain groups over others [and] has at least as much to do with privilege as to personal desire and effort" (p. 14). Horatio Alger's "rags to riches" stories written in the mid-1800s about how impoverished American young boys rose from poverty to achieve middle-class lifestyles were influential, but also fictional (Nackenoff, 1997). The reality is that the United States has lower socioeconomic mobility rates than most other industrial nations (e.g., Canada, Germany, France, Australia, and Japan), which makes it difficult for Americans to move from lower socioeconomic ranks to the middle class (Goldberg, 2021; Rothstein, 2017). For instance, 42% of American boys whose fathers were in the poorest 20% of their generation end up in the poorest 20% of their own generation; by contrast, in Scandinavian countries, only about 25% of these boys end up that way (Diamond, 2019). The reality is that not all Americans start the race to success at the same starting line; some start with social and economic resources that position them much closer to the finish line than others. Said in another way, some are born with a socioeconomic silver spoon in their mouth; others are born with a plastic spoon, and some are born no spoon at all.

"Being born in the elite in the U.S. gives you a constellation of privileges that very few people in the world have ever experienced. Being born poor in the U.S. gives you disadvantages unlike anything in Western Europe, Japan, and Canada."

—DAVID I. LEVINE, ECONOMIST AND SOCIAL MOBILITY RESEARCHER

Gender Diversity: Women

Although women are not a minority group in terms of their percentage in the overall population, they have faced significant discrimination throughout history. To combat it, the Women's Civil Rights Movement was formed in 1848 when a young housewife and mother from New York, Elizabeth Cady Stanton, and her female colleagues organized a convention in Seneca Falls, New York. In advance of the convention, Stanton used the Declaration of Independence as a guide to draft her own "Declaration of Sentiments" (Stanton et al., 1889). She tied the women's rights movement directly to the rights of citizens outlined by the nation's founding fathers. Her Declaration of Sentiments included the following injustices:

- Women could not vote.
- Women had to follow laws they had no part in drafting.
- Married women had no property rights.
- Women had to pay property taxes even though they had no representation in levying those taxes.
- Divorce and child custody laws gave no rights to women.
- Women could not be admitted to any college or university to further their education.
- Many professional occupations were completely closed to working women (e.g., the medical and legal professions) and when women were allowed to work, their compensation was only a fraction of what men earned.
- With only few exceptions, women were not permitted to participate in the affairs of the church.
- Husbands had legal power over their wives to the point of being able to imprison or beat them without punishment.
- Women were deprived of self-confidence and self-respect, making them totally dependent on men.

"Rosie the Riveter"—iconic symbol of how women took on and successfully performed men's jobs when men served in the military during World War II. © TinaImages/Shutterstock.com

The initial civil rights convention in 1848 proved to be a success, leading to additional women's conventions held regularly between 1850 and the start of the Civil War. Prominent women in the movement traveled across the country to speak on behalf of equal rights for the next forty years. The movement encountered intense political opposition; it took more than 70 years before the movement was able to secure women's right to vote in 1920 (National Women's History Project, 1998).

However, in the long run, the women's rights movement led to the more expanded opportunities women have today. More women now have the opportunity to work and earn an income than at any other time in American history. The ability of women to enter the workforce has enabled today's middle-class families to have two breadwinners, allowing these families to keep up with inflation and maintain a middle-class lifestyle (Warren & Tyagi, 2003). This is not the first time that women have stepped up to fill a breadwinner's role. During World War II, so many American men were drafted for military duty that women had to fill their vacated jobs, including jobs that involved working in steel mills, ammunition production, and airplane construction. Women became their household's primary breadwinner in many families during the war; they embraced the opportunity to work, demonstrating to themselves and others that they could perform work that went beyond traditional "womanly" duties. However, after the war ended, the U.S. government launched a propaganda campaign urging women to "return to normalcy" and resume their traditional, more limited household roles (Honey, 1984).

Consider This…

At one point in history, all college students were men. In fact, the term "freshman" literally meant "fresh man" because every new college student was, indeed, a man; no females were enrolled in (or could enroll in) college. Even as late as 1955, only 25% of American college students were female. By 2000, that percentage had jumped to almost 66% (Postsecondary Education Opportunity, 2001). Between 1990 and 2009, the proportion of women enrolling in college increased at a rate almost three times faster than that of men (Kim, 2011). Women now earn the majority of bachelor's, master's, and doctoral degrees granted in the United States (National Center for Education Statistics, 2011). Women also hold almost 40% of all management positions in American organizations (Torpey, 2017).

Although women are now working in jobs that were once exclusively reserved for men, they still experience inequities with respect to the wages they earn for the work they do. In 1963, women earned 59 cents for every dollar earned by men, which prompted President John F. Kennedy to sign the Equal Pay Act into law, making it illegal for employers to pay unequal wages to men and women who performed the same jobs. Despite the passage of this Act, a gender wage gap still exists—as evidenced by data gathered by the U.S. Census Bureau in 2019—which showed that women working full-time and year-round earned 81.6 cents for every dollar earned by men (National Committee on Pay Equity, 2021). Wage gaps exist even if women are working in the positions as men and have attained the same level of education (AAUW, 2013). Gender and race also intersect to create further discrimination. For example, black women with some college education are paid less than white women with only a high school degree (Kendi, 2019).

Gender gaps continue to exist with respect to male–female employment in certain careers. For instance, women make up less 25% of the labor force in the fields of science, technology, engineering, and mathematics (STEM), which include some of the highest paid professions (U.S. Department of Commerce, Economics & Statistics Administration, 2011; AAUW, 2015).

Reflection 2.9

Are females likely to be represented in equal numbers as males in the career field(s) you are considering? Why do you think this is so?

On the positive side of the ledger, women have made significant strides in leadership positions. In 2020, America elected its first female vice president and more women were represented in United States Congress in 2018 than at any other time in American history. Nonetheless, women constitute more than half of the American population yet hold less

"Women take care and men take charge."

—LONG-HELD GENDER STEREOTYPE THAT HAS HINDERED WOMEN'S ASCENT TO LEADERSHIP POSITIONS

Women have overcome gender barriers to take on leadership positions © ESB Professional/Shutterstock.com

than one-quarter of seats in Congress, and no woman has ever served as President of the United States; in contrast, about 60 other countries have elected a woman as their nation's leader. In the field of business, women make or influence more than 70% of consumer purchases in America and companies with female leadership earn higher-than-average profits, yet women serve as directors on only 18% of the largest U.S. companies and just 5% of Fortune 500 companies (Credit Suisse Research Institute, 2016). These long-standing gender gaps in leadership roles may be attributed to long-held gender stereotypes about men being more confident, assertive, independent, rational and decisive. In contrast, women are more likely to be stereotyped as emotional, warm, and nurturing; and if they do display assertiveness and decisiveness, run the risk of being viewed as bossy or nasty (Heilman, 2001).

Reflection 2.10

What would you say are the major pros and cons of being a woman in America today?

As a group, what do you think women should be most proud of and most concerned about?

Sexual-Orientation and Gender-Identity Diversity

Sexual orientation is "an inherent or immutable enduring emotional, romantic or sexual attraction to other people" (Human Rights Campaign, 2019); *gender identity* is a person's "innermost concept of self as male, female, a blend of both or neither" (Human Rights Campaign, 2019). Both are important dimensions of sexual diversity. A person's gender identity may be the same or different than the biological sex assigned to that person at birth and a person's *gender expression*—the external appearance of the person's gender identity (as expressed through behavior, clothing, haircut, or voice)—may or may not conform to behaviors and characteristics typically associated with being either masculine or feminine (Human Rights Campaign, 2019).

The reality is that sexual orientation and gender identity are not binary (either-or) characteristics for all humans. Instead, they are more complex and exist along a continuum or spectrum that involves not just external anatomy, but an intricate interplay of internal genetic and chemical factors that vary across individuals and can change within the same individual over time (Montañez, 2017). The fact that sexual orientation and gender identity is not an either-or affair is underscored by the fact that all humans have both male and female hormones coursing through their bloodstream, and by research conducted on more than 1,400 human brains that shows the majority of human brains contain both masculine and feminine structural characteristics (Joel et al., 2015).

The wide variety of ways in which gender and sexual orientation is experienced and expressed has led to the development of a sexual diversity vocabulary that includes terms unfamiliar to many people. **Box 2.2** contains an alphabetical listing of these sexual diversity terms and their meaning.

Box 2.2

Androgynous: A person who has the physical characteristics of both sexes, or who identifies with being both male and female.

Asexual: A person who has no sexual feelings or desires, or does not experience sexual attraction to others.

Bisexual: A person who is sexually attracted to both men and women.

Cisgender (a.k.a. Cis): Persons whose gender identity matches the biological sex they were assigned at birth (as opposed to transgender persons).

Coming Out (a.k.a. Coming Out of the of the Closet): Accepting and revealing one's sexual orientation or gender identity.

Gay: Persons who are attracted to members of their same gender.

Gender Dysphoria: A condition in which a person experiences discomfort or distress (e.g., depression) because of a mismatch between the person's gender identity and the biological sex assigned to that person at birth.

Gender-fluid: Persons who do not identify with one particular gender, or whose gender identity fluctuates between male and female.

Gender Identity: The gender a person identifies with, which may or may not align with the gender that person was assigned at birth.

Genderqueer (a.k.a. Non-binary): Persons who do not identify as completely male or completely female; instead, they identify with both genders or neither gender.

Heterosexism: Prejudice or discrimination against homosexuals based on the belief that heterosexuality is the only acceptable sexual orientation.

Heterosexual: A person who is sexually attracted to members of the opposite sex.

Homophobia: Negative attitudes and feelings (e.g., discomfort or fear) toward people who are attracted to members of their own sex.

Intersex: Individuals born with sexual characteristics that differ from a typical male or female (e.g., different sex chromosomes, hormones, or genital anatomy).

Lesbian: A female who is sexually attracted to other females.

LGBTQ: An acronym for persons who are lesbian, gay, bisexual, transgender, and queer or questioning.

Outing: Disclosing an LGBTQ person's sexual orientation or gender identity without that person's consent.

Pansexual (a.k.a. Omnisexual): a person who is romantically or sexually attracted to people of all genders and sexual orientations.

Queer: a general term that includes all persons who are members of a sexual-orientation or gender-identity minority group that is neither heterosexual nor cisgender.

Questioning: the process engaged in by persons who may be unsure of, or uncomfortable with, labeling or categorizing themselves as having a particular sexual orientation or gender identity.

Sexual Orientation: A person's pattern of sexual or romantic attraction to other people, which may be people of the opposite sex or gender, the same sex or gender, or more than one sex or gender.

Transgender (a.k.a. Trans or Gender-Nonconforming): persons whose gender identity differs from the biological sex they were assigned at birth.

Transphobia: Negative attitudes and feelings (e.g., fear, discomfort, or hostility) toward people who are transgender.

Like other minority groups, transgender persons encounter prejudice and hate. Halfway through the year 2021, 29 transgender or gender-nonconforming people had been murdered, putting the murder rate at a pace to surpass the previous one-year high of 44 killings in 2020 (Human Rights Campaign, 2021). Three-quarters of middle school and high school transgender students report feeling unsafe because they have been targets of harassment and bullying (Kosciew et al., 2016). College campuses across the country are increasing their support for **LGBTQ** (**L**esbian, **G**ay, **B**isexual, **T**ransgender and **Q**ueer or **Q**uestioning) students by creating centers and services whose purpose is to promote their acceptance by the campus community. These campus support services play an important role in combating homophobia and related forms of sexual prejudice on campus.

To acknowledge that individuals span the full spectrum of sexual orientation and gender identity is to accept and appreciate sexual diversity (Dessel et al., 2012). America's growing acknowledgment and acceptance of sexual diversity is reflected in the U.S. Supreme Court's historic 2015 decision to legalize same-sex marriage nationwide (Dolan & Romney, 2015) and in the election of the first transgender person to the U.S. Senate in 2020 (Associated Press, 2020). Professional athletes have also become more comfortable publically acknowledging their sexual orientation, such as professional basketball player Jason Collins who announced that he was gay in 2013 and Carl Nassib who became the first active professional football player to do so in 2021. When Nassib made his declaration, he also announced that he planned to donate $100,000 to the Trevor Project—a non-profit organization whose mission is to prevent suicides among LGBTQ youth (Farmer, 2021).

"Be yourself. Everybody else is taken."

—OSCAR WILDE, IRISH POET, PLAYWRIGHT, AND INAUGURAL HONOREE IN THE RAINBOW HONOR WALK—A WALK OF FAME FOR LGBTQ PEOPLE WHO'VE MADE SIGNIFICANT CONTRIBUTIONS IN THEIR FIELD

The LGBTQ Pride Flag, first hand-stitched in 1978, has become a worldwide symbol for LGBTQ rights and inclusion © New Africa/Shutterstock.com

Consider This...

Alan Turing, a gay man, created what came to be called the "Turing Machine" (forerunner to the modern computer), that played a pivotal role in cracking Nazi-coded messages during World War II and enabled the Allies to win many crucial battles. After the war, Turing was persecuted for his homosexuality, which was illegal in England at the time. He was forcibly treated with hormones and eventually committed suicide by eating a cyanide-laced apple. In 2009, the British government issued a formal public apology for the way Turing was treated; in 2013, he received a royal pardon; and in 2019 he was chosen to be the face on Britain's new 50-pound note. The legislator who led the campaign for Turing's pardon, said: "I hope it will acknowledge his unprecedented contribution to society and science. But more importantly, I hope it will serve as a stark and rightfully painful reminder of what we lost in Turing, and what we risk when we allow that kind of hateful ideology to win" (Associated Press, 2019, p. A3). In a 2021 national survey, a record-high 70% of Americans reported that they now support same-sex marriage (McCarthy, 2021).

Reflection 2.11

What do you think LGBTQ members should be most proud of? What do you think is the major threat or challenge faced by members of the LGBTQ community today?

Religious Diversity

According to data collected by the Pew Research Center (2020b), religious diversity in America consists of the following major denominations and viewpoints.

- Christian: 70.6%
- Non-Christian Faiths: 5.9%
    - Jewish: 1.9%
    - Muslim: .9%
    - Buddhist: .7%
    - Hindu: .7%
    - Other World Religions: .3%
- Unitarian: 1.5%
- New Age: .4%
- Native American Religions: .3%
- Unaffiliated (Religious "Nones"—those reporting not belonging to any organized faith): 22.8%
    - Nothing in Particular: 15.8%
    - Agnostic: 4%
    - Atheistic: 3.1%
    - Don't Know: .6%

"I am very happy with the diversity here, but it also frightens me. I have never been in a situation where I have met people who are Jewish, Muslim, atheist, born-again, and many more."
—FIRST-YEAR COLLEGE STUDENT

Among the first American colonists were Puritans who are typically portrayed in history books as coming to North America seeking religious freedom. That they did, but they were also intolerant of other religious viewpoints and considered members of their religion to be the chosen people with the God-given right to tame the wilderness and take the land of "non-Christian" groups (Feagin, 2005). The Puritans viewed Native Americans as "wild beasts" and "agents of the Devil" who should be exterminated and their land confiscated (Collier, 1947). Like Puritans, America's other early colonists were of Protestant denominations who held biases against other religions, including Christian religions such as Catholicism (O'Conner, 1998). Anti-Catholic bias continued well into the twentieth century (Jenkins, 2003). Today, the two religious groups that are the most frequent targets of prejudice and hate are Jews and Muslims (SPLC, 2020, 2021).

Generational Diversity

Human diversity also exists with respect to the historical period in which different groups of people grow up. The term "generation" refers to a cohort (group) of individuals born during the same historical period whose attitudes, values, and viewpoints have been shaped by events that took place in the world during their formative years of development. **Box 2.3** contains a summary of different generations that have been identified by researchers, the personal characteristics commonly associated with each generational group, and the key historical events they experienced that are likely to have influenced their attitudes, values, and viewpoints (Abrams, 2021; Lancaster & Stillman, 2002).

Box 2.3   Generational Diversity: A Snapshot Summary

The Traditional Generation (a.k.a. "Silent Generation") (born 1922–1945). This generation was influenced by events such as the Great Depression and World Wars I and II. Characteristics associated with people growing up during this historical period include loyalty, patriotism, respect for authority, and conservatism.

The Baby Boomer Generation (born 1946–1964). This generation was influenced by events such as the Vietnam War, Watergate, and the Civil Rights movement. Characteristics associated with people growing up at this time include idealism, emphasis on self-fulfillment, and concern for social justice and equal rights.

Generation X (born 1965–1980). This generation was influenced by Sesame Street, the creation of MTV, the AIDS epidemic, and soaring divorce rates. They were the first "latchkey children"—youngsters who used their own key to let themselves into their home after school—because their mothers (often single mothers) were working outside the home. Characteristics associated with this generation include self-reliance, resourcefulness, and ability to adapt to change.

Generation Y (a.k.a. "Millennials") (born 1981–2002). This generation was influenced by the September 11, 2001, terrorist attack on the United States, the shooting of students at Columbine High School, and the collapse of the Enron Corporation. Characteristics associated with people growing up during this era include a preference for working and socializing in groups, familiarity and facility with technology, and willingness to engage in volunteer service in their community—why they are sometimes referred to as the "civic generation." Millenials are the most ethnically diverse generation, more likely to view diversity positively, and more open to experiencing diversity than previous generations.

Generation Z (a.k.a. "The iGeneration") (born 1994–present). This generation includes the latter half of Generation Y. They grew up during an era of international terrorism, global recession, and climate change. Compared with previous generations, this generation tends to be more distrustful of industrial corporations and political systems, and more likely to engage in political activism. During their formative years, social media was in place, so they are very comfortable using Facebook, YouTube, Twitter, Snapchat, etc. Compared with other generations, they are less likely to be concerned about lack of privacy associated with social networking and more likely to expect that they can get their needs immediately met through technology. For these reasons, they are also referred to as the "digital generation."

"You guys [in the media] have to get used to it. This is a new day and age, and for my generation that's a very common word. It's like saying 'bro.' That's how we address our friends. That's how we talk."

—MATT BARNES, MILLENIAL, BIRACIAL PROFESSIONAL BASKETBALL PLAYER, EXPLAINING TO REPORTERS AFTER BEING FINED FOR USING THE WORD "NIGGAS" IN A TWEET TO SOME OF HIS AFRICAN AMERICAN TEAMMATES

"Whenever I'm bored, I can always find something to do on my iphone."

—GEN Z 17-YEAR-OLD

Reflection 2.12

Look back at the characteristics associated with your generation. Which of these characteristics do you think accurately reflect your personal characteristics and those of your closest friends? Which do not?

Chapter Summary and Highlights

A *racial group (race)* is a group of people that share distinctive physical traits, most notably, the color of their skin. Categorizing people into distinct racial groups is more difficult today than at any other time in history because of the growing number of interracial families. The number of Americans who identify themselves as being members of two or more races is projected to become the fastest-growing racial group category in the United States. It is important to keep in mind that racial categories are social classifications that humans arbitrarily decided to create or construct; in other words, race is a *socially constructed* concept. "Races" are merely categories that societies have elected to devise, based on how humans differ with respect to certain physical characteristics. Although skin color has been used as the primary basis for creating racial categories (and for treating people differently based on their racial category), humans could just as easily have been categorized by eye color, hair color, or body size. No set of genes distinguishes one race from another and no blood test or any other type of biological test can accurately diagnose a person's race. Furthermore, modern genetic sequencing techniques which allow people to trace their racial ancestry reveal that their racial background is more mixed than they realized. In fact, research has shown that there is often more genetic similarity between members of different racial groups than among members of the same racial group.

An *ethnic* group is a social group who shares the same cultural characteristics (e.g., language, food, art). In contrast to a racial group whose members shared characteristics are inherited (e.g., their skin color), members of an ethnic group share characteristics that have been learned or acquired through shared social experiences (e.g., their forms of artistic expression). Similar to categorizing people into racial groups, classifying people into ethnic groups often reflects subjective, socially constructed interpretations (or misinterpretations). For instance, the U.S. Census Bureau classifies Hispanics as an ethnic group and members of the white race, but when Hispanics complete national census surveys that ask them to identify their race, almost one-half of them check the box "other," suggesting that they do not perceive themselves as white or others perceive them as white. This illustrates how race and ethnicity are subjective, socially constructed concepts that reflect how society decides to perceive and treat certain social groups, which, in turn, affects how members of these groups perceive themselves.

There is only one ethnic or racial group whose members can legitimately call themselves U.S. "natives" and they are the *American Indians*. Native American Indians now comprise slightly less than 1% of the American population and consist of more than 550 different tribes that differ in terms of income, level of education, geographic location, and traditional customs.

Hispanic Americans are people whose heritage lies in one of the many countries where Spanish is the primary language. Because many Hispanics have Latin American origins, they are also referred to generally as *Latinos* (male Hispanics) and *Latinas* (female Hispanics), and more recently as *Latinx*—a term that can be used to refer to any person of Latin American descent. Currently, Hispanics constitute 15% of the U.S. population, making them the largest minority population in the United States; the Hispanic population in America is projected to nearly triple between 2008 and 2050 and comprise one-third of the U.S. population by the middle of the 21st century. Today, when most Americans think and talk about immigrants, they typically focus on immigrants from Hispanic countries, and white Americans are more likely to oppose Hispanic immigrants than immigrants from European nations. Undocumented Hispanic immigrants, in particular, are currently encountering intense prejudice.

African Americans or blacks consist of people whose skin color ranges from ebony to a shade paler than many whites. Only a small percentage of Americans categorized as "blacks" actually have black-colored skin; most have skin tones that are some shade of brown. In contrast to American immigrants who chose to come to the United States voluntarily, the original blacks who came to America were brought against their will, sold as slaves, forced to perform unpaid labor, and denied all civil rights. Anti-black prejudice has been the most extreme an extensive form of racism in American history, and is most prevalently manifested today in the form of systemic racism.

Asians are defined by the U.S. Census Bureau as a single "race," but its members come from a wide variety of origins and backgrounds that include Chinese and Japanese Americans, as well as Asian citizens who immigrated to the United States from East Asia, Southeast Asia, South Asia, Central Asia, and the Pacific Islands. Asians now represent America's fastest-growing racial group. Similar to other minority groups, Asian immigrants have experienced prejudice and discrimination. Since the COVID pandemic began in 2019, racially motivated attacks against Asian Americans have increased dramatically.

Racial and ethnic minorities now account for more than 45 percent of the total American population—an all-time high. By the middle of the 21st century, minority groups are projected to comprise 57% of the American population and more than 60% of American children.

Diversity also exists among groups in terms of their *socioeconomic status (SES)*—as measured by the group's level of education, amount of income, and the occupational prestige of jobs they hold. Groups occupying lower social strata have fewer economic resources and less access to social privileges, such as connections with influential people who can advance their economic prospects. *Socioeconomic mobility* refers to the ability of people to move up the socioeconomic ladder (e.g., from poverty to the middle class). Since 1980, rates of intergenerational socioeconomic mobility in America have steadily declined. The United States is now one of the hardest industrialized nations for children born into poverty to escape poverty by the time they reach adulthood. People of all racial and ethnic groups experience poverty; however, members of racial and ethnic minority groups experience it at significantly higher rates. This illustrates the concept of *intersectionality*—membership in two or more disadvantaged social categories (e.g., race and social class) often intersect in a way that their combined effect further disadvantages people who hold joint membership in the intersecting groups.

With higher socioeconomic status also come greater privileges. A *privilege* may be defined as an advantage acquired that was not earned, such as having access to money or inheriting money from a family member. Children born into higher-income families acquire these unearned privileges and benefit from them throughout life. The reality is that not all Americans start the race to success at the same starting line; some start with social and economic resources that place them much closer to the finish line than others.

Although *women* are not a minority group in terms of their percentage in the overall population, they have faced significant discrimination throughout history. The women's rights movement has led to the more expanded opportunities women have today. Currently, more women have the opportunity to work and earn an income than at any other time in American history. However, a gender wage gap still exists: women working full-time and year-round earned about 80% of what men earn. Wage gaps still exist if women are working in similar positions as men and have attained similar levels of education. Gender gaps also continue with respect to male–female employment in certain careers. Women make up less 25% of the labor force in the fields of science, technology, engineering, and mathematics (STEM), which include some of the highest paid professions. On the positive side of the ledger, women have made significant strides in leadership positions. In 2020, America elected its first female vice president and more women were represented in United States Congress in 2018 than at any other time in American history. Nonetheless, women make up more than half of the American population, yet hold less than one-quarter of seats in Congress, and no woman has ever served as President of the United States; in contrast, about 60 other countries have elected a woman as their nation's leader.

Sexual orientation—what gender people are sexually attracted to and *gender identity* —what gender a person identifies with, are forms of human diversity. A person's gender identity may be the same or different from the biological sex assigned to that person at birth. The scientific reality is that sexual orientation and gender identity are not binary (either-or) characteristics for all humans. Instead, these human characteristics are more complex and exist along a continuum or spectrum that involves not just external anatomy, but an intricate interplay of internal genetic and chemical factors that vary from person to person and can change within the same person over time.

Internet Resources

Race and Ethnicity: https://www.diffen.com/difference/Ethnicity_vs_Race

Transgender peer support: https://transflifeline.org/

Understanding privilege: https://www.verywellmind.com/what-is-white-privilege-5070460

Income inequality: https://inequality.org/facts/income-inequality/

Gender bias in the workplace: https://builtin.com/diversity-inclusion/gender-bias-in-the-workplace

References

"A Long, Bloody History of Anti-Latino Violence in the U.S." (2019, August 18). *Los Angeles Times*, p. A14.

American Association of University Women. (2013). *The simple truth about the gender pay gap. Author.*

American Association of University Women. (2015). *Solving the equation: The variables of women's success in engineering and computing.* Author.

Abrams, S. J. (2021, January 31). Generation Z's surprising optimism is reason for hope. *Los Angeles Times*, A15.

Adler, R. B., Rosenfield, L. B., & Proctor, R. F. (2004). *Interplay: The process of interpersonal communication.* Oxford, England: Oxford University Press.

American Psychological Association. (2019). *Socioeconomic status.* https://www.apa.org/topics/socioeconomic-status/

Anderson, M. (2016). *White rage: The unspoken truth of our racial divide.* Bloomsbury.

Anderson, M., & Fienberg, S. (2000). Race and ethnicity and the controversy over the U.S. Census. *Current Sociology, 48*(3), 87–110.

Andrews, W. L. (2019). *Slavery and class in the American South.* Oxford University Press.

Associated Press. (2019, July 16). From ignominy to big money. *Los Angeles Times*, A3.

Associated Press. (2020, November 6). LGBTQ candidates notch milestone wins across U.S. *Los Angeles Times*, A14.

Banks, J. A. (2016). *Cultural diversity and education: Foundations, curriculum, and teaching* (6th ed.). Routledge.

Barker, D. K. (1997). Kill the Indian, save the child: Cultural genocide and the boarding school. In D. Morrison (Ed.), *American Indian studies: An interdisciplinary approach to contemporary issues* (pp. 47–68). Peter Lang Publishing.

Board of Governors of the Federal Reserve System. (2019). *106th annual report.* Author.

Bobo, L. D., & Huthcings, V. L. (1996). Perceptions of racial group competition: Extending Blum's theory of group position to a multiracial social context. *American Sociological Review, 61*(6), 951–972.

Bonilla-Silva, E. (2018). *Racism without racists: Color-blind racism and the persistence of racial inequality in America.* Rowman & Littlefield.

Bourne, R. S. (1916).Trans-national America. *Atlantic Monthly, 118,* 95.

Blanco, M. (2010). *Before Brown there was Mendez: The lasting impact of Mendez v. Westminster in the struggle for desegregation.* Immigration Policy Center, American Immigration Council. https://www.americanimmigrationcouncil.org/sites/default/files/research/Mendez_vWestminster_032410.pdf

Bowman, P. J., Muhammad, R., & Ifatunji, M. (2004). Skin tone, class, and racial attitudes among African Americans. In C. Herring, V. Keith, & H. Norton (Eds.), *Skin deep: How race and complexion matter in the "color-blind" era* (pp. 128–158). University of Illinois Press.

Brader, T., Valentino, N. A., & Suhay, E. (2008). What triggers public opposition to immigration? Anxiety, group cues, and immigration threat. *American Journal of Political Science, 52*(4), 959–978.

Bridgeman, B. (2003). *Psychology and evolution: The origins of mind.* Sage.

Bronfenbrenner, U. (Ed.). (2005). *Making human beings human: Bioecological perspectives on human development.* Sage.

Brookings Institution. (2019). *The US will become "minority white" in 2045, census projects.* http://www.brookings.edu/blog/the-avenue/2018/03/14/the-us-will-beomce-minority-white-in2045-census-projects/

Bruenig, N. (2019). *Wealth inequality higher than ever.* https://www.jacobinmag.com/2017/wealth-inequality-united-states-federal-reserve

Budiman, A., & Ruiz, N. G. (2021). *Key facts about Asian origin groups in the U.S.* Pew Research Center. https://www.pewresearch.org/fact-tank/2021/04/20/key-facatgs-about-asian-origin-groups-in-the-u-s

Camorata, S. A. (2012). *Immigrants in the United States, 2010: A profile of America's foreign-born population.* Center for Immigration

Caplan, P. J., & Caplan, J. B. (2009). *Thinking critically about research on sex and gender* (3rd ed.). HarperCollins College Publishers.

Carrigan, W. D., & Webb, C. (2013). *Forgotten dead: Mob violence against Mexicans in the United States, 1848–1928.* Oxford University Press.

Charter, S. (1975). *The legacy of the blues.* De Capo Press.

Cho, S., Crenshaw, K. W., & McCall, L. (2013). Toward a field of intersectionality studies: theory, applications, and praxis. *Journal of Women in Culture and Society, 38*(4), 785–810.

Cianciotto, J. (2005). *Hispanic and Latino same-sex couple households in the United States: A report from the 2000 census.* The National Gay and Lesbian Task Force Policy Institute and the National Latino/a Coalition for Justice.

Collier, J. (1947). *The Indians of the Americas.* W.W. Norton & Company.

Colombo, G., Cullen, R., & Lisle, B. (2013). *Rereading America: Cultural contexts for critical thinking and writing* (9th ed.). Bedford Books of St. Martin's Press.

Conley, D. (2005). *The pecking order: A bold new look and how family and society determine who we become.* Random House.

Corak, M. (2010). *Chasing the same dream, climbing different ladders: Economic mobility in the United States and Canada.* Economic mobility project of the Pew Charitable Trusts. http://www.pewtrusts.org/en/research-and-analysis/reports/0001/01/01/chasing-the-same-dream-climbing-different-ladders

"COVID's Financial Effects Varied." (2021, May 18). *Los Angeles Times,* A9.

Credit Suisse Research Institute. (2016). *The global health report 2016.* https://www.credit-suisse.com/about-us-news/en/articles/news-and-expertise/the-global-wealth-report-2016-201611.html

Crenshaw, K. (1991). Mapping the margins: Intersectionality, identity politics, and violence against women of color. *Stanford Law Review, 43*(6), 1241–1299.

Cubberly, E. P. (1909). *Changing conceptions of education.* Houghton Mifflin.

Diamond, J. (2019). *Upheaval: Turning point for nations in crisis.* Little, Brown and Company.

DiAngelo, R. (2018). *White fragility: Why it's so hard for white people to talk about racism.* Beacon Press.

Dingemann, M. K., & Rumbaut, R. G. (2010). The immigrant-crime nexus and post-deportation experiences: En(countering) stereotypes in Southern California and El Salvador, 31. *University of La Verne Law Review, 31*(2), 363–402.

Do, A. (2021, March 17). A wave of hate against Asians. *Los Angeles Times*, B1-B2

Drachsler, J. (1920). *Democracy and assimilation.* Macmillan.

Edsall, T. B. (2012, March 11). The reproduction of privilege. *New York Times.* https://campaignstops.blogs.nytimes.com/2012/03/12/the-reproduction-of-privilege/

Farmer, S. (2021, June 22). NFL player is first to come out as gay. *Los Angeles Times*, A1 & A7.

Feagin, J. R. (2006). *Systemic racism: A theory of oppression.* Routledge.

Feagin, J., & Feagin, J. B. R. (2011). *Race and ethnic relations* (9th ed.). Pearson.

Francis-Fallon, B. (2000, November 29). The political fight over 'Latinx': Why naming and identity matter in a complex community. *Los Angeles Times*, A16.

Goldberg, N. (2021). Is life fair? One-third of Americans think so. *Los Angeles Times*, A13.

Gómez, L. E. (2020). *Inventing Latinos: A new story of American racism.* The New Press.

Guerrero, J. (2021, June 21). Stop deporting workers who are essential to America. *Los Angeles Times*, A13.

Hagerty, M. R. (2000). Social comparisons of income in one's community: Evidence from national surveys of income and happiness. *Journal of Personality and Social Psychology, 78*, 764–771.

Hallowell, J., Layard, R., & Sachs, J. (2016). *World happiness report 2016.* https://s3.amazonaws.com/happiness-report/2016/HR-V1_web.pdf

Hanushek, E. A., Peterson, P. F., Tapepy, L. M., & Woessmann, L. (2019). *The unwavering SES achievement Gap: Trends in U.S. student performance.* NBER Working Paper No. 25648. National Bureau of Economic Research. https://www.nber.org/papers/w25648

Heilman, M. E. (2001). Description and prescription: How gender stereotypes prevent women's ascent up the organizational ladder. *Journal of Social Issues, 57*, 657–674.

Honey, M. (1984). *Creating Rosie the Riveter: Class, gender, and propaganda during World War II.* University of Massachusetts Press.

Horn, J. (2018). 1619: *Jamestown and the forging of American democracy.* Basic Books.

Human Rights Campaign. (2021). *Fatal violence against the transgender and gender non-conforming community in 2021.* https://www.hrc./resources/fatal-violence-agains-the-transgender-and-gender-non-conforming-community-in-2021

"Immigrants from 1776 Onward." (2019, July 4). *Los Angeles Times*, A10.

Jablonski, N. G., & Chaplin, G. (2002). Skin deep. *Scientific American* (October), 75–81.

Jacobson, M. F. (1998). *Whiteness of a different color: European immigrants and the alchemy of race.* Harvard University Press.

Jardina, A. (2019). *White identity politics.* Cambridge University Press.

Jenkins, P. (2003). *The new-anti-Catholicism: The last acceptable prejudice.* Oxford University Press.

Joel, D., Berman, Z., Tabor, I., Wexler, N., Gaber, O., Stein, Y., Shefi, N., Pool, J., Urchs, S., Margulies, D. S., Liem, F., Hänggi, J., Jäncke, L., & Assaf, Y. (2015). Sex beyond the genitalia: The human brain mosaic. *Proceedings of the National Academy of Sciences*, vol. 11, no. 50, pp. 15468–15473.

Jones, L. (1963). *Blues people.* William Morrow.

Kendi, I. X. (2016). *Stamped from the beginning: The definitive history of racist ideas in America.* Bold Type Books.

Kendi, I. X. (2019). *How to be an antiracist.* One World.

Kim, Y. M. (2011). *Minorities in higher education: Twenty-fourth status report, 2011 supplement.* American Council on Education.

Klein, L. G., & Knitzer, J. (2007). *Promoting effective learning: What every policymaker and educator should know.* National Center for Children in Poverty. http://nccp.org/publications/pub_695.html

Kochhar, R., & Cilluffo, A. (2018, July 12). *Key findings on the rise of income inequality within America's racial and ethnic groups.* Pew Research Center. https://www.pewresearch.org/fact-tank/2017/0712/-key-findings-on-the-rise-of-income-inequality-within-america-racial-and-ethnic-groups/

Kochhar, R., Fry, R., & Taylor, P. (2011). Wealth gaps rise to record highs between Whites, Blacks, Hispanics, twenty-to-one. *Pew Research Social and Demographics Trends* (July). http://www.pewsocialtrends.org/2011/07/26/wealth-gaps-rise-to-record-highs-between-whites-blacks-hispanics/

Kolbert, E. (2018, October 22). There's no scientific basis for race—it's a made-up label. *National Geographic.* https://www.nationalgeographic.co.uk/people-and-culture/2018/04/theres-no-scientific-basis-race-its-made-label

Koplowski, C. (2006, November). Talk about it. *NEA Today Magazine.* http://www.nea.org/home/14449.htm

Kosciew, J. G., Greytak, E. A., Giga, N. M., Villenas, C., & Danischewski, D. J. (2016). *The national 2015 school climate survey: The experiences of gay, lesbian, bisexual, transgender, and queer youth in our nation's schools.* GLSEN.

Leadbitter, M. (1971). *Nothing but the blues.* Hanover Books.

Lee, D. (2021, April 4). A widening gap among Asian Americans. *Los Angeles Times,* A6.

López, I. H. (2014). *Dog whistle politics: How coded racial appeals have reinvented racism & wrecked the middle class.* Oxford University Press.

Luhman, R. (2007). *The sociological outlook.* Rowman & Littlefield.

Martin, S. F. (2011). *A nation of immigrants.* Cambridge University Press.

Martinez, G. (1997). Mexican Americans and whiteness. In R. Delgado & J. Stefanic (Eds.), *Critical white studies* (pp. 201–213). Temple University Press.

Martinez Muñoz, M. (2018). *The injustice never leaves you: Anti-Mexican violence in Texas.* Harvard University Press.

May, S. (2012). Critical multiculturalism and education. In J. A. Banks (Ed.), *Encyclopedia of diversity in education* (volume 1, pp. 472–478). Sage.

McCarthy, J. (2021, June 8). *Record-high 70% support same-sex marriage.* Gallup. https://news.gallup.com/poll/350486/record-high-support-same-sex-marriage.aspx

Mendez, F. L., Krahn, T., Schrack, B., Krahn, A. M., Veeramah, K. R., Woerner, A. E., Fomine, F. L. M., Bradman, N., Thomas, M. G., Karafet, T. M., & Hammer, M. F. (2013). An African American paternal lineage adds an extremely ancient root to the human Y chromosome phylogenetic tree. *American Journal of Human Genetics, 92,* 454–459.

Meredith, M. (2011). *Born in Africa: The quest for the origins of human life.* Public Affairs.

Minnich, E. K. (2005). *Transforming knowledge* (2nd ed.). Temple University Press.

Mitnik, P. A., & Gruskey, D. B. (2015). *Economic mobility in the United States.* The Pew Charitable Trusts and the Russell Sage Foundation. http://www.pewtrusts.org/~/media/assets/2015/07/fsm-irs-report_artfinal.pdf

Montañez, A. (2017). Beyond XX and XY. *Scientific American, 317*(3), 50–51.

Nackenoff, C. (1997). The Horatio Alger myth. In P. Gerster & N. Cords (Eds.), *Myth America: A historical anthology,* Volume II. Brandywine Press.

Nájera, J. R. (2015). *The borderlands of race: Mexican segregation in a south Texas town.* University of Texas Press.

Nájera, J. R. (2020, October 1). Why abuse and neglect in ICE detention grow. *Los Angeles Times,* A11.

National Assessment of Educational Progress. (2015a). *2015 Reading Grade 12 Assessment Report Card: Summary Data Tables for National and Pilot State Sample Sizes, Partici-*

pation Rates, Proportions of SD and ELL Students Identified, Demographics, and Performance Results. https://www.nationsreportcard.gov/reading_math_g12_2015/files/Appendix_20

National Assessment of Educational Progress. (2015b). *2015 Mathematics Grade 12 Assessment Report Card: Summary Data Average scores and achievement-level results in NAEP mathematics for twelfth-grade students, by selected characteristics: Various years, 2005–2015.* https://www.nationsreportcard.gov/reading_math_g12_2015/files/Appendix_20

National Assessment of Educational Progress. (2019). *Results from the 2019 mathematics and reading assessments. The National Report Card.* National Center for Education Statistics. https://www.nationsreportcard.gov/mathematics/supportive_files/2019_infogra

National Center for Education Statistics. (2008). *Table 41: Percentage distribution of enrollment in public elementary and secondary schools by race/ethnicity and state or jurisdiction: Fall 1996 and fall 2006.* U.S. Department of Education.

National Center for Education Statistics. (2011). *Table 317: Bachelor's, master's, and doctor's degrees conferred by degree-granting institutions, by sex of student and discipline division: 2010-11.* Digest of Education Statistics.

National Committee on Pay Equity. (2021). *Gender wage gap still persists.* https://www.pay-equity.org/

National Council for the Social Sciences. (1991). *Curriculum guidelines for multicultural education.* Prepared by the NCSS Task Force on Ethnic Studies Curriculum Guidelines. www.socialstudies.org/positions/multicultural

National Education Association. (2002–2019). *Strategies for closing the achievement gaps.* http://www.nea.org/home/13550.htm

Nicholas, R. W. (1991). Cultures in the curriculum. *Liberal Education, 77*(3), 16–21.

O'Conner, T. H. (1998). *Boston Catholics: A history of the church and its people.* Northeastern University Press.

Oluo, I. (2019). *So you want to talk about race.* Seal Press.

Orfield, G., & Lee, C. (2005). *Why segregation matters: Poverty and educational inequality.* The Civil Rights Project at Harvard University.

Painter, N. I. (2015, June 20). What is whiteness? *New York Times.* https://www.nytimes.com/2015/06/sunday/whyat-is-whiteness.html

Palmer, R. (1981). *Deep blues.* Viking Press.

Peoples, J., & Bailey, G. (2011). *Humanity: An introduction to cultural anthropology.* Wadsworth, Cengage Learning. http://www.aacu.org/leap/documents/2009-employer-survey.pdf

Peter G. Peterson Foundation. (2019, October 4). *Income and wealth in America: An overview of recent data.* https://www.pgpf.org/blog/2019/10/income-and-wealth-in-the-united-states-an-overview-of-data

Pew Research Center. (2020a). *About one-in-four U.S. Hispanics have heard of Latinx, but just 3% use it.* https://www.pewresearch.org/hispanic/2020/08/11/about-one-in-four-u-s-hispanics-have-heard-of-latinx-but-just-3-use-it/

Pew Research Center. (2020b). *Religious landscape study.* https://www.pewforum.org/religious-landscape-study/

Pinker, S. (2000). *The language instinct: The new science of language and mind.* Perennial.

Postsecondary Education Opportunity. (2001). *Enrollment rates for females 18 to 34 years, 1950-2000.* Number 113 (November). Center for the Study of Opportunity in Higher Education.

Reid, G. B. R., & Hetherington, R. (2010). *The climate connection: Climate change and modern evolution.* Cambridge University Press.

Rothstein, R. (2017). *The color of law*. Liveright Publishing.

Salisbury, N. (1982). *Manitou and providence: Indians, Europeans, and the making of New England, 1500-1643*. Oxford.

Segall, M. H., Campbell, D. T., & Herskovits, M. J. (1996). *The influence of culture on visual perception*. Bobbs-Merrill.

Shiraev, E. D., & Levy, D. (2013). *Cross-cultural psychology: Critical thinking and contemporary applications* (5th ed.). Pearson Education.

Siler, J. (2019). *The white devil's daughters: The women who fought slavery in San Francisco's Chinatown*. Knopf.

Skelton, G. (2020). How best to confront our ugly, racist past? *Los Angeles Times*, B1–B2.

Smith, D. (2015). *Diversity's promise for higher education: Making it work* (2nd ed.). Johns Hopkins University Press.

Snow, C. (2005, July/August). From literacy to learning. *Harvard Education Letter*.

SPLC (Southern Poverty Law Center). (2020). *The year in hate and extremism, 2019*. A Report from the Southern Poverty Law Center. Montgomery, Alabama.

SPLC (Southern Poverty Law Center). (2021). *The year in hate and extremism, 2020*. A Report from the Southern Poverty Law Center. Montgomery, Alabama.

Stanton, E. C., Anthony, S. B., &. Cage, M. J. (1889). *A history of woman suffrage, vol. 1*. Fowler and Wells.

Stiglitz, J. E. (2012). *The price of inequality: How today's divided society endangers our future*. Horton.

Takaki, R.T. (2008). *A different mirror: A history of multicultural America* (1st revised ed.). Back Bay Books/Little, Brown, & Company.

Templeton, A. R. (1998). Human races: A genetic and evolutionary perspective. *American Anthropologist, 100*(3), 632–650.

Torpey, E. (2017). *Women in management*. https://www.bls.gov/careeroutlook/2017/data-on-display/women-managers.htm

U.S. Census Bureau. (2008). *An older and more diverse nation by midcentury*. http://www.census.gov/Press-release/www/releases/archives/ population/012496.html

U.S. Census Bureau. (2013). *About race*. https://www.census.gov/topics/population/race/about.html

U.S. Census Bureau. (2015, March). *Projections of the size and composition of the U.S. population: 2014 to 2060*. http://www.census.gov/content/dam/ Census/library/publications/2015/demo/p25-1143.pdf

U.S. Census Bureau. (2018). *Older people projected to outnumber children for first time in U.S. history*. https://www.census.gov/newsroom/press-releases/2018/cb18-41-population-projections.html

U.S. Census Bureau (2020). *Race*. https://www.census.gov/topics/population/race/about.html

U.S. Department of Commerce, Economics and Statistics Administration. (2011). *Women in STEM: A gender gap to innovation*. www.esa.doc.gov

U.S. Department of Education, National Center for Education Statistics. (2013). *The condition of education 2013*. https://nces.ed.gov/pubs2013/2013037.pdf

Valentino, N. A., Brader, T., & Jardina, A. E. (2013). Immigration opposition among U.S. whites: General ethnocentrism or media priming of attitudes about Latinos? *Political Psychology, 34*(2), 149–166.

Valenzuela, A. (1999). *Subtractive schooling: U.S.-Mexican youth and the politics of caring*. State University of New York Press.

Warren, E., & Tyagi, A. W. (2003). *The two-income-trap: Why middle class parents are going broke*. Basic Books.

Washington Center for Equitable Growth. (2019). *The distribution of wealth in the United States and implications for a net worth tax.* https://quitablefowth.org/the-distribution-of-wealth-in-the-united-states-and-implications-for-a-net-worth-tax/

Weatherford, J. (1991). *Native roots: How the Indians enriched America.* Crown Publishers.

Wheelright, J. (2005). Human, study thyself. *Discover,* (March), pp. 39–45.

Wilkerson, I. (2020). *Caste: The origins of our discontents.* Random House.

Wilkinson, R., & Pickett, K. (2009). *The spirit level: Why greater equality makes societies stronger.* Bloomsbury.

Wu, H. (2015, December 14). The 'model minority myth': Why Asian American poverty goes unseen. https://mashable.com/2015/12/14/asian-american-poverty/

Zajonc, R. B. (1968). Attitudinal effects of mere exposure. *Journal of Personality and Social Psychology, 9,* Monograph Supplement, No. 2, Part 2.

Zajonc, R. B. (1970). Brainwash: Familiarity breeds comfort. *Psychology Today* (February), pp. 32–35, 60–62.

Zajonc, R. B. (2001). Mere exposure: A gateway to the subliminal. *Current Directions in Psychological Science, 10,* 224–228.

Reflections and Applications

Name
_____

Date
_____

2.1 Review the sidebar quotes contained in this chapter and select two that you think are particularly meaningful or inspirational. For each quote you selected, provide an explanation why you chose it.

2.2 Rate the amount or variety of racial and ethnic diversity you have experienced in the following settings:

The high school you attended	High	Moderate	Low
The college or university you are attending	High	Moderate	Low
The neighborhood in which you grew up	High	Moderate	Low
Places where you have been employed	High	Moderate	Low

Which of these settings had the *most* and *least* diversity? What do you think accounted for this difference?

2.3 a) What forms of diversity do you see represented on campus?

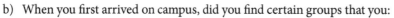

b) When you first arrived on campus, did you find certain groups that you:
- didn't expect to see?
- didn't expect to see in such large numbers?
- didn't expect to be so open about their group membership?

2.4 a) Write down (in question form) one thing you have always wondered about, or would like to know more about the following groups of people:

- Native Americans (American Indians)
- Hispanic Americans (Latinos and Latinas)
- African Americans (Blacks)
- Asian Americans
- Transgender persons

b) Which of these groups would you feel *most* comfortable approaching to ask about their experiences?

c) Which of these groups would you feel *least* comfortable approaching? Why?

2.5 Diversity Interview

a) Find a person on your campus from an ethnic or racial group that you've had little previous contact. Ask that person for an interview, and during the interview, include the following questions.

- What does "diversity" mean to you?
- What prior experiences have affected your current viewpoints or attitudes about diversity?
- What would you say have been the major influences and turning points in your life?
- Who would you cite as your positive role models, heroes, or sources of inspiration?
- What societal contributions made by your ethnic or racial group would you like others to be aware of and acknowledge?
- What do you hope will never again be said about or happen to your ethnic or racial group?

b) If you were the interviewee instead of the interviewer, how would you have answered the above questions?

2.6 In 2021, 17 million Americans earned the minimum wage of $7.25, which has not increased since 2009. Given the growing income inequality gap in the United States, some states and cities have set their minimum wage higher.

a) Do you think the current minimum wage should be raised? If yes, why? If no, why not?

b) What do you think the minimum hourly wage should be set at so that working adults can afford food, housing and transportation, and make a decent living?

The Benefits of Diversity

Chapter Purpose and Preview

This chapter defines multicultural education and explains how it not only promotes acceptance and appreciation of minority groups, but also deepens learning and elevates the critical and creative thinking skills of all students. In addition to documenting the cognitive benefits of diversity, the chapter demonstrates how appreciating diversity serves to reduce societal prejudice, preserve democracy, enhance emotional intelligence and self-awareness, and cultivate intercultural competencies essential for career success in the 21st century.

Reflection 3.1

Do you think that members of a majority group that has never been a victim of prejudice or discrimination, benefit from experiences with diversity? If yes, why? If no, why not?

What Are the Educational Benefits of Diversity?

The term "multicultural education" is often associated with cultural appreciation activities, such as schools celebrating Black History Month or students bringing artifacts to school representing their culture. While these are useful experiences that should be continued, learning from diversity involves more than periodic celebrations of cultural differences. It empowers students to evaluate ideas in terms of their cultural validity and cultural bias, and it engages students in learning experiences that foster interaction among diverse student groups (Banks et al., 2001). Education for and with diversity is an ongoing learning process that takes place both inside and outside the classroom. When students encounter multiple cultural perspectives and interact with students from diverse backgrounds during the learning process, the learning of any academic subject is broadened and deepened. Thus, experiencing and valuing diversity is not just the socially sensitive or "politically correct" thing to do, it's the educationally effective thing to do; it enriches the quality and impact of a college education.

National surveys show that by the end of their first year in college, almost two-thirds of students report having "stronger" or "much stronger" knowledge of people from different races and cultures than they did before entering college. The majority of first-year students also report being more open to experiencing diverse cultures, viewpoints, and values than they had been previously (HERI, 2013, 2014). This chapter identifies the multiple advantages of experiencing diversity; keep these benefits in mind and use them as a source of motivation to seek out and capitalize on the power of diversity throughout your college experience.

Gaining greater self-awareness (self-knowledge) is a major goal of a college education and experiences with diversity help students achieve this goal. © Kendall Hunt Publishing Company

Diversity Increases Self-Awareness and Self-Knowledge

One of the most frequently cited purposes of a college education is to "know thyself" (Cross, 1982)—to engage in introspection, to become more self-aware, and to gain deeper knowledge of oneself. Scholars consider this capacity for self-insight to be a form of human intelligence, known as "intrapersonal intelligence" (Gardner, 1999).

Multicultural experiences supply us with multiple opportunities to deepen self-knowledge. When we encounter diverse groups and ideas from different cultures, it sheds brighter light on our personal identity, prompting us to ask self-searching questions such as: *Who am I? How am I different from others? What has made me the person I am?* Diversity experiences that prompt these questions enable students to "develop more sophisticated understandings of why they are the way they are, why their ethnic and cultural groups are the way they are, and what ethnicity and culture mean in their daily lives" (National Council for the Social Sciences, 1991, p. 18).

 Consider This...

The more we learn about people different than ourselves, the more we learn about ourselves.

Our self-knowledge is deepened by experiences with people from diverse backgrounds because it enables us to compare and contrast our life experiences with persons whose experiences differ sharply from our own. Viewing ourselves in relation to others with different backgrounds helps liberate us from an ethnocentric and egocentric perspective by supplying us with a *comparative perspective*—a reference point that positions us to step outside ourselves and see more clearly how our particular cultural background has shaped who we are. As Ginsberg and Wlodkowski (2009) point out: "When we meet others whose family or community norms vary from our own, it is akin to holding up a mirror, provoking questions we might not otherwise think to ask. Such contrast and dissonance present [opportunities] to examine assumptions, making it possible to more deeply understand who we are in relation to one another" (p. 7). Supporting this assertion is research showing that when college students interact with students of different races and ethnic backgrounds, they often experience "unexpected" or "jarring" self-insights that enable them to learn more about themselves (Light, 2001).

Gaining greater insight into the distinctiveness of our personal experiences also enables us to see how we may be uniquely advantaged or disadvantaged relative to others. For example, by learning about differences in financial resources and educational opportunities that exist across different cultural groups, we gain greater awareness of how privileged (or not) we actually are.

> "It is difficult to see the picture when you are inside the frame."
> —AN OLD SAYING (AUTHOR UNKNOWN)

> "When you go to high school in L.A., everyone's poor so it doesn't seem weird. But then you go to college and meet students who live in mansions, or they were middle class, and I realized, 'Wow, I didn't know how poor I was"
> —FIRST-YEAR UNIVERSITY STUDENT WHO GREW UP IN A LOW-INCOME LOS ANGELES NEIGHBORHOOD (LOPEZ, 2018)

Diversity Widens, Deepens, and Accelerates Learning

Simply stated, humans learn more from diversity than they do from similarity or familiarity. Restricting the diversity of people with whom we decide to interact because of stereotypes or prejudices restricts the variety of our socially acquired knowledge, and in so doing, constricts the breadth and depth of our learning. Similar to how our physical performance is strengthened by supplying the body with a diversified diet of foods from different nutritional groups, our mental performance is strengthened by supplying our mind with a diversified diet of ideas from different cultural groups. For example, our knowledge about how to manage stress has been strengthened by our learning from Indian Buddhist culture that meditation is an effective, drug-free, stress-management strategy (Bodian, 2006). Indian Buddhist culture has also fueled the current use of mindfulness in America as a self-awareness and self-growth strategy (Gunaratana, 2011).

From Eskimos, we learned about the health value of fish by learning how their extraordinarily low rate of cardiovascular disease was related to their fish-rich diet—which contains a type of unsaturated fat that flushes out and washes away cholesterol-forming fats from the bloodstream (Feskens & Kromhout, 1993; Khoshaba & Maddi, 1999–2004). We have also learned from studying the culture of Intuits or Yupiks, another Eskimo group, that a diet high in unsaturated fats (and low in saturated fats) reduces our risk for nongenetic forms of cardiovascular disease, such as high blood pressure, heart attacks, and strokes (American Heart Association, 2006). A good example of how unwillingness to learn from other cultures can slow down the rate at which we acquire and apply knowledge took place in 1771 when an African slave named Onesimus was brought to during the smallpox pandemic and asked if he had smallpox:

> "Yes and no," Onesimus answered. He explained how in Africa before his enslavement, a tiny amount of pus from a smallpox victim had been scraped into

his skin with a thorn—an African hundreds of years old that was used to build up healthy recipients' immunity to the disease. This form of inoculation—a precursor to modern vaccination—was an innovative practice that prevented untold numbers of deaths in West Africa. Racist European scientists at first refused to recognize that African physicians could have made such advances . . . . It would take several decades and many more deaths before British physician Edward Jenner, the so-called father of immunology, validated inoculation (Kendi, 2016, p. 71).

> "The more eyes, different eyes, we can use to observe one thing, the more complete will our concept of this thing, our objectivity, be."
>
> —FRIEDRICH NIETZSCHE, GERMAN PHILOSOPHER

These examples illustrate the importance of being open to learning about and from diverse cultures for expanding our acquisition and application of knowledge.

Diversity not only widens our knowledge base, it also deepens and accelerates learning. Deep learning takes place when strong connections are made between the knowledge we have already stored in our brain and the new knowledge we are trying to acquire (see **Figure 3.1**). New information can be more easily assimilated and integrated if a wider range of interconnections have already been formed in their brain (Rosenshine, 1997). When we acquire diverse perspectives, it broadens and differentiates our knowledge base, increasing its capacity for making new connections. In other words, diversity adds to the multiplicity and variety of the brain's neural pathways, providing it with more routes through which to connect new ideas, which accelerates and deepens the learning process.

Figure 3.1 Knowledge is stored in the brain in the form of neurological connections. Exposure to diverse perspectives adds to the multiplicity and variety of the brain's neural network, providing more pathways through which we can connect (learn) new ideas. © Andrii Vodolazhskyi/Shutterstock.com

Diversity also deepens learning by "stretching" the brain beyond its normal comfort zone, pushing it to work harder. Encountering something unfamiliar forces our brain to take an extra step to make sense of it—by comparing, contrasting, and trying to relate it to something we know (Acredolo & O'Connor, 1991; Nagda et al., 2005). This added expenditure of mental energy results in the creation of stronger and more durable neurological connections that serve to deepen learning (Willis, 2006).

Diversity Strengthens Our Ability to Think Critically from Multiple Perspectives

When the world is viewed through the lens of a single (monocultural) perspective, it is seen only from the narrow, ethnocentric perspective of the viewer (Paul & Elder, 2002). Diversity emancipates us from the narrow lens of ethnocentrism, replacing it with a kaleidoscopic lens through which we can view the world from a more comprehensive, multicultural and cross-cultural perspectives. For instance, our perception of the dimension of time becomes more comprehensive and complete when we view it from cross-cultural perspectives. Western cultures (e.g., United States and Canada) tend to view time from a "monochronic" perspective, focusing primarily on the present (the "here and now"), seeing chronological events as a series of successive episodes rather than as an evolving chain of interconnected experiences. In contrast, Eastern cultures (e.g., China and India) are more likely to take a "polychromic" perspective on time, viewing it less in terms of separated, discrete segments and more like a spectrum or continuum in which the three dimensions of time (past, present, future) merge together to form a continuous flow of interdependent experiences (LeBaron, 2003; Novinger, 2001). One consequence of these different views of time is that people in Western cultures are more prone to think in a linear fashion, focusing on the future and moving in the direction of end goals. In contrast, members of Eastern cultures think in a more circular or swirling manner (the yin and yang). This circular thought process leads people from these cultures to view opposite or counteracting thoughts and feelings in a more interconnected manner in which complement one another to maintain balance (Pedrotti, 2015). For instance, in Eastern cultures happiness is more likely to be viewed and pursued with the idea that it cannot take place without being balanced by occasional feelings of unhappiness, which ultimately gives rise to feelings of happiness. Thus, a happy person is someone who accepts and expects to experience this circularity of feelings, not someone who expects to progress linearly toward the goal of achieving stable, and permanent state of happiness (Lopez et al., 2015).

> "Mono-perspective analyses of complex ethnic and cultural issues can produce skewed, distorted interpretations and evaluations."
> —NATIONAL COUNCIL FOR THE SOCIAL SCIENCES, *CURRICULUM GUIDELINES FOR MULTICULTURAL EDUCATION*

These examples illustrate how viewing time and life experiences through the lenses of different cultures helps us develop a more nuanced and integrated understanding of our world and ourselves. When such diverse perspectives are brought into the thinking process, it also enhances the quality and accuracy of our decision-making (Banks, 2016; Smith, 2015). For instance, when group discussions take place among diverse people who bring multiple cutural perspectives to the table, group decisions become less polarized (one-sided) (Baron, 2005) and less susceptible to "groupthink"—the tendency for people with similar viewpoints not to challenge their similar perspective—which can lead to decisions that overlook flaws or biases in the group members' thought process (Janis, 1982). Groupthink is what led American doctors to erroneously conclude that acupuncture was quackery (International Wellness Directory, 2009), delaying the recognition and America's approval of this Chinese method of pain relief as an effective alternative to pain-killing drugs.

"When all men think alike, no one thinks very much."
—WALTER LIPPMANN, DISTINGUISHED JOURNALIST AND ORIGINATOR OF THE TERM "STEREOTYPE"

 Consider This…

Because our views are shaped, limited, and often biased by our own cultural vantage point, seeking out multicultural perspectives enables us to think beyond the boundaries of our monocultural and ethnocentric perspective, empowering us to become more open-minded, multi-dimensional thinkers.

Reflection 3.3

Do you intentionally seek out ideas from others who have different cultural backgrounds than your own? If yes, why? If no, why not?

One key purpose of a college education is to expose students to different cultural perspectives and worldviews. Not surprisingly, research shows that higher levels of education are associated with lower levels of ethnocentrism (Bobo & Licari, 1989) and group prejudice (Feldman & Huddy, 2005), and higher tolerance for alternative viewpoints (Hetherington & Weiler, 2009). Other studies show that students who have more experiences with diversity—such as taking multicultural courses, participating in diversity programs on campus, and interacting with peers from different racial and ethnic backgrounds—are more likely to experience greater gains in:

- thinking *complexity*—ability to think about all parts of a problem and approach issues from multiple vantage points (Association of American Colleges & Universities, 2004; Gurin, 1999),
- *reflective* thinking—ability to think deeply about both personal and global issues (Kitchener et al., 2000), and
- *critical* thinking—ability to evaluate the validity of one's own reasoning and the reasoning of others (Gorski, 1995–2019; Pascarella et al., 2001).

These cognitive benefits of diversity experiences are likely due to the fact that when we encounter perspectives that differ from our own, it creates "cognitive dissonance"—a state of mental disequilibrium or imbalance that disrupts our habitual ways of thinking (Langer,

1997). This internal instability forces our mind to deal with contrasting perspectives simultaneously, which disrupts and displaces single-dimensional thinking, replacing it with thinking that is more multidimensional and complex (Brookfield, 1987; Gorski, 1995–2019).

In addition, when we view information reported to us from diverse cultural perspectives, it enables us to become more critically aware of how information is "constructed" from the reporter's particular cultural perspective and better equipped to challenge that perspective (Banks, 1995). A multicultural education helps us critically evaluate what we hear and see by asking such questions as: "Whose voice is speaking, and whose voice am I not hearing?" and "What cultural perspective (or bias) is the author or producer bringing to their book, website, or movie?" (Gorski, 1995–2019).

Diversity Enhances Creative Thinking and Problem-Solving

In addition to promoting critical thinking, research shows that diversity enhances creative thinking (Leung et al, 2008; Maddux & Galinsky, 2009). Acquiring knowledge about multiple cultures and gaining access to diverse cultural perspectives positions us to think "outside the box" of our own cultural framework, equipping us with a wider range of vantage points to view problems and a more versatile set of thinking tools to solve them (Kelly, 1994).

When people from different cultural backgrounds participate in an exchange of ideas about a problem to be solved, it often has a "cross-stimulation" effect—the ideas exchanged crisscross to stimulate innovative solutions that transcend cultural boundaries (Brown et al., 1998). Said in another way, cross-

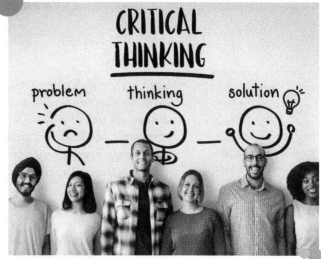

Diversity cultivates critical and creative thinking skills and problem-solving ability. © Rawpixel.com/Shutterstock.com

cultural ideas "cross-fertilize" and germinate new ideas for attacking old problems (Harris, 2010). Research also suggests that when people are exposed to diverse perspectives and alternative viewpoints, they become more open to considering different goal options and more willing to experiment with different goal-achievement strategies (Stoltz, 2014).

In contrast, when alternative cultural perspectives are dismissed or devalued, the variety of lenses through which we view issues or problems is restricted. This restricted range of viewpoints reduces *divergent* thinking—thinking that moves in different directions—a hallmark of creative thinking. When interactions and conversations take place exclusively among groups of people with similar cultural experiences, their ideas are less likely to diverge; instead they tend to "converge" and merge into the same lane or line of thought—the one occupied by the homogeneous cultural group doing the thinking. It could be said that segregation of racial and ethnic groups not only separates people socially, it also separates them mentally and suppresses their collective creativity. This is well illustrated in the book (and movie) *Hidden Figures*, which documents how a group of talented black female mathematicians were initially and intentionally segregated from their white male coworkers at NASA. When they were eventually integrated into the work team, they made crucial, creative contributions to the successful launching of America's first astronaut (Shetterly, 2017). Similarly, creativity research conducted in Japan (a country that has fluctuated widely from being very closed to very open to immigration) reveals that bursts of creative discoveries in a variety of fields took place in the country soon after it adopted more open immigration policies (Simonton, in Epstein, 2019).

Consider This...

When people from diverse backgrounds are given the opportunity to bounce ideas off one another, it stimulates divergent (out-of-the-box) thinking and generates synergy (multiplication of ideas) that leads to serendipity (unexpected discoveries of innovative and effective ideas). While it may be true that "birds of the same feather flock together," when birds of a different feather flock together, they fly higher—to higher levels of creative thinking.

Diversity Expands Social Networks and Builds Emotional Intelligence

Acquiring knowledge about other cultures and interacting with members of diverse cultural groups widens our social circle and expands the pool of people with whom we can develop relationships and form friendships. A more diverse and extensive pool of interpersonal contacts supplies students with greater social capital—a larger network of human connections that can support college success and career advancement (Smith, 2015). Research in college settings shows that the more frequently students have experiences and have positive intergroup contact, the higher is their level of satisfaction with campus life and the college experience (Astin, 1993; Cheng & Zhao, 2006; Dovidio et al., 2000; Enberg, 2004). Furthermore, studies show that when students widen the cultural circle of peers with whom they interact, they gain greater self-confidence and improved ability to adapt to new people and situations (Miville et al., 1992). In contrast, students who limit their social experiences to members of their own culture are left with "few opportunities to acquire more than stereotypes about ethnic and cultural groups other than their own" (National Council for the Social Sciences, 1991, p. 22). Reinforcing these findings is research conducted by social psychologists which show that less-prejudiced people report higher levels of life satisfaction (Feagin & McKinney, 2003)—probably because they have less social distrust or fear and are more comfortable interacting with different social groups (Baron et al., 2006).

Interacting with others whose life experiences, circumstances, and challenges differ from our own develops empathy—awareness of, and sensitivity to the feelings of others (Levine, 2005), which is an essential element of *emotional intelligence*—an attribute that research shows is a stronger predictor of personal and professional success than intellectual ability (Goleman, 1995, 2006).

> "Variety is the spice of life."
> —AN OLD AMERICAN PROVERB

> "Viva la difference!" (Long live difference!)
> —A FAMOUS FRENCH SAYING

> "When diverse and conflicting perspectives are juxtaposed, students are able to develop empathy and an understanding of each group's perspective and point of view."
> —JAMES BANKS, FOUNDING DIRECTOR OF THE CENTER FOR MULTICULTURAL EDUCATION AT THE UNIVERSITY OF WASHINGTON

Reflection 3.4

Would you say that your amount of interaction with peers from diverse backgrounds is "frequent," "occasional," or "rare?" What do you think contributes to, or detracts from, your amount of interaction?

Diversity Enhances Career Preparation

Learning about, with, and from members of diverse cultures also has a very practical long-term benefit: It develops skills needed for career success in the 21st century work world. Whatever line of work today's college graduates decide to pursue, they are likely to find themselves working with employers, co-workers, customers, and clients from diverse cultural backgrounds. America's workforce is now more racially and ethnically diverse than at any time in the nation's history, and it will grow ever more diverse throughout the remainder of the current century. By 2050, the proportion of American workers from minority ethnic and racial groups is estimated to jump to 55% (U.S. Census Bureau, 2008).

National surveys show that today's business leaders, and employers are seeking to hire people who are more than just "aware" or "tolerant" of diversity. They seek employees who have actual experience with diversity and are able to collaborate with diverse co-workers, clients, and customers (Association of American Colleges & Universities, 2002; Education Commission of the States, 1995; Hart Research Associates, 2013).

In addition to the growing domestic diversity of the workforce within the United States, today's global economy calls for employees with cross-cultural skills and knowledge of international diversity. Due to unprecedented and ongoing advances in electronic technology, there is more economic interdependence among nations, more international trading, more multinational corporations, more international travel, and more instantaneous worldwide communication between nations (Dryden & Vos, 1999; Friedman, 2005). Even smaller companies and corporations are becoming more international in nature (Brooks, 2009). As a result, employers in all sectors of the economy are seeking job candidates with the following skills and attributes: sensitivity to human differences, ability to understand and relate to people from different cultural backgrounds, international and intercultural knowledge, and ability to communicate in a second language (Hart Research Associates, 2013; Job Outlook, 2018; NACE, 2019; Office of Research, 1994). Multinational corporations are also seeking executives with international leadership skills and managers who have the ability to interact effectively with culturally diverse employees (House & Javidan, 2004). Collectively, these multicultural and cross-cultural skills are referred to as *intercultural competency*, which encompasses "knowledge of cultures and cultural practices (one's own and others), complex cognitive skills for decision-making in intercultural contexts, social skills to function effectively in diverse groups and personal attributes that include flexibility and openness to new ideas" (Wabash National Study of Liberal Arts Education, 2007). These skills have also been identified as critical for effective political leadership in the 21st century (Blackwell et al., 2002).

> "Actual interaction with peers of different races is far superior to merely reading or watching a movie about racial issues."
> —SPOKESPERSON FOR GENERAL MOTORS CORPORATION COMMENTING ON THE COMPANY'S EXPERIENCE WITH EMPLOYEES

College graduates' future coworkers are likely to come from diverse cultural backgrounds. © Jacob Lund/Shutterstock.com

> "Technology and advanced communications have transformed the world into a global community, with business colleagues and competitors as likely to live in India as in Indianapolis. In this environment, people need a deeper understanding of the thinking, motivations, and actions of different cultures, countries, and regions."
> —PARTNERSHIP FOR 21ST CENTURY SKILLS

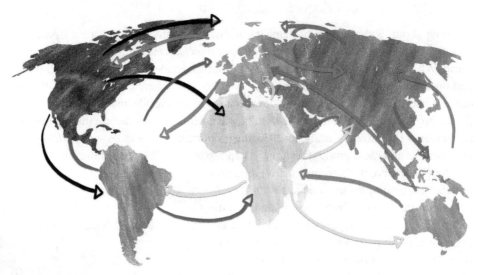

Increases in international communication technology, economic interdependence between nations, and the growth of multinational companies have made intercultural skills an essential career competency for today's college graduates. © Likee68/Shutterstock.com

Reflection 3.5

What intercultural skills or competencies do you think you have already developed? What ones do you think need further development?

Consider This...

Intercultural competence is a skill set that has two powerful features:

1) *Transferability*—it's a portable skill set that "travels well"—it can be carried and applied across a wide range of personal experiences, work situations, and life roles.
2) *Durability*—it's a sustainable skill set that has lifelong value—it can be used continuously throughout life.

Diversity Reduces Group Prejudice and Discrimination

Schools serve as the starting place for promoting social justice and equity in the larger society (Gorski, 1995–2019). Research shows that when students have positive interpersonal interactions with peers from different cultures and engage in open conversations with them about diversity-related topics that challenge their previously held beliefs, it reduces prejudice and increases openness to engaging in further intergroup interaction (Pascarella et al.,

1996; Whitt et al., 2001). However, these positive outcomes do not take place simply by mixing minority and majority students together in the same school environment. School-integration research strongly suggests that mere exposure to, or incidental contact between, majority and minority students does not automatically reduce prejudice and improve interracial relations (Stephan, 1978). Similarly, at the college level, including students from diverse backgrounds in the student body does not guarantee that students will expand their social networks to interact and learn from students with different cultural backgrounds. Instead, they exhibit what social psychologists call the "self-similarity principle": the tendency to associate and develop relationships with others whose backgrounds, beliefs, and interests are similar to one's own (Uzzi & Dunlap, 2005). Thus, the benefits of diversity cannot be achieved solely through college admissions decisions that ensure diverse students are present on campus. To realize the full prejudice-reducing benefits of diversity, students need to move beyond incidental or coincidental intergroup contact to intentional intergroup interaction. As diversity scholar, Patrick Hill puts it:

> Meaningful multiculturalism transforms the curriculum. While the presence of persons of other cultures and subcultures is a virtual prerequisite to that transformation, their "mere presence" is primarily a political achievement, not an intellectual or educational achievement. Real educational progress will be made when multiculturalism becomes *interculturalism* [emphasis added] (1991, p. 41).

Research shows that the self-similarity principle can be overcome if individuals from diverse groups make an intentional effort to engage in intercultural interaction; when they do, it increases multicultural appreciation and the formation of intercultural friendships (Pettigrew et al., 2011). By remaining mindful of the power of intercultural interaction and taking action to initiate it, college students can reduce biases and stereotypes they may consciously or unconsciously hold toward members of other cultural groupsand open themselves to experiencing the social and educational benefits of diversity. (Specific strategies for doing so are presented in Chapter 5.)

Diversity Preserves Democracy

As a democratic nation, the United States is a country built on the principles of social justice, equal rights, and equal opportunity for all citizens. Making a commitment to diversity is to "make a strong, unequivocal commitment to democracy, to basic American values of justice and equality" (Banks in Brandt, 1994, p. 31). America's ability to continue to thrive as a democracy in the 21st century will depend on an educational system that develops and deploys the talents and civic participation of all its citizens, including those from historically underrepresented and disadvantaged cultural backgrounds (American Council on Education, 2008). In contrast to many nations, where the majority of citizens surveyed do not report that diversity benefits their country, the majority of Americans believe that diversity makes the United States a better nation (Drake & Poushter, 2016).

Prejudice and discrimination are both contradictions and threats to the foundational principles of any nation that calls itself a democracy (Myrdal, 1944; Smith, 2004). Lest we forget, it was the efforts of American citizens who had long been targets of prejudice and discrimination, such as the civil rights activists of the 1960s and 1970s, that confronted and compelled America to live up to the democratic ideals stated in its Declaration of Independence, Constitution, and Bill of Rights (Okihiro, 1994).

"The Constitution of the United States knows no distinction between citizens on account of color. In whatever else other nations may have been great an grand, our greatness and grandeur will be found in the faithful application of the principle of perfect civil equality to the people of all races and of all creeds, and to men of no creeds."

—FREDERICK DOUGLASS, FORMER SLAVE AND SUBSEQUENT ABOLITIONIST, AUTHOR, AND ADVOCATE FOR EQUAL RIGHTS FOR ALL AMERICANS

© Olga Utchenko/Shutterstock.com

Members of minority racial and ethnic groups are more likely to develop pride and allegiance to their country, and are more likely to participate in its democratic form of governance, when their group identity and culture are validated (Kymlicka, 2004). Multicultural education validates the cultures of all social groups, including those that have been historically minimized or marginalized. In so doing, it helps America fulfill its democratic promise.

 **Consider This…**

Diversity and democracy go hand-in-hand; when the former is valued, the latter is preserved.

Chapter Summary and Highlights

Multicultural education empowers students to evaluate ideas in terms of their cultural validity and cultural bias, and engages students in learning experiences that foster interaction among diverse student groups. When students encounter multiple cultural perspectives and interact with students from diverse backgrounds during the learning process, the learning of any academic subject is broadened and deepened. More specifically, diversity enhances learning and personal development in the following major ways.

Diversity increases self-awareness and self-knowledge. The more we learn about people different than ourselves, we learn more about ourselves and deepen our self-knowledge, gaining a *comparative perspective*—a reference point that positions us to step outside ourselves and see more clearly how our particular cultural background shaped who we are and prompting us to ask self-searching questions such as: Who am I? How am I different from others? What has made me the person I am?

Diversity widens, deepens, and accelerates learning. Simply stated, humans learn more from diversity than they do from similarity or familiarity. In contrast, restricting the diversity of people with whom we interact because of stereotypes or prejudices restricts the variety of our socially acquired knowledge, and in so doing, constricts the breadth and depth of our learning. Experiencing diverse perspectives broadens and differentiates our knowledge base and increases its capacity for making new connections. Diversity adds to the multiplicity and variety of the brain's neural pathways, providing it with more routes through which to connect new ideas, which accelerates and deepens the learning process. Diversity also strengthens learning by "stretching" the brain beyond its normal comfort zone, pushing it to work harder. Encountering something unfamiliar forces the brain has to take an extra step to make sense of it—by comparing, contrasting, and trying to relate it to something it already knows. This added expenditure of mental energy results in the creation of stronger, more durable neurological connections that deepen learning.

Diversity strengthens our ability to think critically from multiple perspectives. When the world is viewed through the lens of a single (monocultural) perspective, it is seen only from the narrow, ethnocentric perspective of the viewer. Diversity emancipates the viewer from the narrow lens of ethnocentrism, replacing it with a more comprehensive and powerful kaleidoscopic lens through which the world can be viewed from multicultural and cross-cultural perspectives. Because our viewpoints are shaped, limited, and often biased by our own cultural vantage point, seeking out multicultural perspectives enables us to think beyond the boundaries of a monocultural and ethnocentric perspective, allowing us to become more open-minded, multi-dimensional thinkers. Encountering perspectives that differ from our own creates "cognitive dissonance"—a state of mental disequilibrium or imbalance that disrupts our habitual ways of thinking, enabling us to become more critically aware of how information reported to us is "constructed" from the reporter's particular cultural perspective, and that equips us to challenge perspective. A multicultural curriculum helps us critically evaluate what we hear and see by asking such questions as: "Whose voice is speaking, and whose voice am I not hearing?" and "What cultural perspective (or bias) is the author or producer bringing to their book, website, or movie?"

Diversity enhances creative thinking and problem-solving. Acquiring knowledge about multiple cultures and gaining access to diverse cultural perspectives positions us to think "outside the box" of our own cultural framework, supplying us with a wider range of vantage points to view problems and a more versatile set of thinking tools to solve them. When people from different cultural backgrounds exchange ideas about how a problem may be solved, it often has a "cross-stimulation" effect—the ideas exchanged crisscross to stimulate innovative solutions that transcend cultural boundaries. In contrast, when alternative cultural perspectives are dismissed or devalued, the variety of lenses through which we view issues or problems is restricted, which reduces *divergent* thinking—thinking that moves in different directions—a hallmark of creative thinking. In short, when people from diverse backgrounds are given the opportunity to bounce ideas off one another, it stimulates divergent (out-of-the-box) thinking and generates synergy (multiplication of ideas) that leads to serendipity (unexpected discoveries of innovative and effective ideas).

Diversity expands social networks and builds emotional intelligence. Acquiring knowledge about other cultures and interacting with members of diverse cultural groups widens our social circle and expands the pool of people with whom we develop relationships and form friendships. A more diverse and extensive pool of interpersonal contacts supplies students with increased social capital—a larger network of human connections that can support their college success and career advancement. Interacting with others whose life experiences, circumstances and challenges differ from our own develops empathy—awareness of, and sensitivity to the feelings of others, which is an essential element of *emotional intelligence*—an attribute that research has shown to be is a stronger predictor of personal and professional success than intellectual ability.

Diversity enhances career preparation. Learning about, with, and from members of diverse cultures also has a very practical long-term benefit: It develops skills needed for career success in the twenty-first century work world. Whatever line of work today's college graduates decide to pursue, they are likely to find themselves working with employers, co-workers, customers, and clients from diverse cultural backgrounds. America's workforce is now more racially and ethnically diverse than at any time in the nation's history, and it will grow ever more diverse throughout the remainder of the current century. In addition to the growing domestic diversity of the workforce within the United States, today's global economy calls for employees with cross-cultural skills and knowledge of international diversity. Collectively, multicultural and cross-cultural skills are referred to as *intercultural competency*, which encompasses as knowledge of cultures and cultural practices (one's own and others), complex cognitive skills for decision-making in intercultural contexts, social skills to function effectively in diverse groups and personal attributes such as flexibility and openness to new ideas.

Diversity reduces group prejudice and discrimination. Research shows that when students have positive interpersonal interactions with peers from different cultures and engage in open conversations with them about diversity-related topics that challenge their previously held beliefs, it reduces prejudices increases openness to engage in further intergroup interaction. However, these positive outcomes do not take place simply by mixing minority and majority students together in the same school environment. To experience these outcomes, students need to move beyond incidental or coincidental intergroup contact to intentional intergroup interaction. By remaining mindful of the power of intercultural interaction and taking action to initiate it, college students can reduce biases and stereotypes they may consciously or unconsciously hold toward members of other cultural groups and open themselves up to experiencing the social and educational benefits of diversity.

Diversity preserves democracy.
Diversity and democracy go hand-in-hand; when the former is valued, the latter is preserved. As a democratic nation, the United States is a country built on the principles of social justice, equal rights, and equal opportunity for all citizens. Prejudice and discrimination are contradictions and threats to the foundational principles of any nation that calls itself a democracy. Members of minority racial and ethnic groups are more likely to develop pride and allegiance to their country, and are more likely to participate in its democratic form of governance, when their group identity and culture are validated. Multicul-

tural education validates the cultures of all social groups, including those that have been historically minimized or marginalized. In so doing, it helps America fulfill its democratic promise.

Internet Resources

Why diversity is important: https://diversity.social/why-is-diversity-important/

How diversity makes us smarter: https://greatergood.berkeley.edu/article/item/how_diversity_makes_smarter

Importance and value of diversity in the fields of Science, Technology, Engineering & Mathematics (STEM): https://blogs.scientificamerican.com/voices/diversity-in-stem-what-it-is-and-why-it-matters/

Diversity competencies for the workplace: https://petworld-online.com/diversity-competencies-in-the-workplace

Benefits of diversity for democratic citizenship: http://www-personal.umich.edu/~pgurin/benefits.html

References

Acredolo, C., & O'Connor, J. (1991). On the difficulty of detecting cognitive uncertainty. *Human Development, 34,* 204–223.

American Council on Education. (2008). *Making the case for affirmative action.* http://www.acenet.edu/bookstore/descriptions/making_the_case/works/research.cfm

American Heart Association. (2006). *Fish, levels of mercury and omega-3 fatty acids.* http://americanheart.org/presenter.jthml?identifier =3013797

Association of American Colleges & Universities. (2002). *Greater expectations: A new vision for learning as a nation goes to college.* Author.

Association of American Colleges & Universities. (2004). *Our students' best work.* Author.

Astin, A. W. (1993). *What matters in college?* Jossey-Bass.

Banks, J. A. (1995). *Multicultural education and curriculum transformation. The Journal of Negro Education, 64*(4), 390–400.

Banks, J. A. (2016). *Cultural diversity and education: Foundations, curriculum, and teaching* (6th ed.). Routledge.

Banks, J. A., Cookson, P., Gay, G., Hawley, W., Irvine, J. J., Nieto, S., Schofield, J. W., & Stephan, W. (2001). Diversity within unity: Essential principles for teaching and learning in a multicultural society. *Phi Delta Kappan, 83*(3), 196–203.

Baron, R. S. (2005). So right it's wrong: groupthink and the ubiquitous nature of polarized group decision making. *Advances in Experimental Social Psychology, 37,* 219–253.

Baron, R. A., Byrne, D., & Branscombe, N. R. (2006). *Social psychology* (11th ed.). Pearson.

Bennett, M. J. (2004). From ethnocentrism to ethnorelativism. In J. S. Wurzel (Ed.), *Toward multiculturalism: A reader in multicultural education* (2nd ed., pp. 62–78). Intercultural Resource Corporation.

Blackwell, A. G., Kwoh, S., & Pastor, M. (2002). *Searching for the uncommon common ground: New dimensions on race in America.* Norton.

Bobo, L. D., & Licari, F. C. (1989). Education and political tolerance: Testing the effects of cognitive sophistication and target group affect. *Public Opinion Quarterly, 53*(3), 285–308.

Bodian, S. (2006). *Meditation for dummies* (2nd ed.). Wiley Publishing.

Brandt, R. (1994). On educating for diversity: A conversation with James Banks. *Educational Leadership, 52*(9), 31–35.

Brookfield, S. D. (1987). *Developing critical thinkers.* Jossey-Bass.

Brooks, I. (2009). *Organizational behavior* (4th ed.). Prentice Hall.

Brown, T. D., Dane, F. C., & Durham, M. D. (1998). Perception of race and ethnicity. *Journal of Social Behavior & Personality, 13*(2), 295–306.

Cheng, D. X., & Zhao, C. (2006). Cultivating multicultural competence through active participation, multicultural activities, and multicultural learning. *NASPA Journal, 43*(4) 13–38.

Chisholm, I. M. (1994). Preparing teachers for multicultural classrooms. *Journal of Educational Issues of Language Minority Students, 14,* 43–68.

Cross, K. P. (1982). Thirty years passed: Trends in general education. In B. L. Johnson (Ed.), *General education in two-year colleges* (pp. 11–20). Jossey-Bass.

Cuseo, J. (1992, Spring). Cooperative learning vs. small-group discussions and group projects: The critical differences. *Cooperative Learning & College Teaching Newsletter, 2*(3), pp. 4–10. (Reprinted in Jones & Price [1995], *Introduction to accounting: A user's perspective.* Prentice-Hall.)

Dean, C. B., Hubbell, E. R., Pitler, H., & Stone, B. (2012). *Classroom instruction that works: Research-based strategies for increasing student achievement* (2nd ed.). Association for Supervision and Curriculum Development.

Dovidio, J. F., Kawakami, K., & Gaertner, S. L. (2000). Reducing contemporary prejudice: Combating explicit and implicit bias at the individual and intergroup level. In S. Oskamp (Ed.), *Reducing prejudice and discrimination* (pp. 137–164). Erlbaum.

Drake, B., & Poushter, J. (2016). In views of diversity, many Europeans are less positive than Americans. *Pew Research Center,* 1–2. www.pewresearch.org/fact-tank/2016/07/12/in-views-of-diversity-many-europeans-are-less-positive-than-americans

Dryden, G. & Vos, J. (1999). *The learning revolution: To change the way the world learns.* The Learning Web.

Education Commission of the States. (1995). *Making quality count in undergraduate education.* ECS Distribution Center.

Enberg, M. E. (2004). Improving intergroup relations in higher education: A critical examination of the influence of educational interventions on racial bias. *Review of Educational Research, 74*(4), 473–524.

Epstein, J. (2019). *Upheaval: Turning points for nations in crisis.* Little, Brown and Company.

Feagin, J. R., & McKinney, M. D. (2003). *The many costs of racism.* Rowman & Littlefield.

Feldman, S., & Huddy, L. (2005). Racial resentment and white opposition to race-conscious programs: Principles or prejudice? *American Journal of Political Science, 49*(1), 168–183.

Feskens, E. J., & Kromhout, D. (1993). Epidemiologic studies on Eskimos and fish intake. *Annals of the New York Academy of Science, 683,* 9–15.

Friedman, T. L. (2005). *The world is flat: A brief history of the twenty-first century.* Farrar, Straus & Giroux.

Gardner, H. (1999). *Intelligence reframed: Multiple intelligences for the 21st century.* Basic Books.

Ginsberg, M. B., & Wlodkowski, R. J. (2009). *Diversity & motivation* (2nd ed.). Jossey-Bass.

Goleman, D. (1995). *Emotional intelligence: Why it can matter more than IQ.* Random House.

Goleman, D. (2006). *Emotional intelligence: Why it can matter more than IQ* (2nd ed.). Bantam Books.

Gorski, P. C. (1995–2019). *Key characteristics of a multicultural curriculum.* Critical Multicultural Pavilion: Multicultural Curriculum Reform (An EdChange Project). www.edchange.org/multicultural/curriculum/characteristics.html

Gunaratana, B. (2011). *Mindfulness in plain English.* Wisdom Publications.

Gurin, P. (1999). New research on the benefits of diversity in college and beyond: An empirical analysis. *Diversity Digest* (spring). http://www.diversityweb.org/Digest/Sp99/benefits.html

Harris, R. (2010). *On the purpose of a liberal arts education.* wisdomandfollyblog.com/.../seven-reasons-for-the-liberal-arts-part-2/

Hart Research Associates. (2013). *It takes more than a major: Employer priorities for college learning and student success.* Author.

Hetherington, M. J., & Weiler, J. D. (2009). *Authoritarianism and polarization in American politics.* Cambridge University Press.

Hill, P. J. (1991). Multiculturalism: The crucial philosophical and organizational issues. *Change, 23*(4), 38–47.

House, R. J., & Javidan, M. (2004). *Overview of GLOBE.* In R. J. J House, P. J. Hanges, M. Javidan, P. W. Dorfman, V. Gupta, & Associates (Eds.), *Culture leadership, and organizations: The GLOBE study of 62 societies* (pp. 9–28). SAGE.

International Wellness Directory. (2009). *The history of quackery.* https://www.mnwelldir.org/docs/history/quackery.htm

Janis, I. L. (1982). *Groupthink: Psychological studies of policy decisions and fiascoes.* (2nd ed.). Houghton Mifflin.

Job Outlook. (2018). *Are college graduates "career ready?"* National Association of Colleges & Employers. https://www.naceweb.org/career-readiness/competencies/are-college-graduates-career-ready/

Johnson, D. W., & Johnson, R. T. (1989). *Cooperation and competition: Theory and research.* Interaction Book Company.

Kelly, K. (1994). *Out of control: The new biology of machines, social systems, and the economic world.* Addison-Wesley.

Kendi, I. X. (2016). *Stamped from the beginning: The definitive history of racist ideas in America.* Bold Type Books.

Khoshaba, D. M., & Maddi, S. R. (1999–2004). *HardiTraining: Managing stressful change.* The Hardiness Institute.

Kitchener, K., Wood, P., & Jensen, L. (2000, August). *Curricular, co-curricular, and institutional influence on real-world problem-solving.* Paper presented at the annual meeting of the American Psychological Association, Boston.

Kymlicka, W. (2004). *Multicultural citizenship: A liberal theory of minority rights.* Oxford University Press.

Langer, E. (1997). *The power of mindful learning.* De Capo Press.

LeBaron, M. (2003). *Bridging cultural conflicts: New approaches for a changing world.* Jossey-Bass.

Leung, A. K., Maddux, W. W., Galinsky, A. D., & Chie-yue, C. (2008). Multicultural experience enhances creativity: The when and how. *American Psychologist, 63*(3), 169–181.

Levine, D. (2005). *Teaching empathy.* Solution Tree Press.

Light, R. J. (2001). *Making the most of college: Students speak their minds.* Harvard University Press.

Lopez, S. (2018, September 9). Dreaming of a life better than their own. *Los Angeles Times,* B-1-B2.

Lopez, S. J., Pedrotti, J. T., & Snyder, C. R. (2015). *Positive psychology: The scientific and practical explorations of human strengths.* Sage.

Maddux, W. W., & Galinsky, A. D. (2009). Cultural borders and mental barriers: The relationship between living abroad and creativity. *Journal of Personality and Social Psychology, 96*(5), 1047–1061.

Marzano, R., Pickering, D. J., & Pollock, J. (2001). *Classroom instruction that works: Research-based strategies for increasing student achievement.* Association for Supervision and Curriculum Development.

Miville, M. L., Molla, B., & Sedlacek, W. E. (1992). Attitudes of tolerance for diversity among college students. *Journal of the Freshman Year Experience, 4*(1), 95–110.

Myrdal, F. (1944). *An American dilemma: The Negro problem and modern democracy.* Harper and Row.

National Association of Colleges & Employers. (2019). *Career readiness defined.* http://www.naceweb.org/career-readiness/competencies/career-readiness-defined/

Nagda, B. R., Gurin, P., & Johnson, S. M. (2005). Living, doing and thinking diversity: How does pre-college diversity experience affect first-year students' engagement with college diversity? In R. S. Feldman (Ed.), *Improving the first year of college: Research and practice* (pp. 73–110). Lawrence Erlbaum Associates.

National Council for the Social Sciences. (1991). *Curriculum guidelines for multicultural education.* Prepared by the NCSS Task Force on Ethnic Studies Curriculum Guidelines. www.socialstudies.org/positions/multicultural

Novinger, T. (2001). *Intercultural communication: A practical guide.* University of Texas Press.

Office of Research. (1994). *What employers expect of college graduates: International knowledge and second language skills.* Office of Educational Research and Improvement (OERI), U.S. Department of Education.

Okihiro, G. (1994). *Margins and mainstreams: Asians in American history and culture.* University of Washington Press.

Pascarella, E., Edison, M., Nora, A., Hagedorn, L, & Terenzini, P. (1996). Influences on students' openness to diversity and challenge in the first year of college. *Journal of Higher Education, 67,* 174–195.

Pascarella, E., Palmer, B., Moye, M., & Pierson, C. (2001). Do diversity experiences influence the development of critical thinking? *Journal of College Student Development, 42,* 257–291.

Paul, R., & Elder, L. (2002). *Critical thinking: Tools for taking charge of your professional and personal life.* Pearson Education.

Pedrotti, J. T. (2015). Cultural competence in positive psychology: History, research, and practice. In J. C. Wade, L. I. Maks, & R. D. Hetzel (Eds.), *Positive psychology on the college campus* (pp. 81–98). Oxford University Press.

Pettigrew, T. F., Tropp, L. R., Wagner, U., & Christ, O. (2011). Recent advances in intergroup contact theory. *International Journal of Intercultural Relations, 35*(3), 271–280.

Putnam, R. (2007). E pluribus unum: Diversity and community in the twenty-first century. The 2006 Johan Skytte Prize Lecture, *Scandinavian Political Studies, 30,* 137–74.

Rosenshine, B. (1997). Advances in research on instruction. In J. W. Lloyd, E. J., Kameanui, & D. Chard (Eds.), *Issues in educating students with disabilities* (pp. 197–221). Lawrence Erlbaum.

Shetterly, M. L. (2017). *Hidden figures: The American dream and the untold story of the black women mathematicians who helped win the space race.* HarperCollins.

Slavin, R. E. (1990). *Cooperative learning: Theory, research, and practice.* Prentice-Hall

Smith, P. (2004). *The quiet crisis: How higher education is failing America.* Anker.

Smith, D. (2015). *Diversity's promise for higher education: Making it work* (2nd ed.).Johns Hopkins University Press.

Stephan, W. (1978). School desegregation: An evaluation of predictions made in Brown vs. Board of Education. *Psychological Bulletin, 85,* 217–238.

Stoltz, P. G. (2014). *Grit: The new science of what it takes to persevere, flourish, succeed.* Climb Strong Press.

Thompson, A., & Cuseo, J. (2014). *Diversity and the college experience.* Kendall Hunt.

U.S. Census Bureau. (2008). *An older and more diverse nation by midcentury.* http://www.census.gov/Press-Release/www/releases/archives/population/012496.html

Uzzi, B., & Dunlap, S. (2005). How to build your network. H*arvard Business Review, 83*(12), 53–60.

Wabash National Study of Liberal Arts Education. (2007). *Liberal arts outcomes.* http:www.liberalarts.wabash.edu/ study-overview/

Whitt, E., Edison, M., Pascarella, E., Terenzini, P., & Nora, A. (2001). Influences on students' openness to diversity and challenge in the second and third years of college. *Journal of Higher Education, 72,* 172–204.

Willis, J. (2006). *Research-based strategies to ignite student learning: Insights from a neurologist and classroom teacher.* ASCD.

Reflections and Applications

Name

_____

Date

_____

3.1 Review the sidebar quotes contained in this chapter and select two that you think are particularly meaningful or inspirational. For each quote you selected, provide an explanation of why you chose it.

3.2 Reflect on the following benefits of multicultural education cited in this chapter and rate them on a scale of 1–5 in terms of their importance to you (1 = low importance; 5 = high importance).

a) Increases self-awareness and self-knowledge

b) Deepens and accelerates learning

c) Strengthens ability to think critically

d) Fosters creative thinking

e) Expands social networks and builds emotional intelligence

f) Enhances career preparation

g) Reduces societal prejudice and discrimination

h) Preserves democracy

For any item you gave a rating of "5," briefly explain why you gave that item the highest possible rating.

3.3 How would you defend, support, or explain the following statement? "Humans learn more from diversity than they do from similarity or familiarity."

3.4 Intercultural competence has been defined as the ability to appreciate and learn from human differences and to interact effectively with people from diverse cultural backgrounds. What points would you make to persuade your peers that they need to develop intercultural competence with respect to be successful in their future career?

3.5 Describe what you think is the key point being made by the author of the following quote: "Meaningful multiculturalism transforms the curriculum. While the presence of persons of other cultures and subcultures is a virtual prerequisite to that transformation, their 'mere presence' is primarily a political achievement, not an intellectual or educational achievement. Real educational progress will be made when multiculturalism becomes *interculturalism*."

3.6 Defend or support the following statement: "Diversity and democracy go hand-in-hand; when the former is valued, the latter is preserved."

Barriers to Diversity Appreciation: Implicit Bias, Stereotypes, Prejudice, and Discrimination

Chapter Purpose and Preview

This chapter analyzes and synthesizes common forms of personal bias, stereotyping, prejudice, and discrimination. The chapter also examines the roots of prejudice—what causes its formation in the first place and what holds it in place once it has been formed. The chapter concludes by analyzing the underlying causes of bias, which is a form of critical thinking—an important outcome of a college education and a key characteristic of a well-educated person.

Introduction

Prejudice and discrimination displayed by humans toward other members of their own species has a long and continuing trail. (See **Box 4.1** on p. 101.) Although some of the more flagrant forms of prejudice and discrimination have been eliminated (e.g., slavery and race-based lynchings), the United States still remains a country fraught with other forms prejudice that continue to divide its citizens along the lines of race, culture, and social class. Studies show that these prejudicial divisions are increasing as the proportion of ethnic and racial minorities in the American population is increasing (Brookings Institute, 2008). America's public schools, for instance, are more segregated today than they were in the late 1960s (Kisida & Piontek, 2019; Vox Media, 2019).

Stereotyping and Implicit Bias

The word *stereotype* derives from two roots: *stereo*—to look at in a fixed way, and *type*—to categorize or group together (as in the word "typical"). Thus, to stereotype a group of people is to look at members of the same group (type) in the same (fixed) way and to overlook differences among individuals who make up that group (Hamilton et al., 1994). Stereotyping dismisses individuality; instead, all individuals in the same group (e.g., race or gender) are viewed as having similar personal characteristics—as reflected in comments like: "You know how they are; they're all alike."

All stereotypes involve *bias,* which literally means "slant." A bias (slant) can tilt toward the positive or the negative and it may be a conscious or unconscious—also known as *implicit bias*. Positive bias results in favorable stereotypes (e.g., "Asians are great in science and math"); negative bias leads to unfavorable stereotypes (e.g., "Asians are nerds who do nothing but study"). While most people do not engage in blatant stereotyping, many individuals do hold overgeneralized beliefs about particular social groups. Even individuals who strongly believe in the importance of equal rights and equitable treatment of all human groups have been found to hold implicit racial biases (Banaji & Greenwald, 2013). For example, one major study showed that whites who reported positive attitudes toward other racial groups on surveys were found to engage friendlier and more comfortable conversations with black people than did whites who held negative interracial attitudes when their interactions were videotaped. However, when the video recordings of whites with positive interracial attitudes interacting with blacks were reviewed with the sound off, their nonverbal communication (body language) revealed higher levels of discomfort and stress than when they interacted with whites. Thus, they did not express *explicit* bias (verbally) but demonstrated *implicit* bias (nonverbally) (Dovidio et al., 2002).

When stereotypes are negative, they can be internalized by members of the stereotyped group and have negative effects on their self-confidence and performance, as illustrated in the following personal experience.

Personal Experience

I was six years old when a six-year-old girl (a member of a different racial group than me) told me that people of my race (black) could not swim. Since I couldn't swim at that time and she could, I assumed she was correct. I asked a boy (a member of the same racial group as the girl) whether her statement was true. He responded emphatically: "Yes, it's definitely true!" Since I grew up in an area where few other African Americans were around to counteract this belief about my racial group, I continued to buy into this stereotype until I finally took swimming lessons as an adult. After many lessons, I am now a lousy swimmer because I didn't even attempt to swim until reaching an advanced age. Moral of the story: Negative group stereotypes can limit the personal confidence and performance potential of individuals in the group that has been stereotyped.

—Aaron Thompson

The above story illustrates a particular form of stereotyping known as "stereotype threat"—a negative stereotype about members of a group can threaten the performance of individuals in that group and increase the likelihood they will confirm or conform to the negative stereotype (Steele, 2004).

Reflection 4.1

Have you ever been stereotyped based on your appearance or group membership?

(a) If yes, what was the stereotype? How did being stereotyped make you feel?

(b) If no, why do you think you have never been stereotyped?

Prejudice

When members of a stereotyped group are pre-*judged*, the stereotype becomes *prejudice*. In fact, the word "prejudice" literally means "pre-judge." Thus, stereotyping can lead to prejudice by causing people to form beliefs about another social group before the facts are known. Typically, prejudice is associated with negative pre-judgments result in *stigmatizing*—ascribing inferior or unfavorable traits to members of the same group (Goffman, 1963). Studies show that young children often enter school with prejudicial attitudes that reflect those held by the adults in their family and community (Aboud, 1998, 2009; Stephan & Stephan, 2004). Studies also show that stigmatizing can affect students' behavior in school and have adverse effects on their academic performance (Inzlicht & Good, 2006; Mendoza-Denton et al., 2006).

Prejudice negative effects on the health on members of racial and ethnic groups that are targets of prejudice (Lewis, 2002) as well as the health of those who hold group prejudices—by causing them to experience a rush of stress hormones when they come in contact with members of the groups toward which they are prejudiced (Page-Gould, 2010). For instance, in one study, European Americans took a survey over the Internet that assessed their prejudice toward African Americans. The European Americans who completed the survey then participated in an interview conducted by an African American or a European American. When the interviewer was African American, European Americans who scored low on the prejudice test showed no bodily increase in stress hormones;

"I grew up in a very racist family. Even a year ago, I could honestly say, 'I hate Asians' with a straight face and mean it. My senior AP teacher taught me not to be so judgmental. He got me to open up to others, so much so that my current boyfriend is half Chinese."
—FIRST-YEAR COLLEGE STUDENT

those who scored higher on the prejudice tests showed a spike in their bodily levels of cortisol—a stress hormone that weakens immune function and increases the risk of heart disease (Mendes et al., 2007). Thus, prejudice is bad not only for the health of those who are targets of prejudice, it's also bad for the health of those who are the holders of prejudice.

Personal Experience

I was 15 years old when I first became aware of the racial prejudice that existed among members of my extended family. I grew up in New York during the 1950s and became an avid fan of the New York Giants baseball team. When I was 8, the team left New York and moved to San Francisco. Even though the Giants left my hometown, I still considered them to be my team. As a result, I was teased frequently by members of my extended family about rooting for an out-of-town team and not being loyal to New York.

During one teasing episode that took place in the presence of my cousins and uncles, I defended my team by pointing out they were in first place and that I expected them to win the double-header they were to play later that day. My 19-year-old cousin, Jimmy, interrupted me and sarcastically proclaimed that the Giants' double-header was going to be cancelled because Malcolm X (black civil rights leader) was holding a meeting. Several of my older cousins and my uncles began laughing, but I couldn't figure out what was so funny. Then I suddenly got the "joke." At that time, the Giants were a team that had more black and Latino players than any other team in baseball. They were the first major league team to have multiple players from the Dominican Republic, and they had players from Puerto Rico and Cuba. I began to realize that all the teasing I received about being a Giants fan had less to do with the fact that I was rooting for an out-of-town team and had more to do with the fact that I was rooting for a "colored" team.

Before hearing that joke at my family get-together, I never thought of the Giants' players as colored; I just thought they were colorful. They had unique playing styles and distinctive surnames and nicknames, such as: Willie Mays ("The Say Hey Kid"), Willie "Stretch" McCovey, Orlando Cepeda (the "Baby Bull"), and Juan Marichal (the "Dominican Dandy"). As a young boy, I saw these players as being refreshingly different and exciting. However, after my cousin's wisecrack that day, and the encouraging reaction it received from many members of my family, I became more color-conscious. It also transformed me from a Giants fan to Giants fanatic. I was not only rooting for a team; I was rooting for a cause. Later that year, the Giants added a pitcher by the name of Masanori Murakami—the first Asian player ever to play major league baseball in America. I was proud to be rooting for the most diverse team in history. I didn't realize it at the time, but that encounter with racial prejudice in my own family was what launched my later-life advocacy for diversity and and was likely the original source of motivation for my co-writing this book.

—Joe Cuseo

Discrimination

The root meaning of the word *discrimination* is to "divide" or "separate." In contrast to prejudice, which is a biased belief, attitude, or opinion, discrimination is a biased *action*. Technically, discrimination can be either negative or positive—for example, a discriminating eater may be careful about consuming only healthy foods and avoiding consumption of unhealthy foods. However, discrimination is more often associated with negative forms of behavior in which unfair or unjust acts are committed against a group of people that are targets of prejudice. Thus, it could be said that discrimination takes prejudice (an attitude) and puts it into practice (an action). For example, not hiring or selling property someone because of that person's racial group, gender, or sexual orientation is an act of discrimination.

Discrimination is often driven by implicit bias and expressed in subtle ways without people being fully aware they are discriminating. For example, in a series of classic studies, it was discovered that some white, male college professors treated white male students differently from female students and students of color. These studies showed that females and minority students taught by white male instructors:

- received less eye contact in class,
- were called on less frequently in class,
- were given less time to respond to questions the instructors asked in class, and
- had less interpersonal contact with the instructors outside of class (Hall & Sandler, 1982, 1984; Sedlacek, 1987; Wright, 1987).

In the vast majority of these cases, the discriminatory treatment that female and minority students received was subtle and was not done intentionally or consciously by the instructors (Green, 1989). Nonetheless, these unintended actions are still discriminatory because they send a tacit message to students from certain groups that less is expected of them or they're not as capable as other students (Sadker & Sadker, 1994).

Discrimination can take place not only through individual actions, but also through institutional actions that are built or "baked" into organizational policies and practices of an institution (e.g., a corporate organization or an institution of higher education). An interesting example of institutional racism once took place in the music industry. Auditions for orchestras were typically conducted with the identity of the applicants visible to the judges (employers). However, in one audition, the son of a man who worked for the orchestra was applying for a position as a musician and there was concern that if his identity were visible, nepotism (biased favoritism of a relative) would affect the hiring process. To guard against this unfair practice, screens were placed in front of the auditioning musicians to conceal their identities. Other orchestras heard about this practice and soon began implementing the same procedure for all their auditions. After the practice of concealing the identity of auditioning musicians became common, something unexpected happened: more women and racial minorities began to be hired by classical orchestras. Because the applicants' identity was concealed, employment decisions that were previously biased by institutional

> "A lot of us never asked questions in class before—it just wasn't done, especially by a woman or a girl, so we need to realize that and get into the habit of asking questions and challenging—regardless of the reactions of the professors and other students."
> —ADULT FEMALE COLLEGE STUDENT

© Iuliia Vanhaber/Shutterstock.com

racism or sexism began to be replaced by applicants' actual qualifications—the merit of their performance (Gladwell, 2005).

Even if job applicants are not intentionally discriminated against in the hiring process on the basis of race or gender, research reveals that people of color still have less access to jobs, particularly higher-paying ones, because many of these positions are obtained through word of mouth. This networking advantage (sometimes referred to as "social capital") favors people who live and socialize with people holding similar positions and who make hiring decisions for such positions—people who are predominantly white. Research shows that employers in most organizations tend to hire people like themselves because they perceive them (either consciously or unconsciously) to be better qualified (Harper, 2012). Sociologists refer to this phenomenon as *homosocial reproduction*—the tendency to replace departing members of an organization with candidates whose characteristics are similar to the departing employee or the employer doing the hiring (Elliot & Smith, 2004; Kanter, 1977). This works to the advantage of white male candidates, providing them with a *privilege* (an unearned advantage) that is denied to groups that have been historically discriminated against in the job market, such as women and people of color. Similarly, privilege can take the form of "privileged legacies"—people who have the privilege of benefitting from their relationship to a family member—such as inheriting money from a wealthy parent or getting admitted to a college because a family member previously attended that college. These privileged benefits less available to certain groups of people, such as women and people of color, whose family members grew up during times of race and gender discrimination (Minnich, 2005).

Racial discrimination can also pervade multiple institutions and entire societal systems, referred to as *systemic racism*. For instance, practices used the housing, education, and criminal justice systems continue to have a discriminatory impact on people of color. (Detailed documentation of these forms of systemic racism is provided in Chapters 7 and 8.)

Reflection 4.2

Have you ever observed or been a victim of discrimination? What did the act of discrimination involve and why do you think it occurred?

Microaggression

A microaggression is a discriminatory act that takes the form of an indirect or subtle put-down—delivered intentionally or unintentionally to members of a social group—particularly a group that has been historically marginalized or stigmatized (Sue, 2010). Chester Pierce, a black Harvard University psychiatrist, first coined the term to describe insults and dismissals that he witnessed being aimed at blacks (Treadwell, 2013), but the term has been expanded to other groups who are also common targets of microaggressions. For example, an anti-Hispanic microaggression would be if a white American asked a Hispanic American: "Where are you really from?" The microaggression exhibited here is the indirect suggestion or insinuation that the person may be an illegal immigrant who doesn't belong in America. A common anti-transgender microaggression is intentionally misgendering a transgender person by referring to that person with a pronoun that does not represent the gender person identifies with.

Microaggressions may also take the form of subtly annoying actions taken toward members of a particular group, such as the one described by Eduardo Bonilla-Silva, a Duke University sociologist: "I, a black-looking Puerto Rican, am monitored in stores or asked numerous time by clerks, "May I help *you* (a way of letting me know that they are checking me). How can I charge discrimination when the behavior seems to be 'polite'"? (Bonilla-Silva, 2018, p. 51). Research shows that when people of color repeatedly experience microaggressions such as these, it begins to wear on their mental and physical health (Lui & Quezada, 2019; Nadal et al., 2014; Sue et al., 2007).

Nativism

The United States often proudly calls itself "a nation of immigrants" but America has a long history of opposing immigration and resisting immigrants' assimilation into the dominant culture (Giroux, 1998; Moghaddam, 2008). Opposition to immigration typically increases when the number of immigrants increases, and if the immigrants have darker skin, unfamiliar traditions, and speak a foreign language. For example, an immigration act passed in 1924 sharply reduced the number of "undesirable" (darker-skinned whites) immigrants from southern and eastern Europe, which included Italians, Jews, Hungarians, and Slavs. This immigration policy ensured that most of the immigrants coming to America during the following decades would be from Western Europe and Canada (Jardina, 2019). Throughout U.S. history, white Americans have been more opposed to immigration than people of color (Abrajano & Hajnal, 2015; Schuman et al., 1985) and national surveys conducted by the Pew Research Center reveal that Americans living in geographic areas with relatively low numbers of foreign-born people are those who are most likely to view immigrants as a burden to America and a threat to American culture (Benjamin, 2009).

Research conducted by the Southern Poverty Law Center indicates that anti-immigrant prejudice has risen to levels not seen in America since the 1920s, and anti-immigrant hate groups have increased dramatically since the late 1990s (SPLC, 2020).

 Consider This…

More than one-third of all American Nobel Prize winners have been foreign-born and more than half were either immigrants themselves or children of immigrants (Diamond, 2019).

Hate Groups

The Federal Bureau of Investigations (FBI) defines a *hate group* as "a social group [whose] primary purpose is to promote animosity, hostility, and malice against persons belonging to a race, religion, disability, sexual orientation, or ethnicity/national origin which differs from that of the members of its organization" (FBI, 2015).

The Southern Poverty Law Center (SPLC) Intelligence Project has been tracking hate groups for many years, identifying a hate group based on: (a) publications (in print or online) of its professed principles, (b) statements made by the group's official leader, (c) how the group's followers show support for the group (e.g., making donations or paying membership dues), and (c) the group's participation in activities (e.g., meetings and rallies). Based on these criteria, the SPLC's Intelligence Project has identified more than 800 hate groups in the United States, the largest percentage of which are white supremacy groups, whose members believe their goal is to protect and preserve the white race and that people of color, immigrants, and other minority groups are inferior and threatening. The number of white supremacist and white nationalist groups has been growing due to fear of the growing number of non-whites in the U.S. population. They believe this growth in the non-white population is part of "the great replacement" plot to displace white people from their home country. Some white supremacist groups believe that Jews are promoting this change in racial demographics, as demonstrated at the 2017 "Unite the Right" in Charlottesville, Virginia, where white supremacists repeatedly chanted: "Jews will not replace us." An increasing number of white supremacists also refer to themselves as "accelerationists" who are preparing for an apocalyptic and violent race war that they believe will be inevitable as America continues to become an increasingly multicultural nation (SPLC, 2020, 2021). Also contributing to the growth of white nationalist groups are social media sites designed to recruit new members and provide them with a supportive community (Swain, 2002; Swain & Nieli, 2003).

"Overestimation of one's own position and the hate for all who differ from it is narcissism. He is nothing, but if he can identify with his nation, or can transfer his personal narcissism to the nation, then he is everything."

—ERICH FROMM, PROMINENT GERMAN SOCIAL PSYCHOLOGIST AND PSYCHOANALYST

 ## Consider This…

Facebook's standards on hate speech now state: "We don't allow content that contains hate speech. This includes attacks on people because of their race, ethnicity, religion, caste, physical or mental ability, gender, or sexual orientation."

White supremacy and white nationalist groups make up the largest percentage of hate groups in America. © Clive Chilvers/Shutterstock.com

Box 4.1 contains a summary of different hate groups and organizations that were active in America in 2021.

Box 4.1 — Major Hate Groups in the United Students, 2021

White Nationalists: A collection of a number of different hate groups that believe in the superiority of the white race (a.k.a. white supremacy).

Ku Klux Klan (KKK): the oldest of America's hate groups; its members have a long history of prejudice and violence, that originally focused primarily on blacks, but also includes Jews, immigrants, and the LGBTQ community.

Neo-Nazi: groups who share a hatred of Jews and admiration for Adolf Hitler and Nazi Germany. (These groups also harbor hatred toward people of color and members of the LGBTQ community.)

The Ku Klux Klan (KKK) is America's oldest hate group and is still active today. © Everett Collection/Shutterstock.com

Racist Skinheads: an especially violent white nationalist group that is planning (and hoping) for a race war; its members typically have shaved heads, wear black boots, and adorn their bodies with racist tattoos.

Neo-Confederates: a branch of white nationalism that uses symbols of the Southern Confederacy to convey their racist ideology, seeks to preserve monuments devoted to confederate war heroes, and opposes renaming Army bases named after confederate military officers.

Anti-Muslim Groups: emerging after the September 11th, 2001 terrorist attack, these groups view all Muslims as terrorist threats and believe that the U.S. government is being infiltrated by Islamic extremists. (Muslims are now the second-largest target of religious hate crimes following Jews.)

Neo-Nazi hate groups share a hatred of Jews and love for Adolf Hitler. © mark reinstein/Shutterstock.com

Anti-LGBTQ Groups: oppose LGBTQ rights (e.g. the right to marry or serve in the military), often because they believe that LGBTQ people are threats to children, society, and public health. Anti-LGBTQ groups are one of the fastest-growing hate groups in America.

Proud Boys: a self-described "Western chauvinist" men's club that demonizes trans people, is misogynistic, anti-Muslim, anti-immigrant, and anti-Semitic—as evidenced by one of its members protesting the results of the 2020 national election at the nation's capitol while wearing a shirt with the message, "6MWE"—an anti-Semitic slogan standing for "Six Million Weren't Enough."

Boogaloo Boys: a loosely defined group who believes that America is headed toward a second civil war; they show up at protests heavily armed and wearing Hawaiian shirts to symbolize the "big luau"—a term they modified to create the group's name, "Boogaloo." They describe themselves as race-blind, anti-government libertarians who are preparing to engage in armed insurrection against governmental tyranny. Its members also include white nationalists preparing for a race war.

Sources: Miller (2020); SPLC (2019, 2020)

Hate Crimes

The Federal Bureau of Investigation defines a *hate crime* as a "criminal offense against a person or property motivated in whole or in part by an offender's bias against a race, religion, disability, sexual orientation, ethnicity, gender, or gender identity" (FBI, 2015). Individuals who commit hate crimes may not be members of hate groups, but their motivation for committing hate crimes is often inspired or ignited by a hate group ideology (SPLC, 2019). Hate-crime laws are now in place at the federal level and in all states except Arkansas, South Carolina, and Wyoming. Civil rights activists in Wyoming have been pushing the state to pass hate-crime legislation ever since Matthew Shepard, a gay college student, was targeted and murdered in 1998. (See details about his case on p. 124.) They have not been successful in getting a state law passed, but their efforts have drawn national attention to anti-gay violence, leading many states to add sexual orientation to the groups covered by their hate crime laws (Kaleem, 2021).

Since the FBI began collecting hate crime statistics, blacks have been the number one target of racial hate crimes. Jews have been the major target of religion-based hate crimes (Hier & Cooper, 2019), and anti-Muslim hate crimes have increased sharply since the September 11th attack on the United States (SPLC, 2021). Anti-Asian hate crimes have increased dramatically since the outbreak of the COVID-19 pandemic (Center for the Study of Hate and Extremism, 2021).

Listed below are examples of significant hate crimes that have been committed against different social groups in recent years.

- *Anti-Asian*: In 2020, Chinese and Korean restaurants were vandalized with anti-Asian graffiti (e.g., "Stop eating dogs"), and an Asian American woman was attacked on a bus by a woman and three teenage girls who struck her with an umbrella, accusing her of starting the COVID pandemic (Kaleem et al., 2021).
- *Anti-Jewish (Anti-Semitic)*: In 2018, while shouting anti-Semitic slurs, a gunman opened fire in a Pittsburgh synagogue, killing 11 and wounding six others. Prior to the attack, he posted on social media that Jews were the "enemy of the people" (Hussain, 2019).
- *Anti-Muslim*: In 2019, a white nationalist in New Zealand went on a shooting rampage at two mosques, killing 51 and injuring many others. He then livestreamed the shooting, leaving a 74-page manifesto detailing how he grew to hate Muslims, intends to kill them, and encourages others to kill them as well (Hussain, 2019).
- *Anti-Hispanic*: In 2019, at a Walmart outlet in El Paso, Texas, where Hispanic parents and children were taking advantage of a tax-free shopping day before the start of the school year, a 21-year-old man with an assault rifle, killed 22 and injured 26 others. Just before the attack, the gunman posted comments about the need for "ethnic displacement," his disapproval of "race-mixing," and his intention to do something about the "Hispanic invasion of Texas" (SPLC, 2020).
- *Anti-Black:* In 2015, a 21-year-old white supremacist attended a Bible study at a black Methodist church in Charleston, South Carolina. Following the service, he proceeded to shoot nine African Americans, killing three (including the senior pastor and a state senator) while shouting racial epithets during the attack. Explaining why he targeted the church, he stated that he had "no choice" but to target blacks because they were "stupid and violent" (Bacon, 2015).
- *Anti-LGBTQ*: In 2016, 49 people were killed and 53 injured at a Miami nightclub frequented by members of the LGBTQ community. It was the deadliest attack on the LGBTQ people in U.S. history (Associated Press, 2021).

Consider This...

Terrorism refers to the unlawful use of violence and intimidation, especially against civilians, that is driven by political ideology. *Domestic terrorism* is a form of terrorism in which terrorists target citizens of their own country (Jackson, 2012). Currently, domestic terrorism is not recognized as a hate crime.

Reflection 4.3

Do you think the extreme forms of prejudice displayed by hate groups and hate crimes are the result of growing prejudice in our society, or do you think they reflect implicit biases that have always been held and people have become more comfortable expressing them explicitly or openly? Why?

Box 4.2 contains definitions and examples of the variety of biases, prejudicial beliefs, and discriminatory behaviors that have plagued humankind and serve as barriers to acceptance and appreciation of diversity. As you read through the list, place a checkmark next to any form of prejudice that you have experienced, have seen others experience, or have seen others demonstrate.

Box 4.2 Definitions and Examples of Biases, Prejudicial Beliefs, and Discriminatory Behaviors

Ageism: prejudice or discrimination toward certain age groups, particularly the elderly.

Example: believing that "old" people have dementia and should not hold decision-making jobs or political positions.

Ableism: prejudice or discrimination displayed toward people who are disabled and handicapped (physically, mentally, or emotionally).

Example: Intentionally avoiding social contact with people in wheelchairs.

Anti-Semitism: prejudice or discrimination toward Jews and other people who practice the religion of Judaism.

Example: Disliking or disdaining Jews because they are the people who "killed Christ."

Apartheid: an institutionalized system of "legal racism" supported by a nation's government. (Apartheid derives from a word in the Afrikaans language which means "apartness.")

Example: South Africa's national system of racial segregation and discrimination that existed from 1948 to 1994.

"Never, never, and never again shall it be that this beautiful land will again experience the oppression of one by another."

—NELSON MANDELA, ANTI-APARTHEID ACTIVIST, FIRST BLACK PRESIDENT OF SOUTH AFRICA AFTER APARTHEID, AND RECIPIENT OF THE NOBEL PEACE PRIZE

Classism: prejudice or discrimination toward a group based on their social class, particularly toward people of lower socioeconomic status.

Example: Acknowledging the contributions made by politicians and wealthy industrialists to America, while ignoring or minimizing the contributions of poor immigrants, farmers, slaves, and pioneer women.

Colorism: a form of racism that involves bias toward people of color with darker-colored skin.

Example: Darker-skinned Mexican Americans more often being the targets of "go back to Mexico" chants than lighter-skinned Mexican Americans.

Discrimination: unequal and unfair treatment of a particular social group.

Example: Women being paid less than men for performing the same job, even though if they have exactly the same level of education and job qualifications.

Ethnocentrism: viewing one's own culture or ethnic group as "normal" or "superior" and other cultures as "abnormal" or "inferior."

Example: Viewing another culture as "abnormal" or "uncivilized" because its members eat certain animals that are unacceptable to eat in our culture, even though we eat animals that are unacceptable to eat in their culture.

Genocide: mass murdering of a particular ethnic or racial group.

Example: The Holocaust, in which millions of Jews were systematically murdered in Nazi Germany. Other examples include the murdering of Cambodians under the Khmer Rouge regime, the murdering of Bosnian Muslims in the former country of Yugoslavia, the slaughter of the Tutsi minority by the Hutu majority in Rwanda, and the massive killing of Native Americans during America's western expansion.

"A war of extermination will continue to be waged . . . until the Indian race becomes extinct."
—PETER BURNETT, FIRST ELECTED GOVERNOR OF CALIFORNIA, 1851

Hate Crimes: criminal action motivated solely by prejudice toward the victim being a member of a particular social group.

Example: Acts of vandalism or assault aimed at members of a particular ethnic group or persons of a particular sexual orientation.

Hate Groups: organizations whose primary purpose is to stimulate prejudice, discrimination, or aggression toward certain groups of people based on their ethnicity, race, religion, etc.

Example: The Ku Klux Klan—an American terrorist group that perpetrates hatred toward all non-white races.

Heterosexism: belief that heterosexuality is the only acceptable sexual orientation.

Example: Denying gays the same legal rights as heterosexuals.

Homophobia: extreme fear or hatred of homosexuals.

Example: Anti-gay websites and "gay bashing"—engaging in violent acts that target gays.

"Jim Crow" Laws: formal and informal laws created by whites to segregate blacks after the abolition of slavery.

Example: laws that required blacks to use separate bathrooms and be educated in separate schools.

Microaggression: a brief, indirect or subtle put-down, delivered intentionally or unintentionally to members of certain group—particularly groups that have been historically marginalized or stigmatized.

Example: Asking a student of color if he got into college as a "special admit" or an employee of color if she got her job because of affirmative action.

Nationalism a.k.a. Jingoism: excessive belief in the superiority or exceptionality of one's own nation (without acknowledging its mistakes or weaknesses) and disdain for other nations, often accompanied by favoring aggressive foreign policies that neglect the needs of other nations or the common needs of all nations.

Example: "Blind patriotism"—not seeing the shortcomings of one's own country and viewing any questioning or criticism of it as being disloyal or "unpatriotic." (As reflected in such slogans as: "America: right or wrong!" "America: love it or leave it!")

Nativism: a political ideology or policy that serves or advances the interests of native inhabitants at the expense of immigrants and that opposes immigration based on fears that immigrants—particularly those from certain nations—will disrupt or displace the cultural norms and values of one's own nation. (Note: People holding this political position do not view it as prejudice, but as patriotism.)

Example: The Chinese Exclusion Act—a federal law passed in 1882 that prohibited Chinese immigrants from entering the United States—the first anti-immigration law implemented in America that banned all members of a particular ethnic or national group from entering the country.

Prejudice: a negative pre-judgment about members of another social group.

Example: White coaches thinking that black football players cannot play quarter-back because they lack the intelligence.

Racial Profiling: using a person's social group as grounds for suspecting a criminal offense.

Example: Police making a traffic stop or conducting a car search based solely on an individual's racial characteristics.

Racism: belief that one's racial group is superior to other groups, which that may be expressed as an attitude (prejudice) or demonstrated in action (discrimination).

Example: Historic confiscation of land from American Indians based on the belief that they were "savages" or enslaving African Americans based on the belief that they were "subhuman."

Regional Bias: prejudice or discrimination based on the geographical region in which a group of people is born and raised.

Example: A northerner who thinks that all southerners are racists.

Religious Intolerance: denying a group of people the fundamental right to hold religious beliefs or to hold a certain religious belief that differs from one's own.

Example: Atheists who force non-religious (secular) beliefs on others, or members of a religion who believe that members of other religions are infidels or "sinners."

Segregation: intentional decision made by a group to separate itself (socially or physically) from another group.

Example: "White flight"—whites moving out of neighborhoods when people of color move in.

"Patriotism is when love of your own people comes first; nationalism is when hate for people other than your own comes first."
—CHARLES DE GAULLE, FORMER PRESIDENT OF FRANCE AND ARMY OFFICER WHO LED FRENCH FORCES AGAINST NAZI GERMANY IN WWII

"The teaching of nationalism often results in students learning misconceptions, stereotypes, and myths about other nations and acquiring negative and confused attitudes toward them."
—JAMES BANKS, FOUNDING DIRECTOR OF THE CENTER OR MULTICULTURAL EDUCATION AT THE UNIVERSITY OF WASHINGTON

"Let us all hope that the dark clouds of racial prejudice will soon pass away and . . . in some not too distant tomorrow the radiant stars of love and brotherhood will shine over our great nation."
—MARTIN LUTHER KING, JR., CIVIL RIGHTS LEADER, HUMANITARIAN, AND RECIPIENT OF THE NOBEL PEACE PRIZE

Sexism: prejudice or discrimination based on a person's sex or gender.

Example: Believing that women should not pursue careers in fields traditionally occupied by men (e.g., engineering or politics) because they lack the innate qualities or natural skills to be successful.

Slavery: forced labor in which people are viewed as property, held against their will, and deprived of the right to receive wages.

Example: The legal enslavement of African Americans in the United States until 1865.

Stereotyping: viewing all (or virtually all) members of the same group in the same way—such as having the same type of personal traits or characteristics.

Example: "If you're Italian, you must be in the Mafia or have a family member who is."

Systemic Racism: racial discrimination rooted in societal systems that discriminate against certain groups.

Example: Race-based discrimination in mortgage lending, bank loans, and housing opportunities.

Terrorism: intentional acts of violence committed against civilians that are motivated by political prejudice.

Example: The September 11th, 2001 attacks on the United States.

White Supremacy: the belief that whites are a superior racial group, should dominate other racial groups, or live in a whites-only society.

Example: The view held by hate groups, such as the Ku Klux Klan and neo-Nazis.

White Genocide: (a.k.a. "Replacement Theory") a racist conspiracy theory contending that white people all over the world are being displaced by immigrants and people of color, often with the secret assistance of prominent Jews.

Example: Erroneous claims that the South African government is attacking and seizing the land of white farmers.

Xenophobia: fear or hatred of foreigners, outsiders, or strangers.

Example: belief that immigrants should be banned from entering the country or deported from the country because they take away jobs from native citizens and commit crimes.

Reflection 4.4

Looking back at the above list, which forms of prejudice you have experienced or have seen others experience?

Causes of Prejudice and Discrimination

All different forms of prejudice and discrimination have one thing in common: they involve biases unsupported by factual evidence and critical thinking. Less clear, however, is why or how these biases develop in the first place. There is no single, definitive answer to this question, but research suggests that the following factors play a key role in the formation and preservation of prejudice:

1. Discomfort with the unknown or unfamiliar
2. Selective perception and selective memory
3. Categorizing people into "in" groups and "out" groups
4. Perceiving members of unfamiliar groups as more alike than members of one's own group
5. Majority group members overestimating the frequency of negative behavior exhibited by minority group members
6. Rationalizing prejudice and discrimination as justifiable
7. Strengthening self-esteem by identifying or associating with a "superior" group

Discomfort with the Unknown or Unfamiliar

Studies show that when humans encounter something unfamiliar or uncommon, they're likely to experience feelings of discomfort or anxiety; in contrast, when they experience repeated exposure to something and become more familiar with it, they perceive it more positively and judge it more favorably (Zajonc, 2001). This phenomenon is so prevalent and powerful that social psychologists have come to call it the "familiarity principle" (Zajonc, 1968, 1970). It is the same principle that underlies the slogan "advertising pays"—the more exposure a product receives, the more familiar the product becomes, and the more likely people are to favor it (and buy it) (Grimes & Kitchen, 2007).The familiarity principle also accounts for why research on people's voting patterns shows that the amount of public exposure a candidate gets, the more familiar the candidate becomes, and the more votes the candidate receives (Bornstein & Carver-Lemley, 2004).

Comfort with familiarity is likely "wired into" the human brain because it played an important role in the survival and evolution of the human species (Kahneman, 2011). When our early ancestors encountered something or somebody unfamiliar, it was advantageous for them to react with anxiety because that emotion produced a rush of adrenaline in the body that prepared them to deal with a potential predator by helping them fight it or flee from it (the "fight-or-flight" response), thus increasing their chances of survival and the future survival of the human species (Jansen et al., 1995). The fight-or-flight response to the unfamiliar is so deeply rooted in our evolutionary history that it continues to manifest itself in newborn babies. When infants between 6 and 12 months encounter someone unfamiliar, it triggers "stranger anxiety"—they cry, their heart rate accelerates, and their breathing rate increases rapidly (Brooker et al., 2013).

The fight-or-flight response also explains why people of all ages tend to form rapid judgments (within 40 milliseconds) about anyone they encounter who they think may be personally threatening (Bar et al., 2006; Gladwell, 2005). It may also account for why negative pre-judgments (prejudice) form so quickly toward members of less familiar racial or cultural groups (Aronson et al., 2013). Fear of the unfamiliar is difficult to consciously control because it is a wired-in automatic emotional reaction involving lower (subconscious)

"See that man over there?
Yes, I hate him.
But you don't know him.
That's why I hate him."
—GORDON ALLPORT, SOCIAL PSYCHOLOGIST, THE *NATURE OF PREJUDICE*

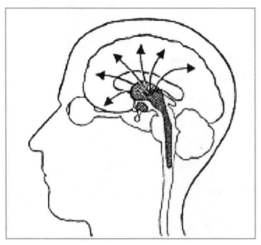

Figure 4.1 Information entering the human brain is first processed emotionally at a subconscious level (lower shaded area) before reaching higher areas of the brain responsible for conscious, rational thinking. However, by being consciously aware of, and reacting rationally to, fear or anxiety triggered by encounters with unfamiliar social groups, irrational prejudices can be short-circuited before becoming enduring attitudes.
© Kendall Hunt Publishing Company

"For the most part we don't first see, and then define, we define first and then see."
—WALTER LIPPMANN, AMERICAN WRITER AND REPORTER WHO COINED THE TERM "STEREOTYPE"

"We see what is behind our eyes."
—CHINESE PROVERB

centers of the brain that trigger it before higher sections of the brain (responsible for conscious awareness and rational thinking) can get involved (see **Figure 4.1**). Consequently, people who hold prejudice toward a social group typically distance themselves from members of that group, leaving them with little or no opportunity for them to become familiar with and to have positive experiences with members of the group that could contradict or disprove their prejudice. This results in a self-perpetuating cycle in which the prejudiced person continues to avoid contact with members of the stigmatized group, which, in turn, continues to maintain and reinforce the person's prejudice.

However, by remaining aware of the fear-of-the-unfamiliar reaction when it occurs, we can train the conscious part of our brain to gain greater control of this implicit bias, respond to it rationally, and prevent it from morphing into full-blown prejudice and discrimination toward members of groups who are unfamiliar to us, or with whom we've have had limited previous contact.

Selective Perception and Selective Memory

In addition to fear of the unfamiliar, personal prejudice can form and be maintained through a psychological process known as *selective perception*—the tendency for biased people to see what they *expect* to see and fail to see what contradicts their bias (Hugenberg & Bodenhausen, 2003). Have you ever noticed how fans rooting for their favorite sports team tend to focus on, "see," and react strongly to calls by referees that go against their own team (bias), but don't seem to react (or even notice) calls that go against the opposing team? This is an innocuous everyday example of how selective perception operates. In the more pernicious case of prejudice, selective perception takes the form of the old adage, "seeing is believing" and turns it into "believing is seeing," leading prejudiced people to continue "seeing" things that are consistent with their prejudicial belief while remaining "blind" to experiences and evidence that contradict it.

Compounding selective perception is the process of *selective memory*—the tendency for prejudiced people to recall information that reinforces their prejudicial belief and forget information that refutes it (Judd et al., 1991). The dual processes of selective perception and selective memory work jointly to preserve prejudice, and they typically operate *unconsciously* (Baron et al., 2009). As a result, people holding a prejudice may not even be aware they are using these processes and that their use of them is perpetuating their prejudice, which ensures their prejudice goes unchallenged and unchanged. The power of the prejudice-preserving process of selective perception and selective memory can be so strong that even if a prejudiced people happens to have a positive experience with a member of the group they have stigmatized, that positive experience is dismissed as the "exception that proves the rule" (Crisp & Hewstone, 2007; Hewstone, 1994).

Have you ever witnessed selective perception or selective memory—people seeing or recalling what they believe to be true due do bias, rather than what is actually true?

If yes, what bias was involved and how was selective perception or selective memory used to support the bias?

Categorizing People into "In" Groups and "Out" Groups

Humans have a long history of grouping fellow humans into social categories. This habit of categorizing may result from the human brain's natural tendency to: (a) seek patterns and associations that make the complex social world simpler to understand—a phenomenon known as "implicit social cognition" (Bless et al., 2004; Greenwald & Banaji, 1995), and (b) use mental shortcuts to more easily manage all the incoming information it must deal with—a process referred to "cognitive bias" (Haselton et al., 2005).

The good news is that grouping people into categories does help our brain organize and simplify our social relationships. The bad news is that it can also oversimplify those relationships by creating group stereotypes. Group stereotyping can then lead to binary, black-or-white thinking that involves mentally creating *in*-groups ("us") and *out*-groups ("them") (Dutton, 2021) that contribute to *ethnocentrism*—viewing one's own cultural group as the central and "normal" in-group and other cultures as marginal or "abnormal" out-groups (National Council for the Social Sciences, 1991). Ethnocentrism, in turn, can lead to prejudice and discrimination toward members of other racial and ethnic groups (Bigler & Hughes, 2009; Stephan & Stephan, 2004).

 Consider This...

We should be on guard to prevent ourselves (and others) from falling into the ethnocentric trap of viewing groups that are culturally *different* as culturally *deficient* groups.

Perceiving Members of Unfamiliar Groups as More Alike than Members of One's Own Group

Research in the field of social psychology demonstrates that humans tend to perceive members of different (less familiar) groups as more alike in attitudes and behavior than members of their own (familiar) group (Baron et al., 2006). For example, members of younger age groups perceive members of older age groups as more alike in their attitudes and beliefs than members of their own age group (Linville et al., 1989). This tendency likely stems from the fact that we have more experience with members of our own group, which gives us more opportunities to observe and interact with a wider variety of individuals within our group. In contrast, we have less frequent contact with members of unfamiliar groups, so we are less likely to observe the variety of individual differences that exist among other, less familiar groups. As a result, we may come to the conclusion that members of an unfamiliar group are more alike in attitudes and behavior than they actually are and that the behavior of an individual member of that group typifies the group as a whole.

When the unfamiliar to us is a different racial group, it can also lead us to the erroneous conclusion that "they all look alike." Studies show that humans are better able to recognize individuals of their own race than individuals of other races—a phenomenon known as "own-race bias" (Aronson et al., 2013). However, racial identification errors are much less likely to take place if members of different races interact with and become familiar with one another, particularly at an early age (Sangrigoli et al., 2005).

Given the significant racial segregation that still exists in our society (Massey, 2004), people remain susceptible to making facial identification errors when identifying individuals of other races (Malpass, 1992). The most likely explanation for cross-race facial recognition errors is that when the face of a member of an unfamiliar race is viewed, the viewer's perception is influenced less by the person's individual facial features and more by the general facial features associated with the member's racial group (e.g., Asian eyes or African lips) (Levin, 2000).

Cross-race facial identification errors have led to false criminal convictions of individuals from racial minority groups that were based on eyewitness testimony provided by members of the majority racial group. DNA evidence discovered later proved that the crime was committed by another member of the same racial group as the falsely accused person (Ramsey & Frank, 2007). A famous example of such an error involved Lenell Geter, an African American engineer who received a life sentence for a crime he never committed. The arresting officer (a white man) mistakenly swore under oath that Geter was a career criminal suspected of dozens of holdups. Four other white witnesses also misidentified him for a different black man who actually committed the crime and was later apprehended.

Such miscarriages of justice resulting from the misperception that minority-group members "all *look* alike" are stunning and newsworthy. However, the belief that minority-group members "all *act* alike" is a much more pervasive, prejudice-forming misconception. This misconception is the underlying foundation for negative group stereotyping (e.g., Indians are savages; blacks are violent), which led to some of the most extreme forms of racial discrimination and domination that have taken place in America (Baron et al., 2006).

Majority Group Members Overestimating the Frequency of Negative Behavior Exhibited by Minority Group Members

Studies show that if negative or socially threatening behavior occurs at the same rate among members of both a majority and minority group (e.g., criminal behavior occurring in both groups at a rate of 10 percent), members of the majority group are more likely to think that the rate is higher in the minority group and are more likely to develop negative attitudes (prejudice) toward members of the minority group (Baron et al., 2006). For example, it has been found that whites in the United States underestimate the crime rate of white men and overestimate the crime rates of black men (Hamilton & Sherman, 1989).

One possible explanation for this overestimation error is that minorities represent a smaller proportion of the population and, therefore, are more likely to stand out. Thus, behavior exhibited by members of a minority group is more likely to be noticed (and remembered). If that behavior happens to be negative or potentially threatening, it is more likely to attract the attention of majority group members and trigger prejudice toward members of the minority group (McArthur & Friedman, 1980).

Rationalizing Prejudice and Discrimination as Justifiable

Rationalization is a psychological strategy that humans use to try to explain or justify personal behavior that is clearly illogical or unethical. For instance, slavery was both and illogical and unethical; it clearly contradicted the democratic principles and ideals on which America was founded. To reconcile this contradiction and allow the United States to use unpaid labor to advance its economic prosperity, the concept of different human "races" was introduced. American business and political leaders used the argument that people of a darker color (race) were inferior to the "white race" and not full human beings; therefore, it was justifiable (and legal) to enslave them and use them like beasts of burden or profit-making property (Feagin, 2005). The United States used this rationale (rationalization) to become the first nation in the world to adopt a system of slavery based exclusively on skin color. Similar rationalizations were used to justify the extermination of Native Americans, the forced takeover of land from Mexicans, and the intentional exclusion of Asian immigrants (California Newsreel, 2003).

These historical examples illustrate the extent to which humans can rationalize clearly unconscionable prejudicial beliefs and actions. What was offered as a rationale (rational explanation) for atrocious acts of discrimination was nothing more than a rationalization (self-serving justification) for behavior that was neither rational nor ethical.

Strengthening Self-Esteem by Identifying or Associating with a "Superior" Group

A person's self-identity (Who am I?) and self-esteem (How do I feel about myself?) are strongly influenced by the group(s) the person identifies with and has membership in. If people believe they are a member of a group that is better than or superior to other groups, their self-image is strengthened (Tafjel, 1982; Tafjel & Turner, 1986). Belonging to a self-proclaimed "superior" group enables its members to more positive self-image by comparing themselves to members of other groups that viewed as being "less than" or inferior to their own group (Brislin, 1993). The reasoning goes like this: My group is better, and since I belong to a better group, I am better (I feel better about myself).

Building up one's self-image by identifying with a "superior" group is particularly important to people with low self-esteem, struggling economically, or experiencing personal frustration, because they can boost their self-image by finding flaws or weaknesses in members of other "inferior" groups (Rudman & Fairchild, 2004). Members of the inferior (stigmatized) group can serve as a scapegoat for their frustrations and failures (Gemmil, 1989). The word "scapegoat" dates back to Biblical times and the old practice of releasing a goat into the wilderness as part of the Jewish ceremony of Yom Kippur (Day of Atonement). Before the goat was released, a high priest symbolically laid the sins of the people on its head; after the goat was freed, the people were symbolically freed (forgiven) for their sins. This ritual led to the term *scapegoat*, which now refers to an innocent person or group of people on whom the flaws and misfortunes of others are transferred (the goat), thereby allowing the guilty party to "escape" blame and responsibility.

Research in social psychology has shown that when people experience events that decrease their self-esteem (e.g., when they experience unemployment or a drop in income), their prejudice toward other groups increases (Aronson et al., 2013). This is illustrated by an experimental study in which individuals were given either positive or negative feedback on a task they just performed. After receiving feedback on their performance, they evaluated a female job applicant who was introduced as being Jewish. Results of this experiment revealed that when individuals received negative feedback on their task performance (lowering their self-esteem) were more likely to evaluate the Jewish job applicant negatively; however, if they were later allowed to point out the weaknesses and shortcomings of the Jewish job applicant (the scapegoat), their self-esteem increased (Fein & Spencer, 1997). These results demonstrate that when people have lower self-esteem, it increases the likelihood of scapegoating—which, in turn, elevates the scapegoater's level of self-esteem. These experimental results are consistent with arguably the most extreme and horrific example of scapegoating in human history: In Nazi Germany, when Adolf Hitler's prejudicial ideology about Jews (and other "defective" groups) stirred up ethnic pride among Germans, instilling in them the belief that they were members of a "master race" while Jews and other "inferior" groups were used as scapegoats for the country's economic and social problems.

Reflection 4.6

Have you ever observed someone attempt to bolster their self-esteem or self-image by putting down or scapegoating members of an "inferior" group? If yes, what was the group being scapegoated and what was the group membership of the person doing the scapegoating?

Personal Experience   One of the best-attended events at my college was a presentation delivered by a guest speaker named Floyd Cochran. Originally a member of and recruiter for "Aryan Nation" (a white-supremacist hate group), he eventually quit the group and became a nationally known civil rights activist and educator who toured the country, speaking out against racist organizations and hate crimes at high schools and colleges. After giving his talk on my campus, he asked the jam-packed room of students if they had any questions. No student raised a hand, probably because the audience was so large and the topic so sensitive. I thought that if I broke the ice and asked a question, then students would feel comfortable doing the same. So I asked Cochran: "Based on your experience with the hate-group members you associated with and new members you recruited, what would you say was the number-one reason *why* people joined a hate group?" Without the slightest pause, he immediately and firmly stated that most members of his hate group had a poor self-image and many came from dysfunctional families where their need for social acceptance was never met. Cochran's answer strongly suggests that one root cause of prejudice and discrimination is the need for people with low self-esteem to strengthen their weak-self-image by identifying with a "stronger" or "superior" group.

—Joe Cuseo

 ## Consider This…

Understanding the root causes of bias, prejudice, and discrimination is a key component of multicultural education; it is the component that serves to prevent the formation and combat its continuation, and reduce its proliferation.

Chapter Summary and Highlights

The United States remains a country fraught with forms of prejudice that continue to divide its citizens along the lines of race, culture, and social class. Studies show that these prejudicial divisions are increasing as the proportion of ethnic and racial minorities in the American population is increasing. America's public schools, for instance, are more segregated today than they were in the late 1960s.

Stereotyping is perceiving individual members of the same group (type) in the same (fixed) way while overlooking differences among individuals who make up that group. Stereotyping dismisses individuality; instead, all individuals of the same group (e.g., race or gender) are viewed as having similar personal characteristics. All stereotypes involve *bias*, which literally means "slant." A bias (slant) can tilt toward the positive or the negative and it may be conscious bias or unconscious referred to as *implicit bias*. When stereotypes are negative, they can be internalized by the members of the stereotyped group and have adverse effects on their self-confidence and performance—a phenomenon known as "stereotype threat." While most people do not engage in blatant stereotyping, many do hold overgeneralized beliefs about particular social groups. Even individuals who strongly believe in equal rights and equitable treatment of all human groups have been found to hold implicit racial biases.

When members of a stereotyped group are pre-*judged*, the the stereotype becomes *prejudice*. In fact, the word "prejudice" literally means "pre-judge." Typically, prejudice is associated with negative pre-judgments that involve *stigmatizing*—ascribing inferior or unfavorable traits to members of the same group. Prejudice has been found to adversely affect the health of people who are targets of prejudice and the health of people who hold prejudices.

In contrast to prejudice, which is a biased belief, attitude, or opinion, *discrimination* is a biased action or behavior. Discrimination can take place not only on a personal level, but also on an institutional level by being built or "baked" into the policies and practices of an institution (e.g., a corporation). Racial discrimination can also pervade multiple institutions and entire societal systems, which is referred to as *systemic racism*. For instance, practices used in the housing, education, and criminal justice systems continue to have discriminatory impact on people of color.

Microaggressions are discriminatory acts that are exhibited in the form of indirect or subtle put-down that are delivered intentionally or unintentionally to members of a social group—particularly a group that has been historically marginalized or stigmatized.

A *hate group* is defined by the FBI as a social group whose primary purpose is to promote animosity, hostility, and malice toward persons belonging to a race, religion, disability, sexual orientation, ethnicity, or national origin that differs from its group members. More than 800 hate groups have been identified in the United States, the largest percentage of which are white supremacy groups, whose members see their goal as protecting and preserving the white race and see people of color, immigrants, and other minority groups as inferior and threatening. The number of white supremacist and white nationalist groups has been growing in America due to fear of the growing number of non-whites in the U.S. population. Further contributing to the growth of white nationalist groups is the growing number of social media sites designed to recruit new members and provide them with a supportive community.

A *hate crime* is defined by the FBI as a criminal offense against person or property motivated by the criminal offender's bias against a race, religion, disability, sexual orientation, ethnicity, gender, or gender identity. Hate-crime laws are now in place at the federal level and in all but three U.S. states. Individuals who commit hate crimes may not be members of hate groups, but their motivation to commit hate crimes is often inspired by a hate group's ideology. Since the FBI began collecting hate crime statistics, blacks have been the number-one target of racial hate crimes. Jews have been the major target of religion-based hate crimes, and anti-Muslim hate crimes have increased sharply since the September 11th, 2001 attack on the United States. Anti-Asian hate crimes have also increased dramatically since the outbreak of the COVID-19 pandemic.

There is no single, definitive answer to the question of what causes prejudice and discrimination, but research suggests that the following factors play a key role:

- Discomfort with the unknown or unfamiliar
- Using selective perception and selective memory to support biased beliefs
- Categorizing people into "in" groups and "out" groups
- Perceiving members of unfamiliar groups as more alike than members of one's own group
- Majority group members overestimating the frequency of negative behavior exhibited by minority group members
- Rationalizing prejudice and discrimination as justifiable
- Strengthening self-esteem by identifying or associating with a "superior" group

Internet Resources

Bias and Stereotyping: https://www.psychologytoday.com/us/articles/199805/where-bias-begins-the-ruth-about-stereotypes

Reducing Stereotype Threat: www.reducingstereotypethreat.org/

Microaggressions: https://www.psychologytoday.com/us/basics/microaggression

LGBTQ Acceptance and Support: www.itgetsbetter.org

Stopping Anti-Asian Hate: https://www.stopaapihate.org/

Promoting Civil Rights and Combating Hate Groups in America: https://www.splcenter.org/issues/hate-and-extremism

Promoting Human Rights and Countering Discrimination Worldwide: https://www.amnesty.org/en/what-we-do/

References

Aboud, F. E. (1998). *Children and prejudice*. Basil Blackwell.

Aboud, F. E. (2009). Modifying children's racial attitudes. In J. A. Banks (Ed.), *The Routledge international companion to multicultural education* (pp. 199–209). Routledge.

Abrajano, M., & Hajnal, Z. (2015). *White backlash: Immigration, race, and American politics*. Princeton University Press.

Aronson, E., Wilson, T. D., & Akert, R. M. (2013). *Social psychology* (8th ed.). Pearson/Prentice Hall.

Associated Press. (2021, June 13). Orlando club to become a memorial. *Los Angeles Times*, A14.

"Ask Teaching Tolerance." (2019, Fall). *Teaching Tolerance*, Issue 63, p. 9.

Bacon. (2015, July 7). Dylan Roof indicted in Charleston rampage. *USA Today*. https://ww.usatoday.com/story/news/nation/2015/07/07dylan-roof-indicted--charleston-shootings/29815457/

Banaji, M. R., & Greenwald, A. G. (2013). *Blindspot: Hidden biases of good people*. Banton Books.

Banks, J. A. (2016). *Cultural diversity and education: Foundations, curriculum, and teaching* (6th ed.). Routledge.

Bar, M., Neta, M., & Linz, H. (2006). Very first impressions. *Emotion, 6*(2), 269–278.

Baron, R. A., Brancombe, N. R., & Byrne, D. R. (2009). *Social psychology* (12th ed.). Pearson.

Baron, B. A., Byrne, D., & Branscombe, N. R. (2006). *Mastering social psychology*. Pearson/Allyn and Bacon.

Benjamin, R. (2009). *Searching for whitopia: An improbable journey to the heart of white America*. HarperCollins.

Bigler, R. A., & Hughes, J. M. (2009). The nature and origins of children's racial attitudes. In J. A. Banks (Ed.), *The Routledge international companion to multicultural education* (pp. 186–198). Routledge.

Bless, H., Fiedler, K., & Strack, F. (2004). *Social cognition: How individuals construct social reality*. Psychology Press.

Bonilla-Silva, E. (2018). *Racism without racists: Color-blind racism and the persistence of racial inequality in America* (5th ed.). Rowman & Littlefield.

Bornstein, R. F., & Craver-Lemley, C. (2004). Mere exposure effect. In R. F. Pohl (Ed.), *Cognitive illusions: A handbook on fallacies and biases in thinking, judgement and memory* (pp. 215–234). Psychology Press.

Bowman, B. T. (1995). *Cultural diversity and academic achievement*. http://www.ncrel.org/sdrs/areas/issues/educatrs/leadrshp/le0bow.htm#author

Braddock, J, M., II., & Mikulyuk, A. B. (2012). Segregation, desegregation, and resegregation. In J. A. Banks (Ed.), *Encyclopedia of diversity in education* (vol. 4, pp. 1930–1934). SAGE.

Brislin, R. W. (1993). *Understanding culture's influence on behavior.* Harcourt Brace Jovanovich College Publishers.

Brooker, R. J., Buss, K. A., Lemery-Chalfant, K., Aksan, N., Davidson, R. J., & Goldsmith, H. H. (2013). The development of stranger fear in infancy and toddlerhood: Normative development, individual differences, antecedents, and outcomes. *Developmental Science, 16* (6), 864–78

Brookings Institute. (2008). *Demographic keys to the 2008 election.* Brookings Institute. www.brookings.edu/~/media/Files/events/2008/1020_demographics/20081020_demographics.pdf

California Newsreel. (2003). *Race-the power of an illusion.* http://www.PBS.org/Race

Cannon, W. (1932). *The wisdom of the body.* W.W. Norton & Company.

Cartledge, G., Singh, A., & Gibson, L. (2008). Practical behavior management techniques to close the accessibility gap for students who are culturally and linguistically diverse. *Preventing School Failure, 52*(3), 29–38.

Center for the Study of Hate and Extremism. (2021). *Anti-Asian hate crimes reported to police in America's largest cities: 2020.* https://www.csusb.edu/sites/default/files/FACTSHEET-Anti-Asian Hate 2020 3.2.21pdf

Chabria, A. (2019, September 14). 3 bills on bias are sent to Gov. *Los Angeles Times,* pp. B1, B4.

Crisp, R. J., & Hewstone, N. (2007). Multiple social categorizations. In M. P. Sanna (Ed.), *Advances in experimental and social psychology* (vol. 39, pp. 163–254). Academic Press.

Diamond, J. (2019). *Upheaval: Turning point for nations in crisis.* Little, Brown and Company.

Dovidio, J. F., Kawakami, K., & Gaertner, S. L. (2002). Implicit and explicit prejudice and interracial interaction. *Journal of Personality and Social Psychology, 82,* 62–68.

Dutton, K. (2021). *Black-and-white thinking: The burden of a binary brain in a complex world.* Farrar, Straus, & Gioux.

Elliot, J. R., & Smith, R. A. (2004). Race, gender, and workplace power. *American Sociological Review, 69*(3), 365–386.

Federal Bureau of Investigation. (2015). *Hate crime data collection and guidelines training manual.* https://www.fbi.gov/cile-respository/ucr/ucr-hate-crime-data-collection-guidelines-training-manual-02272015.pdf/view

Feagin, J. (2005). *Systemic racism: A theory of oppression.* Routledge.

Fein, S., & Spencer, S. J. (1997). Prejudice as self-image maintenance: Affirming the self through derogating others. *Journal of Personality and Social Behavior, 73*(1), 31–44.

Friedman, J., Kim, D., & Schneberk, T. (2019). Assessment of racial/ethnic and income disparities in the prescription of opioids and other controlled medications in California. *JAMA Internal Medicine, 179*(4), 469–476. https://jamanetwork.com/journals/jamainternalmedicine/fullarticle/2723625

Gemmil, G. (1989). The dynamics of scapegoating in small groups. *Small Group Behavior, 20,* 406–418.

Giroux, H. A. (1998). The politics of national identity and the pedagogy of multiculturalism in the USA. In D. Bennett (Ed.), *Multicultural states: Rethinking difference and identity* (pp. 178–194). Routledge.

Gladwell, M. (2005). *Blink: The power of thinking without thinking.* Little, Brown and Company.

Goffman, E. (1963). *Stigma: Notes on the management of spoiled identity.* Prentice-Hall.

Gonzalez, G., & Maez, L. (1995, Fall). Advances in research in bilingual education. *Directions in Language and Education, 1*(5), 694–701.

Gordon, R., Piana, L. D., & Keleher, T. (2000). *Facing the consequences: An examination of racial discrimination in U.S. public schools.* Applied Research Center.

Gorski, P. C. (1995–2018). *Key characteristics of a multicultural curriculum.* Critical Multicultural Pavilion: Multicultural Curriculum Reform (An EdChange Project). www.edchange.org/multicultural/curriculum/characteristics.html

Green, M. G. (Ed.). (1989). *Minorities on campus: A handbook for enhancing diversity.* American Council on Education.

Greenwald, A. G., & Banaji, M. R. (1995). Implicit social cognition: Attitudes, self-esteem and stereotypes. *Psychological Review, 102*(1), 4–27.

Grimes, A., & Kitchen, P. J. (2007). Researching mere exposure effects to advertising. *International Journal of Market Research, 4*(2), 191–221.

Hall, R. M., & Sandler, B. R. (1982). *The classroom climate: A chilly one for women.* Association of American Colleges' Project on the Status of Women. Association of American Colleges.

Hall, R. M., & Sandler, B. R. (1984). *Out of the classroom: A chilly campus climate for women.* Association of American Colleges' Project on the Status of Women. Association of American Colleges.

Hamilton, D. L., & Sherman, S. J. (1989). Illusory correlations: Implications for stereotype theory and research. In D. Bar-Tal, C. F. Graumann, A. W. Kruglanski, & W. Stroebe (Eds.), *Stereotyping and prejudice: Changing conceptions* (pp. 59–82). Springer-Verlag.

Hamilton, D. L., Stroessner, S. J., & Driscoll, D. M. (1994). Social cognition and the study of stereotyping. In P. G. Devine, D. J. Hamilton, & T. M. Ostrom (Eds.), *Social cognition: Impact on social psychology* (pp. 291–321). Academic Press.

Harper, S. R. (2012). Race without racism: How higher education researchers minimize racist institutional norms. *Review of Higher Education, 36*(1), 9–30.

Haselton, M. G., Nettle, D., & Andrews, P. W. (2005). The evolution of cognitive bias. In D. M. Buss (Ed.), *The handbook of evolutionary psychology* (pp. 724–746.). Hoboken, NJ: John Wiley & Sons Inc.

Hewstone, M. (1994). Revision and change of stereotypic beliefs. In search of the elusive subtyping model. In W. Stroebe & M. Hewstone (Eds.), *European Review of Social Psychology, 5*(1), 69–109.

Hier, M., & Cooper, A. (2019, January 4). Hatred roars back. *Los Angeles Times*, A9.

Hirschfeld, F. (1997). *George Washington and slavery.* University of Missouri Press.

Hugenberg, K., & Bodenhausen, G. V. (2003). Facing prejudice: Implicit prejudice and the perception of facial threat. *Psychological Science, 14,* 640–643.

Hussain, S. (2019, August 3). Focus on white supremacy: Authorities examine racist ideology as a source of domestic terrorism. *Los Angeles Times*, A2.

Inzlicht, M., & Good, C. (2006). How environments can threaten academic performance, self-knowledge, and sense of belonging. In S. Levin & C. van Laar (Eds.), *Stigma and group inequality* (pp. 129–150). Erlbaum.

Jackson, G. M. (2012). *Predicting malicious behavior: Tools and techniques for ensuring global security.* John Wiley & Sons.

Jansen, A. S. P., Nguyen, X. V., Karpitsky, V., Mettenleiter, T. C., & Loewy, A. D. (1995). Central command neurons of the sympathetic nervous system: Basis of the fight-or-flight response. *Science, 27*(5236), 644–646.

Jardina, A. (2019). *White identity politics.* Cambridge University Press.

Judd, C. M., Ryan, C. S., & Parke, B. (1991). Accuracy in the judgment of in-group and out-group variability. *Journal of Personality and Social Psychology, 61,* 366–379.

Kahneman, D. (2011). *Thinking, fast and slow.* Farrar, Straus & Giroux.

Kaleem, J. (2021, March 20). Hate crime laws back in the spotlight. *Los Angeles Times*, A2.

Kaleem, J., Lee, K., & Etehad, M. (2021, March 5). Anti-Asian hate crimes surge in U.S. *Los Angeles Times*, A5.

Kanter, R. (1977). *Men and women of the corporation.* Basic Books.

Katznelson, I. (2005). *When affirmative action was white: An untold history of racial inequality in twentieth-century America.* Norton.

Kisida, B., & Piontek, O. (2019, May 22). *Is segregation really getting worse?* Education Next. https://www.educationnext.org/is-school-segregation-really-getting-worse/

Kober, N. (2001, April). *It takes more than testing: Closing the achievement gap. A report of the Center on Education Policy.* Center on Education Policy.

Levin, D. T. (2000). Race as a visual feature: Using visual search and perceptual discrimination tasks to understand face categories and the cross-race recognition deficit. *Journal of Experimental Psychology: General, 129*(4), 559–574.

Lewis, M. L. (2002). *Multicultural health psychology: Special topics acknowledging diversity.* Allyn & Bacon.

Linville, P. W., Fischer, G. W., & Salovey, P. (1989). Perceived distributions of the characteristics of in-group and out-group members: Empirical evidence and a computer simulation. *Journal of Personality and Social Psychology, 57,* 165–188.

Lipka, J., Hoganm, M. P., Webster, J. P., Yanez, E., Adams, B., Clark, S., & Lacy, D. (2005). Math in a cultural context: Two case studies of a successful culturally based math project. *Anthropology and Education Quarterly, 36*(4), 367–385.

Lui, P. P., & Quezada, L. (2019). Associations between microaggression and adjustment outcomes: A meta-analytic and narrative review. *Psychological Bulletin, 145* (1), 45–78.

Malpass, R. S. (1992). "They all look alike to me." In M. Merrens & G. Brannigan (Eds.) *The undaunted psychologist.* (pp. 74–88). McGraw-Hill.

Massey, D. (2003). *The source of the river: The social origins of freshmen at America's selective colleges and universities.* Princeton University Press.

Massey, D. S. (2004). Segregation and stratification: A biosocial perspective. *Du Bois Review: Social Science Research on Race, 1*(1), 7–25.

McArthur, L. Z., & Friedman, S. A. (1980). Illusory correlation in impression formation: Variations in the shared distinctiveness effect as a function of the distinctive person's age, race, and sex. *Journal of Personality and Social Psychology, 39,* 615–624.

Mendes, W. B., Gray, H. M., Mendoza-Denton, B., Major, B., & Epel, E. S. (2007). Why egalitarianism might be good for your health: Physiological thriving during stressful intergroup encounters. *Psychological Science, 18,* 991–998.

Mendoza-Denton, R., Page-Gould, E., & Pietrak, J. (2006). Mechanisms for coping with status-based rejection expectations. In S. Levin & C. van Laar (Eds.), *Stigma and group inequality* (pp. 151–170). Erlbaum.

Mervosh, S. (2019, February 27). How much wealthier are white school districts than nonwhite ones? $23 billion, report says. *The New York Times.* https://www.nytimes.com/2019/02/27/education/school-districts-funding-white-minorities.html?module=inline

Miller, C. (2020). The "boogaloo" started as a racist meme. *Hate and extremism in 2020.* Southern Poverty Law Center.

Minnich, E. K. (2005). *Transforming knowledge* (2nd ed.). Temple University Press.

Moghaddam, F. (2008). *Multiculturalism and intergroup relations: Psychological implications for democracy in global context.* American Psychological Association.

Moss, M., & Puma, M. (1995). *Prospects: The congressionally mandated study of educational growth and opportunity: First year report on language minority and limited English proficient students.* U.S. Department of Education.

Nadal, K. L., Griffin, K. E., Wong, Y., Hamit, S., & Rasmus, M. (2014). The impact of racial microaggressions on mental health: Counseling implications for clients of color. *Journal of Counseling and Development, 92(1),* 57–66.

Nagda, B. R., Gurin, P., & Johnson, S. M. (2005). Living, doing and thinking diversity: How does pre-college diversity experience affect first-year students' engagement with college diversity? In R. S. Feldman (Ed.), *Improving the first year of college: Research and practice* (pp. 73–110). Lawrence Erlbaum.

National Collaborative on Diversity in the Teaching Force. (2004). *Assessment of diversity in America's teaching force.* Author

National Council for the Social Sciences. (1991). *Curriculum guidelines for multicultural education.* Prepared by the NCSS Task Force on Ethnic Studies Curriculum Guidelines. www.socialstudies.org/positions/multicultural

Page-Gould, E. (2010). The unhealthy racist. In J. Marsh, R. Mendoza-Denton, & J. A. Smith (Eds.), *Are we born racist? New insights from neuroscience and positive psychology.* Beacon Press.

Pettigrew, T. F. (1998). Intergroup contact theory. *Annual Review of Psychology, 49,* 65–85.

Planty, M., Hussar, W., Snyder, T., Kena, G., Kewal Ramani, A., Kemp, J., Bianco, K., & Dinkes, R. (2009). *The condition of education 2009.* National Center for Education Statistics. https://nces.ed.gov/pubs2009/2009081.pdf

Ramsey, R. J., & Frank, J. (2007). Wrongful conviction: Perceptions of criminal justice professionals regarding the frequency of wrongful conviction and the extent of system errors. *Crime & Delinquency, 53,* 436–470.

Revilla, A. T., & Sweeney, Y. D. L. G. (1997). *Low income does not cause low school achievement: Creating a sense of family and respect in the school environment.* http://www.idra.org/IDRA_Newsletter/June_-_July_1997_High_-_Performing_High_Poverty_Schools/Low_Income_Does_Not_Cause_Low_School_Achievement/

Rivera, B. D., & Rogers-Adkinson, D. (1997). Culturally sensitive interventions: Social skills training with children and parents from culturally and linguistically diverse backgrounds. *Intervention in School and Clinic, 33,* 75–80.

Rudman, L. A., & Fairchild, K. (2004). Reactions to counter-stereotypic behavior: The role of backlash in cultural stereotype maintenance. *Journal of Personality and Social Psychology, 87,* 157–176.

Sadker, M., & Sadker, D. (1994). *Failing at fairness: How America's schools cheat girls.* Charles Scribner's Sons.

Sangrigoli, S., Pallier, C., Argenti, A. M, Ventureya, V.A.G., & de Schonen, S. (2005). Reversibility of the other-race effect in face recognition during childhood. *Psychological Science, 16,* 440–444.

Scharf, A. (2018). *Critical practices for anti-bias education.* Teaching Tolerance: A Project of the Southern Poverty Law Center. https://www.tolerance.org/.../2019-04/TT-Critical-Practices-for-Anti-bias-Education.pdf

Schneider, E. C., Zaslavsky, A. M., & Epstein, A. M. (2002). Racial disparities in the quality of care for enrollees in Medicare managed care. *Journal of the American Medical Association, 287,* 1288–1294.

Schuman, H., Steeh, C., Bobo, L. D., & Krysan, M. (1985). *Racial attitudes in America: Trends and interpretations.* Harvard University Press.

Sedlacek, W. (1987). Black students on white campuses: 20 years of research. *Journal of College Student Personnel, 28,* 484–495.

Shapiro, S. R. (1993). *Human rights violations in the United States: A report on U.S. compliance.* Human Rights Watch, American Civil Liberties Union.

Smith, R. (2005). Saving black boys: Unimaginable outcomes for the most vulnerable students require imaginable leadership. *School Administrator, 62*(1), 1–7.

Smith, D. (2015). *Diversity's promise for higher education: Making it work* (2nd ed.). Johns Hopkins University Press.

Southern Poverty Law Center. (2020). *The year in hate and extremism, 2019.* A Report from the Southern Poverty Law Center.

Southern Poverty Law Center. (2021). *The year in hate and extremism, 2020.* A Report from the Southern Poverty Law Center.

Steele, C. M. (2004). A threat in the air: How stereotypes shape intellectual identity and performance. In J. A. Banks & C. A. M. Banks (Eds.), *Handbook of research on multicultural education* (2nd ed., pp. 692–698). Jossey-Bass.

Steele, C. M., & Aronson, J. (1995). Stereotype threat and the intellectual test performance of African–Americans. *Journal of Personality and Social Psychology, 69,* 797–811.

Stephan, W. G., & Stephan, C. W. (2004). Intergroup relations in multicultural education programs. In J. A. Banks & C. A. M. Banks (Eds.), *Handbook of research on multicultural education* (2nd ed., pp. 782–798). Jossey-Bass.

Sue, D.W. (2010). *Microaggressions in everyday life: Race, gender, and sexual orientation.* John Wiley & Sons.

Sue, D. W., Capodilupo, C. M., Torino, G. C., Bucceri, J. M., Holder, A. M. B., Nadal, K. L., & Esquilin, M. (2007). Racial microaggressions in everyday life: Implications for clinical practice. *American Psychologist, 62*(4), 271–286.

Sumida, S., & Gurin, P. A. (2001). Celebration of power. In D. L. Schoem & S. Hurtado (Eds.), *Intergroup dialogue: Deliberative democracy in school, college, community, and workplace* (pp. 280–293). University of Michigan.

Swain, C. M. (2002). *The new white nationalism in America: Its challenge to integration.* Cambridge University Press.

Swain, C. M., & Nieli, R. (2003). *Contemporary voices of white nationalism in America.* Cambridge University Press.

Tafjel, H. (1982). *Social identity and intergroup behavior.* Cambridge University Press.

Tafjel, H., & Turner, J. C. (1986). The social identity theory of intergroup behavior. In S. Worchel & W. G. Austin (Eds.), *Psychology of intergroup relations* (2nd ed.). Nelson-Hall,

Thompson, A. (2009). *White privilege.* In H. Greene & S. Gabbidon (Eds.), *Encyclopedia of race and crime.* SAGE.

Thompson, A., & Luhman, R. (1997). Familial predictors of educational attainment: Regional and racial variations. In P. Hall (Ed.), *Race, ethnicity, and multiculturalism* (pp. 63–88). Garland Publishing.

Treadwell, H. M. (2013). *Beyond stereotypes in black and white: How everyday leaders can build healthier opportunities for African American boys and men.* Praeger.

U.S. Department of Education. (2016). *The state of racial diversity in the educator workforce.* https://www2.ed.gov/rschstat/eval/highered/racial-diversity/state-racial-diversity-workforce.pdf

Villegas, A. M., & Lucas, T. (2002). *Educating culturally responsive teachers.* State University of New York Press.

Vox Media. (2019). *The data proves that segregation is getting worse.* https://www.vox.com/2018/3/5/17080218/school-segregation-getting-worse-data

Weissglass, J. (2001). Racism and the achievement gap. *Education Week, 20*(43), 49–72.

Wong-Fillmore, L. (1991). When learning a second language means losing the first. *Early Childhood Research Quarterly, 6,* 323–346.

Wright, D. J. (Ed.) (1987). *Responding to the needs of today's minority students.* New Directions for Student Services, No. 38. Jossey-Bass.

Zajonc, R. B. (1968). Attitudinal effects of mere exposure. *Journal of Personality and Social Psychology, 9,* Monograph Supplement, No. 2, part 2.

Zajonc, R. B. (1970). Brainwash: Familiarity breeds comfort. *Psychology Today* (February), 32-35 & 60-62.

Zajonc, R. B. (2001). Mere exposure: A gateway to the subliminal. *Current Directions in Psychological Science, 10,* 224–228.

Reflections and Applications

Name

_____

Date

_____

4.1 Review the sidebar quotes contained in this chapter and select two that you think are particularly meaningful or inspirational. For each quote you selected, provide an explanation of why you chose it.

4.2 Review the following factors discussed in this chapter that research indicates may play an important role in the development of prejudice. Suggest a strategy that might be used to reduce or prevent each of these potential causes of prejudice.

a) Experiencing discomfort with the unknown or unfamiliar

b) Using selective perception and selective memory to support prejudicial beliefs

c) Categorizing people into "in" groups and "out" groups

d) Strengthening self-esteem by identifying or associating with a "superior" group

4.3 Have you ever perceived or treated a person based on a stereotype associated with that person's group?

    a) If yes, what stereotypical assumptions did you make about the person? Was that person aware of or affected by your stereotyping?

    b) If no, why do you think you have been able to avoid perceiving or treating others based on their group stereotype?

4.4 Do you think there are certain groups on your campus that may be especially vulnerable to stereotyping? If yes, what are those groups and what stereotypes are held about them? If no, why not?

4.5 Implicit Bias Self-Assessment

Go to *implicit.harvard.edu/implicit/takeatest.html* This site contains tests for implicit (unconscious) bias toward different groups. Take the implicit bias tests relating to the following: skin tone, race, Asian, Arab-Muslim, sexuality, transgender, gender-career, and disability. After completing each of these tests, answer the following questions:

a) Do you think your results were accurate?

b) Did the results suggest that you held a bias about certain group(s) that you were not aware of?

c) If your answer to the previous question was "yes," what do you think may have caused or contributed to this bias?

d) If your closest family member and best friend took these tests, how do you think their results would have compared with yours?

4.6 Scenario: Free Speech or Hate Speech?

Suppose a white supremacist wanted to come to your campus to make a presentation about how America belongs to whites because whites are the superior race that built this exceptional nation. Do you think your campus should allow this presentation to ensure "free speech" or disallow it because it gives the speaker a platform for "hate speech?" Or, do you think the presenter should be allowed to speak, but only if certain conditions are met? (If so, what conditions would those be?)

4.7 Hate Crime: Homophobic Murder

In October 1998, Matthew Shepard—a 21-year-old University of Wyoming freshman—was fatally beaten a few hours after attending the planning of a Gay Awareness Week meeting on campus. Following the meeting, Matthew went to a local bar where he met two individuals, Aaron James McKinney and Russell Henderson, who pretended to be gay. They lured Matthew to their truck, where McKinney said: "Guess what, we're not gay. You're going to get jacked. It's Gay Awareness Week!" McKinney and Henderson began beating Shepard inside the truck and drove him to an isolated place in the countryside. They tied him to a fence and pistol whipped him with a handgun. The assailants then stole Shepard's wallet and shoes, tied him to a fence, and left him to die. Matthew Shepard died five days after the attack. An autopsy revealed that he had been hit in the head 18 times. He also sustained bruises on the back of his hands while trying to protect himself as well as bruises around his groin—indicating that he'd been kicked numerous times. After the incident, one of the assailants explained his actions to his girlfriend by saying: "Well you know how I feel about gays."

Russell Henderson pleaded guilty and was sentenced to life in prison. McKinney was about to begin trial to determine whether he should be put to death, but Matthew Shepard's parents persuaded the prosecution not to pursue the death penalty and allow him to be sentenced to life in prison instead.

In October 2018—20 years after his slaying—a service and celebration of Matthew Shepard's life was held and attended by more than 2,000 people, and many others watched online. The service was led by Gene Robinson—the first openly gay bishop of the Episcopal Church. For Shepard's family and friends, the 2018 service was their first opportunity to publicly celebrate Matthew's life because at the time of his 1998 slaying, anti-gay protesters disrupted his first funeral service when they confronted and screamed at the funeral-goers. The hostility at the first service was so intense that Matthew's father was advised to wear a bulletproof vest under his suit at the second service.

Source: *NY Times*, October 10 & November 21, 1998; *Los Angeles Times*, October 27, 2018.

Case Reflection Question

a) Why or how do you think the attackers developed such an intense hatred of gay men?

b) What, if anything, could have been done to prevent the attackers' hatred toward gays from developing in the first place?

c) Do you think the attackers could ever be successfully rehabilitated, educated, or treated for their homophobia?

d) Would you say that homophobia and hatred of gays is currently decreasing or increasing? Why?

4.8 Case Study: Anti-Semitic Incident at High School Party

At a house party in southern California, a group of high school juniors played a drinking game with red cups and ping-pong balls. As the students were adding and moving the cups around the floor, one student noted that it was beginning to look like a swastika, so he rearranged a few more cups so that it actually took the shape of a swastika. About a dozen students then gathered around it, raised their arms in a Nazi salute, and had their photo taken. One student put a caption on the photo, titling it "German rage," and posted it on Snapchat. The picture quickly spread throughout social media and triggered outrage among other students, parents, and politicians. Some of the partying students then took to social media to say that it was just a joke and question why people who weren't even Jewish were so upset. Since the incident happened off campus on a weekend, school officials were uncertain about what disciplinary action could or should be taken. The director of a regional Anti-Defamation League reported that he hadn't seen any evidence that these students were Nazis or Nazi sympathizers, but still felt their actions were reprehensible because they served to "normalize" hate. He said: "What starts as jokes then becomes social exclusion then becomes discrimination."

The incident called attention to a nationwide trend of increasing anti-Semitic incidents at American schools. In 2017 alone, there were 457 anti-Semitic incidents in non-Jewish schools across the country, making the K-12 school system the number-one public place where such incidents occurred.

Source: Ormseth, M., Parvini, S., Do, A., & Tchekmedyian, A. (2019, March 5). Shock in O.C. over photos. *Los Angeles Times*, pp. A1 & A12.

Case Reflection Questions

a) Why do you think this incident took place in the first place?

b)   What action (if any) do you think the school district should have taken in response to the incident?

c)   Could this incident have been prevented? If yes, how? If no, why not?

d)   Why do you think anti-Semitic incidents (and hate crimes toward minority groups in general) are on the rise?

Overcoming Bias, Combating Prejudice, and Developing Cultural Competence

Chapter Purpose and Preview

This chapter lays out a systematic, four-step process for increasing awareness of implicit bias and engaging in authentic, culturally competent interracial and intercultural interactions. The chapter concludes with a set of specific, research-based action strategies for promoting interpersonal interaction, friendship formation, and collaboration among members of diverse groups.

A Model for Overcoming Biases and Appreciating Diversity

As discussed previously, *bias* means slant—a leaning toward a view about something or somebody based on inaccurate or incomplete information that often takes place without conscious awareness (Fiarman, 2016). Anyone, including open-minded individuals, can hold biases stemming from their cultural backgrounds and personal upbringing. Only a deep sense of self-examination and self-awareness can uproot and minimize these biases. This self-examination process involves consciously and continually asking ourselves *what* we believe about a group, *why* we hold that belief, and what evidence we have to support it. Making an intentional effort to introspect and inspect our biases is the critical first step toward accepting and appreciating diversity.

The introspective process can be conceptualized as a systematic series of steps that begins with gaining *awareness* of group differences, followed by: *acknowledging* biases (explicit or implicit) toward groups that differ from our own, *accepting* group differences, and taking *action* to initiate positive interaction with members of diverse groups. Thus, the process of overcoming bias and appreciating diversity involves a four-step progression:

1. **Awareness** of our personal beliefs and attitudes toward diverse groups;
2. **Acknowledgment** of how our beliefs and attitudes may affect our interactions with members of diverse groups;
3. **Acceptance** of (including empathy for) members of diverse groups; and
4. **Action** taken to engage with members of diverse groups (see **Figure 5.1.**)

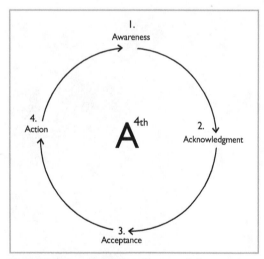

Figure 5.1 The cycle of diversity appreciation.
© Kendall Hunt Publishing Company

"It is possible to override our worst impulses and reduce prejudices. But to do so in a meaningful way requires forethought, and awareness of the unconscious biases passed on through the generations."

—SUSAN FISKE, PROFESSOR OF PSYCHOLOGY, PRINCETON UNIVERSITY

This four-step process is not only sequential; it's also hierarchical—each step builds on the preceding one so that advancing to a higher step becomes possible only after the previous step has been taken. By completing all steps, we move beyond mere acceptance or tolerance of diversity to valuing diversity and reaping its benefits.

Stage 1. Awareness

Biases can be held without our being consciously aware that we are holding them (Fiarman, 2016), and once held, they can lead to acts of discrimination, unintentional though they may be (Baron et al., 2006; Butler, 1993). When students gain greater awareness of the subtle, subconscious biases they may hold, they achieve a key objective of multicultural education: a deeper sense of self-insight (Gorski, 1995–2018).

The first step toward reducing biases is to gain deeper awareness of our culturally influenced beliefs and how those beliefs may be affecting our expectations of, and interactions with, members of other cultural groups. Starting early in life, a variety of cultural agents (family members, peers, media, etc.) shape our attitudes, beliefs, and behaviors, and their influence on us become so ingrained that we no longer evaluate them. In fact, to question or challenge culturally acquired beliefs may make us feel like we're denying or disrespecting our heritage. However, carefully examining our beliefs, and assessing whether or not they are biased, is a key form of critical thinking that liberates us from being blind to and bounded by our biased beliefs.

The process of exploring and unearthing our unconscious biases does not mean we are subjecting ourselves to a self-imposed "guilt trip" or shaming exercises (Jones & Wade, 2015). Nor does it mean that we are holding ourselves personally responsible for the extreme forms of prejudice and discrimination that have taken place at a societal level. Instead, it is simply self-exploration process designed to promote deeper self-insight and potential discovery of subtle beliefs or attitudes that can distort our views of other groups and possibly disadvantage them, even without deliberate or malicious intent (Butler, 1993).

Personal Experience

I once engaged in the process of introspection to become more self-aware of my group biases, and while doing so, I recalled an incident that took place when I was 11 years old. I was comparing baseball cards with a friend of mine who was of Irish descent. As he was showing me his cards, he pulled out certain ones and said, "he's good." After he pulled out the fourth or fifth card, I finally figured out his criterion for determining who was "good." All the cards he pulled out had Irish surnames (e.g., O'Toole, McMahon, Maloney). He certainly didn't pull out any cards that had Italian-sounding names like mine. Later that year, I noticed that some of my Italian classmates were being derisively called "wops" and "guineas." On one particular occasion, an Irish boy in our crowded schoolyard shouted out the following question at me: "Hey, Cuseo, do you know why you don't have any freckles?" The classmate then answered his own question: "Because they'd slide right off your greasy Italian face!" Laughter then broke out among a bunch of kids who overheard the comment.

These childhood incidents have left me with a lingering bias against Irish-Americans. To this day, I cannot bring myself to root for Notre Dame's sports teams because their nickname is the "fighting Irish" or root for Boston's professional basketball team because they're named the Celtics. However, the good news is that I'm become aware of this bias, which has helped prevent it from turning it into anti-Irish prejudice or discrimination. In fact, I remain a close friend of the young Irish American boy who once showed me only the baseball cards of "good" (Irish-named) players.

—Joe Cuseo

A specific strategy for gaining deeper self-awareness of your feelings, beliefs, and biases about diverse groups is to do the following:

- List all things that come to mind about a social group of which you are not a member and with whom you've had very little contact. (You can use the diversity spectrum on p. 2 to identify one such group.)
- Write down all thoughts and feelings you have about the group. Be sure it's what you truly believe and not what seems like the "right" or "socially acceptable" thing to say. Try to be totally honest; don't worry about how your thoughts and feelings might be judged because you will not be sharing them with anyone else.

- Look back on the ideas you wrote down in the previous step, reflect on them, and think deeply about whether they may be biased views about the group, even if the bias is subtle.
- Once you have carefully examined your deepest thoughts and feelings and recorded them in writing, answer the following reflection questions as honestly as possible.

Reflection 5.1

Would you say that any of the thoughts or feelings you wrote down represents a negative bias, stereotype, or prejudice? If yes: (a) Why do you think you hold it? (b) How do you think it developed in the first place?

The process of gaining new knowledge through deep assessment, deep reflection, deep learning, increases your intellectual capacity as a leader. This process can be said to build your IQ.

Once you have honestly answered the above questions, you are ready to advance to the next stage in the process of diversity appreciation: *Acknowledgment*.

Stage 2. Acknowledgment

Appreciating diversity cannot take place without first acknowledging diverse groups and how their life experiences may differ from our own. This acknowledgment takes us beyond the diversity-dismissive question: "We're all human, aren't we?" This question is only partially true. Yes, we are all humans, but humans are members of different social groups with different group identities, and those identities affect the life experiences of individuals who comprise the groups. To ignore group differences is to ignore the fact that members of different groups have different privileges, such as the amount of economic and social resources available to them. For instance, to ignore differences between socioeconomic groups is to fail to acknowledge the reality that individuals born into families with greater wealth and socioeconomic status have the privilege of tapping into networks of influential people who can help them gain access to employment, loans, educational services, and legal assistance.

Acknowledgment also involves acknowledging how our attitudes and behavior toward different groups can, in turn, affect how members of these groups view themselves. George Cooley, famous sociologist, coined the term "looking glass self" to capture the idea that when people see how others react to them and act toward them, it's like looking in a mirror—the actions and reactions (positive or negative) of others reflect back on them and affect how they view themselves (positively or negatively) (Cooley, 1922). Thus, negative biases that aren't unacknowledged have the potential to impact others, even though the impact may be unconscious and unintentional. By taking the time and making the effort to acknowledge our negative biases toward certain groups, we're less likely to put those biases into action and we reduce the risk that our biases have a negative effect on the self-concept or self-esteem of individuals in that group. Engaging in this process builds your social intelligence (SQ).

Once we have acknowledged how our biased thoughts, feelings, and actions may impact members of different groups, we are positioned to progress to the next stage in the process of diversity appreciation: *Acceptance*.

Reflection 5.2

Have you ever been subjected to implicit bias because you were a member of a particular social group?

If you have, what did the implicit bias involve and why do you think it occurred?

If you have never experienced implicit bias, why do you think you haven't?

Stage 3. Acceptance

This stage of diversity appreciation involves developing greater sensitivity to and empathy for others who have been adversely affected by group biases or prejudices. In this stage, we accept the fact that although we cannot actually feel what victims of prejudice have experienced, we can still understand how they feel and why they feel that way. In other words, we develop empathy, a form of emotional intelligence (Goleman, 2006) that promotes acceptance of different human experiences and breaks down biases toward members of other social groups (Batson, 1991; Goleman, 1995).

You can increase empathy for members of marginalized groups that have been targets of bias or prejudice by imagining what it would be like to be a member of that group and undergoing their experience. Better yet, actually take on that experience through role play. For example, spend a day in a wheelchair to experience what it's like for someone with a physical disability, or wear an eye mask for a day to experience what it's like to be blind. A classic example of role play for increasing empathy for groups that have experienced racism was conducted in 1959 by John Howard Griffin, a white novelist from Texas who disguised himself as black and took a six-week journey through the Deep South during the Jim Crow era of racial segregation and discrimination. Griffin kept a journal of his experiences and chronicled them in a book titled, *Black Like Me*. The book became an international bestseller that sold over 12 million copes and was translated into 16 different languages. To disguise himself as black, Griffin sought the help of a dermatologist who gave him an oral medication that deeply darkened his skin after it was exposed to sunlight. It was medication used for patients suffering from a disease that caused white spots

"Radical empathy means putting in the work to educate oneself and listen with a humble heart to understand another's experience from their perspective, not as we imagine we would feel."
—ISABEL WILKERSON, FIRST WOMAN OF AFRICAN AMERICAN HERITAGE TO WIN THE PULITZER PRIZE IN JOURNALISM

to appear on their face and body. Other than darkening his skin and shaving his head, he kept everything else about himself exactly the same, including his identity, clothing, speech patterns, and his educational and professional credentials. Griffin wrote the following about his experience taking on the role of a "black" man:

> Black men told me that the only way a white man could hope to understand this reality was to wake up some morning in a black man's skin. I learned within a very few hours that no one was judging me by my qualities as a human individual and everyone was judging me by my pigment. As soon as white men or women saw me, they automatically assumed I possessed a whole set of false characteristics (false not only to me but to all black men). They saw us as "different" from themselves in fundamental ways: we were irresponsible; we were different in our sexual morals; we were intellectually limited. Always, in every encounter, even with "good whites," we had the feeling that the white person was not talking with us but with his image of us. I could have been a Jew in Germany, a Mexican in a number of states, or a member of any "inferior" group. Only the details would have differed. The story would be the same (1962, pp. 166-167)

Personal Experience

As previously mentioned, one of the best attended events that ever took place on my campus was a presentation made by Floyd Cochran, a former member and recruiter for "Aryan Nation" (a White-supremacist hate group) who eventually left the group and went on to become a nationally known civil rights activist and educator. While he was speaking at my college, Cochran pointed to a key experience that caused him to change his bigoted views. It occurred when his pregnant wife had an early ultrasound that revealed his unborn son had a cleft palate. In the minds of the white supremacist group in which he was a member, the baby was "defective" and if he were to become the father of a defective child, he could no longer be a member of the supremacist group. This left Cochran with two choices: (a) abort his son and remain a member of the group or (b) keep his son and be ostracized by a group whose supremacist beliefs he endorsed. Cochran chose to quit the group, soon thereafter, he renounced his racist beliefs and began speaking out publicly against the hateful prejudices he once firmly believed and taught.

After hearing Cochran's story, it struck me that the experience that triggered his incredible transformation was an exercise in role reversal. When his son was deemed "inferior," he was thrust into a reversed role—he became the recipient rather than perpetrator of hateful discrimination. Cochran's radical reversal from hateful racist to civil rights activist is a dramatic example of how being placed in the role or position of a person experiencing prejudice can be a powerful way to promote empathy for victims of prejudice.

—Joe Cuseo

Connecting with members of other groups at a deep, empathetic levels is a key element of emotional intelligence (EQ).

Stage 4. Action

Once we: (a) become aware of our biases, (b) acknowledge how our biases have affected members of other social groups, and (c) accept the feelings of others who may have been adversely affected by our biases, we can (d) take action to capitalize on the benefits of diversity. The fourth and most advanced stage of this model of diversity appreciation requires stepping beyond mere tolerance and acceptance of diversity. A person who just tolerates diversity simply co-exists with diverse groups. In contrast, someone at this Action Stage of diversity appreciation exhibits *cultural competence* by initiating authentic diversity-related action and interaction with members of diverse groups and does so in ways that benefit both parties. For instance, students who reach this most advanced stage, convert diversity appreciation from attitude to action by seeking out interaction with students from diverse groups, collaborating with them, and learning with them in a way that changes their view of them and themselves (Smith, 1997, 2015). In so doing, they develop cultural competence and achieve an important outcome of multicultural education: self-transformation (Gorski, 1995–2018).

In summary, cultural competence is reached by progressing through successive steps or stages, each of which involves a more advanced level of cultural sensitivity and appreciation—as depicted in **Box 5.1**.

> "It is not enough to be tolerant. You tolerate what you would rather not have to deal with and wish would go away. It is no honor just to be tolerated."
> —ISABEL WILKERSON, PULITZER PRIZE-WINNING AUTHOR AND RECIPIENT OF THE NATIONAL HUMANITIES MEDAL

Box 5.1 **Progressive Steps to Cultural Competence**

Cultural Awareness: awareness of personal biases toward different cultural groups and their effect on oneself and others.

⇩

Cultural Acknowledgment: acknowledging that differences exist between individuals, races, and cultures, and viewing these differences as assets rather than liabilities.

⇩

Cultural Acceptance: accommodating cultural differences (rather than resisting and rejecting them) and looking for commonalities with others who you see as different.

⇩

Cultural Action: moving beyond recognizing and valuing diversity to actually seeking it out and experiencing its benefits.

⇩

Cultural Competence: gaining proficiency in relating to, learning from, and collaborating with people from diverse cultural backgrounds.

In the courses I teach, in the workshops I give, and in the life I live, I strive to value diversity. I am committed to recognizing and appreciating the variety of characteristics that contribute to our humanity and promote our individual and collective achievement. I have learned not only to tolerate groups that differ from me, but value these differences and learn from them. I want to be someone who isn't just "politically correct," but a person who continually self-checks and self-corrects my beliefs about human diversity. I will continue to challenge myself to strive toward increasingly higher levels of cultural competence.

—Aaron Thompson

If we were to view the attainment of cultural competence not only as a personal accomplishment, but as a *societal* achievement, it could be visualized as an ascending stairway composed of 12 steps (see **Figure 5.2**). Throughout history, human societies have held beliefs about different social groups that have reflected (and continue to reflect) the lower steps of this stairway. It should be the goal of humankind to climb this staircase, ascend to its pinnacle, and never descend to its lower levels.

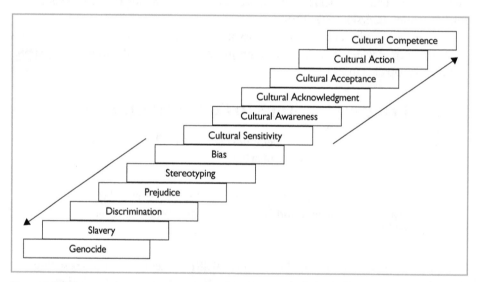

Figure 5.2 Stairway to Cultural Competence
© Kendall Hunt Publishing Company

Reflection 5.3

Looking at the steps of the stairway in **Figure 5.2**, which step do you think our society is at right now? Why? To move to the highest steps of the staircase, what major changes do you think our society needs to make?

Specific Strategies for Developing and Demonstrating Cultural Competence

Attaining cultural competence is the ultimate goal of diversity appreciation. Here are specific ways to advance toward that goal and eventually reach it.

Make a conscious attempt to perceive and interact with others on a person-to-person basis, not according to their group membership. Research shows that humans tend to perceive individuals from less familiar social groups in a more stereotypic fashion—seeing them as being more alike than members of their own group (Taylor et al., 2006). To combat this tendency, an intentional effort must be made to view, treat, or judge people from other members of other groups not in terms of their cultural or racial category, but as unique individuals.

Supporting this recommendation is research showing that when whites intentionally practice identifying the faces of others on a person-by-person basis instead of them by race, they are able to improve their ability to distinguish the faces of individuals from different races and reduce their level of implicit racial bias (Lebrecht et al., 2009).

Apply effective human relations skills and principles of social intelligence to develop positive relationships with members of other cultures. Human intelligence was once considered to be a general intellectual trait that could be measured by a single intelligence test (IQ). Scholars have since discovered that the singular word "intelligence" is incomplete and should be replaced by the more inclusive term "intelligences" to reflect the fact that humans demonstrate intelligence in multiple forms that cannot be captured by a single general-intelligence test score. One of these multiple forms of intelligences is *social intelligence* (aka "interpersonal intelligence"): the ability to effectively communicate with and relate to other human beings (Gardner, 1993, 1999; Goleman, 2006).

Interpersonal communication and human relations skills are the two key pillars of social intelligence. These skills are important for all human interactions, but they are even more important when interaction takes place between people from different cultures because poor interpersonal communication skills can lead to a cross-cultural communication breakdown and possible termination of a potentially fruitful intercultural relationship. When people attempt to communicate across different cultures, they're often so concerned about saying the "right thing" (what to say), they forget about saying it the "right way" (how to say it) (Du Praw & Axner, 1997).

Described below are human relations practices that research indicates are effective ways to enhance the quality of interpersonal relationships in general and intercultural relationships in particular.

Learn and remember the *names* of people you meet. How can you encourage members of diverse groups to view you as approachable and open to forming relationships with them? The first step is to learn their names.

> "You can't judge a book by the cover."
> —1962 HIT SONG BY ELLAS MCDANIEL, AKA BO DIDDLEY (NOTE: A "BODIDDLEY" IS A ONE-STRINGED AFRICAN GUITAR)

© marekuliasz/Shutterstock.com

When you learn and remember the names of individuals, and refer to them by name, it affirms their individuality and personal uniqueness. This is particularly important for members of minority groups because their individuality can often be masked or dismissed due to stereotypes held by their groups by members of the majority group.

It is common to hear people say that they have a good memory for faces but not names, suggesting they are not good at remembering names and never will be. The truth is that the ability to retain and recall names isn't an innate talent or inherited ability. Instead, it's a skill developed through intentional effort and effective use of strategies for remembering, such as the following

- When you first meet people, pay close attention to their name when you first hear it. The crucial initial step to remembering someone's name is to get that person's name into your brain in the first place. As obvious as this may seem, when we first meet someone, instead of listening actively and closely for the person's name, we're often more concerned about the first impression we're making or thinking about what we're going to say next (Demarais & White, 2004). Consequently, we often *forget* a person's name because we never did *get* the person's name (into our brain) in the first place. In other words, we were absentminded—our mind was literally "absent" (off somewhere else, thinking about something else), instead of being present and paying attention to the person's name when we first hear it.

- Say the person's name soon after you first hear it. For example, if your friend Gertrude just introduced you to Geraldine, you might say: "Geraldine, how long have you known Gertrude?" Stating the person's name shortly after you first hear it helps you remember the name because it prevents forgetting at a time when forgetting is most likely to occur—during the first moments after our brain takes in new information (Averell & Heathcote, 2011). In addition to improving your memory of the person's name, there is another benefit of saying the person's name right after you've heard it: It makes the person feel acknowledged and welcomed.

- Associate the person's name with something else about the person. For instance, a name could be remembered by associating it with: (a) some physical characteristic of the person (e.g., "tall Paul"), (b) the place where you first met the person, or (c) your first topic of conversation. Making a mental connection between the person's name and something else associated with the person improves memory of the name by capitalizing on the brain's natural tendency to store (retain) pieces of information as part of an interconnected network of related information (Zull, 2011).

- Keep a name journal that includes the names of people you meet accompanied in something you learned about them. We write down things we don't want to forget, such as tasks we need to complete or items we want to buy at the store, so why not use this same strategy to help us not forget the names of people we want to remember?

Refer to people by name when you see them and interact with them. Once you learn a person's name, be sure to continue referring to the person by name. If you happen to see Waldo, saying, "Hi, Waldo" will mean a lot more to him than simply saying "Hi" or "Hi, there"—which sounds like you've just encountered an unidentifiable object floating "out there" in public space or like you're addressing a personal correspondence to someone you know as "to whom it may concern." Continuing to refer to people by name after first learning their names not only serves to strengthen your memory of their names it also shows them that you haven't forgotten who they are (and that they're important to

"We should be aware of the magic contained in a name. The name sets that individual apart; it makes him or her unique among all others. Remember that a person's name is to that person the sweetest and most important sound in any language."

—DALE CARNEGIE, AUTHOR OF THE BEST-SELLING BOOK, *HOW TO WIN FRIENDS AND INFLUENCE PEOPLE*, AND FOUNDER OF THE DALE CARNEGIE COURSE—A WORLDWIDE LEADERSHIP TRAINING PROGRAM FOR BUSINESS PROFESSIONALS

"When I joined the bank, I started keeping a record of the people I met and put them on little cards, and I would indicate on the cards when I met them, and under what circumstances, and sometimes [make] a little notation which would help me remember a conversation."

—DAVID ROCKEFELLER, PROMINENT AMERICAN BANKER, PHILANTHROPIST, AND FORMER CEO OF THE CHASE MANHATTAN BANK you). This is a particularly powerful message to send to minority students who may feel marginalized.

Show interest in others by remembering what they share with you and by referring to what they have shared with you in subsequent conversations. Listen closely to and try to retain what people share with you, especially what seems important to them, or what really interests them (whether it be school, sports, family, or friends) and bring up these topics next time you see them. Try to move beyond the mindless routine of asking the standard, generic questions people always ask each other when they meet again (e.g., "How are you?" "What's new?"). Instead, ask personalized questions about something specific the person shared with you previously (e.g., "How did things go on that math test you were worried about?").

Studies of college students from underrepresented or marginalized groups indicate that they are more likely to succeed in college when they experience *personal validation*—the feeling of being recognized as individuals and that members of the campus community care about them (Rendón-Linares & Muñoz, 2011). Majority students can provide minority students with personal validation by knowing them by name, referring to them by name, showing interest in them, and remembering what their interests are. By recalling what other students share with you, it shows them that they matter to you; and by showing interest in their lives and talking with them about their interests, they become more interested in you and continuing their relationship with you.

> "You can make more friends in 2 months by becoming interested in other people than you can in 2 years by trying to get other people interested in you."
> —DALE CARNEGIE, *HOW TO WIN FRIENDS AND INFLUENCE PEOPLE*

Reflection 5.4

Since you have been on campus, do you feel that you have received personal validation from other members of your campus community?

If yes, from whom?

If no, why do you think you haven't?

Be an active and empathic listener. When people take surveys that ask them to identify qualities or characteristics of a good friend, "good listener" consistently ranks among the top characteristics cited (Berndt, 1992). Effective listening skills have also been found to characterize effective problem solvers (Steil & Bommelje, 2007) and effective leaders (Johnson & Bechler, 1998), and it ranks among the top skills sought by employers (Gabric & McFadden, 2001; Wolvin, 2010).

Despite the well-documented importance of listening skills, scholars in the field of interpersonal communications and human relations report that most people spend too much time talking and not enough time listening or listening actively and empathically (Nichols, 1995; Nichols & Stevens, 1957; Wolvin, 2010). Humans can understand spoken words at a rate more than twice as fast as the rate at which others can speak them (Barker & Watson,

> "We have been given two ears and but a single mouth in order that we may hear more and talk less."
> —ZENO OF CITIUM, ANCIENT GREEK PHILOSOPHER

> "Most people do not listen with the intent to understand; they listen with the intent to reply."
> —STEPHEN COVEY, AUTHOR, *THE 7 HABITS OF HIGHLY EFFECTIVE PEOPLE*

2000; Headlee, 2016). This leaves plenty of time for our mind to wander and slip into *passive listening*—hearing the words being spoken, but not listening closely to what the words actually mean. *Active listening* is a human relations strategy for minimizing attention drift passive listening that involves: (a) focusing our *full attention* on the speaker's message—as opposed to "half-listening" and waiting for our turn to talk or thinking about what we're going to say next; (b) listening *empathically*—by paying close attention not only to what the speaker is communicating verbally but also to the speaker's nonverbal messages; and (c) listening with *engagement*—by expressing interest in the speaker, checking our understanding of the speaker's words and feelings, and encouraging the speaker to elaborate.

Consider This…

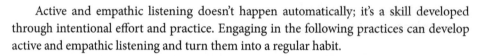

Listening actively and empathically to others from diverse backgrounds enables you to give their thoughts and feelings your undivided attention, sending them a clear message that you hear them and respect what they have to say.

Active and empathic listening doesn't happen automatically; it's a skill developed through intentional effort and practice. Engaging in the following practices can develop active and empathic listening and turn them into a regular habit.

- **Periodically check to see if you're understanding the speaker's message.** Good listeners take personal responsibility for following the speaker's message. In contrast, poor listeners put all the responsibility on the speaker to make the message clear and interesting. To check if you're following the speaker's message, occasionally paraphrase what you hear being said in your own words (e.g., "What I hear you saying is …"). These check-in statements ensure that you're following what's being said; they also assure the speaker that you're listening closely and taking what's being said seriously.

- **In addition to checking your understanding of what the speaker is saying, check your understanding of what the speaker is feeling.** Pay particularly close attention to nonverbal messages—such as tone of voice and body language—which often provide clues to the emotions behind the words. For example, if the speaker's rate of speech and volume increase, it may suggest that there are strong emotions underlying the words being said. In which case, you might check in with a statement like: "It seems like you have strong feelings about . . ."

- **Avoid interrupting the speaker when you have something you want to say.** Wait until the speaker pauses for a period of time to be sure that the speaker's point has been completed otherwise you may disrupt the speaker's train of thought or send the message that what you have to say is more important. Also, if the speaker pauses, leading you think it's okay for you to start talking, but you both begin speaking again at the same time, let the speaker continue and say something like: "Sorry, didn't mean to interrupt. You were saying . . ."

- **When asking questions, allow the speaker ample time to answer.** Silent spots may feel uncomfortable, but give the speaker time to formulate thoughts and figure out how to express them before answering. Allowing pause time for a response is particularly important for those who may be communicating cross-culturally or cross-linguistically (e.g., a speaker whose first language isn't English).

- **Avoid "selective listening"**— selectively tuning into topics we find interesting and ideas we agree with, and tuning out topics and ideas that disinterest us or that we disagree with. Ignoring or blocking out information and ideas that we do not immediately find interesting or do not support our point of view is not only a poor social skill, it's also a poor critical-thinking skill. As discussed in Chapter 3, our thinking becomes deeper and more complex when we're exposed to perspectives that don't mirror or duplicate our own.

- **Use effective "body language" to send a clear message that you're listening with attention and interest.** Communication experts estimate that more than two-thirds of all human communication is nonverbal and that nonverbal communication sends stronger and truer messages than verbal communication (Driver, 2010; Navarro, 2008). When a speaker perceives inconsistency between a listener's verbal and non-verbal messages (e.g., one signals interest and the other disinterest), the speaker is more likely to place more weight on the nonverbal message (Ekman, 2009). Consequently, body language may be the most powerful way we can communicate genuine interest in what's being said and respect for the speaker. (For a short summary of effective nonverbal messages to send while listening, see **Box 5.2**.)

> "Listening well is as important to critical thinking as is contributing brilliantly."
> —STEPHEN BROOKFIELD, AUTHOR, *DEVELOPING CRITICAL THINKERS*

Box 5.2 — Nonverbal Signals Associated with Active Listening

Good listeners listen not only with their ears; they listen their whole body to send signals to the speaker that they are paying full attention to what is being said. Communication experts have created the acronym "SOFTEN" to summarize all the key body-language signals that should be sent while listening. Listed below are the signals represented by each letter of the SOFTEN acronym.

S=Smile. Smiling communicates acceptance and interest. However, smiling should be done periodically, not continuously. (A continuous, non-stop smile can appear artificial or inauthentic.)

Sit Still. Fidgeting or squirming sends the message that you're bored or growing impatient (and can't wait for the speaker to finish).

O=Open Posture. Avoid closed-posture positions, such as crossing your arms or folding your hands. These nonverbal signals can convey a message that you're not open to what the speaker is saying or passing judgment on what's being said.

F=Forward Lean. Leaning forward sends the message that you're looking forward to what the speaker is about to say. In contrast, leaning back can send a signal that you're backing off from (losing interest in) what's being said or, worse yet, that you're evaluating or psychoanalyzing the speaker.

Face the Speaker Directly. Try to line up your shoulders directly or squarely with the speaker's shoulders—as opposed to turning one shoulder toward the speaker and the other shoulder away—which may send the message that you want to get away or giving the speaker the "cold shoulder."

T=Touch. Communication experts advise that a light touch on the arm, particularly to reassure a person who's speaking about something they're worried about or uncomfortable with, is acceptable and a good way to communicate warmth. However, touch sparingly and make it more like a pat rather than a sustained touch or stroke, which could be interpreted as inappropriate intimacy (or sexual harassment).

E=Eye Contact. Lack of eye contact with the speaker can send the message that you're looking elsewhere to find something more interesting or stimulating to do (e.g., looking to check your text messages). However, eye contact shouldn't be continuous or relentless because it can be interpreted as staring. Instead, make periodic eye contact—occasionally look away from the speaker's eyes and then return your eye contact. (Temporarily taking your eyes off the speaker can also send the positive message that you're thinking about what the person is saying.)

N=Nod Your Head. Nodding your head slowly and periodically while listening sends a signal that you're following what's being said and affirming the person saying it. However, rapid and repeated head nodding should be avoided because it may communicate you want the speaker to hurry up and finish.

Sources: Barker and Watson (2000); Nichols (2009); Purdy and Borisoff (1996)

Reflection 5.5

Looking back at the nonverbal listening signals cited in **Box 5.2**:

a) Which signal do you think would most important to send during interactions with people from all cultures? Why?

b) Which signal do you think may not be good to send to members of certain cultures? Why?

 ## Consider This…

There are five keys to building positive interpersonal and intercultural relationships: (1) know and refer to others by name; (2) show interest in others by asking them about their interests; (3) listen actively and empathically; (4) remember what they share with you, and (5) show them that you remembered (and cared about) what they shared with you referring to it in future conversations.

Strategies for Increasing Personal Contact and Interpersonal Interaction with Members of Diverse Groups

Listening to lectures on diversity or reading books about diversity is learning *about* diversity vicariously—through someone else. In contrast, person-to-person interaction with others from diverse backgrounds is learning *from* diversity directly. The difference is comparable to acquiring knowledge about a country by reading about it or hearing an instructor talk about it—as opposed to actually traveling to that country and interacting with its natives. Interpersonal interaction with members of different cultural groups takes us beyond multicultural knowledge to intercultural interaction and transforms diversity appreciation from an attitude to an action. This is why scholars often prefer the term *intercultural* education to multicultural education because the former suggests that appreciating diversity involves genuine *interaction* between members of different cultures and the ability to communicate across cultural boundaries (Banks, 2016).

Research shows that engaging in regular contact between members of different racial or ethnic groups reduces intergroup stereotyping and prejudice (Pettigrew, 1997, 1998; Pettigrew & Tropp, 2006). In one review of over 200 separate studies, face-to-face interaction between members of different racial and ethnic groups was found to reduce intergroup prejudice in 94% of the interactions that took place between the groups (Pettigrew & Tropp, 2000). Furthermore, such interaction have been found to increase intergroup friendships, even among members of groups that have previously experienced intergroup conflict (Paolini et al., 2007). Studies of college students also show that students from minority racial and ethnic groups who form intergroup friendships on campus report a greater sense of belonging and a higher level of satisfaction with their college experience (Mendoza-Denton, 2010).

The need to make conscious and intentional attempts to engage in intercultural interaction is underscored by research in social psychology, which indicates that humans have a strong predisposition to associate with others who share their same ethnicity and socioeconomic status—a phenomenon that scholars refer to as "homophily"—the tendency for people with similar attitudes and beliefs to group together. Homophily has also been found to take place among students on college campuses (Hastings & Cohn, 2015). Additional research shows that when people are asked why they do not interact with others from different racial and ethnic backgrounds, members of both minority and non-minority groups say they have avoided contact because they feared rejection and interpreted the other group's avoidance of them as indicating as that they were not interested in intergroup interaction (Shelton & Richeson, 2005). The tendency for different groups to make incorrect assumptions about each other has long been observed by social psychologists who refer to it as "pluralistic ignorance" (Katz & Allport, 1931). Thus, to combat homophily and pluralistic ignorance, conscious efforts and intentional attempts have to be made to step outside our cultural comfort zone and seek out opportunities to interact with people from diverse cultural backgrounds (Syed & Juan, 2012). Failing to do so is likely to result in our reverting to the default tendency of humans to distance themselves from diversity and deny themselves the opportunity to experience diversity and its benefits.

Reflection 5.6

Would you say your campus climate or culture supports and facilitates intercultural interaction among students from different racial and cultural backgrounds? Is there anything that could be done to improve your campus climate to make it more supportive of, or conducive to, intercultural interaction?

Described below are specific strategies that college students can use to increase their contact and interaction with members of diverse groups.

Seek out the views and opinions of classmates from diverse backgrounds. Group discussions among students of different cultures have been found to reduce prejudice and promote intercultural appreciation, but only if each member's cultural identity and perspective are sought out and valued by members of the discussion group (Baron et al., 2008). You can demonstrate leadership during group discussions by seeking out the views and opinions of classmates from diverse backgrounds and ensuring that their ideas are heard. After discussions have ended, you could also ask students from minority cultural backgrounds if there were points made or positions taken during the discussion that they would have questioned or challenged, but didn't get the opportunity to share, or didn't feel comfortable about sharing.

In classes where there is little or no student diversity, encourage your classmates to approach course topics and issues from diverse perspectives. For instance, you might ask: "If there were international students here, what might they be adding to our discussion?" Or, "If members of certain minority groups were here, would they be offering a different viewpoint?"

When you are allowed to form your own discussion groups and choose group-project members, include students from diverse backgrounds. You can gain greater access to diverse perspectives by intentionally joining or forming diverse learning groups with students who differ in terms with respect to such characteristics as gender, age, race, or ethnicity. Including diversity in your discussion groups is not only a culturally inclusive practice, it's also an effective educational practice because it broadens and deepens learning by exposing group members to wider variety of perspectives. For instance, when a discussion group is composed of members who are diverse with respect to age, older students will bring a broad range of practical life experiences to the discussion that younger students can draw on and learn from; at the same time, younger students will bring a more contemporary and idealistic perspective that can balance and enrich the intergenerational discussion.

Incorporating gender diversity into your discussion groups can infuse different approaches to learning and ways of understanding issues displayed by males and females. Studies show that males are more likely to be "separate knowers"—they tend to "detach" themselves from the concept or issue being discussed so they can analyze it. Females, on the other hand, are more likely to be "connected knowers"—they tend to relate personally to concepts being discussed and connect them with their own experiences and the experiences of others. For example, when interpreting a poem, males are more likely to ask: "What techniques can I use to analyze it?" In contrast, females are more likely to ask: "What is the poet trying to say to me?" (Belenky et al., 1986). By forming gender-diverse discussion groups, both approaches are included in the discussion process, that results in a more a balanced and complete understanding of the topic being discussed.

It has also been found that during group discussions, females are more likely to work collaboratively, often sharing their ideas with others and collecting ideas from others. In contrast, males more often adopt a competitive approach and debate the ideas of others (Magolda, 1992). Consistent with these findings are studies of females in leadership positions, which reveal that women are more likely to adopt a more democratic or participative style of leadership than men (van Engen & Willemsen, 2004).

Form and facilitate collaborative learning teams composed of students from diverse backgrounds. A learning *team* is different than a discussion group. A discussion group simply discusses (tosses around) ideas. A learning team moves beyond discussion to *collaboration*—its members "co-labor" (work together) to reach the same goal. In educational settings, research from kindergarten through college indicates that students' academic performance and interpersonal skills are strengthened when whey work collaboratively in teams (Cuseo, 1996). The physical environment or location where teamwork takes place can further enrich the quality of collaboration and the quality of their work produced by the learning team. Teammates are more likely to interact openly and work collaboratively if their work takes place in a friendly, informal environment that's conducive to relationship building. If possible, have your team come together in a living room or a lounge area. Compared with a sterile classroom, these environments supply a warmer atmosphere that's more conducive to interpersonal interaction and collaboration.

When members of any group work as a team to pursue a common goal, it creates positive interdependence and a sense of camaraderie among teammates that often extends beyond the work task to other social settings. The power of teamwork for promoting positive cross-cultural interaction and relationship building is evidenced by the number of interracial friendships that are formed among athletes who play together on the same team and soldiers who fight together in the same military unit (Putnam, 2007). Formal research studies also show that when members of different racial groups work together on teams in pursuit of the same common goal, racial prejudices decrease and interracial friendships increase among team members (Allport, 1954; Amir, 1969, 1976; Brown et al., 2003; Dovidio et al., 2011; Pettigrew & Tropp, 2000). These positive developments may be explained, at least in part, by the fact that when members of diverse groups join together on the same team, nobody is a member of an "out" group ("them"); instead, everybody is a member of the same "in" group ("us") (Pratto et al., 2000; Sidanius et al., 2000).

It is important to underscore the fact that these positive outcomes occur when the contact between members of different cultural groups involves working collaboratively toward achieving the same goal. If the intergroup contact involves competition for limited resources, whereby one group achieves the goal at the expense of the other, it actually escalates intergroup prejudice (Allport, 1954, 1979; Eberhardt, 2019).

After engaging in group work with diverse teammates, take time to reflect on the experience. The final step in any learning process, whether it be learning from a professor or learning from group work, is to step back from the experience and thoughtfully review it. Deep learning takes place through effortful action followed by thoughtful reflection (Bligh, 2000; Roediger et al., 2007). After working in diverse groups, you can reflect on what you learned from the experience, and encourage other group members to do the same, by asking yourself and other group members the following questions:

- What major similarities in viewpoints did all group members share? (What common themes emerged?)
- What major differences of opinion were expressed by members of the group from different cultural backgrounds? (What were the variations on the common themes?)
- Were there particular topics or issues raised that provoked intense discussion or passionate reaction from diverse members of the group?
- Did the group discussion result in group members changing their mind about ideas or positions they originally held, particularly ideas or positions relating to diversity, awareness and cross-cultural differences?

"Knowledge of characteristics and needs that all human beings share can foster a sense of community among individuals of diverse ethnic identities."

—CHERYL BERNSTEIN COHEN, *TEACHING ABOUT ETHNIC DIVERSITY*

Be a community builder by identifying what unifies the experiences of students from diverse backgrounds. In addition to seeking out and appreciating the distinctive experiences of different racial and cultural groups, look for and point out the common denominators—themes of unity that co-exist with diversity. Find the shared experiences that traverse or transcend group differences and unite all groups—for example, common components and experiences shared by all cultural groups (see Chapter 1, p. 4).

When discussions of diversity focus exclusively on intergroup differences without also attending to intergroup commonalities, it can heighten feelings of divisiveness between groups and cause members of minority groups to feel further isolated or alienated (Smith, 1997, 2015). Studies show that efforts at promoting multicultural appreciation of minority groups can lead some members of nonminority groups to believe their group is being neglected or excluded (Plaut et al., 2011; Stevens et al., 2008). To reduce the risk of this happening, include all groups by digging below the surface of group differences and unearthing the common ground on which all groups stand. Raising awareness of what different groups have in common can help defuse feelings of divisiveness and provide a solid foundation on which open and honest discussions of group differences can be built. Research shows that when members of different groups become more aware of the characteristics and experiences they share as human beings, intergroup prejudices are reduced (Jackson et al., 2020).

Place yourself in situations or locations on campus where you're more likely to encounter and experience diversity. Research in social psychology provides hard evidence for what's obvious: People who are in the same place at the same time are more likely to communicate with one another and form relationships (Latané et al., 1995). You can create these conditions to increase communication and relationships with members of diverse groups by: (a) placing yourself in situations where there are opportunities to interact with students from different cultural backgrounds (e.g., sitting nearby diverse students in class, in the library, or in the campus cafe), (b) joining up with diverse students for group discussions, study groups, or group projects, and (c) joining campus clubs or organizations whose mission is to promote diversity awareness, interaction, and appreciation (e.g., multicultural clubs or international student organizations). By intentionally placing yourself in these social situations, you position yourself you to form relationships with members of different cultural groups, and create opportunities to learn about othem (and vice versa).

Take advantage of social media to "chat" virtually with students from diverse groups. Technology can be a convenient and comfortable way to initiate contact with members of groups with whom you have had little or no prior contact. Interacting initially *online* can sometimes serve to "break the ice" and pave the way for later interaction *in person*. (You can also engage in online exchanges with diverse students living in other countries by visiting http://www.epals.com.)

Engage in extracurricular or co-curricular programs relating to diversity. Studies show that when students participate in out-of-class experiences that involve diversity, it enhances critical thinking (Pascarella & Terenzini, 2005) while reducing implicit bias and unconscious prejudice (Blair, 2002). This reduction of bias and prejudice is likely due to the fact that when students from different cultures participate in extracurricular activities together, sharing membership in the same student club, campus organization, or athletic team, they create a joint or unified membership that cuts across their cultural differences (and biases) and a "superordinate group identity" that transcends their cultural differences, uniting them under the same social umbrella (Banks, 2016).

If you're a member of a minority group on campus, join or form a campus club or organization with other members of your minority group. Research shows that student clubs and organizations that bring together members of the same minority group provide its members with valuable social support, promote pride in their group identity, and elevates their personal well-being—particularly if they are feeling excluded or marginalized (Grills et al., 2016; Williams et al., 1999). When college students from minority racial or ethnic groups form their own support groups, it doesn't mean that they are attempting to self-segregate or distance themselves from members of other groups; instead, they are simply creating one social place or space on campus where they can spend some time not being in the minority (Smith, 2015). There is a difference between separatism and segregation. The latter is an attempt by a dominant majority group to reduce contact and maintain dominance over a minority group; the former is an attempt on the part of members of a minority group to value their own culture while, at the same time, remaining open to and valuing interaction with members of the majority group (Banks, 2016). In a major study of college campuses where Latinx (Latina/Latino) students formed their own club or organization *and* socialized with white students, students on these campuses reported experiencing less racial tension and a more welcoming campus climate (Hurtado, 2002).

Participate in volunteer experiences that bring you in contact with people living in diverse communities or neighborhoods. Better yet, take a leadership role by organizing volunteer experiences in which you and other students participate together. Research on students who engage in volunteer service experience indicates that they experience significant gains in self-esteem and sense of purpose (Astin et al., 2000; Vogelgesang et al., 2002). Studies also show that individuals who devote time and energy to be of service to others are more likely to report higher levels of personal happiness and life satisfaction (Myers, 1993).

Furthermore, volunteering provides students with an experiential learning opportunity that develops career-relevant skills, such as teamwork, problem-solving, decision-making, intercultural competence, and leadership (Astin et al., 2000; National Association of Colleges & Employers, 2019).

Consider This...

Volunteerism and service learning experiences can help students explore and identify career paths that are consistent with their personal values, interests and talents, as well as develop their employability skills. By engaging in service to diverse communities, students not only serve others, they also build cultural competence and career readiness.

Chapter Summary and Highlights

Anyone, including open-minded individuals, can hold biases rooted in their cultural backgrounds. Only a deep sense of self-examination and self-awareness can uproot and offset these biases. Making an intentional effort to introspect and inspect our biases is the critical first step toward accepting and appreciating diversity. This introspective process can be conceptualized as a systematic series of steps that begins with gaining *awareness* of group differences, followed by: *acknowledging* biases (explicit or implicit) toward groups that differ from our own, *accepting* group differences, and moving from acceptance to *action* by initiating interaction with members of diverse groups. This introspective process entails the following four-step progression: (1) **awareness** of our personal beliefs and attitudes toward diverse groups; (2) **acknowledgment** of how our beliefs and attitudes may affect our interactions with members of diverse groups; (3) **acceptance** of (including empathy for) members of diverse groups; and (4) **action** taken to engage with members of diverse groups.

Attaining cultural competence is the ultimate goal of diversity appreciation. Specific ways to advance toward and eventually reach that goal include the following.

Make a conscious attempt to perceive and interact with others on a person-to-person basis, not according to their group membership. Research shows that humans tend to perceive individuals from less familiar social groups in a more stereotypic fashion—seeing them as being more alike than members of their own group. To combat this tendency, an intentional effort has to be made to view, treat, and judge people from other cultural groups not in terms of their cultural or racial category, but as unique individuals.

Apply effective human relations skills and principles of social intelligence to develop positive intercultural relationships. One form of human intelligence is *social intelligence* (aka "interpersonal intelligence")—the ability to effectively communicate with and relate to other human beings.

Interpersonal communication and human relations skills are the two key pillars of social intelligence and there are keys to building positive interpersonal and intercultural relationships are: (1) knowing others by name and referring to them by name; (2) showing interest in others by asking them about their interests; (3) listening actively and empathically when others share their thoughts with you; (4) remembering what others share with you, and (5) showing them that you remembered (and cared about) what they shared with you by referring to it in future conversations. These are five effective ways to enhance the quality of interpersonal relationships in general and intercultural relationships in particular.

Learn and remember the *names* of people you meet. By learning and remembering the names of individuals, and referring to them by name, it affirms their individuality and uniqueness. This is particularly important for members of minority groups because their individuality can often be masked or dismissed due to stereotypes held about their group held by members of the majority group.

Refer to people by name when you see them and interact with them. Once you learn a person's name, be sure to continue referring to that person by name. This serves to strengthen your memory of names and shows them that you haven't forgotten who they are (and that they're important to you). This is a particularly powerful message to send to members of minority groups because they may feel marginalized.

Show interest in others, remember what they share with you, and refer to what they have shared with you in subsequent conversations. By remembering what other students share with you, it shows them that their interests and concerns matter to you, and increases the likelihood they become interested in you and continuing their relationship with you.

Be an active and empathic listener. When people answer surveys that ask them to identify the characteristics of a good friend, "good listener" consistently ranks among the top characteristics cited. Listening actively and empathically to others from diverse backgrounds enables you to give their thoughts and feelings your undivided attention, sending them a clear message that you hear them and respect what they have to say.

Seek out the views and opinions of classmates from diverse backgrounds. Group discussions among students of different cultures have been found to reduce prejudice and promote intercultural appreciation, but only if each member's cultural identity and perspective is sought out and valued by members of the discussion group. You can demonstrate leadership during group discussions in class by seeking out the views and opinions of classmates from diverse backgrounds and ensuring that their ideas are heard.

When you're allowed to form your own discussion groups and choose teammates for group projects, include students from diverse backgrounds. You can gain greater access to diverse perspectives by intentionally joining or forming learning groups with students who differ with respect to such characteristics as gender, age, race, or ethnicity. Including diversity in your discussion groups is not only a culturally inclusive practice, it's also an effective educational practice that serves to broaden and deepen learning by exposing group members to wider variety of perspectives.

Form and facilitate collaborative learning teams composed of students from diverse backgrounds. A discussion group simply discusses (tosses around) ideas. A learning team moves beyond discussion to *collaboration*—its members "co-labor" (work together) to reach a common goal. Studies also show that when members of different racial groups work in teams toward the same goal, racial prejudices decrease and interracial friendships increase among team members.

After engaging in group work with diverse teammates, take time to reflect on the experience. The final step in any learning process, whether it be learning from a professor or learning from group work, is to step back from the experience and thoughtfully review it. After working in diverse groups, you can reflect on what you learned from the experience and encourage other group members to do the same, particularly regarding what they learned from different members of the group.

Be a community builder by identifying commonalities in the experiences of students from diverse backgrounds. When discussions of diversity focus exclusively on intergroup differences without also attending to intergroup commonalities, it can heighten feelings of divisiveness between member of different cultural groups and cause members of minority groups to feel further isolated or alienated. Raising awareness of what different groups have in common can help defuse feelings of divisiveness and provide a solid foundation on which open and honest discussions of group differences can be built.

Place yourself in situations or locations on campus where you're more likely to encounter and experience diversity. Putting yourself in the same space or place with members of diverse groups increases opportunities to interact with them and learn about them (and vice versa).

Take advantage of social media to "chat" virtually with students from diverse groups. Technology can be a convenient and comfortable way to initiate contact with members of groups with whom you have had little or no prior contact. Interacting initially *online* can also serve to "break the ice" and pave the way for later interaction *in person*.

Engage in extracurricular and co-curricular programs relating to diversity. Studies show that when students participate in out-of-class experiences that involve diversity, it enhances critical thinking while reducing implicit bias and unconscious prejudice.

If you're a member of a minority group on your campus, join or form a campus club or organization with other members of your minority group. Research shows that student clubs and organizations that bring together members of the same minority group provide these students with valuable social support, promotes pride in their group identity, and elevates their personal well-being, particularly if they are feeling excluded or marginalized on campus.

Participate in volunteer experiences that bring you in contact with people in diverse communities or neighborhoods. Research indicates that students who engage in volunteer and service experiences show gains in self-esteem and sense of purpose. Engaging in service to diverse communities also builds cultural competence and career readiness.

Internet Resources

Becoming aware of implicit bias: https://www/youtube.com/watch?v=kKHSJHkPeLY

Cultural Competence: https://extension.psu-edu/what-is-cultural-competence-and-how-to-develop-it

Cross-cultural communication challenges & strategies: http://www.pbs.org/ampu/crosscult.html

Interpersonal Communication Skills: https://www.skillsyouneed.com/ips/what-is-communication.html

Social Intelligence: https://www.verywellmind.com/what-is-social-intelligence-4163839

Emotional Intelligence: https://www.psychologytoday.com/us/basics/emotional-intelligence

References

Allport, G. W. (1954). *The nature of prejudice.* Addison-Wesley.

Allport, G. W. (1979). *The nature of prejudice* (3rd ed.). Addison-Wesley.

Amir, Y. (1969). Contact hypothesis in ethnic relations. *Psychological Bulletin, 71,* 319–342.

Amir, Y. (1976). The role of intergroup contact in change of prejudice and ethnic relations. In P. A. Katz (Ed.), *Towards the elimination of racism* (pp. 245–308). Pergamon Press.

Astin, A. W., Vogelgesang, L. J., Ikeda, E. K. & Yee, J. A. (2000). *How service learning affects students.* University of California Los Angeles, Higher Education Research Institute.

Averell, L., & Heathcote, A. (2011). The form of the forgetting curve and the fate of memories. *Journal of Mathematical Psychology, 55*(1), 25–35.

Banks, J. A. (2016). *Cultural diversity and education: Foundations, curriculum, and teaching* (6th ed.). Routledge.

Barker, L., & Watson, K. W. (2000). *Listen up: How to improve relationships, reduce stress, and be more productive by using the power of listening.* St. Martin's Press.

Baron, R. A., Branscombe, N. R, & Byrne, D. R. (2008). *Social psychology* (12th ed.). Pearson.

Bass, B. M., & Riggio, R. E. (2005). *Transformational leadership* (2nd ed.). Lawrence Erlbaum Associates.

Batson, C. D. (1991). *The altruism question: Toward a social-psychological answer.* Lawrence Erlbaum Associates.

Belenky, M. F., Clinchy, B., Goldberger, N. R., & Tarule, J. M. (1986). *Women's ways of knowing: The development of self, voice, and mind.* Basic Books.

Berndt, T. J. (1992). Friendship and friends' influence in adolescence. *Current Directions in Psychological Science, 1*(5), 156–159.

Blair, I. V. (2002). The malleability of automatic stereotypes and prejudice. *Personality and Social Psychology Review, 6*(3), 242–261.

Bligh, D. A. (2000). *What's the use of lectures?* Jossey-Bass.

Bowman, B. T. (1995). *Cultural diversity and academic achievement.* http://www.ncrel.org/sdrs/areas/issues/educatrs/leadrshp/le0bow.htm#author

Brown, K. T, Brown, T. N., Jackson, J. S., Sellers, R. M., & Manuel, W. J. (2003). Teammates on and off the field? Contact with Black teammates and the racial attitudes of White student athletes. *Journal of Applied Social Psychology, 33,* 1379–1403.

Butler, J. E. (1993). Transforming the curriculum: Teaching about women of color. In J. A. Banks & C. Banks (Eds.), *Multicultural education: Issues and perspectives.* Allyn & Bacon.

Cooley, C. H. (1922). *Human nature and the social order.* Scribner's.

Cuseo, J. B. (1996). *Cooperative learning: A pedagogy for addressing contemporary challenges and critical issues in higher education.* New Forums Press.

Demarais, A., & White, V. (2004). *First impressions: What you don't know about how others see you.* Bantam.

Dovidio, J. F., Eller, A., & Hewstone, M. (2011). Improving intergroup relations through direct, extended and other forms of indirect contact. *Group Processes & Intergroup Relations, 14*, 147–160.

Driver, J. (2010). *You say more than you think: A 7-day plan for using the new body language to get what you want.* Crown Publishers.

Du Praw, M. & Axner, M. (1997). *Toward a more perfect union in an age of diversity: Working on common cross-cultural communication challenges* http://www.pbs.org/ampu/crosscult.html.

Eagly, A. H., & Carli, L. L. (2003). The female leadership advantage: An evaluation of the evidence. *Leadership Quarterly, 14*, 807–834.

Eberhardt, J. L. (2019). *Biased: Uncovering the hidden prejudice that shapes what we see, think, and do.* Viking.

Ekman, P. (2009). *Telling lies: Clues to deceit in the marketplace, politics, and marriage* (revised ed.). W. W. Norton.

Fiarman, S. E. (2016). Unconscious bias: When good intentions aren't enough. *Educational Leadership, 74*(3), 10–15.

Gabric, D., & McFadden, K. L. (2001). Student and employer perceptions of desirable entry-level operations management skills. *American Business Law Journal, 16*(1), 50–59.

Gardner, H. (1993). *Multiple intelligences: The theory of multiple intelligences* (2nd ed.). Basic Books.

Gardner, H. (1999). *Intelligence reframed: Multiple intelligences for the 21st century.* Basic Books.

Ginsberg, M. B., & Wlodkowski, R. J. (2009). *Diversity and motivation: Culturally responsive teaching in college.* Jossey-Bass.

Goleman, D. (1995). *Emotional intelligence: Why it can matter more than IQ.* Random House.

Goleman, D. (2006). *Social intelligence: The new science of human relationships.* Dell.

Gorski, P. C. (1995–2018). *Key characteristics of a multicultural curriculum.* Critical Multicultural Pavilion: Multicultural Curriculum Reform (An EdChange Project). www.edchange.org/multicultural/curriculum/characteristics.html

Griffin, J. H. (1962). *Black like me.* Penguin Group.

Grills, C., Cook, D., Douglas, J., Subica, A., Villanueva, S., & Hudson, B. (2016). Culture, racial socialization, and positive African American youth development. *Journal of Black Psychology, 42*, 343–373.

Hastings, S. L., & Cohn, T. J. (2015). Social development and relationship development. In J. C. Wade, L. I. Marks, & R. D. Hetzel (Eds.), *Positive psychology on the college campus* (pp. 3239–3260). Oxford University Press.

Headlee, C. (2016, February 16). *Ten ways to have a better conversation* [TED talk]. https://www.ted.com/talks/celeste_headlee_10_ways_to_have_a_better_conversation

Hogan, R., Curphy, G. J., & Hogan, J. (1994). What we know about leadership: Effectiveness and personality. *American Psychologist, 49*, 493–504.

Hurtado, S. (2002). Creating a climate of inclusion: Understanding Latina(o) college students. In W. A. Smith, P. T. Altbach, & K. Lometey (Eds.), *The racial crisis in American higher education: Continuing challenges for the twenty-first century* (pp. 121–136). State University of New York Press.

Jackson, J. C., Castelo, N., & Gray, K. (2020). Could a rising robot workforce make humans less prejudiced? *American Psychologist, 75*(7), 969–982.

Johnson, S., & Bechler, C. (1998). Examining the relationships between listening effectiveness and leadership emergence: Perceptions, behaviors, and recall. *Small Group Research, 29*(4), 452–471.

Jones, J. E., & Wade, J. C. (2015). Positive supervision and training. In J. C. Wade, L. I. Marks, & R. D. Hetzel (Eds*.), Positive psychology on the college campus* (pp. 191–218). Oxford University Press.

Katz, D., & Allport, F. H. (1931). *Student attitudes*. Craftsman.

Latané, B., Liu, J. H., Nowak, A., Bonevento, N., & Zheng, L. (1995). Distance matters: Physical space and social impact. *Personality and Social Psychology Bulletin, 21*, 795–805.

Lebrecht, S., Pierce L. J, Tarr, M. J., & Tanaka, J. W. (2009). Perceptual other-race training reduces implicit racial bias. *PLoS ONE 4*(1), e4215. https://doi.org/10.1371/ journal. pone.0004215

Locks, A. M., Hurtado, S., Bowman, N., & Osequera, L. (2008). Extending notions of campus climate and diversity to students' transition to college. *Review of Higher Education, 31*(3), 257–285.

Magolda, M. B. B. (1992). *Knowing and reasoning in college*. Jossey-Bass.

Mendoza-Denton, R. (2010). Framed! Understanding achievement gaps. In J. Marsh, R. Mendoza-Deton, & J. A. Smith (Eds.), *Are we born racists? New insights from Neuroscience and positive psychology* (pp. 24–33). Boston: Beacon Press.

Myers, D. G. (1993). *The pursuit of happiness: Who is happy—and why?* Morrow.

National Association of Colleges & Employers. (2019). *Career readiness defined.* http:// www.naceweb.org/career-readiness/competencies/career-readiness-defined/

Navarro, J. (2008). *What every BODY is saying.* Harper Collins.

Nichols, M. P. (1995). *The lost art of listening.* Guilford Press.

Nichols, M. P. (2009). *The lost art of listening: How learning to listen can improve relationships.* The Guilford Press.

Nichols, M. P., & Stevens, L. A. (1957). *Are you listening?* McGraw-Hill.

Paolini, S., Hewstone, M., & Cairns, E. (2007). Direct and indirect intergroup friendship effects: testing the moderating role of the affective-cognitive bases of prejudice. *Personality and Social Psychology Bulletin, 33*(10), 1406–1420.

Pascarella, E. T., & Terenzini, P. T. (2005). *How college affects students: A third decade of research* (vol. 2). San Francisco: Jossey-Bass.

Pettigrew, T. F. (1997). Generalized intergroup contact effects on prejudice. *Personality and Social Psychology Bulletin, 23*, 173–185.

Pettigrew, T. F. (1998). Intergroup contact theory. *Annual Review of Psychology, 49*, 65–85.

Pettigrew, T. F., & Tropp, L. R. (2000). Does intergroup contact reduce prejudice: Recent meta-analytic findings. In S. Oskamp (Ed.), *Reducing prejudice and discrimination* (pp. 93–114). Lawrence Erlbaum Associates.

Pettigrew, T. F., & Tropp, L. R. (2006). A meta-analytic test of intergroup contact theory. *Journal of Personality and Social Psychology, 90*(5), 751–783.

Plaut, V. C., Garnett, F. G., Buffardi, L. E., & Sanchez-Burks, J. (2011). "What about me?" Perceptions of exclusion and Whites' reactions to multiculturalism. *Journal of Personality and Social Psychology, 101*(2), 337–353.

Pratto, F., Liu, J. H., Levin, S., Sidanius, J., Shih, M., Bachrach, H., & Hegarty, P. (2000). Social dominance orientation and the legitimization of inequality across cultures. *Journal of Cross-Cultural Psychology, 31*, 369–409.

Purdy, M., & Borisoff, D. (Eds.). (1996). *Listening in everyday life: A personal and professional approach.* University Press of America.

Putnam, R. D. (2007). E Pluribus Unum: Diversity and Community in the 21st Century: The 2006 Johan Skytte Prize Lecture. *Scandinavian Political Studies, 30*, 137–174. https://doi.org/10.1111/j.1467-9477.2007.00176x

Rendón-Linares, L. I., & Muñoz, S. M. (2011). Revisiting validation theory: Theoretical foundations, applications, and extensions. *Enrollment Management Journal, 5*(2), 12–33.

Roediger, H. L., Dudai, Y., & Fitzpatrick, M. (Eds.). (2007). *Science and memory: Concepts.* Oxford University Press.

Shelton, J. N., & Richeson, J. A. (2005). Intergroup contact and pluralistic ignorance. *Journal of Personality and Social Psychology, 88*(1), 91–107.

Sidanius, J., Levin, S., Liu, H., & Pratto, F. (2000). Social dominance orientation, anti-egalitarianism, and the political psychology of gender: An extension and cross-cultural replication. *European Journal of Social Psychology, 30*, 41–67.

Slavin, R. E. (2012). Cooperative learning. In J. A. Banks (Ed.), *Encyclopedia of diversity in education* (vol. 1, pp. 453–456). SAGE.

Smith, D. (1997). How diversity influences learning. *Liberal Education, 83*(2), 42–48.

Smith, D. (2015). *Diversity's promise for higher education: Making it work* (2nd ed.). Johns Hopkins University Press.

Steil, L. L., & Bommelje, R. (2007). *Listening leaders: The ten golden rules to listen: Lead and succeed.* Beaver Pond Press.

Stevens, F. G., Plaut, V. C., & Sanchez-Burks, J. (2008). Unlocking the benefits of diversity: All-inclusive multiculturalism and positive organizational change. *Journal of Applied Science, 44*(1), 116–133.

Syed, M., & Juan, M. J. D. (2012). Birds of an ethnic feather? Ethnic identity homophily among college-age friends. *Journal of Adolescence, 35*(6), 1505–1514.

Taylor, S. E., Peplau, L. A., & Sears, D. O. (2006). *Social psychology* (12th ed.). Pearson/Prentice-Hall.

van Engen, M. L., & Willemsen, T. M. (2004). Sex and leadership styles: A meta-analysis of research published in the 1990s. *Psychological Reports, 94*, 3–18.

Vogelgesang, L. J., Ikeda, E. K., Gilmartin, S. K., & Keup, J. R. (2002). Service-learning and the first-year experience: Outcomes related to learning and persistence. In E. Zlotkowsky (Ed.), *Service-learning and the first-year experience: Preparing students for personal success and civic responsibility* (pp. 27–36; Monograph No. 34). University of South Carolina, National Resource Center for the First-Year Experience and Students in Transition.

Williams, D., Spencer, M., Jackson, J., & Ashnore, R. (1999). Race, stress, and physical health: The role of group identity. In R. Contrada & R. Ashmore (Eds.), *Self-social identity and physical health* (pp. 71–100). Oxford University Press.

Wolvin, A. D. (2010). *Listening and communication in the 21st century.* Blackwell.

Zull, J. E. (2011). *From brain to mind: Using neuroscience to guide change in education.* Stylus.

Reflections and Applications

Name

_____

Date

_____

5.1 Review the sidebar quotes contained in this chapter and select two that you think are particularly meaningful or inspirational. For each quote you selected, provide an explanation of why you chose it.

5.2 Self-Assessment of Interpersonal Relationship Skills

On a scale of 1–5 (1 = low, 5 = high), rate yourself on each of the following characteristics.

____ I am good at initiating relationships.

____ I am approachable.

____ I am a good listener.

Provide a reason or explanation for each of your ratings that describes:

(a) what you're doing well,

(b) what you'd like to improve, and

(c) what you could do to improve (or what campus resource you could use to help you improve).

5.3 One way in which college students can increase contact with members of diverse groups is to place themselves in locations on campus where they are more likely to encounter and experience diversity. On your campus, where would those locations be? How comfortable would you feel about placing yourself in those locations? Why?

5.4 Review the strategies for *increasing personal contact and interpersonal interaction with members of diverse groups* on p. 140. Select three that you think are most important and hope to put into practice.

5.5 What would you say are the two most powerful principles or practices of effective cross-cultural communication? Why?

5.6 What interpersonal skills do you think you have already developed that would be particularly useful when interacting with members of other cultural groups? What intercultural skills do you need to develop further in order to maximize your ability to interact effectively with members of diverse groups?

Racism: Current Forms, Historical Roots, and Underlying Causes

Chapter Purpose and Preview

This chapter defines and describes the major forms of racism, identifies their historical roots, and examines their underlying psychological causes. It traces the development of racism to the original beliefs and ideologies that led to its initial formation and examines the factors that continue to preserve and perpetuate racism today.

Introduction

Anti-black racism is the primary focus of this because much more research has been conducted on this form of racism toward any other racial group (Jardina, 2019) and because this extensive body of research shows that anti-black is a unique and most extreme form of racism (Bobo & Huthcings, 1996). The point is not to dismiss or minimize racism experienced by other racial groups. The chapter does include some discussion of racism toward other racial groups, but detailed racism aimed at other racial and ethnic groups is discussed primarily in Chapter 2.

Racism Defined

Although the term "racism" was not formally defined and used until the mid-1900s, beliefs about the superiority of whites and the inferiority of other races has existed since the birth of America. Thomas Jefferson, who penned the phrase "all men are created equal" in the Declaration of Independence, stated in 1785: "The blacks, whether originally a distinct race, or made distinct by time and circumstances, are inferior to the whites in the endowment of both body and mind" (Kendi, 2019, p. 20). Beliefs about the inferiority of blacks continued into the 19th century was clearly demonstrated in the classic Supreme Court case of *Plessy vs. Ferguson* in 1896. Homer Plessy, a black man who looked white, went to court to argue that his 14th amendment rights to equal treatment were being violated by a Louisiana state law that forced him to ride in a railcar instead of passenger cars reserved only for whites. A Louisiana judge had first ruled in defense of the law, claiming that the "foul odors of blacks in close quarters" made the law reasonable. The Louisiana Supreme Court ruled then uphold the segregation law, with one judge claiming that it was an acceptable "social law" that recognized the "distinction" between the races. Plessy's case eventually reached the U.S. Supreme Court, which also ruled against Plessy, issuing the following explanation for the decision: "If one race be inferior to the other socially, the constitution of the United states cannot put them on the same plane" (Anderson, 2016, p. 35).

> "The worst disease is the treatment of the Negro. Everyone who freshly learns of this state . . . feels not only the injustice, but the scorn of the principle of the Fathers who founded the United States on the principle that 'all men are created equal'."
>
> —ALBERT EINSTEIN, STATEMENT MADE AFTER IMMIGRATING TO THE UNITED SATES

In his study of the origins of the term racism, George Fredrickson (2002) discovered that it first began being used during the 1930s to describe the ideology behind the Nazis' persecution of Jews. According to Fredrickson, it was "Hitler who gave racism a bad name." In 1944, Gunnar Myrdal, a Swedish sociologist, published a highly acclaimed book titled, *An American Dilemma*, in which he made the case that race represented nothing more than superficial physical differences between groups (such as the color of their outer layer of skin) and had nothing to do with their personal and psychological characteristics, such as their intelligence or morality. At about the same time that Myrdal made this point, Ruth Benedict, a famous anthropologist, published the first formal definition of "racism," calling it "an unproved assumption of the biological and perpetual superiority of one human group over another" (Benedict, 1940).

Origins and Root Causes of Racism

To get a deep and complete understanding of the forms of racism that exist today, it is necessary to trace them back to their historical roots, which include a variety of economic, political, religious and scientific racist beliefs.

Economic Exploitation

America's democratic system was built on the foundational principle pronounced in its Declaration of Independence that "all men are created equal and from that equal creation they derive rights inherent and inalienable, among which are the preservation of life, and liberty, and the pursuit of happiness." At the time this principle was proclaimed, slavery already had become a legal and well-established feature of America's economy. In fact, our nation's first president, George Washington "owned" more than 300 slaves at the time of his death (Hirschfeld, 1997).

The truth is that America's original economy was built on the free labor provided by black slaves and free land provided and free land taken by the forcible removal of Native Americans. The slavery system reaped economic benefits not just for slave owners, but also for white merchants, bankers, and shippers in both the South and the North, including New York City—where Wall Street served as a center for slave selling and buying. Slaves also built America's first mansions, its first college and university buildings, and the White House—including the "Statue of Freedom" that sits atop the Capitol Dome (Rogers, 1961). As Feagin (2005) points out, "In one way or another, the majority of whites benefited from the slavery-centered economic complex, which encompassed the slave trade, trade with and support of slave plantations, the international trade in slave-produced products, and the panoply of slavery-support occupations and businesses" (p. 13).

After blacks were exploited for economic purposes, beliefs about their racial inferiority were then introduced as the reasons for justifying their exploitation (Coates, 2015). Thus, the system of slavery was used first to advance America's early economy, racist beliefs about black inferiority followed as an ideology to rationalize the enslavement of blacks. The powerful role that economics played as a driving force behind the implementation and justification of slavery is well illustrated in the case of the South's first industrial labor dispute in 1847. This dispute involved an iron manufacturing company in Richmond, Virginia that put enslaved blacks in skilled positions to cut labor costs. In protest, white workers went on strike, demanding pay raises and the removal of blacks from the skilled-work positions. The white strikers thought that the company executives would care more about race than profit and would side with their own race rather than with blacks. They were wrong; the white executives fired the white strikers and justified their firing by claiming that the strikers were pro-black abolitionists who were interfering with their legal right to use slave labor. This event was just one of multiple similar incidents of workplace conflict, many of which were violent, that took place in industrial cities across the United States which triggered by employers trying to suppress organized labor and strikes by white workers attempting to gain fairer wages and better working conditions. White unions often sought to strengthen their bargaining positions by excluding black workers. As a countermeasure, industry owners hired blacks as replacements or strikebreakers, which created anti-black hostility (Schechter, 1994).

The economic roots of racism ran so deep and wide that they led to some of the worst race riots in American history, such as those described in **Box 6.1**.

"The ultimate goal of racism was the profit and comfort of the white race, specifically of rich white men. The oppression of people of color was an easy way to get this wealth and power, and racism was a good way to justify it."

—IJEOMO OLUO, AUTHOR, *SO YOU WANT TO TALK ABOUT RACE*

Box 6.1 **Race Riots Rooted in Economics**

1917: *East St. Louis Massacre*. Labor-related racial violence took place in East St. Louis, Illinois triggered by the employment of black workers in a factory holding government contracts. At least 40 blacks were killed and approximately 6,000 were left homeless. During multiple days of violence, blacks were beaten, some hung from street lamps, and others shot while trying to flee, including those attempting to swim across the Mississippi river to St. Louis, Missouri.

1919: *The Elaine Massacre*. The deadliest racial confrontation in Arkansas history and possibly the bloodiest racial conflict in U.S. history took place in the city of Elaine, Arkansas, where approximately 100 African Americans, mostly sharecroppers on the plantations of white landowners, attended a union meeting to discuss how to seek fair payment for their cotton crops that were being purchased by white plantation owners—who were dominant during the Jim Crow era and often exploited black sharecroppers by paying them poorly, or not paying them at all, for cotton crops the sharecroppers cultivated. Leaders of the black union workers placed armed guards around the church where the meeting was being held to prevent disruption of their meeting by white opponents. A shootout then took place in front of the church between the armed black guards and whites parked in a vehicle parked in front of the church, resulting in the killing of one white man and the wounding of another.

The next morning, the county sheriff sent out a posse to arrest those suspected of being involved in the shooting. The posse encountered minimal resistance from the black residents of the area around Elaine, but fear that blacks outnumbered whites in the Elaine area led an estimated 500–1,000 armed white people—mostly from the surrounding Arkansas counties but also from across the river in Mississippi—to travel to Elaine and put down what they called an "insurrection." Local authorities also sent telegrams to the state governor, requesting that U.S. troops be sent to Elaine; he obliged by sending more than 500 battle-tested troops to the area. In the ensuing battle, an estimated five whites and hundreds of blacks were killed, including members of the local black community who had nothing to do with the union efforts but happened to be in the area at the time. The military also placed several hundred African Americans in makeshift stockades until they were vouched for by their white employers.

1921: *Tulsa Race Massacre*. White mobs burnt down 1,256 black residences, churches, schools, and businesses in a 40-block area of Greenwood, Oklahoma—an economically prosperous section of Tulsa known as "Black Wall Street." Envious of the area's wealth and incited by a local newspaper's report about a black man being accused of stepping on a white girl's foot or attempting to rape a white woman (reports varied), a mob of hundreds of white men gathered around the jail where the suspect was being held. A group of black men, some of whom were armed, came to the jail to ensure that the man would have a fair trial and not be lynched, which was a common practice during the Jim Crow era. The sheriff persuaded the group to leave the jail, assuring them that he had the situation under control. However, an exchange of gunfire ensued, during which two blacks and ten whites were killed.

News about the deaths spread throughout the city, leading to a mob of white rioters invading the Greenwood area, where they burned and looted homes. The area was also bombed by airplanes. By the time the riot had ended, an estimated 10,000 blacks were displaced from their homes; 300 blacks were killed and many others were injured but denied treatment in local white-only hospitals. The bodies of blacks who died in the massacre were dumped into mass graves.

Decades of silence followed the event and no mention of it was made in local, state, and national histories. In 1996, the Oklahoma state legislature authorized formation of the Oklahoma Commission to Study the Tulsa Race Riot. Its members investigated the events, interviewed survivors, heard testimony from the public, and prepared a detailed report of the events that took place at the riot. In 2001, the Commission's final report indicated that the city had conspired with the mob of white citizens against black citizens. Oklahoma then passed legislation to establish some scholarships for descendants of survivors, encourage economic development of Greenwood, and develop a memorial park in Tulsa dedicated to victims of the massacre. In 2020, the massacre was finally added to the Oklahoma school curriculum.

Furniture and belongings of a displaced black family following the 1921 Tulsa race massacre. © Everett Collection/Shutterstock.com

Reflection 6.1

Were you aware of any of the race-related incidents discussed in **Box 6.1**? If yes, where did you learn about them? If no, why do you think you hadn't?

Political Racism

From America's beginnings, whiteness has been associated with the nation's identity: To be white was to be "American" (Masuoka & Junn, 2013). In 1790, just one year after the U.S. Constitution was adopted, Congress passed the Naturalization Act (the nation's first citizenship law) which declared that naturalized American citizens included all "free white persons" living in the United States for two or more years but excluded "free" blacks or Native American Indians (Omni & Winant, 1986). In 1861, Alexander Stephens, a prominent Southern politician, proudly made this statement about the United States: "Its corner-stone rests upon the great truth that the negro is not equal to the white man; that slavery subordination to the superior race is his natural and normal condition. This, our new government, is the first, in the history of the world, based upon this great physical, philosophical, and moral truth" (Wilkerson, 2020, p. 335).

America's emphasis on whiteness was so extreme that it extended to darker-skinned people who are now considered to be members of the white race. In the mid-1800s, darker-skinned white immigrants first came to America from Eastern and Southern Europe (e.g., Hungarians, Jews, Greeks, and Italians). Following their arrival, America's first anti-immigration ("nativism") movement emerged among U.S. citizens of Western European descent, such as such as the English and Scottish (Bennett, 1988) who viewed and categorized the newly arrived Eastern and Southern immigrants as "non-white" (Martin, 2011). Congress eventually passed the Immigration Act of 1924, which limited the number of American immigrants to no more than two percent of the total number of people presently living in the United States. This ensured that a very limited number of immigrants would enter America from countries in Eastern and Southern Europe, as well as Asia and India, all of whom were not considered to be "white" by American standards. Arguing for the passage of the 1924 immigration bill, one U.S. senator delivered a passionate speech in which he flatly stated: "Thank God we have in America perhaps the largest percentage of any country in the world of the pure, unadulterated Anglo-Saxon stock; certainly the greatest of any nation in the Nordic breed" (Jardina, 2019, p. 155).

Later in the 20th century, non-Western European immigrants who came to America distanced themselves from blacks by identifying themselves as white, allowing them to gain the social and political privileges of being members of the white majority and "mainstream" American culture (Roediger, 2006). Nevertheless, a national poll conducted in 1945 still showed that Americans were much more enthusiastic about lighter-skinned immigrants coming from Scandinavian countries such as Holland, Belgium and England, and much less enthusiastic about darker-skinned Polish, Russian, and Greek immigrants—who were less likely to be considered "white" at that time (Roper Center for Public Opinion Research, 2015).

More recent research on implicit (unconscious) bias shows that Americans today still automatically and unconsciously associate being "American" with being "white" (Devos & Banaji, 2005). In 2018, the 45th president of the United States questioned why immigrants were coming to America from countries whose citizens are predominantly people of color, asking: "Why are we having all these people from shithole countries come here?" He then suggested that the United States should instead accept more people from countries like Norway (Beckwith, 2018).

Strategic Racism (a.k.a. White Identity Politics)

Strategic racism has been defined as "purposeful efforts to use racial animus as leverage to gain material wealth, political power, or heightened social standing" (López, 2014, p. 46). It is "new" or "soft" form of racism that's more subtle and sophisticated than the blatant racism of the Jim Crow era but still works to preserve or promote racial inequality and injustice (Bonilla-Silva, 2018).

Social scientists link the emergence of this new form of racism to America's changing racial demographics (Jardina, 2019). Throughout the 20th century, whites made up more than 80% of the U.S. population. Since then, their proportion in the U.S. population has been declining. It is projected that by 2040, for the first time in history, whites will be a minority group in America (Alba et al., 2005). This growing presence of people of color in the United States, coupled with the tendency for whites to overestimate the size of America's dark-skinned population (Gallagher, 2003), has led some whites to become more conscious of their race (Jardina, 2019) and feel threatened by an increasingly multiracial society in which they see their race becoming a minority of its nation's citizens, a minority of its voters and, perhaps, a minority of its elected political leaders (Feagin, 2005).

Research shows that when higher-status groups perceive threats to the status quo, it increases their level of anxiety (Scheepers & Ellemers, 2005). Even informing or reminding whites that their proportion of the population is shrinking has been found to increase: (a) their sense of group threat (Myers & Levy, 2018), (b) their prejudicial attitudes toward other racial groups (Craig & Richeson, 2017), and (c) their opposition to policies and politicians that aim to advance racial equity. It can also lead whites to identify more strongly with their racial group and engage in "white identity politics" the practice of supporting political officials and political policies that advance the self-interests and social status of whites (López, 2014). White identity politics was likely responsible for the "white backlash" that followed the election of America's first black president, Barack Obama. In president Obama's first year in office alone, there was a 400 percent increase in death threats to the president. Facebook even had to close down a page where hundreds of its users answered "yes" to a posted question: "Should Obama be killed?" In addition, president Obama's personal Twitter account was flooded with death threats, such as: "Kill yourself you tree swinging nigger" (Anderson, 2016, p. 156). White backlash was also evidenced by the growth of more than 200 hate groups after Obama was elected (SPLC, 2021).

However, most whites engaging in white identity politics are not full-blown racists who harbor intense hatred toward people of color; in fact, many of them are willing to acknowledge that that being white has provided them with unearned privileges associated with being members of a dominant racial group (Jardina, 2019). Nevertheless, their strong sense of white consciousness serves to heighten their sense of in-group identity and outgroup bias (Effron & Knowles, 2015) which, in turn, leads them to advocate for policies that preserve or promote forms of systemic racism that maintain their group's dominance (Miller et al., 1981) and to strongly oppose governmental attempts to reduce systemic racism and racial inequalities (Jardina, 2019). Thus, despite not being overt racists, they still perpetuate racism. As sociologist David Wellman (2009) puts it in his book, *Portraits of White Racism*: "Prejudiced people are not the only racists."

Research on group identity also shows that people typically judge others whom they see as similar to themselves (their "in group") as being nicer and more trustworthy that they expect they'll be treated more favorably by members of their in-group because they share the same self-interests (Yamagishi & Mifune, 2008). When this type of in-group bias is adopted by a dominant racial group, it can lead to an in-group vs. out-group, "rob from Peter to give to Paul" mentality in which members of the in-group (white) see the distribution of societal resources as a zero-sum game where any economic or political gains made by the out-group (non-whites) result in losses to the in-group (whites)—such as loss of jobs, income, and social status privileges (Jardina, 2019). However, there is little evidence supporting this "divide-and-conquer" or "teeter-totter" belief that increased advantages for people of color come at the expense of lost advantages for whites. In fact, history shows that the exact opposite typically takes place: both groups become more advantaged. For instance, white labor unions mistakenly believed that they would benefit economically by excluding blacks from joining. However, it actually disadvantaged white workers because whenever they attempted to strike to improve their wages, employers had the option of employing non-unionized blacks at even lower wages (Wise, 2011). Thus, white workers' discriminatory decision to keep blacks out their unions allowed employers to under-pay blacks and use them as a tool for "wage control" to suppress wages of all workers, both white and black (Johnson, 1936). Instead of attempting to compete against blacks in a win–lose game of tug-of-war, working class whites would have better off allowing blacks to unionize with them and play a win–win game in which a "rising tide lifts all boats." As Kendi (2016) notes, "It is not coincidental that slavery kept the vast majority of southern Whites poor. It is not coincidental that more White Americans thrived during the anti-racist movements from the 1930s to the early 1970s than ever before or since" (p. 504).

More recently, this same type of win–lose mindset hurt working-class whites who opposed governmental policies designed to improve their health benefits because they saw those policies as advantaging undeserving racial minorities. By opposing these policies, they actually disadvantaged themselves by reducing their access to more affordable, higher-quality health care. In a study of one state where citizens voted for elected officials who opposed expanding the state's restrictive healthcare benefit policies, an estimated 4,599 black lives and 12,013 white lives were lost during a five-year period after the election that could have been saved if healthcare benefits had been expanded (Metzl, 2019).

DiAngelo (2018) reports that whites holding economic power have intentionally encouraged economically struggling working-class whites to blame people of color for their economic struggles, using it as a political strategy to distract them from the fact that a growing percentage of America's wealth is shifting to a smaller percentage of wealthy elites, creating the largest rich-poor wealth gap in our nation's history. Kendi (2019) argues that those in political power promote "racist ideas to suppress resistance to policies that are detrimental to White people by convincing average White people that inequity is rooted in 'personal failure' and is unrelated to policies . . . and that equalizing policies are anti-White" (Kendi, 2019, p. 130).

Similar to how the wealthy elite endorsed racism to advance their economic self-interests, so have politicians opportunistically used racism to advance their political careers. Members of the voting public who hold racist beliefs favor politicians who endorse racist policies, and politicians use racist public opinions to their advantage by adopting policy positions and political platforms that cater to voters with racist beliefs (Jardina, 2019). For instance, in the 1980s and 1990s, politicians exploited Americans' economic and personal safety insecurities by using racial stereotypes such as "crack heads," "crack babies," and "welfare queens" to gain

"For too long, we've . . . bought the view that America is a zero-sum game: If you succeed, I fail; if you get ahead, I fall behind; if you get the job, I lose mine. Maybe worse of all: If I hold you down, I lift myself up."
—JOE BIDEN, 45TH PRESIDENT OF THE UNITED STATES

"The history of racist ideas is the history of powerful policy-makers erecting racist policies out of self interest, then producing racist ideas to defend and rationalize inequitable effects of their policies, while everyday people consume those racist ideas, which in turn sparks ignorance and hate."
—IBRAM X KENDI, AWARD-WINNING AUTHOR AND DIRECTOR OF THE, CENTER FOR ANTIRACIST RESEARCH AT BOSTON UNIVERSITY

political support for reducing income-assistance programs and to support an unneeded and unsuccessful "war on drugs" (Alexander, 2020). (For specific details, see Chapter 8.)

The term "dog whistle" is a metaphor to describe a message that operates on two levels: on one level, it's not loud enough to be clearly heard, yet on another level it's audible enough to send a clear message to members of the audience who want to hear it. Politicians often use "racial dog whistles" or coded racial language to appeal to racist voters and block civil rights policies without appearing to be racist themselves. Dog whistling is subtle enough in its intention and consequences to enable the whistler to escape accusations of racism and, if accused, it allows the whistler to claim innocence and indignantly deny being called a racist (López, 2014). In the 1960s, one political strategist described this racial dog-whistle strategy in the following way: "You start out in 1954 by saying 'nigger, nigger, nigger.' By 1968, you can't say 'nigger'—that hurts you. Backfires. So you say stuff like forced busing, states' rights and all that stuff . . . and a byproduct of them is blacks get hurt worse than whites" (Anderson, 2016, p. 119). This strategy was used by Alabama governor George Wallace who originally defended racial segregation by vigorous claims about white superiority. However, his political career began to suffer because it was clear to many that he was a full-blown racist. Soon thereafter, he stopped talking about the need for racial segregation and started talking about states' rights, which was the same coded language used by southern statesmen before the Civil War to defend their use of slavery. Wallace's revamped (or recoded) platform revived his political career to the point that he was chosen as a candidate in four consecutive presidential elections from 1968 through 1976 (López, 2014). Wallace's new strategy prompted one political analyst to say: "He can use all the other issues—law and order, running your own schools, protecting property rights—and never mention race. But people will know he's telling them 'a nigger's trying to get your job, trying to move into your neighborhood.' What Wallace is doing is talking to them in a kind of shorthand, a kind of code" (Kinder & Sanders, 1996, p. 227). President Richard Nixon used the same coded "state rights" strategy to defend segregated schools and oppose support for school integration (Jardina, 2019). So did former president Ronald Reagan code his defense of racial discrimination in housing under the cloak of "personal rights," saying: "If an individual wants to discriminate against Negroes or others in selling or renting his house, it is his right to do so" (Longley et al., 2007). Not surprisingly, political scientists have observed that racist dog-whistle messages (e.g., media depictions of black criminals and welfare recipients) tend to appear more frequently during election years (Gilens, 1999).

"Time and time again, powerful and brilliant men and women have produced racist ideas in order to justify the racist policies of their era, in order to redirect the blame for their era's racial disparities away from those policies and onto Black People."

—IBRAM X. KENDI, AUTHOR, *STAMPED FROM THE BEGINNING: THE DEFINITIVE HISTORY OF RACIST IDEAS IN AMERICA* (P. 9)

Scientific Racism

Attempts have also been made to support racist beliefs and justify racist policies with reinforcing them with alleged scientific evidence, which scholars refer to as "scientific racism" (Eberhardt, 2019). There is a long history of such attempts, dating as far back as 1576 when a prominent French academic introduced "climate theory," claiming that the heat in Africa caused blacks to become hypersexual and prone to behaving like savage beasts (de Miramon, 2009). Proponents of climate theory also assumed (incorrectly) that whites were the original and "normal" race that other races should aspire to become and that Africans' dark skins could return to their original white complexion by living in cooler European climates (Stuurman, 2000, 2001).

In 1776, when the United States first became an independent nation, a glaring inconsistency existed between its humane democratic ideals about equality and its inhumane enslavement of blacks. In an attempt to reconcile or justify this contradiction, Thomas Jefferson (who, himself, owned hundreds of slaves) held the belief that whites were a superior race and solicited out scientists to support his belief (DiAngelo, 2018). One prominent scientist he sought out was a physician named Samuel Morton, known today as the "father of scientific racism." Morton collected and studied human skulls during the first half of the 1800s, and on the basis of these "craniometry" studies, he concluded that whites or "Caucasians" were the most intelligent of all races and blacks were at the bottom. Morton's ideas were soon adopted and circulated by slavery advocates and defenders. When Morton died in 1851, a South Carolina medical journal praised him for "giving the negro his true position as an inferior race" (Kolbert, 2018).

During the 1850s, another team of scientific racists attempted to explain racial inequalities by promulgating a theory "polygenism"— the theory different racial groups had different biological origins. In a book written by one polygenist titled, *The Classification of Mankind, By the Wool of Their Heads*, the author argued that whites and blacks belonged to distinctive species because whites had hair and blacks had "wool," which he claimed was proof that blacks were members of an inferior, animal-like species (Browne, 1850). Another prominent anthropologist at the time, Franz Boas, claimed that there was an evolutionary spectrum or continuum among higher primates, with monkeys and apes being the least evolved on the lowest end, whites being the most evolved on the highest end, and people of African descent falling in-between (Lott, 1999). Jennifer Eberhardt, a contemporary social psychologist, spent several years reviewing illustrations of blacks in old science books that touted polygenism and had this to say about what she discovered: "I was not prepared for the primitive sketches, hailed as proof of permanent inferiority. The images repulsed me. The animalistic depictions of black anatomy bore no resemblance to any person I'd ever seen" (Eberhardt, 2019, p. 140). The stereotype of blacks being "ape-like" is no longer openly verbalized, yet researchers have found that it's still used in metaphors and visual tropes (Goff et al., 2008), including one in which former president Obama being was referred to as the "primate in chief" (Sauer, 2011) and former first lady, Michelle Obama as an "ape in heels" (Uwumarogie, 2016).

Much of this early "science" on racial classifications used to prove the inferiority of the black race was sponsored by universities (Zuberi, 2001) and was used by the universities to justify their decision to disallow blacks from attending their institutions (Karabel, 2005). Eventually, Charles Darwin's landmark book *On the Origin of Species* (1859) provided indisputable evidence for "monogenism"—that all races make up one and the same human species, thus refuting polygenism. Darwin also disproved climate theory by tracing the origin of the human species to Africa, not Europe. Nonetheless, prejudicial beliefs about the purity and superiority of the white race continued into the 1900s. In a widely read book published in the United States during World War I, its author, Madison Grant, claimed that different races varied not only in their physical appearance but also in their intellectual and moral capacity and that the more successful and superior nations achieved their success because they had a higher percentage of citizens with superior Nordic blood (Grant, 1916). Grant was also a eugenicist who argued that "inferior stocks" should be sterilized and quarantined in a "rigid system of elimination of those who are weak or unfit . . . or perhaps worthless race types" (Wilkerson, 2020, p. 81). In 1924, Adolf Hitler read Grant's book while in jail following his failed attempt to overthrow Germany's democracy. When he later rose to power as dictator, Hitler called Grant's book "my Bible" and publicly thanked Grant for writing it (Spiro, 2009). Eerily, in 2020, at a political rally in Minnesota—

a state whose population contains a high percentage of Americans of Nordic descent, the 45th President of the United States praised the almost all-white attendees at his rally by saying: "You have good genes, you know that right? You have good genes in Minnesota" (Mehta, 2020, p. A5).

Not only were blacks considered to be inferior to whites intellectually, but also *physically*. Up until the middle of the 1800s, many Europeans, including Charles Darwin, believed that humans of European origin were generally stronger than darker-skinned people, and they cited the physically challenging performances of white explorers as evidence for this position. In the American South, it was also believed that whites, because of their superior genetic endowment, were superior to blacks in athletic performance. Records of plantation doctors who treated black slaves contained statements about blacks having naturally weaker hearts, lungs, and muscle strength—unless they were forced to strengthen their slack muscles through work imposed on them by whites. However, once blacks were emancipated from slavery, a new and totally opposite view emerged about blacks having beast-like strength that made them potentially dangerous criminals (Hoberman, 1997).

Eventually, the belief that blacks were advantaged physically expanded to include the view that they were advantaged athletically—due to their more primitive origins. After Jesse Owen's spectacular performance in the 1936 Olympics, one white track-and-field athletic coach publicly stated: "The Negro excels in the events that he does because he is closer to the primitive than the white man. It was not so long ago that his ability to spring and jump was a life-and-death matter to him in the jungle" (in Hoberman, 1997, p. 199). This view of superior black physicality was sometimes supported by the belief that slave traffickers selected the most physically endowed blacks to capture and import to America as slaves. However, historians have found very little evidence that slave traffickers took the time to find, capture, and import only the most physically endowed Africans (Herskovits, 1941). Nevertheless, the belief in black physical prowess has persisted and the increasing number of black athletes pursuing and achieving excellence in certain sports, along with increasing media coverage of their exploits, has further fueled the belief that blacks are naturally (biologically) endowed with superior athletic ability. However, their celebrated athletic achievements are often accompanied by the racist view that they have superior physical ability but inferior mental ability; in other words, whites have the brain and blacks have the brawn (Hoberman, 1997).

> "Western racism inflicted on African Americans a physicalized (and eventually athleticized) identity from which they have yet to escape. The cult of black athleticism continues a racist tradition that has long emphasized the motor skills and manual training of African Americans."
>
> —JOHN HOBERMAN, PROFESSOR, UNIVERSITY OF TEXAS AUSTIN AND AUTHOR OF *DARWIN'S ATHLETES*

Reflection 6.2

Why do you think there is a disproportionate number of black athletes in such sports as basketball and football? How do you think most people would respond to this question?

Religious Racism

Racism has also been fueled by religious beliefs about humans being arranged in a racial hierarchy of superior and inferior groups by divine ordination or intention (López, 2014). America's first white colonists identified themselves as Christians and claimed they were different from and superior to non-Christian "Indians" and "Negroes" (Feagin, 2005). Early American theologians also asserted that God created whites first in his image and likeness before creating blacks. Later, during the mid-1800s, theological leaders began to build religious beliefs about white-superiority around the scientific theory of "polygenism" (different racial groups had different biological beginnings), leading to two prominent theologians (Nott & Gliddon, 1854) to write a widely read book in which they modified the biblical story of creation by claiming that Adam and Eve were white and God created other inferior races, placing them in different regions of the world.

These religious beliefs helped to justify black slavery, but Charles Darwin's influential work on the origins of the human species weakened the scientific theory of polygenism and religious beliefs based on that theory (Eberhardt, 2009). Soon thereafter, another religious-based racist belief emerged that revolved around a biblical story about Noah condemning his son Ham's supposedly black descendants to be servants to the white descendants of Noah's other sons (Feagin, 2005). This belief was also used to justify slavery by drawing on a biblical passage found in Genesis 9:18–29, which read: "Negroes were the children of Ham, the son of Noah's curse, which produces Ham's colour and the slavery God inflicted upon his descendants" (Kendi, 2016, p. 21). In his classic book, *Black Like Me* published in 1960, John Howard Griffin reported visiting a monastery to discuss religious-based racism. Griffin told a Trappist monk about how often he heard racists in the Jim Crow South cite some passage from the Bible to support their segregationist prejudices and practices. The monk laughed and responded by saying: "Didn't Shakespeare say something about every fool in error can find a passage of Scripture to back him up." The monk's reply promoted Griffin to sarcastically wonder how religious segregationists would envision heaven for blacks and whites: "What about the Negro? Do they have another Heaven for him? Or possibly just a section of Heaven set aside for the Negro's quarters?" (Griffin, 1962, pp. 136 & 165).

Cultural Racism

World War II vividly demonstrated the horrific consequences of racist beliefs about about the genetic inferiority and superiority of different human races. Consequently, a new form of racism emerged that had less to do with the biological makeup of different racial groups and more to do with their cultural characteristics; in particular, white supremacists began focusing on the deficient "black culture" (López, 2014). Black culture was denigrated as devaluing commitment to family, education, and hard work, and valuing drug use and crime (Anderson, 2016). These "deficiencies" of black culture continue to be publicized by political figures and certain media outlets, despite being unsupported by carefully conducted research (Larson, 2006). For instance, research on black families shows that blacks have a long history of strong kinship bonds, such as incorporating elderly family members into the nuclear family, relying on extended family networks, and informally caring for children beyond the nuclear family. All these familial practices have helped blacks survive the marginalization and oppression they experienced across multiple

"We believe that God created all people. But white Anglo-Saxon Christians are the apple of His eye."

—COMMENT MADE TO A BLACK JOURNALIST VISITING A CHRISTIAN IDENTITY CHURCH SERVICE IN 2008 (BENJAMIN, 2009)

"Between the Christianity of this land, and the Christianity of Christ, I recognize the widest possible difference."

—FREDERICK DOUGLAS, RENOWNED BLACK ORATOR AND ABOLITIONIST

"African American families have often been maligned today as 'broken' or 'disorganized' by the descendants of those whites who sought to destroy those families in earlier eras."

—JOE FEAGIN, PROFESSOR OF SOCIOLOGY, TEXAS A&M UNIVERSITY

generations (Hill, 1999), including multiple generations of black families that were systematically broken up throughout a century of slavery.

While it is true that blacks experience higher rates of unemployment and poverty, and there are higher crime rates in black ghettos, advocates of cultural racism attribute these outcomes to failings in black culture, while failing to acknowledge the fact that culture shaped by environmental or structural conditions and that the behavior exhibited by blacks are often reflections of, and adaptations to disadvantaged conditions which have been created by systemic racism in housing, education, and employment. (See Chapters 7 and 8 for specific details and documentation.) Sociologist Katherine Beckett offers the following description of how failure to acknowledge these disadvantaged conditions was used to support cultural racism: "The (alleged) misbehaviors of the poor were transformed from adaptations to poverty into character failings that accounted for poverty in the first place" (Beckett, 1997, p. 34).

Underlying Psychological Causes of Racism

Extensive research has been conducted in the social sciences about the psychological factors that contribute to racist attitudes and beliefs. In addition to the causes of bias and prejudice discussed in Chapter 4, research points to three psychological processes playing a key role in the formation and perpetuation of racism: group bias, implicit bias, and media messaging.

Group Bias

As mentioned in Chapter 4, a person's sense of self-esteem is influenced by the group(s) that person identifies with; consequently, if individuals can identify with a "superior" group, they can feel superior and feel better about themselves (Tajfel & Turner, 1986). The greater the degree to which a person identifies with a group, the more important that group is to the person's self-image (Turner, 1985). Known as *social identity theory*, this psychological process motivates individuals to make social comparisons between their group and other groups, and to view their "in group" as superior in comparison to the other inferior "out groups." As Thomas Jefferson once said about slavery: "It raises white men to the same general level that dignifies and exalts every white man by the presence of a lower race" (Feagin, 2005, p. 73).

Noted psychologist, Eric Fromm reports that members of less affluent and less educated groups are more likely to identify with what they think is a superior racial group because it enables them to conclude that although they may have lower socioeconomic status, they still belong to a racial group (white) that has higher status than non-white groups; by comparing themselves to a lower-status group, their sense of self-esteem and self-importance is bolstered. According to Wilkerson (2020), their comparative thought process works this way: "Who are you if there is no one to be better than?" (p. 183). When this thought process is applied to anti-black prejudice held by low socioeconomic-status whites, it goes like this: "I may not be rich, but at least I am not a nigger" (Kendi, 2019, p. 155).

Wise (2011) points out how this form of racist thinking was propagated by white elites in colonial America to support and sustain their privileged socioeconomic status. White elites passed laws to divide white and black workers and convince white indentured servants from Europe (who were just one step above black slaves in socioeconomic status) that they had more in common with the elite whites who owned them than the black slaves who worked next to them. Similarly, prior to the Civil War, the Southern ruling class persuaded the white working class to fight for the Confederacy to preserve black slavery, even though slavery actually harmed the wages of lower-income whites by forcing them to compete with no-cost labor. Creating such racial divisions among workers continued into the 20th century, enabling employers to reduce the risk that workers would unite in an organized effort to secure fairer wages (Smith, 1949). W.E.B. Du Bois, black sociologist and civil rights activist, called this practice the "psychological wage"—a deliberate strategy used by the white ruling class immediately following the abolition of slavery to keep the attention of poor working-class whites focused on fighting against black equality rather than fighting for their own economic equality and ability to earn higher wages:

> They [the working class] were given public deference and titles of courtesy because they were white. They were admitted freely with all class of white people to public functions, public parks, and the best schools. The police were drawn from their ranks, and the courts, dependent upon their votes, treated them with such leniency as to encourage lawlessness. While all this had little effect upon their economic situation, it had great effect upon their personal treatment. The newspapers specialized on news that flattered the poor whites and almost utterly ignored the Negro except in crime and ridicule (Du Bois, 1935, p. 700).

Implicit Racial Bias

As defined in Chapter 4, implicit bias is a subconscious prejudgment about members of a group. Neuroscience research shows that a person's *racial* group is the first characteristic that the brain notices when viewing another person—before the person's age, gender, or any other group characteristic (Johnson, 2010). Infants as young as six month look longer at faces of another race than faces of their own racial group, suggesting that humans are innately wired to detect racial differences even before they're able to speak (Katz & Kofkin, 1997). Because a person's race is so easily visualized and immediately detectable, it's often the fastest and most automatic feature used by people to categorize (and judge) others (Apfelbaum et al., 2008).

Reflection 6.3

When you visualize the face of a black person, what first thoughts that come to mind?

Why do you think those thoughts immediately came to mind?

Since the brain detects race rapidly and automatically, it can lead to implicit racial biases. The effect is so strong that individuals who sincerely want to avoid holding anti-black bias, or who strongly believe they don't hold any bias against blacks, still exhibit bias on implicit bias tests (Nosek et al., 2002). But what causes implicit anti-black bias to develop in the first place? Certainly family and peers play an obvious and important role, but research points the media as playing a key and long historical role in creating anti-black bias.

Role of Media in Promoting Racial Bias

Studies show that approximately 80% of white Americans have been exposed to negative media messages about blacks and other marginalized groups by the time they reach adulthood. The messaging is so pervasive that as many as one-third of black Americans also hold implicit biases about members of their own race (Eberhardt, 2019). Communication researchers note that since whites have limited personal contact with blacks, their impressions of blacks are heavily influenced by how they are portrayed in the media (Wilkerson, 1992), which can often be negatively biased. In one analysis of early newspaper reports about race-related rapes, it was discovered that not a single newspaper article announced the acquittal of a black man charged with rape, yet one-third of acquitted white rape suspects received newspaper coverage. Furthermore, these "newspaper reports of rape constructed white defendants as individual offenders and black defendants as representative of the failing of their racial group" (Block, 2001–2002, p. 146). After the Tulsa race riot of 1921, during which 300 blacks were killed and 800 injured, the headline of a Tulsa newspaper read, "Two Whites Dead in Race Riot" and reporters wrote that "there were no known negro fatalities" (Perry, 2007). After two race riots took place in 1919, a 672-page report titled *The Negro in Chicago* was released. One of the report's major recommendations was that the press refrain from using epithets when referring to blacks and treat black stories and white stories with the same standards and "sense of proportion" (Chicago Commission on Race Relations, 1922).

1919 Chicago Race Riot. The black victim was chased by a group of white segregationists who stoned him to death as he attempted to find shelter in his home near a white neighborhood. Such stories were often not reported in city newspapers, or were reported in a way that derogated blacks. © Everett Collection/Shutterstock.com

The commission that issued the report did not have the authority to enforce its recommendation, so there was no follow through on its recommendations (Wilkerson, 2010). During 1940s and 1950s in Detroit, multiple incidents of mob violence were directed at blacks who attempted to buy homes in white neighborhoods. Most of these incidents were not reported by the city's major newspapers and only came to the public's attention when stories were written about them in black weekly newspapers (Sugrue, 2005).

In a 2017 study of poor people depicted in the news, it was found that 59% of those depicted were blacks, even though blacks made up about 27% of the nation's poor; in contrast, poor whites accounted for 17% of the poor people depicted, yet made up 66% of America's poor (Wilkerson, 2020). Research also shows that blacks are disproportionately featured in news stories about street crime (Alexander, 2020). The impact that such imbalanced media coverage can have on the development of anti-black bias is suggested by research in social psychology. In one research study, people were provided with a fictional news report about a street crime with no photo of the criminal included in the news report. Later, when people who were exposed to this story were asked about its details, 60% of them falsely recalled seeing an image of a criminal associated with the story, and 70% of those who falsely recalled

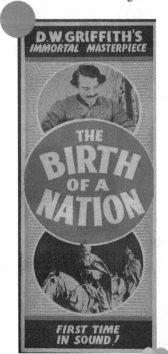

© David W. Griffith Corp./Epoch Producing Corporation / Everett Collection / Bridgeman Images

seeing the criminal's image thought the image was that of an African American (Gilliam & Iyenagar, 2000).

Anti-black bias has also been conveyed in history books. Among the first major books written about slavery were authored by a Georgia native, Ulrich Bonnell Phillips. He portrayed slavery not as a brutal and oppressive racist system that drove the South's economy, but as a relatively low-profit enterprise practiced by benevolent planters who cared for and helped civilize a group of barbaric people who were content with the treatment they received. Phillips' book, *American Negro Slavery* (1918) was widely read and he continued to be viewed as the leading authority on slavery into the mid-1900s (Kendi, 2016).

At the turn of the twentieth century, a book titled *The Clansman: An Historical Romance of the Ku Klux Klan* was published; it became a national bestseller and was later turned into a widely viewed 3-hour film, *The Birth of a Nation* (1915). The film depicted blacks (whose roles were played mainly by white actors in blackface) as unintelligent and sexually aggressive toward white women, and it portrayed the Ku Klux Klan (KKK) as a heroic force that protected American values and prevented social disorder (Armstrong, 2010). The film helped to stoke fears held by whites after the Civil War that freed black slaves would be violent and attempt to rape white women. Within a year after the film's release, the Ku Klux Klan was revived in Georgia and Klansmen soon began openly holding public parades before cheering white crowds across different states in the South (Wilkerson, 2020).

In 1912, the popular novel, *Tarzan of the Apes* was published, which tells the fictional story of a white orphan abandoned in Africa and raised by ape-like Africans who call him "Tarzan" (meaning "white skin" in their language). Tarzan protects Jane, a white woman, from ravishing black men and apes, and teaches Africans how to grow food. The widely read novel was later turned into a series of blockbuster films, the first of which appeared in 1918; it was followed by multiple sequels and a comic book series, all which served to create an association between blacks, helplessness, and savagery in the public's mind (Kendi, 2016). In 1929, Lincoln Perry became the first black movie star, casted as a shiftless character named "Stepan Fetch it" whose role was that of the "laziest man in the world"—a man who hardly did any work, frustrating the supporting cast of white characters who ended up doing the work themselves (Watkins, 2006).

In 1939, one of the most widely viewed and highest grossing films of all time was released: *Gone with the Wind*. The movie was set on a plantation in Georgia during the Civil War and the post-war Reconstruction era period. It portrayed the pre-Civil War South as a time of peaceful tranquility for both whites and blacks, and depicted the Civil War as an intrusion of Northern forces on the Southern way of life. The black servants in the film were presented as compliant and content, committed more to their white masters than to other enslaved blacks, and uninterested in leaving the plantation when they were emancipated following the Civil War. The film also depicts slaves freed after the War as immoral and dangerous, similar to how they were portrayed in the earlier blockbuster film, "The Birth of a Nation" (Bailey, 2021).

University of Texas professor, John Hoberman, argues that contemporary media coverage of black athletes contributes to negative black stereotyping and anti-black bias: "While it is assumed that sport has made an important contribution to racial integration, this has been counterbalanced by the merger of the athlete, the gangster, rapper, and the criminal into a single black persona that the sports industry, the music industry, and the advertising industry have made into the predominant image of black masculinity in the United States and around the world" (Hoberman, 1997, p. xxvii).

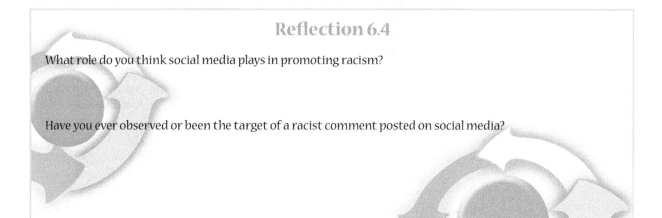

Reflection 6.4

What role do you think social media plays in promoting racism?

Have you ever observed or been the target of a racist comment posted on social media?

Current Forms and Varieties of Racism

Racism can be exhibited as personal prejudice and discrimination (e.g., racist beliefs and hateful actions), or embedded in societal institutions and systems (e.g., systemic racism in the health care industry and criminal justice system). This chapter focuses primarily on the first of these forms of racism; the second form (systemic racism) is discussed extensively in Chapters 7 and 8.

Racial Segregation

When members of one racial group intentionally decide to separate themselves from another racial group, either socially or physically, they are practicing racial segregation. Scholars consider segregation to be the most foundational and consequential form of racism because it minimizes (or eliminates) contact between members of the segregated groups. This intergroup isolation and insulation can serve as an incubator for hatching and fomenting racial prejudices and inequities. As Bonilla-Silva (2018) notes: "How can whites develop empathy and gain an understanding of blacks if so few of them develop meaningful interactions with them?" (p. 119). Little or no contact with members of a segregated minority group increases the likelihood that the minority group will be perceived as "unfamiliar" (or "strange") which, in turn, can trigger feelings of anxiety (Zajonc, 2001). Anxiety is an unpleasant emotion and when that unpleasant emotion becomes associated with members of the segregated group, it can lead to further avoidance of them (Pettigrew, 1998). In a long-term study of more than 2,500 students enrolled the University of Michigan, it was found that white students who attended highly segregated high schools also had the most segregated friendship patterns in college (Matlock, 1997). In contrast, studies show that when children are raised in interracial communities, they grow up holding less prejudicial racial attitudes, are more likely to live in interracial neighborhoods as adults, and are more likely to send their own children to interracial schools (Braddock & Mikulyuk, 2012).

Blacks have experienced racial segregation for a longer period of time than any other racial group and they remain America's most segregated racial group—at all income levels (Logan, 2003) and all ages (Feagin, 2005). Segregation of blacks has a long and ongoing history starting with slavery when blacks were housed in separate quarters. Even the minority of slaveholders and political figures who thought slavery was inhumane and inconsistent with America's democratic principles and argued that slaves should be emancipated, would not endorse any emancipation program that was involved with racial integration; instead, the program was most commonly endorsed involved exporting blacks to Africa or other places outside the United States (Feagin, 2005). When slavery was abolished, whites immediately created formal and informal laws that allowed them to separate themselves from emancipated blacks, including prohibiting blacks from attending schools with whites, eating at restaurants with whites, and using the same bathrooms as whites. These "Jim Crow" laws (named after "Jump Jim Crow"—a song-and-dance character played by a white man with a black face) were first enacted following the Civil War were kept in place for almost a full century (Thompson, 2009).

Forty years after the U.S. Supreme Court's decision to support racial segregation of public transportation in the *Plessy v. Ferguson* case in 1896, legendary black blues musician, B.B. King described his train ride back to Mississippi upon his return from military service in World War II:

> The trip back was an eye-opener for me. German prisoners of war were on the same train. But unlike us, they weren't forced to sit in separate and inferior compartments. They sat with the white folk. And these were our sworn enemies! Men who, only weeks before, were looking to shoot us dead! It hurt my heart to see what happened if too many whites got on the train and had to sit in the black section. They'd put up a partition to hide us from view. The train officials were telling the white passengers, "You can look at enemy soldiers who were ready to cut your throat, but you can't look at the black American soldiers willing to die for you." It upset me even worse when I saw how the German prisoners were used to pick cotton in the Delta. We blacks picked till nightfall—seven or eight in the evening. But the Germans were allowed to

take off at three in the afternoon. Plantation owners worried about overworking them. That made us feel less than human. We were seen as beasts of burden, dumb animals, a level below the Germans. To watch your enemy get better treatment than yourself was a helluva thing to endure (King & Ritz, 1996, p. 91)

The ferocity of the South's segregationist ideology continued well into the 1960s and was tellingly captured in the infamous words of Alabama governor, George Wallace, during a speech he gave when being sworn into office in 1963: "It is very appropriate then that from this Cradle of the Confederacy, this very Heart of the Great Anglo-Saxon Southland . . . . In the name of the greatest people that have ever trod this earth, I draw the line in the dust . . . I say segregation today . . . segregation tomorrow . . . segregation forever" (NPR, 2013).

Segregation, however, was in no way limited to the South; it was a national phenomenon. America's armed forces and federal employees were segregated up to 1948, and even though there were no formal Jim Crow outside the South, Midwestern and Northern states used informal segregation practices to prevent "race mixing" (Alexander, 2020). In fact, "Jim Crow"-type segregation was in place in the North well before the term was coined in the South. Informal segregation practices were used in Northern towns and cities to separate and subordinate its growing number of black residents since the early 1800s, well before it was formally legalized in the South following the Civil War (Feagin, 2005). In the early 1900s, when many Southern black families moved North during the "Great Migration," Northern schools were not segregated formally by law, but black children were often kept separate from white children in classroom settings (Wilkerson, 2020). In 1928, one researcher noted that in Northern schools, "Colored pupils sometimes occupy only the front seats or the back seats. They are grouped on one side, or occupy alternate rows; sometimes they are seated without regard to race; or they share seats with white pupils, a method used regularly by one teacher for punishing white pupils" (Daniel, 1928, p. 183).

Segregation laws prohibiting blacks from swimming in the same water as whites were also prevalent and forcefully enforced. In 1919, one of America's worst race riots took place in Chicago when a young white man stoned a black swimmer who drifted toward a section of a public beach that the community decided was off limits to blacks. The black swimmer drowned after the stoning, but when policemen arrived at the scene, they refused to arrest the attacker. Race riots followed soon thereafter, leading to the death of 38 people, 23 of whom were black (Rothstein, 2017). In 1935, the town of Newton, Kansas went to the state supreme court to keep blacks out of a new public pool that the town recently built. Whites in the town would only swim in a pool after blacks used if the water was drained and the tank scrubbed. Members of Newton's city council argued that blacks had to be excluded from using the new public pool because it was a "circulatory type of pool" whose water could only changed once during the swimming season. Since this couldn't be done each time a black person used this type of pool, the town decided to ban blacks from using it altogether. The Kansas Supreme Court sided with the town and for almost 30 years, the city's only public pool remained segregated and could be legally used by whites (Wiltse, 2007).

Racial segregation policies was rigidly applied to all blacks, regardless of their fame or national accomplishments. In 1936, Black track-and-field star, Jesse Owens won four gold medals at the Olympic Games in Berlin. After the games ended, a ticker-tape parade was held in New York to honor Owens and other American Olympians; following the parade, to get to his own reception was held at the Waldorf Astoria hotel in New York City, and Owens had to ride the freight elevator instead of the normal hotel elevator reserved for whites only. Owens later commented that after he won his medals at the Olympics in Berlin, white supremacist Adolf Hitler refused to shake hands with him like he had with white medal winners, but he was able to reside in the same housing facilities as his white teammates, which was something he could not have done in his home country (Wilkerson, 2010).

Ohio Restaurant, 1938. Source: Library of Congress

Segregationist practices were so widespread nationwide that a black New York City mailman wrote *The Negro Motorist Green Book*, an annual guidebook for black auto travelers that was used by blacks from 1936 to 1966. The book provided black travelers with information about where they could "travel without embarrassment." The book guided them to places across the United States that would accommodate their requests for food and lodging, and guided them away from places that refused to accommodate them, including many places in the North, Midwest, and far West (Driskel, 2015).

Racial segregation continues to exist in the United States today (Massey, 2003; Nagda et al., 2005). Although America has become an increasingly diverse nation, 80% of its major cities were more segregated in 2019 than they were 30 years earlier (Mendenian et al., 2021) and despite the increasing racial diversity of students attending America's schools, students of color are much more likely to attend schools where they constitute the majority of their school's population (Mervosh, 2019); in contrast, white students attend schools where 75% of their schoolmates are white (Orfield et al., 2012).

Even religious services have long been, and continue to be racially segregated. In 1965, the famous black writer and activist, James Baldwin observed: "I don't know if white Christians hate Negros or not, but I know that we have a Christian church which is black. I know the most segregated hour in American life is high noon on Sunday" (Foulks, 2015). Baldwin's observation still applies today: in 2020, the majority of American religious congregations still remain racially segregated (Granderson, 2021).

Miscegenation Laws

Another way in which racial segregation was practiced in the United States was through passage and enforcement of miscegenation laws that forbid marriage, or even sexual contact, between members of different racial groups. The majority of America's states (41 of 50) once had laws on the books that outlawed marriage between blacks and whites, punishable by fines up to $5,000 and 10 years in prison. These laws were in place until the U.S. Supreme Court overturned them in 1967. One southern state did not officially repeal its

"I think it is one of the tragedies of our nation, one of the shameful tragedies, that 11o'clock on Sunday morning is one of the most segregated hours, if not the most segregated hour, in Christian America. Any church that stands against integration and that has a segregated body is standing against the spirit and the teachings of Jesus Christ."

—MARTIN LUTHER KING, JR.

law against intermarriage until 2000, and even then, 40% of the state's citizens who voted on the referendum, voted in favor of keeping the marriage ban on the books (Wilkerson, 2020). Although interracial marriage is now legal and increasing, national surveys still show that whites are more likely to oppose interracial marriage than any other form of interracial integration (Schuman et al., 1997).

Consider This...

In 1955, a black 14-year-old named Emmett Till was kidnapped, tortured, and killed in Mississippi after being falsely accused of whistling at a white woman. The two white men responsible for Till's murder were acquitted by an all-white jury. Till's mother decided to give her son an open-casket funeral so that the world could be witness to the image of his disfigured body. In 2007, a marker was placed at the site where the teenager's body was recovered to memorialize his unjust death. Since the marker was put in place, it has been vandalized at least three times. In 2021, a proposal to offer a public apology for Till's murder did not receive enough votes from a Mississippi legislative committee.

The United States was the only country in the world to adopt the principle of "racial absolutism"—the belief that a single drop of black blood could taint the purity of a white person. This form of racist ideology is based on the myth that inferior mental capacities and character traits are correlated or associated with dark skin color; thus, any infusion of non-white "blood" into a white person's body could taint or contaminate a white person's racial purity (and superiority) (Drake, 1987). This "one drop" rule meant that no matter how white a person of color looked, if that person had at least one black ancestor, the person was considered to be black, to be treated as black, and to have the same rights (or lack thereof) as blacks (Herring, 2004). During the slavery period, large numbers of black women were raped by white slaveowners and aristocrats (with impunity). Because of the one-drop rule, the children resulting from these rapes were classified as "black" and were enslaved, sometimes by the very men who fathered them (Feagin, 2005).

It is noteworthy that this rigid insistence on preserving the purity and privilege of the white race was not practiced anywhere else in the world besides America. Even the German Nazis, who praised and emulated America's commitment to racial purity, thought that the "one-drop rule" was too harsh and unforgiving (Whitman, 2017). Other nations with racist ideologies that discriminated against blacks typically granted lighter-skinned blacks of mixed black-white ancestry more privileges than dark-skinned Africans (Rodriguez & Cordero-Guzman, 1999). For example, in South Africa during the era of Apartheid, blacks who had some white heritage were granted more civil rights. In Latin American countries, the mixing of races is viewed positively as a way of promoting racial equality and national identity among its different colored citizens (Knight, 1990).

"I have a dream that my four little children will one day live in a nation where they will not be judged by the color of their skin, but by the content of their character."

—MARTIN LUTHER KING, JR., CIVIL RIGHTS LEADER AND WINNER OF THE NOBEL PEACE PRIZE

Consider This…

In 1967, the U.S. Supreme Court ruled in the case of *Loving v. Virginia* (1967) that laws banning interracial marriage were illegal. The case involved Mildred Loving, a woman of color, and her white husband Richard Loving, who were both sentenced to a year in prison in 1958 for marrying because their marriage violated Virginia's Racial Integrity Act of 1924, which criminalized marriage between people classified as "white" and "colored." The Supreme Court's decision to overturn the Virginia's interracial marriage law decision is considered to be a pivotal turning point that helped dismantle "Jim Crow" segregation laws in the South (Nowak & Rotunda, 2012).

Reflection 6.5

If you are non-black, would you be willing to marry someone who is black? Why or why not?

If you are black, would you be willing to marry someone who is non-black? Why or why not?

Colorism

Colorism may be defined as a type or subset of racism that ascribes positive attributes and privileges to lighter-skinned people of color with more Anglo facial features (Herring, 2004). For instance, after Mexico was first colonized by Spain, colorism was experienced by its darker-skinned Mexican citizens (Hunter, 2004). In India, its darker-skinned citizens were ascribed to lower levels of the caste system (Hall, 1995). The origins of colorism can be traced to the racist belief that whites of European descent were biologically superior and more advanced than races with darker skin tones (Gossett, 1963). Scholars have noted that this age-old association between blackness and inferiority or depravity is reflected in current terms such as "blackmail," "blackballing," and "black sheep" (Cole et al., 2013). Experimental research also shows that people are more likely to quickly and subconsciously associate the color black with immorality (Sherman & Clore, 2009).

In America, colorism has its roots in the slavery system, which whites rationalized as being justifiable because blacks were an inferior and subservient race (Ernst, 1980; Ridgeway & Balkwell, 1997). White slave owners encouraged slaves of black-white ancestry (mulattos) to feel superior to blacks (Berlin, 1976) and allowed mulattos to perform more "privileged" slave labor that required less laborious work and more direct contact with whites, such as serving as house servants. These lighter-skinned blacks were supplied better food, clothing, and sometimes were given opportunities to learn how to read and write (Franklin, 1980). Because of these privileges it was not surprising that a higher percentage of mulattos went on to become leaders of the civil rights movement (Landry, 1987), such as Frederick Douglass and Benjamin Banneker (Horton & Sykes, 2004).

A sizable body of research indicates that colorism exists today and continues to have different consequences for people of color with lighter and darker skin tones. In a major study conducted by the American Sociological Foundation, it was found that the degree of racial segregation in the United States between whites and people of color is related to darkness of their skin color, with the highest level of segregation taking place between whites and blacks, an intermediate level of segregation between whites and Hispanics (Latinx), and the lowest level of segregation between whites and Asians (DiAngelo, 2018).

Research also shows that compared with lighter-skinned blacks, darker-skinned blacks experience: (a) lower levels of educational attainment (Keith & Herring, 1991), (b) lower levels of income (Hughes & Hertel, 1990), and (c) higher levels of job discrimination (Herring, 2004). Also, darker-skinned black men: (a) report lower levels of self-efficacy—the degree to which they believe they can influence or control the outcomes of their lives (Thompson & Keith, 2004), (b) are more likely to be viewed by employers as potentially uncooperative, dishonest, and violent (Kirschenman & Neckerman, 1991), and (c) receive harsher sentences for crimes committed—even when controlling for their socioeconomic status, the severity of the crime committed, and mitigating circumstances surrounding the crime; and if the crime involves a homicide and the victim is white, defendants who look "more black" are twice as likely to receive the death penalty (Eberhardt, 2019).

Both lighter-skinned blacks and lighter-skinned Latinos experience less residential segregation, have higher levels of education, are more likely to be perceived as intelligent during job interviews, and have higher incomes—even when other sociocultural factors are taken into account (Bonilla-Silva, 2018; Hannon, 2015; Hunter, 2005; Telles & Murguia, 1990). Research on how colorism affects women of color indicates that African American females with lower levels of education and income report lower levels of self-esteem in general, but their level of self-esteem is higher if their skin color is lighter (Thompson & Keith, 2004). Lower levels of self-esteem experienced by darker-skinned African American females may be explained, at least in part, by the fact that lighter-skinned African American women are more likely to be perceived as "attractive" and more likely to marry men of higher socioeconomic status (Hunter, 1998). Studies show that as early as age six, black girls are twice as likely as black boys to be sensitive to the attractiveness of their skin color (Russell et al., 1992). Black women have been found to spend considerable amounts of money on beauty products, as do white women, but unlike beauty products purchased by white women, many products sold to and bought by women of color are designed to have a "whitening" effect on their appearance, such as skin creams or bleaches, hair straighteners, and light-colored contact lenses (Hunter, 2004). Some women of color also elect to have cosmetic surgery to gain a more white and Anglo-like appearance (Davis, 1995) Similarly, cosmetic marketing companies target darker skinned Mexican-American women with skin-bleaching creams, including one company whose advertising pitch claimed that Mexican American women "with lighter, more healthy skin tones will become much more successful in business, love and society" (Ruiz, 1998, p. 57).

Consider This…

Gisela Meza Salinas' father was born in Puerto Rico and her mother in Mexico. Whenever Gisela visited Mexico as a child, her grandmother's friends would make note of her light skin tone, saying things like, "She's so pretty, she's so white." Describing how she feels now about her lighter-skinned appearance as a 22-year-old woman, Gisela said: "It's really uncomfortable, but I can't imagine my discomfort compared to my cousins who are darker skinned. My discomfort is because I'm hyper-aware of the benefit I'm receiving. I can't imagine being on the other side of the spectrum." Commenting further about the increasing number of anti-Hispanic hate incidents in the United States, Gisela said that she has never been the target of a racist incident because of her light skin tone: "They have to know I'm Hispanic to target me, and because I'm white passing, I'm pretty much in a bullet-proof vest."

Source: Mejia (2018)

Research shows that there is a "what is beautiful is good" stereotype in which people who are seen as physically attractive are also more likely to be seen as having attractive personal characteristics, such as intelligence, confidence, and self-esteem (Langlois et al., 2000). When the beautiful-is-good stereotype gets applied to women of color, it lowers dark-skinned women's sense of self-esteem (Thompson & Keith, 2004). However, darker-skinned women of color with higher levels of education and income are much less likely to experience low levels of self-esteem; their higher socioeconomic status heightens their self-esteem to the same level as black women of lighter color (Thompson & Keith, 2004).

Some lighter-skinned people of color may also attempt to take advantage of colorism by self-identifying as white, or claiming to be white to gain white privileges (Herring, 2004). In one of the first well-known cases of a person of color trying to do so took place during the Jim Crow era when William Hannibal Thomas, a light-skinned black man, wanted to be accepted by whites as one of their own. He wrote a book titled, *The American Negro*, which claimed that black people were inferior to whites, but he and other light-skinned blacks were able to overcome their "inferior" biological heritage (Kendi, 2019). Today, the term "passing" is used to refer to a person of color whose skin is light enough to be perceived as white and is able to blend into white culture. The fact there is no corresponding term for a dark-skinned white person who attempts to "pass" as a person of color "highlights the fact that, in a racist society, the desired direction is always toward whiteness and away from being perceived as a person of color" (DiAngelo, 2018, p. xvi).

A number of researchers have found that lighter-skinned African Americans, Mexican Americans, and South Americans who self-identify as white tend to hold more conservative political attitudes and are less involved in civil rights activism than their darker-skinned counterparts (Bonilla-Silva, 2018; Hall, 1994). Ijeomo Oluo, a light-skinned African American woman, offers the following advice to light-skinned blacks who may be tempted to use colorism to obtain personal privilege or refrain from equal-rights activism:

> If black people of all shade ranges were viewed as equally intelligent until proven otherwise by their actions, then that privilege would cease to exist. But when somebody treats me as "more intelligent" and treats a darker-skinned black person as "less intelligent," if I don't challenge that, if I just

accept the unearned compliment (and the better grade, the job offer, the access to more financially successful areas of society) with a smile and don't ask why it was given to me or why it's not also given to my darker-skinned counterparts—I'm benefitting from unfair privilege and helping perpetuate it further. The darker-skinned person does not really have much power to challenge that privilege (Oluo, 2019, p. 64).

On the other hand, some light-skinned people of color feel ostracized from other members of their race because they're not viewed as a "true" person of color. In fact, the term "ethnic authenticity" has come into use as a term for describing darker-skinned African Americans and Mexican Americans who are viewed and accepted as "authentic" members of their racial or ethnic group—as opposed to lighter-skinned people of color who may be viewed as not being "black enough" or "Chicano enough" (Hunter, 2004).

Personal
Experience

I was sitting in a coffee shop in Chicago O'Hare airport while proofreading my first draft of this chapter. I looked up from my work for a moment and saw what appeared to be a white girl about 18 years of age. As I lowered my head to return to work, I did a double-take and looked at her again because something about her physical appearance seemed different or unusual. When I looked more closely at her the second time, I noticed that although she had white skin, the features of her face and hair appeared to be those of an African American. After a couple of seconds of puzzlement, I figured it out: she was an *albino* African American. That satisfied my curiosity for the moment, but then I began to wonder: Would it still be accurate to say she was "black" even though her skin was not black? Would her hair and facial features be sufficient for her to be considered or classified as black? If yes, then what would be the "race" of someone who had black skin tone, but did not have the hair and facial features characteristic of black people? Could or should person of African American descent still be called "black", even when that person's skin color appears is actually white?

—Joe Cuseo

Reflection 6.6

Has the lightness or darkness of your skin color affected the way others have viewed or treated you at any time in your life? If yes, in what way(s)?

Has the lightness or darkness of other people's skin affected the way you've viewed or treated them? If yes, in what way(s)?

Chapter Summary and Highlights

Although the term "racism" was not formally defined and used until the mid-1900s, beliefs about white superiority and the inferiority of other races have existed before and after the birth of America. America's original economy was built on the slavery system that reaped economic benefits not just for Southern slave owners but also for white merchants, bankers, and shippers in all parts of the nation. After blacks had been exploited for economic purposes, beliefs about their racial inferiority were then introduced as a reason for justifying their exploitation. In other words, slavery was used first to advance America's early economy, then racist beliefs about black inferiority followed as an ideology to rationalize the slavery system.

From America's beginnings, whiteness has been associated with the nation's identity: To be white was to be "American." Just one year after the U.S. Constitution was adopted, Congress passed the Naturalization Act (the nation's first citizenship law) which declared that naturalized American citizens included all "free white persons" living in the United States for two or more years but excluded "free" blacks or Native American Indians. Politically motivated, pro-white racism continues today in the form of *strategic racism*, defined as "purposeful efforts to use racial animus as leverage to gain material wealth, political power, or heightened social standing." This represents a newer and "softer" form of racism is more subtle and sophisticated than the blatant racism of the slavery Jim Crow era, but it still serves to preserve or promote racial inequality and injustice. The emergence of this new form of racism has been linked to America's changing racial demographics. Throughout the 20th century, whites made up more than 80% of the U.S. population; since then, their proportion has been declining and by 2040, for the first time in history, whites will become a minority group in America. This growing presence of people of color, coupled with the tendency of whites to overestimate the size of America's dark-skinned population, has led some whites to become more conscious of their race and feel threatened by the increasingly multicultural makeup of the country. This has led more whites to engage in "white identity politics"— the practice of supporting political officials and political policies that advance the self-interests and social status of whites. Most people who engage in white identity politics are not full-blown racists who harbor intense hatred toward people of color; in fact, many may even acknowledge that that being white has provided them with unearned privileges because of their membership in a dominant racial group. Nevertheless, their strong sense of white consciousness heightens their sense of in-group identity and out-group bias, leading them to advocate for policies that preserve their group's dominance and oppose governmental attempts to reduce systemic racism and racial inequalities in American society.

Similar to how wealth whites endorsed racism to advance their economic opportunities, so have politicians opportunistically used racism to and advance their political careers, often using "racial dog whistles" or coded racial language to appeal to racist voters and to block civil rights policies without appearing to be racist themselves.

Racist beliefs and political policies have also been advanced by relying on alleged scientific findings, referred to as *scientific racism*. "Climate theory" was once a scientific theory that claimed that the heat in Africa caused blacks to become hypersexual and prone to behaving like savage beasts. At one time, prominent anthropologists claimed that there was an evolutionary spectrum or continuum among higher primates, with monkeys and apes being the least evolved on the lowest end of the scale, whites being the most evolved on the highest end, and people of African descent falling in-between. Physicians who treated black slaves also believed that blacks had naturally weaker hearts, lungs, and muscle strength—unless they were forced to strengthen their slack muscles through work imposed on them by whites. Once blacks were emancipated from slavery, however, a new and totally opposite view emerged about blacks having beast-like strength that made them potentially dangerous criminals. Beliefs about black physical prowess eventually expanded to include the view that they were advantaged athletically—due to their more primitive origins, and their athletic achievements were often accompanied by the racist view that they are endowed with superior physical abilities, but inferior mental abilities (i.e., whites have the brain and blacks have the brawn).

Religious beliefs have also fueled racism by disseminating the idea that human beings have been arranged in a racial hierarchy of superior and inferior groups through divine ordination or intention (López, 2014). America's first white colonists identified themselves as "Christians," claiming that they were distinctly different from and superior to non-Christian "Indians" and "Negroes." Early American theologians also asserted that God created whites first in his image and likeness, then later created blacks separately. This belief was used to justify slavery, often by citing a biblical story about Noah who condemned his son Ham's black descendants to be servants to the white descendants of Noah's other sons.

After World War II vividly demonstrated the horrific consequences of racism based on beliefs about the genetic inferiority of certain human racial groups, a new form of racism emerged. Referred to as *cultural racism*, this form of racism was based less on a group's biology and more on the group's cultural characteristics. In particular, references were made to deficiencies in "black culture" that devalued family and hard work, and valued violence and drug use. Advocates of cultural racism attributed blacks' lower socioeconomic failings of their culture, while failing to acknowledge that "culture" is shaped by environmental conditions and that behavior exhibited by blacks often are reflections of and adaptations to disadvantaged conditions created by systemic racism in housing, education, and employment.

Extensive research in the social sciences points to three key *psychological* processes playing a critical role in the formation and perpetuation of racism: group bias, implicit bias, and media messaging.

A person's sense of self-esteem is influenced by the group(s) the person identifies with; consequently, if individuals identify with a "superior" group, they can feel superior and feel better about themselves. Known as "social identity theory," this psychological process motivates individuals to make social comparisons between their group and other groups, and viewing their "in group" as better than other "out groups"—which, in turn, can trigger prejudice toward other racial groups.

Neuroscience research shows that a person's *racial* group is the first characteristic that the brain notices—before the person's age, gender, or any other group characteristic. Because a person's race is so easily visualized and immediately detectable, it is one of the fastest and most automatic feature used by people to categorize (and judge) others. Since the brain detects race rapidly and automatically, it can lead to *implicit (unconscious)* racial biases. The effect is so strong that even individuals who sincerely want to avoid anti-black bias, or who strongly believe they don't hold racial bias, still exhibit bias on implicit bias tests. But what causes implicit anti-black bias to develop in the first place? Certainly family and peers play an important role, but research points the media as also playing a long historical and pivotal role in creating anti-black bias. Since most whites have limited personal contact with blacks, their impressions of blacks are heavily influenced by how blacks are portrayed in the media. Studies show that approximately 80% of white Americans have been exposed to negative media messages about blacks and other marginalized groups by the time they reach adulthood. These media messages have often conveyed negative and misleading impressions of blacks. In one study of poor people depicted in the news, it was found that 59% of those depicted were blacks, even though blacks made up about 27% of the nation's poor; in contrast, poor whites accounted for 17% of the poor people depicted, yet made up 66% of America's poor.

Segregation is a form of racism that is still prevalent today. When members of one racial group intentionally decide to separate themselves from another racial group, either socially or physically, they are practicing racial segregation. Scholars consider segregation to be the most foundational and consequential form of racism because it minimizes (or eliminates) contact between members of the segregated groups, which can foment racial distrust, prejudice, and discrimination.

Blacks have experienced racial segregation for a longer period of time than any other racial group and remain America's most segregated racial group—at all income levels and ages. Although the United States has become an increasingly diverse nation, 80% of its major cities were more segregated in 2019 than they were 30 years earlier, and despite the increasing racial diversity of students attending America's schools, students of color are still much more likely to attend schools where they constitute the majority of the school's population.

Colorism may be defined as a type or subset of racism that ascribes positive attributes and privileges to lighter-skinned people of color with more Anglo facial features. A sizable body of research shows that colorism exists today and has different consequences for people of color with lighter and darker skin tones. For instance, the degree of racial segregation in the United States between whites and people of color is related to the amount of darkness in their skin, with the highest level of segregation taking place between whites and blacks, an intermediate level of segregation between whites and Hispanics (Latinx), and the lowest level of segregation between whites and Asians. Research also shows that compared with lighter-skinned blacks, darker-skinned blacks experience: lower levels of educational attainment, lower levels of income, and higher levels of job discrimination. Darker-skinned black men are more likely to be viewed by employers as potentially uncooperative, dishonest, and violent, and they are more likely to receive harsher sentences for crimes committed—even after controlling for their socioeconomic status, the severity of the crime committed, and mitigating circumstances surrounding the crime; if the crime involves a homicide and the victim is white, defendants who look "more black" are twice as likely to receive the death penalty.

Internet Resources

History of Racial Segregation in the United States:
https://www.history.com/topics/black-history/segregation-united-states

Racism in America Today: https://www.futurity.org/7-factors-racism-united-states-2384462/

Scientific Racism: https://library.harvard.edu/confronting-anti-black-racism/scientific-racism

Colorism: https://www.nccj.org/colorism-0

Implicit Racial Bias: https://perception.org/research/implicit-bias/

References

Alba, R. D., Rumbat, R. G., & Marotz, K. (2005). A distorted nation: Perceptions of racial/ethnic group sizes and attitudes toward immigrants and other minorities. *Social Forces, 84*(2), 901–019.

Alexander, M. (2020). *The new Jim Crow: Mass incarceration in the age of colorblindness.* The New Press.

Anderson, C. (2016). *White rage: The unspoken truth of our racial divide.* Bloomsbury.

Apfelbaum, E. P., Sommers, S. R., & Norton, M. I. (2008). Seeing race and seeming racists? Evaluating strategic colorblindness in social interaction. *Journal of Personality & Social Psychology, 95*(4), 918–932.

Armstrong, E. M. (2010, February 26). *Revered and reviled: D. W. Griffith's "The Birth of a Nation."* https://web.archive.org/web/20100529224316/http:/themovingarts.com/revered-and-reviled-d-w-griffiths-the-birth-of-a-nation/

Bailey, J. (2021, May 25). "Gone with the Wind" and controversy: What you need to know. *The New York Times.* https://www.nytimes.com/2020/06/10/movies-gone-with-the-wind-controversy.html

Beckett, K. (1997). *Making crime pay: Law and order in contemporary politics.* Oxford University Press

Beckwith, R. T. (2018). *President Trump called El Salvador, Haiti "shithole countries": Report.* https://time.com/5100058/donald-trump-shithole-countries/

Benjaimin, R. (2009). *Searching for whitopia: An improbable journey to the heart of white America.* HarperCollins.

Bennett, D. H. (1988). *The party of fear: From nativist movements to the new right in American history.* University of North Carolina Press.

Berlin, I. (1976). The structure of the free negro caste in the antebellum United States. *Journal of Social History, 9*(3), 297–318.

Block, S. (2001–2002), Rape and race in colonial American newspapers, 1728-1776," *Journalism History 27*(4), 146–155.

Bobo, L. D., & Huthcings, V. L. (1996). Perceptions of racial group competition: Extending Blum's theory of group position to a multiracial social context. *American Sociological Review, 61*(6), 951–972.

Bonilla-Silva, E. (2018). *Racism without racists: Color-blind racism and the persistence of racial inequality in America.* Rowman & Littlefield.

Braddock, J, M., II., & Mikulyuk, A. B. (2012). Segregation, desegregation, and resegregation. In J. A. Banks (Ed.), *Encyclopedia of diversity in education* (vol. 4, pp. 1930–1934). SAGE.

Browne, P.A. (1850). *The classification of mankind by the hair and wool of their heads.* A. Hart.

Chicago Commission on Race Relations. (1922). *The Negro in Chicago: A study of race relations and a race riot.* University of Chicago Press.

Coates, T. (2015). *Between the world and me.* Spiegel & Grau.

Cole, K., Wilson, M., & Hall, R. (2013). *The color complex: The politics of skin color in the new millennium.* Random House.

Craig, M. A., & Richeson, J. A. (2017). Information about the US racial demographic shift triggers concerns about anti-white discrimination among the prospective white "minority." *PLOS One, 12*(9), e0185389. https://pubmed.ncbi.nlm.nih.gov/28953971/

Daniel, W. A. (1928). Schools. In T. J. Woofter (Ed.), *Negro problems in the cities*. McGrath Publishing.

Davis, K. (1995). *Reshaping the female body*. Routledge.

De Miramon, C. (2009). Noble dogs, noble blood: The invention of the concept of race in the late middle ages. In M. Eliav-Feldon, B. H. Isaac, & J. Ziegler (Eds.), *The origins of racism in the west*. Ambridge University Press.

Degler, C. N. (1991). *In search of human nature: The decline and revival of Darwinism in American social thought*. Oxford University Press.

Devos, T., & Banaji, M. R. (2005). "American = White?" *Journal of Personality and Social Psychology, 88*(3), 447–466.

DiAngelo, R. (2018). *White fragility: Why it's so hard for white people to talk about racism*. Beacon Press.

Drake, S. C. (1987). *Black folk here and there*, volume one. Center for Afro American Studies, University of California.

Driskel, J. (2015). *An atlas of self-reliance: The negro motorist green book (1937-1964)*. National Museum of African American History. https://americanhistory.si.edu/blog/negro-motorists-green-book

Du Bois, W. E. B. (1935). *Black reconstruction in America: Toward a history of the part which black folk played in the attempt to reconstruct democracy in America 1860-1880*. Harcourt, Brace, and Company.

Eberhardt, J. L. (2019). *Biased: Uncovering the hidden prejudice that shapes what we see, think, and do*. Viking.

Effron, D. A., & Knowles, E. D. (2015). Entitativity and intergroup bias: How belonging to a cohesive group allows people to express their prejudices. *Journal of Personality and Social Psychology, 108*(2), 234–253.

Ernst, K. (1980). Racialism, racialist ideology, and colonialism, past and present. In *Sociological theories: Race and colonialism* (pp. 453–472). UNESCO.

Feagin, J. (2005). *Systemic racism: A theory of oppression*. Routledge.

Foulks, B. (2015). *James Baldwin speaks about racism and the church*. https://syncopated-hustle.org/2015/03/11/james-baldwin-quote/

Franklin, J. H. (1980). *From slavery to freedom*. Knopf.

Fredrickson, G. M. (2002). *Racism: A short history*. Princeton University Press.

Fromm, E. (1964). *The heart of man: Its genius for good and evil*. Harper & Row.

Gallagher, C. (2003). Miscounting race: Explaining whites' misperceptions of racial group size. *Sociological Perspectives, 46*(3), 381–396.

Gilens, M. (1999). *Why Americans hate welfare: Race, media, and the politics of anti-poverty policy*. University of Chicago Press.

Gilliam, F. D. & Iyenagar, S. (2000). Prime suspects: The influence of local television news on the viewing public. *American Journal of Political Science, 44*, 560–573.

Goff, P. A., Williams, M. J., Eberhardt, J. L., & Jackson, N. C. (2008). Not yet human: Implicit knowledge, historical dehumanization, and contemporary consequences. *Journal of Personality and Social Psychology, 94*(2), 292–306.

Gossett, T. F. (1963). *Race: The history of an idea in America*. Southern Methodist University Press.

Granderson, L. Z. (2021, February 14). Ending the tribalism of Sunday mornings. *Los Angeles Times*, A16.

Grant, M. (1916). *The passing of the great race or the racial basis of European history*. Charles Scribner's Sons.

Griffin, J. H. (1962). *Black like me*. Signet.

Hall, R. (1995). The bleaching syndrome: African Americans' response to cultural domination vis-à-vis skin color. *Journal of Black Studies, 26*, 172–184.

Haney López, I. (2014). *Dog whistle politics: How coded racial appeals have reinvented racism and wrecked the middle class*. Oxford University Press.

Hannon, L. (2015). White colorism. *Social Currents, 2*(1), 13–21.

Herring, C. (2004). Skin deep: Race and complexion in the "color-blind" era. In C. Herring, V. M. Keith, & H. D. Horton (Eds.), *Skin deep: How race and complexion matter in the "color blind" era* (pp. 1–21). Institute on Race and Public Policy, University of Illinois at Chicago. University of Illinois Press.

Herring, C., Thomas, M., Durr, M., & Horton, H. D. (1998). Does race matter? The determinants and consequences of self-reports of discrimination victimization. *Race & Society, 1*(2), 109–123.

Herskovits, M. J. (1941). *The myth of the negro past*. Beacon Press.

Hill, R. B. (1999). *The strengths of black families: Twenty-five years later*. University Press of America.

Hoberman, H. (1997). *Darwin's athletes: How sport has damaged black America and preserved the myth of race*. Houghton Mifflin.

Horton, H. D. & Sykes, L. L. (2004). Toward a critical demography of neo-mulattoes: Structural change and diversity within the black population. In C. Herring, V. M. Keith, & H. D. Horton (Eds.), *Skin deep: How race and complexion matter in the "color blind" era* (pp. 159–173). Institute on Race and Public Policy, University of Illinois at Chicago. University of Illinois Press.

Hughes, M., & Hertel, B. R. (1990). The significance of color remains: A study of life chances, mate selection, and ethnic consciousness among Black Americans. *Social Forces, 68*(4), 1105–1120.

Hunter, M. (1998). Colorstruck: Skin color stratification in the lives of African American women. *Sociological Inquiry, 68*(4), 517–535.

Hunter, M. (2004). Light, bright, and almost white: The advantages and disadvantages of light skin. In C. Herring, V. M. Keith, & H. D. Horton (Eds.), Skin/*deep: How race and complexion matter in the "color blind" era* (pp. 22–44). Institute on Race and Public Policy, University of Illinois at Chicago. University of Illinois Press.

Hunter, M. (2005). *Race, gender, and the politics of skin tone*. Routledge.

Jardina, A. (2019). *White identity politics*. Cambridge University Press.

Johnson, C. S. (1936). *A preface to racial understanding*. Friendship Press.

Johnson, K. (2010). Prejudice versus positive thinking. In J. Marsh, R. Mendoza-Denton, & J. A. Smith (Eds.), *Are we born racist? New insights from neuroscience and positive psychology*. Beacon Press.

Karabel, J. (2005). *The chosen: The hidden history of admission and exclusion at Harvard, Yale, and Princeton*. Houghton Mifflin.

Katz, P., & Kofkin, J. (1997). Race, gender and young children. In S. S. Luthar, J. A. Burack, D. Cicchetti, & J. Weisz (Eds.), *Developmental psychopathology: Perspectives on risk and disorder* (pp. 51-74). Cambridge University Press.

Keith, V., & Herring, C. (1991). Skin tone and stratification in the black community. *American Journal of Sociology, 97*(7), 760–778.

Kendi, I. X. (2016). *Stamped from the beginning: The definitive history of racist ideas in America*. Bold Type Books.

Kendi, I. X. (2019). *How to be an antiracist*. One World.

Kinder, D. R., & Sanders, L. M. (1996). *Divided by color: Racial politics and democratic ideals*. University of Chicago Press.

King, B. B., & Ritz, D. (1996). *Blues all around me: The autobiography of B.B. King*. HarperCollins.

Kirschenman, J., & Neckerman, K. M. (1991). "We'd love to hire them but . . .": The meaning of race for employers. In C. Jencks & P. Peterson (Eds.), *The Urban Underclass* (pp. 203–234). Brookings Institution.

Knight, A. (1990). Racism, revolution, and indigenismo: Mexico, 1910-1940. In R. Graham (Ed.), *The idea of race in Latin America* (pp. 1–6). University of Texas Press.

Kolbert, E. (2018, October 22). There's no scientific basis for race—it's a made-up label. *National Geographic*. https://www.nationalgeographic.co.uk/people-and-culture/2018/04/theres-no-scientific-basis-race-its-made-label

Landry, B. (1987). *The new black middle class*. University of California Press.

Langlois, J. H., Kalakanis, L., Rubenstein, A. J., Larson, A., Hallam, M., & Smoot, M. (2000). Maxims or myths of beauty: A meta-analytic and theoretical review. *Psychological Bulletin, 126*, 390–423.

Larson, S. G. (2006). *Media and minorities: The politics of race in news and entertainment*. Rowman and Littlefield.

Logan, J. R. (2003). Ethnic diversity grows, neighborhood integration lags. In B. Katz & R. Lang (Eds.), *Redefining urban and suburban America: Evidence from census 2000* (pp. 235–256). Brookings Institution Press.

Longley, K., Mayer, J. D., Schaller, M., & Sloan, J. W. (2007). *Deconstructing Reagan: Conservative mythology and America's fortieth president*. Routledge.

López, I. H. (2014). *Dog whistle politics: How coded racial appeals have reinvented racism & wrecked the middle class*. Oxford University Press.

Lott, T. L. (1999). *The invention of race: Black culture and the politics of representation*. Blackwell Publishers.

Martin, S. F. (2011). *A nation of immigrants*. Cambridge University Press.

Massey, D. (2003). *The source of the river: The social origins of freshmen at America's selective colleges and universities*. Princeton University Press.

Masuoka, N., & Junn, J. (2013). *The politics of belonging: Race, public opinion, and immigration*. University of Chicago Press.

Matlock, J. (1997). Student expectations and experiences: The Michigan study. *Diversity Digest* (summer). http://www.diversityweb.org/Digest/Sm97/research.html

McClatchy Newspapers. (2013). *Dutch use of "Black Peter" helper for Santa stirs protest*. http://digital.olivesoftware.com/olive/Tablet/LexingtonHeraldLeader/SharedArticle.aspx?href=LHL%2F2013%2F11%2F17&id=Ar00403

Mehta, S. (2020, October 5). Blowing the "racehorse theory" whistle. *Los Angeles Times*, A5.

Mejia, B. (2018, November 23). Dark-skinned Latinos see deeper shade of bias. *Los Angeles Times*, A1 & A11.

Mendenian, S., Gailes, A., & Gambhir, S. (2021). *The roots of structural racism: Twenty-first century residential segregation in the United States*. Belonging Berkeley Segregation Report. https://www.amren.com/news/2021/08/the-roots-of-structural-racism-project/

Mervosh, S. (2019, February 27). How much wealthier are white school districts than nonwhite ones? $23 billion, report says. *The New York Times*. https://www.nytimes.com/2019/02/27/education/school-districts-funding-white-minorities.html?module=inline

Metzl, J. M. (2019). *Dying of whiteness: How the politics of racial resentment is killing America's heartland*. Basic Books.

Miller, A. H., Gurin, P., Gurin, G., & Malanchuk, O. (1981). Group consciousness and political participation. *American Journal of Political Science, 25*(3), 494–511.

Myers, D., & Levy, M. (2018). Racial population projects and reactions to alternative news accounts of growing diversity. *Annals of the American Academy of Political and Social Science, 677*(May), 215–228.

Nagda, B. R., Gurin, P., & Johnson, S. M. (2005). Living, doing and thinking diversity: How does pre-college diversity experience affect first-year students' engagement with college diversity? In R. S. Feldman (Ed.), *Improving the first year of college: Research and practice* (pp. 73–110). Lawrence Erlbaum.

Nosek, B., Banaji, M., & Greenwald, A. (2002). Harvesting implicit group attitudes and beliefs from a demonstration web site. *Group Dynamics: Theory, Research, and Practice, 6*(1), 101–115.

Nott, J. C., & Gliddon, G. R. (1854). *Types of mankind.* Lippincott, Grambo.

Nowak, J. E., & Rotunda, R. D. (2012). *Treatise on constitutional law: Substance and procedure* (5th ed.). West Thomson/Reuters.

National Public Radio. (2013, January 10). *"Segregation forever": A fiery pledge forgiven, but not forgotten.* Radio Diaries. https://www.npr.org/2013/01/14/169080969/segregation-forever-a-fiery-pledge-forgiven-but-not-forgotten

Oluo, I. (2019). *So you want to talk about race.* Seal Press.

Omni, M., & Winant, H. (1986). *Racial formation in the United States.* Routledge and Kegan Paul.

Orfield, G., Kucsera, J., & Siegel-Hawley, G. (2012). *E pluribus . . . separation: Deepening double segregation for more students.* The Civil Rights Project/Proyecto Derechos Civiles, University of California, Los Angeles. http://civil-rightsproject.ucla.edu/research/k-12-eduction/integration-and-diversity/mlk-national/e-pluribus . . . separation-deepening-double-segregation-for-more-students

Perry, A. M. (2007). *Know your price: Valuing black lives and property in America's black cities.* Brookings Institute Press.

Pettigrew, T. F. (1998). Intergroup contact theory. *Annual Review of Psychology, 49,* 65–85.

Ridgeway, C., & Balkwell, J. (1997). Group processes and the diffusion of status beliefs. *Social Psychology Quarterly, 60*(1), 14–31.

Rodriguez, C., & Cordero-Guzman, H. (1999). Placing race in context. In G. A. Gallagher (Ed.), *Rethinking the color line: Readings in race and ethnicity* (pp. 57–63). Mayfield.

Roediger, D. R. (2006). *Working toward whiteness: How America's immigrants became white.* Basic Books.

Rogers, J. A. (1961). *Africa's gift to America.* H. M. Rogers.

Roper Center for Public Opinion Research. (2015). *Huddled masses: Public opinion & the 1965 U.S. Immigration Act.* https://ropercenter.cornell.edu/huddled-masses-public-opinion-and-the-1965-u-s-immigration-act/

Rothstein, R. (2017). *The color of law.* Liveright Publishing.

Ruiz, V. (1998). *From out of the shadows: Mexican women in twentieth century America.* Oxford University Press.

Russell, K., Wilson, M., & Hall, R. (1992). *The color complex: The politics of skin color among African Americans.* Harcourt Brace Jovanovich.

Sauer, A. (2011). *Primate in chief: A guide to racist Obama monkey photoshops.* https://www.theawl.com/2011/04/primate-in-chief-a-guide-to-racis-obama-monkey-photoshops/

Schechter, P. A. (1994). Free and slave labor in the Old South: The Tredegar ironworkers' strike of 1847. *Labor History, 35*(2), 165–186.

Scheepers, D., & Ellemers, N. (2005). When the pressure is up: The assessment of social identity threat in low and high status groups. *Journal of Experimental Psychology, 41*(2), 192–200.

Schuman, H., Steeh, C., Bobo, L., & Krysan, M. (1997). *Racial attitudes in America: Trends and interpretations.* Harvard University Press.

Sherman, G. D. & Clore, G. L. (2009). The color of sin. *Psychological Science, 20*(8), 1019–1025.

Smith, L. (1949). *Killers of the dream.* W. W. Norton.

Spiro, J. P. (2009). *Defending the master race: Conservation, eugenics, and the legacy of Madison Grant.* University Press of New England.

Southern Poverty Law Center. (2021). *The year in hate and extremism, 2020.* A Report from the Southern Poverty Law Center. Montgomery, Alabama.

Stuurman, S. (2000). Francois Bernier and the invention of racial classification. *History Workshop Journal, 50,* 1–2.

Stuurman, S. (2001). A new division of the earth. *History Workshop Journal, 51,* 247–250.

Sugrue, T. J. (2005). *The origins of the urban crisis: Race and inequality in postwar Detroit.* Princeton University Press.

Tajfel, H., & Turner, J. C. (1986). The social identity theory of intergroup behavior. In S. Horschel & W. G. Austin (Eds.), *Psychology of intergroup relations* (pp. 7–24). Nelson-Hall.

Telles, E. E., & Murguia, E. (1990). Phenotypic discrimination and income differences among Mexican Americans. *Social Science Quarterly, 71*(4), 682–696.

Thompson, A. (2009). *White privilege.* In H. Greene & S. Gabbidon (Eds.), *Encyclopedia of race and crime.* SAGE.

Thompson, M., & Keith, V. (2001). The blacker the berry: Gender skin tone, self-esteem and self-efficacy. *Gender and Society, 15*(3), 336–357.

Thompson, M., & Keith, V. (2004). Copper brown and blue black: Colorism and self-evaluation. In C. Herring, V. M. Keith, & H. D. Horton (Eds.), *Skin deep: How race and complexion matter in the "color blind" era* (pp. 45–64). Institute on Race and Public Policy, University of Illinois at Chicago. University of Illinois Press.

Turner, J. C. (1985). Social categorization and self-concept: A social cognitive theory of group behavior. In E. J. Lawler (Ed.), *Advances in group process: Theory and research* (pp. 77–121). JAI Press.

Udry, R., Bauman, K., & Chase, C. (1971). Skin color, status, and mate selection. *American Journal of Sociology, 76*(4), 722–733.

Uwumarogie, V. (2016). *If I have to read about one more bigot calling the Obamas "monkeys."* https://madamenoire.com/745029/obamas-monkeys-racism/

Watkins, M. (2006). *Stepin Fetchit: The life and times of Lincoln Perry.* Vintage Books.

Wellman, D. T. (2009). *Portraits of white racism* (2nd ed.). Cambridge University Press.

Whitman, J. Q. (2017). *Hitler's American model: The United States and the making of Nazi race law.* Princeton University Press.

Wilkerson, I. (1992, June 21). The tallest fence: The feeling of race on a white neighborhood. *The New York Times.* https://www.nytimes.com/1992/06/21/us-the-tallest-fence-feeling-on-race-in-a-white-neighborhood.html

Wilkerson, I. (2010). *The warmth of other suns: The epic story of America's great migration.* Vintage Books.

Wilkerson, I. (2020). *Caste: The origins of our discontents.* Random House.

Wiltse, J. (2007). *Contested waters: A social history of swimming pools in America.* University of North Carolina Press.

Wise, T. (2011). *White like me: Reflection on race from a privileged son* (3rd ed.). Soft Skull Press.

Yamagishi, T., & Mifune, N. (2008). Does share group membership promote altruism? Fear, greed, and reputation. *Rationality and Society, 20*(1), 5–30.

Zajonc, R. B. (2001). Mere exposure: A gateway to the subliminal. *Current Directions in Psychological Science, 10,* 224–228.

Zuberi, T. (2001). *Thicker than blood: How racial statistics lie.* University of Minnesota Press.

Reflections and Applications

Name

_____

Date

_____

6.1 Review the sidebar quotes contained in this chapter and select two that you think are particularly meaningful or inspirational. For each quote you selected, provide an explanation why you chose it.

6.2 Think of someone you know or have met who could be accurately called a "racist."

   a)   What beliefs attitudes or behaviors did that person display that were indicative of racism?

   b)   What factors do you think led to the development of, or was responsible for this person's racist viewpoints?

6.3 Is racism a topic that you think about much or talk about much with others? Why? If you do think about or discuss the topic of racism, what is the situation or context in which it usually takes place?

6.4 Racial bias can be subtle and may only begin to surface when the social or emotional distance between members of different groups grows closer. Honestly rate your level of comfort with the following situations.

Someone from another racial group:

a)	going to your school	High	Moderate	Low
b)	working in your place of employment	High	Moderate	Low
c)	living on your street as a next-door neighbor	High	Moderate	Low
c)	living with you as a roommate	High	Moderate	Low
d)	socializing with you as a personal friend	High	Moderate	Low
e)	being an intimate friend or romantic partner	High	Moderate	Low
f)	being your partner in marriage.	High	Moderate	Low

For items you rated "high," why would you feel comfortable?
For items you rated "low," why would you feel uncomfortable?

6.5 Case Study: Celebrating a Tradition or Perpetuating a Racial Stereotype?

In an old Dutch Christmas tradition, Sinterklaas (St. Nicholas) is accompanied by a character known as Zwart Piet (Black Pete)—a black helper—whose role is typically played by a white person in blackface with a frizzy wig, big gold earring, and very large red lips.

An intense debate has taken place among the Dutch people, some of whom think Black Pete is an offensive stereotype and symbolic of slavery, while others claim that it's just a beloved part of the Dutch Christmas tradition. The head of a working group at the United Nations Office for Human Rights has called for an end to the tradition, stating that members of her working group "cannot understand why it is that the people in The Netherlands cannot see it is a throwback to slavery."

Organizers for the Dutch Christmas festivals have tried to defuse the situation by asking the Black Petes not to wear golden earrings, remove their large curly wigs, and encourage children attending the festivals to paint their faces in various colors.

Source: McClatchy Newspapers (2013)

a)   How or why do you think the Black Pete tradition began in the first place?

b)   Do you think that the presence of Black Pete at Christmas festivals may affect Dutch children's views or attitudes toward black people in any way?

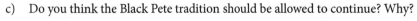

c)   Do you think the Black Pete tradition should be allowed to continue? Why?

6.6 Hate Crime: Racially Motivated Murder

Jasper County, Texas, has a population of approximately 31,000 people. In this county, 80% of the people are White, 18% are black, and 2% are of other races. In 1998, the mayor, the president of the Chamber of Commerce, and two councilmen were black. From the outside, Jasper appeared to be a town with racial harmony, and its black and white leaders were quick to state that there was no racial tension in Jasper.

However, one evening, James Byrd Jr.—a 49-year-old African American man—was walking home along a road and was offered a ride by three white males. Rather than taking Byrd home, Lawrence Brewer (age 31), John King (age 23), and Shawn Berry (age 23)—three men linked to white-supremacist groups—took Byrd to an isolated area and began beating him. They then dropped his pants to his ankles, painted his face black, chained Byrd to their truck, and dragged him for approximately three miles. The truck was driven in a zigzag fashion to inflict maximum pain on the victim. Byrd was decapitated after his body collided with a culvert in a ditch alongside the road. His skin, arms, genitalia, and other body parts were strewn along the road, and his torso was found dumped in front of a black cemetery. Medical examiners testified that Byrd was alive for much of the dragging incident.

When the three assailants were brought to trial, their bodies were covered with racist tattoos. Following his murder, Byrd's family created the James Byrd Foundation for Racial Healing, and a wrought iron fence that had separated black and white graves for more than 150 years in Jasper Cemetery was removed in a special racial unity service. Members of the racist Ku Klux Klan have since visited the gravesite of Byrd several times, leaving racist stickers and other marks that angered Byrd's family and other members of the Japser community.

Source: Louisiana Weekly (February 3, 2003)

Reflection Questions

a)   What factors do you think were responsible for this incident?

b)   Could this incident have been prevented? If yes, how? If no, why not?

c) How likely do you think an incident like this could take place in your hometown or the community that surrounds your campus?

d) If this event happened to take place in your hometown, how do you think members of your hometown community would react? Why?

Understanding Systemic Racism, Part I: Housing, Education, and Employment

Chapter Purpose and Preview

This chapter explains how racism takes place on a scale wider than individual prejudice, extending to racism exhibited by the practices of an organization or institution and systemic racism that pervades entire social systems. The chapter focuses on three particular forms of systemic racism: housing, schooling, and employment, tracing their historical development and documenting their current impact on people of color.

What Is Systemic Racism?

Racism can take place at different levels, ranging from individuals who exhibit it on a person-to-person basis to *institutional* racism that takes place within a particular institution or organization—such as a school or corporate organization, and *systemic* racism that cuts across entire societal systems (Feagin, 2005)—such as housing, health care, and criminal justice systems. Even if people do not engage in intentional discrimination on a personal basis, racism can still be practiced and perpetuated by policies and procedures implanted in organizational and societal structures that operate automatically and systematically to exert collective discriminatory impact on different racial groups (DiAngelo, 2018; Kendi, 2016).

Societal systems in the United States have been shaped by historical events and political decisions that originally put practices decades ago that continue to maintain racial inequities and injustices today. Such historically rooted and still lingering forms of systemic racism need to be understood and acknowledged before they can be effectively uprooted. This requires knowledge not only of the psychology of personal racism, but also the politics, economics, and sociology of systemic racism.

Currently, systemic racism exists in the following social systems:

- *Economic* system: Employment, wages, and wealth
- *Housing* system : Residential choice and home ownership opportunities
- *Education* system: Quality of schools and equality of learning opportunities
- *Health care* system: Access to quality medical care and equal medical treatment
- *Electoral* system: Voting rights and political representation
- *Criminal justice* system: Policing practices, legal representation, and sentencing policies

In the following pages, these current forms of systemic racism will be examined in terms of their impact on black Americans because it is this racial group that has been subjected to, and most affected by, systemic racism in America. However, as documented in the previous chapter, colorism has also impacted other people as well, thus many of the findings about to be presented likely to apply to people of color that are not black, although not as systematically and extensively.

It is important to keep in mind that specific forms of racism need to be traced to their historical roots. Careful examination of the history of systemic racism is critical because it is the residue or remnants of past racist policies and practices that continue to adversely impact the lives of people living now (Kendi, 2016). The historical roots of systemic racism are the underlying and often unacknowledged causes of current systemic racism. Gaining knowledge of these roots is also the key first step to weeding them out the systemic racism that still persists in society today.

> "When we think of racism we think of water hoses, lynchings, racial epithets, and "whites only" signs . . . Our understanding of racism is shaped by the most extreme expressions of individual bigotry, not by the way in which it functions naturally, almost invisibly . . . when it is embedded in the structure of a social system."
> —MICHELLE ALEXANDER, AUTHOR, THE NEW JIM CROW: MASS INCARCERATION IN THE AGE OF COLORBLINDNESS (P. 227 & 228)

> "History is a process ongoing . . . we must grapple with the past as a means of engaging with the present."
> —THOMAS SUGRUE, PROFESSOR OF HISTORY AND SOCIOLOGY, UNIVERSITY OF PENNSYLVANIA

> "The truth is, you don't even have to be 'racist' to be a part of a racist system."
> —IJEOMO OLUO, AUTHOR, *SO YOU WANT TO TALK ABOUT RACE* (P. 28)

Reflection 7.1

Prior to reading this chapter, were you familiar with the term "systemic racism?" If you were, was your understanding of it similar to the way it has been just described?

The Economic System: Systemic Racism in Employment, Income, and Wealth

Employment and Income

In 2015, the hourly wage gap between black and white workers was the largest it's been since 1979 (Wilson & Rogers, 2016). In 2018, the median household income for whites was $70,642 compared with $41,361 for blacks, and the poverty rates for blacks (20.8%) was more than twice than that of whites (10.1%) (Peter G. Peterson Foundation, 2019). Blacks are overrepresented in low-wage jobs, earning between 11% and 17% less than whites (Khouri, 2020a), yet the black–white wage gap exists even when blacks and whites hold the same types of jobs and have similar levels of education (Espinosa & Mitchell, 2020; Moss & Tilly, 2001), and when blacks move up to higher-status jobs, the black–white wage gap increases further (Grodsky & Pager, 2001). It has also been found that black women with some college education make less than white women with only a high school degree (Kendi, 2019). When gender and race combine or intersect in this fashion, it is referred to as *gendered racism* (Thomas et al., 2008).

Wealth

Even larger than the black–white gap in income is the black–white gap in wealth—defined as the value of all assets owned, such as savings, stocks, and home equity. In 2009, the average white family had a net worth of $113,149—about 20 times higher than the average black family (Kochlar et al., 2011). In other words, "for every dollar held by whites, blacks had a lonely nickel in their pocket" (López, 2014, p. 43). The racial gap in wealth today is the largest it's been since 1968 and the gap exists between black and white families at all economic levels, including low-income households. In 2016, for example, the net worth of lower-income white households was $22,900 compared to only $5,000 for lower-income blacks (Serwer, 2020). Contrary to the belief of some people, this wealth gap has little to do with how effectively black and white families save money; it has a lot to do with the fact that white wealth has been accumulated primarily through the opportunities they've had to buy homes and accrue home equity (Meizhu et al., 2006). Blacks have acquired considerably less home equity than whites as a result of many decades of racially discriminatory governmental home-ownership policies and private real-estate practices (Flipen, 2004). (See pp. 207-214 for documentation and details.)

Black families whose parents and grandparents were denied participation in the home equity opportunities in the past now have great difficulty catching up because when it comes to wealth, there is low intergenerational mobility—the ability of a current generation with lower wealth to move up to higher levels of wealth. Low intergenerational mobility also means that already wealthy families are almost always able to hang on to and pass on their wealth to the next generation, providing them with "headstart" assets to pay for such important wealth-building opportunities as a college education and making a downpayment on a house. Access to these headstart assets can then be used to maintain and gain wealth that, in turn, is passed onto the next generation and so forth down the generational line (Feagin, 2005). Rothstein (2017) points out other important ways in which intergenerational wealth generated through home-equity provides advantages to white families that are often not available to black families:

> White families are more often able to borrow from their home equity, if necessary, to weather medical emergencies, and send their children to college, retire without becoming depending on those children, aid family members experiencing hard times, or endure brief periods of joblessness without fear of losing a home or going hungry. If one of these emergencies consumes their savings or home equity, families can bequeath wealth to the next generation (p. 185).

Less wealthy black families are particularly vulnerable to downturns in the national economy. For instance, during the Great Recession of 2008, household wealth fell by 53% for blacks compared to 16% for whites (Kochlar et al., 2011). Similarly, the COVID-19 recession had greater negative impact on black businesses because they had smaller cash reserves and less access to credit. Black-owned businesses are also less able to access government aid since they are less likely to have preexisting relationships with bigger banks that distribute loans and are more likely to be targets of racially discriminatory lending practices. For example, compared with black business owners who requested loans during the COVID-19 pandemic, white requesters were offered more loan options and more encouragement to apply for them. Consequently, more black businesses stopped operating during the pandemic; this stoppage is expected to have negative economic impact on the business owners themselves as well as the people living in cities and neighborhoods where black businesses are located—because these businesses employ a higher proportion of black employees than white businesses (Serwer, 2020).

> "In terms of wealth, America is now the most unequal country in the industrialized world."
>
> —RICH BENJAMIN, AUTHOR, *SEARCHING FOR WHITOPIA*

Reflection 7.2

Prior to reading this chapter, were you aware of the distinction between income and wealth? If so, was your understanding of that distinction similar to the distinction you have just read?

Root Causes for Racial Gaps in Income and Wealth

The gaps in income and wealth between whites and blacks in America today has its origins in the slavery when blacks worked for no wages at all. In fact, most of the enormous wealth accumulated in America prior to the Emancipation Proclamation was built up through almost a century of free labor obtained from unpaid slaves. In 1860, for example, 80 percent of America's gross national product was tied to slavery and two-thirds of the wealthiest Americans lived in the slaveholding South (Davis, 2010). After slavery was abolished in 1863, some Northern members of Congress argued that portions of the estates owned by wealthy Southern Confederates should be provided to freed black slaves as a small form of compensation for centuries of forced labor without wages. Northern Congressmen supported their argument by noting that after the American Revolution in 1776 that emancipated United States from England, white soldiers received post-war grants to purchase land, but not black soldiers—not even those recognized for distinguished military service. In fact, four of five enslaved blacks who served in the American Revolution were forced back into slavery after the war ended (Wise, 2011).

Adding insult to injury, once the Civil War ended, freed slaves in the South were subjected to "Black Codes"—laws adopted by Southern states that were intentionally designed to maintain control of the black labor force by restricting blacks' employment options almost exclusively to plantation labor. These laws also made it illegal for blacks to acquire their own land and permitted whites in some southern states to engage in a practice called "whitecapping"—driving blacks from areas not dominated by white plantation owners and confiscating the land they had occupied (Anderson, 2016).

Thus, the only employment option for freed blacks was to sign annual labor contracts with plantation, mill, or mine owners. These contracts contained clauses that forbade blacks from securing better wages and working condition from any other employer; if they decided to leave, they were jailed for breach of contract. Freed blacks were also banned from jobs that involved specialized work skills they acquired and used as slaves, such as carpentry or blacksmithing. Furthermore, they were prohibited from hunting and fishing, thus ensuring they remained totally dependent on whites for their economic and physical survival (Anderson, 2016).

Consequently, most freed slaves ended up working as sharecroppers, which required that they work for low wages or a share of the crop they harvested on land owned by whites. Wages were not paid until the end of the year to prevent black laborers from seeking employment elsewhere and the wages they received frequently were so-called "shared" wages—not a flat and fair salary, but a share of the harvested crop's profit for the year. If the harvest was poor, black workers received paltry payments or no payment at all for their year's work. Furthermore, black sharecroppers were required to purchase all their work supplies and food items from their landowners (often at inflated prices and interest rates) who often defrauded them by imposing arbitrary fines for "poor work" and by capitalizing on their inability to determine if they were being cheated because of their illiteracy. As a result, black sharecroppers often were left with little pay or ended up in debt at the end of the growing season (Anderson, 2016).

So, in effect, the old system of slavery was transformed into a new system of economic subjugation enforced by intimidation. Blacks who were allegedly "free" were still forced to engage in plantation labor, but unlike slaves who didn't pay for the land they worked on, sharecroppers had to rent plots of land on which to labor and had to pay for necessities they didn't have to pay for as slaves, such as clothing, housing, and food. After the Civil War, a Northern journalist visiting the South noted "the only difference between freedom and slavery is that then [during slavery] the negroes were obliged to work for nothing; now they have to pay for what they used to have for nothing" (Foner, 2014, p. 131).

Later, when sharecropping came to an end and blacks were given the legal right to purchase land, they then faced discrimination from the U.S. Department of Agriculture (USDA) whose local loan officers denied them credit and loans that were routinely provided to whites. This discriminatory practice led black farmers to describe the U.S.D.A. as "the last plantation" (Bittman, 2021). Thus, blacks emerged from slavery without a legal right to purchase land, and after that right was finally granted, they lacked the income and ability to obtain credit to purchase, even at the very low prices for land that existed after the Civil War (Foner, 2014). It's ironic that blacks own only two percent of agricultural land in America today (Gilbert et al., 2002) despite the fact that their ancestors tilled the soil, cultivated the crops, and built the vast agricultural wealth of the South.

The Great Migration

During World War I (1914–1918), "The Great Migration" took place in which large numbers of black Americans migrated from rural farmlands in the South to urban areas of the North, hoping to take advantage of new job opportunities created by the war industry. Blacks were eager to escape the South because of its intensely discriminating "Jim Crow" laws and its loss of employment opportunities due to the mechanization of agriculture. Furthermore, blacks could earn wages working at industrial jobs in the North that far exceeded the wages they received for agricultural work in the South. A black autoworker in Detroit, for example, could earn in one week than what a prosperous black sharecropper could earn in more than two months in the South (Bates, 2012).

In response to the growing number of black workers leaving the South for the North, Southern states did whatever they could to prevent blacks from leaving to find better employment opportunities elsewhere. Northern-bound trains were blocked, their schedules were disrupted, ticketed black passengers were dragged off trains, and laws were passed that empowered police to arrest blacks for vagrancy if they were found trying to board northern-bound trains. Additional laws were passed that allowed Southern law officers to arrest Northern labor agents who came south to recruit black workers that were needed to meet the North's growing demands for industrial production. Meanwhile, World War I was intensifying, furthering the demand for the manufacturing of industrial products needed for military use that were critical for winning the war. Yet, by blocking blacks from departing for th North, Southern capitalists and political leaders placed a higher priority on their local economic interests than supporting the national war effort and allowing blacks the opportunity to earn higher wages elsewhere (Anderson, 2016).

Blacks who managed to leave the South for Northern cities often encountered employment racial discrimination and racist ideas similar to those they left behind in the South. Blacks were placed at the very bottom of the working class, below pre-War immigrants from Southern and Eastern Europe who were already in Northern cities and were members of unions that blocked blacks from certain trades. Yet these unions welcomed poor Southern whites who also migrated to the North looking for better-paying industrial jobs and who often brought their Jim Crow-based racial prejudices with them. In fact, the growing number of blacks that migrated North seeking employment actually served to elevate the status of poor Northern whites and the acceptance of poor European white immigrants. As Wilkerson (2010) describes it, "Black southerners stepped into a hierarchy that assigned them a station beneath everyone else, no matter that their families had been in the county for centuries. Their arrival unwittingly diverted anti-immigrant antagonism their way, as they were an even less favored outsider group than the [European] immigrants they encountered in the North and helped make formerly ridiculed groups more acceptable by comparison" (p. 419).

Northern industries took advantage of the large influx of blacks seeking employment by hiring them at lower wages and using them as union strikebreakers. Once the strikes were over, black migrants were resented even more by white union workers and were often subjected to violence. For instance, a major labor riot erupted in East Saint Louis in

1917, during which a carload of whites fired shots into black homes. The next day, a full-scale riot took place, during which black men were clubbed, stabbed, and hung from telephone poles (Wilkerson, 2010).

For the minority of blacks who found work in urban areas after the abolition of slavery, the only jobs available to them were manual laborers, servants, or porters. They received wages much lower than whites, experienced unemployment rates far higher than whites, and had no opportunities for job advancement or upward socioeconomic mobility (Richardson, 2018). Anti-black discriminatory employment practices continued well into the 20th century. Through the mid-1950s, employment agencies and newspapers listed openings for "colored" and "white" applicants; the colored agencies and ads almost always announcing jobs calling for domestic and service workers (Sugrue, 2005). Once hired, employers often took advantage of blacks' limited employment options to hire them for lower-wage unskilled or semiskilled work that involved the least desirable and most dangerous work (Wilkerson, 2020). One auto company employer hired blacks only to work in the dangerous paint room, saying that "some jobs white folks will not do so they have to take niggers in, particularly duce work—spraying paint on car bodies. This soon kills a white man." When asked if it also kills black men, the employer said: "It shortens their lives; it cuts them down, but they're just niggers" (Widick, 1976, p. 54). These twentieth-century Northern employment practices reflected long-held practices of legally guaranteeing "white" jobs, dating back to slavery laws that stipulated that for every "six Negroes" on a plantation, at least one white worker had to be hired and trained for a skilled job (Allen, 1997).

White union workers also supported the practice of limiting blacks' job opportunities by engaging in wildcat strikes whenever employers hired or upgraded black workers to jobs that had been restricted to whites (Sugrue, 2005). When white-only unions became illegal in 1964, blacks did not receive compensation for their previously suppressed wages (Rothstein, 2017) and received and no credit for the seniority they had built up over many years of work (Kendi, 2016). Furthermore, union discrimination continued despite it being technically prohibited by law. For instance, in 1967, no skilled black workers were hired to work on the building of San Francisco's Bare Area Rapid Transit System (BART). The contractor building BART said he was "committed to equal opportunity" but was unwilling to stop the discrimination because it might provoke a union work stoppage and delay completion of the project. No penalty was imposed on the BART contractor despite federal regulations stipulating that a contractor could be terminated for discrimination (Rothstein, 2017). The fact that events such as these were taking place in places like San Francisco and other western and northern cities clearly demonstrates that systemic racism was not just a "southern" problem; it was a *national* problem.

Deindustrialization

Prior to 1970, inner-city workers without advanced education could find industrial employment close to home. Thereafter, jobs began shifting away from America's cities—a phenomenon referred to as deindustrialization. This shift dramatically damaged black employment opportunities. One study revealed that in 1970, more than 70 percent of all blacks working in urban areas held blue-collar jobs; by 1987, black employment in these areas had dropped sharply to 28 percent (Kasarda, 1990). Employment opportunities began shifting to America's growing suburbs (Benjamin, 2009), creating a "spatial mismatch" between where job growth was taking place and where black job seekers lived

(Holzer, 1991). Information about job opportunities in the distant suburbs is less likely to reach residents of the inner city, and even if it did, the costs incurred to get there—in terms of both transportation time and money—were often prohibitive, particularly for workers in minimum wage-paying jobs (Pager, 2007). The government spent billions to build interstate highways and freeways through America's inner cities, but insufficient funds were allotted to build affordable transportation networks that urban blacks could use to travel to and from the growing number of suburban jobs. Blacks who did manage to secure work in the suburbs were left with less disposable income than their white co-workers because of their higher commuting costs from the central city to the outer suburbs (Rothstein, 2017). One black male eventually had to quit his suburban job because, as he put it, "I was spending more money getting to work than I earned working" (quoted in Alexander, 2020, p. 188).

Current Racial Gaps in Employment

In addition to the growing relocation of jobs from the city to suburbia, jobs began shifting to foreign countries—where employers could hire workers at much lower rates than they could in United States (Milkman, 1997). Further compounding the loss of urban employment opportunities were advances in technology that enabled machines to do many of the jobs once performed by unskilled or semi-skilled workers (Wilson, 1996). The emergence of technology created a new knowledge-based economy that required workers with higher levels of education and who had the advantage of attending schools that prepared them for college, which were not the segregated, poorly funded schools attended by black children in inner cities (Irons, 2002).

The combination of the growing use of technology and the relocation of jobs to suburbs and other nations had dramatic negative impact on black employment and income. In 1954, the unemployment rates of black and white youth were about equal. By 1984, the unemployment rate of white youth increased slightly, but among black youth, it almost quadrupled (Duster, 1997). According to Michelle Alexander (2020), "This was *not* due to a major change in black values, behavior, or culture; this dramatic shift was the result of deindustrialization [declining industrial activity in the city], globalization, and technological advancement. Urban factories shut down as our nation transitioned to a service economy [and] African Americans were trapped in jobless ghettos" (p. 271).

Since the early 1970s, unemployment rates among low-income blacks have continued to rise. This increase can be traced to increased racial segregation of blacks in inner city areas at the same time that city-located business and job opportunities shifted to the suburbs (Bowman et al., 2004). These developments compounded decades of previous discriminatory labor practices that tracked black males into low-paid machinery jobs, many of which now have been eliminated by automation, restructuring, or relocating manufacturing jobs in other countries. Today, the unemployment rate of black teens and young adults is about twice as high as it is for whites, particularly in low-income urban neighborhoods where there are few business establishments. Young inner-city blacks now have fewer job options and must compete with older blacks for entry-level positions (Eberhardt, 2019).

The COVID-19 pandemic is expected to further widen the black–white employment gap because compared with whites, more blacks and other people of color lost their jobs during the pandemic (Levey, 2020). It is noteworthy that among Americans with similar levels of education, unemployment rates are higher for blacks than higher than whites, suggesting that these differences have to do with their race, not to differences in their educational qualifications (Wilson, 2015).

Reflection 7.3

Has the COVID-19 pandemic affected the employment of any members of your family? Do you think that family's race has had any impact on whether or not the pandemic affected their employment?

Hiring Bias

In addition to the aforementioned factors, racial bias in hiring practices also contributes to higher black unemployment rates. In a classic and extensive study designed to detect racial bias in the hiring process, researchers took job ads from newspapers in two major cities and constructed fictitious resumes so that the applicants' qualifications and experiences closely matched the job requirements. The applicants were also given fictitious first names that sounded white (e.g., Brad and Jill) or black (e.g., Jamal and Tamika). Results of the study revealed that job applicants with black-sounding names received 50 percent fewer callbacks than those with white-sounding names in both cities where the ads were placed (Boston and Chicago). This difference was found for all job categories (clerical, administrative assistant, sales, and customers service) and for both entry-level and management positions (Bertrand & Mullainathan, 2004). Similar results were reported in a meta-analysis of multiple studies that involved more than 54,000 job applicants applying for more than 25,000 jobs. This synthesis of multiple studies revealed that whites received 36% more callbacks than blacks and 24% more than Latinos. These results held true for both male and female applicants, applicants with different levels of education, and applicants seeking employment in different job categories (Quillian et al., 2017).

Even if job applicants are not intentionally discriminated against in the hiring process, research reveals that people of color are still denied equal access to jobs, particularly higher-paying positions, because many of these jobs are obtained through word of mouth. This networking opportunity (sometimes referred to as "social capital") advantages job applicants who live and socialize with people holding similar positions and with people who make hiring decisions—who are still predominantly white. As discussed in chapter 4, research shows that employers in most organizations are more likely to perceive applicants with characteristics similar to themselves as being better qualified (Harper, 2012) and are more likely to hire these applicants (Elliott & Smith, 2008; Royster, 2003). Eberhardt (2019) describes this process as being "skewed toward prioritizing a comfortable fit and away from valuing differences. They [employers] are practicing in-group favoritism . . . and that's the sort of mind-set that allows bias to flourish, under the radar and unchecked" (pp. 269–270). Even if people of color detect or strongly suspect they may have been subjected to racial bias in the hiring process, research shows they are unlikely to make a claim or win a claim, particularly if they are low-wage workers who lack the financial or political resources to do so (Pager, 2007).

Reflection 7.4

Have you or your family members ever experienced racial bias in hiring that increased or decreased the chances of being hired for a position? If yes, why? If no, why not?

Conclusion

Black–white differences in unemployment, income, and wealth that exist today are deeply rooted in political policies, economic developments, and employment practices that have either intentionally or inadvertently disadvantaged blacks, particularly blacks living in America's inner cities. These policies and developments reduced blacks' access to employment and fair wages, while leaving them more vulnerable to employment layoffs, less eligible for unemployment benefits if laid off, and less able to acquire the political power needed to improve their economic conditions (Anderson, 2008; Sugrue, 2005).

Another major consequence of racially discriminatory employment and wage-earning opportunities is that it has left working-class blacks without the fiscal resources to choose to live in places other than segregated, low-income communities. Political policies and economic practices that helped create income and wealth disparities between blacks and whites have also contributed to systemic racism in home-ownership opportunities and residential choice (Rothstein, 2016), which will be discussed next.

The Housing System: Residential Choice and Home Ownership Opportunities

The historical roots of systemic racism in housing can be traced back to slavery when blacks were housed against their will in separate slave quarters owned by white plantation owners. Even free blacks in the North at the time did not have the legal right to own their property (Northrup, 2012). After the Civil War, Thaddeus Stevens, a Republican statesman, urged the federal government to transfer portions of land owned by wealthy former Confederates to just-freed slaves to provide them with some small compensation for the many decades of forced, non-paid labor foisted on them and their ancestors. Stevens argued that civic justice alone would not promote equality for blacks unless it was accompanied by economic justice. He warned that without economic empowerment, freed black men would again find themselves at the mercy of their former masters. Stevens' proposal was not approved by Congress; furthermore, freed blacks were not even allowed to purchase their own land to farm in the rural South. Consequently, many blacks migrated to urban areas in hopes of finding an employment alternative to plantation labor and better living conditions. Blacks who made this move had to compete with already-present city residents who had long-held jobs; consequently, the only employment option for black urban migrants involved menial, low-wage jobs that didn't pay them enough to afford decent housing. Their only housing option was to live in shanty towns on the outskirts of the city. This resulted in the creation of a new, segregated urban geography that consisted of the main town, inhabited primarily by whites who occupied the best-built homes and what came to be called "free town," also referred to as "Liberia," which consisted of wretched log cabins occupied by blacks (Foner, 2014).

White Resistance to Residential Integration

During World War I, large numbers of black Americans migrated from the rural South to urban areas in the North to find employment in the growing number of jobs created by the war industry. By the time World War I ended, the number of blacks that had moved North far exceeded the amount of housing available to them. A study of housing in the Chicago area in 1917 revealed that on a typical day, only 50 houses were available for 664 black applicants. This combination of low supply and high demand resulted in blacks having to pay exorbitant rents for dilapidated, overcrowded apartment dwellings. Black professionals, tired of living in cramped conditions and paying exorbitantly high prices for low-quality housing, attempted to move into the only middle-class homes available, which were located in white neighborhoods. Their attempts to reside in those neighborhoods were countered by intense white resistance and white-led race riots that drove blacks back to the overcrowded slums. For instance, Dr. Alexander Turner, a black surgeon, tried to move into a white area in Detroit. Within five hours, he was assailed by a rock- and brick-throwing mob, after which he was forced at gunpoint to sign a deed relinquishing ownership of the property. The police did nothing about the incident—other than escorting Dr. Turner and his family back to the black part of town after the riot (Bates, 2012).

During World War II, a second wave of blacks migrated from the rural South to the North to seek the growing number of industrial jobs opening up in urban areas. Similar to what took place during World War I, Northern whites fiercely resisted their residential integration. Using military-like language, they took it upon themselves to "defend" their residential areas against the black "invasion," often referring to their neighborhoods as "battlegrounds" where they would fight to protect their property. Associations of white homeowners elected block "captains" and formed community organizations that functioned both as social clubs and neighborhood militia. These groups were formed not only to defend white turf, but also to "protect" white women and innocent children—which stemmed from prejudicial beliefs about black hypersexuality (Sugrue, 2005).

White resistance to black integration often involved staging large-sized demonstrations in front of homes that blacks purchased and vandalizing black property by breaking windows, splashing paint on building walls, tearing down fences, trampling gardens, and setting fires. In Chicago, during the first five years after World War II, there were over 350 reported incidents of violence directed toward blacks attempting to rent or buy resi-

Billboard erected in a Detroit neighborhood, just before arrival of the first black families in 1942.
Source: Library of Congress

dences; in 1947 alone, there were 46 attacks on black homes in white communities that bordered black neighborhoods (Rothstein, 2017). Whites also threatened "race traitors"—whites who rented or sold property to blacks. In one instance, they threatened to boycott a department store if its owner did not fire a white woman who had sold her house to a black family.

Even blacks who could afford to buy homes in middle-class white neighborhoods faced intense resistance. The fact that whites resisted the presence of middle-class blacks in their neighborhoods shows that their resistance was not about people of lower socioeconomic status entering their community or fearing that neighbors of "lower-class" standing would reduce their property value. Instead their resistance was based entirely on race (Rothstein, 2017).

Consider This...

In 1951, Harvey Clark, a black bus driver and military veteran, attempted to rent an apartment in Cicero—an all-white Chicago suburb. He and his wife (both college-educated) and their two children had been living in a crammed, two-room apartment in a segregated black neighborhood. They were paying rent that was about 50% higher than tenants in white neighborhoods paid for the same amount of living space. Wanting to get out of their overcrowded and overpriced apartment, they found a place with five times more space in suburban Cicero that costs just $4 more per month. When the Clark's moving truck arrived in Cicero, white protesters met them and tried to stop him from unloading the truck. Chicago police officers sided with the protestors and would not let him move in, threatening to arrest him if he did. After being forced to leave, Clark got a court order to block the police from interfering with his right to live there and to receive protection from whites who were threatening him and his family. After he got the court order, the Clark family tried to move in again and they were met by about 100 housewives who heckled him and a group of teenagers who pelted his apartment with stones. Police ignored his court order and made no effort to protect his family. Gradually, the number of protesters expanded into a mob of 4,000 Cicero residents who then started a riot, raided his apartment, burned the couple's marriage license and the children's baby pictures, threw all the family's belongings out the window and onto the ground and set them on fire. The National Guard had to be called in to restore order. More than 100 rioters were arrested, but not one was indicted by the county grand jury. The jury did, however, indict Mr. Clark, his real estate agent, his attorney, the white landlady who rented him the apartment and her landlady's attorney—all of whom were charged with inciting a riot and conspiring to lower property values. The Cicero riot attracted worldwide attention and condemnation from citizens in other countries.

Sources: Rothstein (2016); Wilkerson (2020)

Police continued to tolerate and even abet resistance to racial integration throughout the twentieth century. For instance, in 1964, when an apartment was rented by black college students in Bridgeport, Illinois—an all-white suburb of Chicago that was home to Chicago mayor Richard Daley—a mob gathered around the apartment and peppered it with rocks. Instead of defending the students, the Chicago police entered the apartment while the students were in class, removed their belongings from the apartment, and informed them when they returned from school that they had been evicted. Local politicians also regularly endorsed white resistance to integration. When the mayor of a Detroit suburb was first elected 1941 (and reelected thirteen times through 1973), he pledged to keep his suburb "lily white" making a crude statement at a public form about why blacks should stay in the inner-city slums and stay out of white suburbs: "When you remove garbage from the backyard, you don't dump it in your neighbor's" (quoted in Sugrue, 2005, p. 76).

Racial Zoning Ordinances

In addition to violent white resistance to black families from moving into their neighborhoods, local housing policies were put in place to block integration. One such policy involved the adoption of "racial zoning ordinances" that prohibited African Americans from buying homes on blocks where whites were a majority (and vice versa). In 1910, Baltimore became the first city to adopt this policy. The city's mayor at the time explained the policy in a way that clearly revealed its racist nature: "Blacks should be quarantined in isolated slums in order to reduce the incidence of civil disturbance, to prevent the spread of communicable disease into the nearby White neighborhoods, and to protect property values among the White majority" (quoted in Perry, 2020, p. 69). In 1917, the Supreme Court struck down explicit racial zoning laws, but they were quickly replaced with more subtle, but equally discriminatory "exclusionary zoning" regulations that restricted neighborhood housing to single-family homes. Because of racial gaps in wealth, such homes were unaffordable to lower-income people of color, thereby enabling whites to keep them out of their residential areas.

Exclusionary zoning ordinances still exist in all parts of the country today, particularly in the form of neighborhood zoning agreements that only allow building of single-family homes in a neighborhood, thus preventing the building of more duplexes and apartments that would be affordable to lower-income people of color. In 2020, the California Assembly proposed a bill to help with the state's long-standing housing shortage of available housing for low- and middle-class families (many of whom are families of color) that would permit the building of more affordable duplexes in suburbs dominated by single-family zoning ordinances. The bill drew strong criticism from white homeowners who said it would "change the character" of their neighborhood. Even the 45th President of the United States opposed eliminating single-family zoning, claiming it would lead to the demise of the suburbs and bring crime to suburban neighborhoods—despite the fact that research shows little or no link between building more affordable housing in a neighborhood and more neighborhood crime (Khouri, 2020b). Restricting neighborhoods exclusively to single-family housing continues to be a hotly contested issue in California and other parts of the country. However, lawmakers in some areas of the country have passed laws that ban exclusive single-family zoning, such as Oregon, Minneapolis, and Berkeley (Logan, 2021).

Restrictive Covenants

Another discriminatory policy that has been used to preserve white residential segregation are "restrictive covenants"—written agreements among all homeowners in a neighborhood that were designed to maintain the neighborhood's "desirable residential characteristics." Similar to zoning ordinances, restrictive covenants prohibited building of multiple residences in neighborhoods with single-family homes, but covenants also prohibited construction of commercial buildings, division of residences into rental units, and renting, selling, or transferring property to "any person not of the Caucasian race." If the covenant was violated, the violator could be sued or forced to move (Eberhardt, 2019; Sugrue, 2005). For instance, in 1942, the Oklahoma Supreme Court blocked a black American's purchase of a home that was restricted by a racial covenant and then charged him for all court and attorney fees, including the costs incurred by the while seller. In hundreds of cases like this, judges did not strike down restrictive covenants as a violation of blacks' constitutional rights, claiming they were just "private agreements." Interestingly, however, the courts did rule that it was illegal for covenants to exclude other people of color, such as Mexican-Americans, because they were judged to be of the "Caucasian" race (Rothstein, 2017). Such was the case in 1945 when a white homeowner in the Detroit area filed a racial-covenant suit against a middle-class black couple who tried to buy a house in his all-white neighborhood. The white homeowner claimed that the husband "appears to have colored features" and the wife "appears to be a mulatto type." The couple's defense attorney argued that "there is no simple way to determine whether a man is a member of the Mongoloid, Caucasoid, or Negroid race" but the county court ruled that the couple was "colored" and, therefore, could be excluded by the racial covenant. Thus, racial covenants were used to systematically discriminate against and segregate only people who were judged to be "black" (Sugrue, 2005).

Racially discriminatory covenants were officially outlawed by the federal government in 1948, but the law did not stop banks and private companies to continued adopting restrictive covenants in all parts of the country where they remained in place until the 1970s (Feagin, 2005). In fact, although restrictive covenants are longer unenforceable, the original deeds of homeowners today still contain restrictive-covenant clauses that prohibit purchase of the home by "non-Caucasians" (Rothstein, 2017).

> "If you inquire into the history of the metropolitan area in which you live, you will probably find ample evidence of how the federal, state, and local governments unconstitutionally used housing policy to create or reinforce segregation in ways that still survive."
> —RICHARD ROTHSTEIN, AUTHOR OF *THE COLOR OF LAW*

 ## Consider This…

In 1957, Willie Mays, a popular hall-of-fame baseball player, attempted to buy a home in San Francisco. He found a newly built house to his liking in an all-white neighborhood. The developer agreed to sell Mays the new home but then backed out of the agreement after neighbors learned of the potential sale and started objecting. One white homeowner in the neighborhood openly stated: "Certainly I objected. I happen to have quite a few pieces of property in that area and I stand to lose a lot if colored people move in. I certainly wouldn't like to have a colored family near me." The mayor of San Francisco learned about it and publicly criticized the developer's decision to succumb to the neighbors' objections and not sell the home to Mays. After the mayor intervened, the developer reversed course and offered the home to Mays for $37,500—$5,000 more than was asked of a potential white buyer. Mays accepted the offer, paid in cash, and moved into the house. A year and half after the sale, a bottle containing a racial hate note was thrown through the front window of his home.

Sources: LaBounty (2000); O'Rourke (2016)

Restrictive racial discrimination has also been practiced by homeowners using the Airbnb advertising platform to rent their homes to travelers who are visiting their part of the country. Unlike booking a hotel, where the traveler chooses where to stay, Airbnb homeowners decide who get to temporarily reside in their homes based on the applicant's personal profile and guest photo, and the hosts can accept or reject an applicant's request to book their home. In 2016, many blacks posted stories on Twitter, Facebook, and other social media about how frequently they applied to stay at homes advertised on the Airbnb platform and were told that the home was currently unavailable. However, when they asked white friends to book the same residence for the same time period, it was advertised as being available. Some blacks tried posing as whites by changing their photograph and name; when they did, they found they could book places that were previously told was unavailable when they applied as blacks (Eberhardt, 2019). These anecdotal reports from black families have been confirmed by researchers at Harvard who made up guest profiles for Airbnb applicants with names that sounded black or white. Then they used these profiles to apply to almost 6,400 Airbnb listings in five different parts of the country. In each part of the country where the profiles were sent, for every priced property being advertised (high cost or low), whether it be for renting a room or an entire house, black applicants were less likely to be accepted than white applicants (Edelman et al., 2017). When Airbnb conducted its own investigation, their researchers also found evidence that requests from blacks were the least likely to be accepted. To address the problem, Airbnb adopted and encouraged its applicants to use an "instant book" option similar to that used by hotels. This option informs the applicant if the accommodation is available, the applicant pays for it and books the residence without having to submit a guest photo or personal profile. When this option was used, Airbnb reported that racial differences in acceptance rates virtually disappeared (Eberhardt, 2019).

Reflection 7.5

Would you say that the neighborhood where your family lives is racially segregated? If yes, why? If no, why not?

The Federal Government's Role in Promoting Racial Segregation in Housing

In addition to *de facto* segregation practiced by American citizens, the American federal government promoted *de jure* segregation by adopting discriminatory federal housing policies. Alarmed by the Russian revolution in 1917, U.S. government officials came to believe that communism could be prevented from taking hold in America if many white Americans became homeowners. If citizens owned property, it was thought that they would become more invested in the nation's capitalistic system. Thus, the government launched an "Own Your Own Home" campaign, which included widespread dissemination of pamphlets on "How to Own Your Own Home" while avoiding "racial strife." The government encouraged racial homogeneity by urging potential home buyers to consider the "general type of people living in the neighborhood" before purchasing a house. In 1930, President Hoover held a presidential conference on home building and home ownership during which he announced that single-family homes were "expressions or racial longing." In conjunction with the conference, the government published a "Better Home Homes Manual," which stated that apartments were the worst kind of housing and were frequently overcrowded because of the "ignorant racial habit" of African Americans (Rothstein, 2017). This was the federal government's first attempt to exclude blacks from single-family suburban living. It was later reinforced and extended by federal housing policies implemented as part of the "New Deal" (1933–1938), which will be discussed next.

The New Deal and Redlining

During the Great Depression of the 1930s, many families owning homes could not make their mortgage payments and were on the verge of eviction; other families couldn't afford homes at all. To help increase homeownership, part of the New Deal created by President

Roosevelt included low-interest, government-backed loan programs were created to provide fiscal support to help existing homeowners pay their mortgages and help new home-buyers purchase a home. This led to a real estate practice called "redlining"—the marking of red lines on a map to indicate neighborhoods where banks would not invest or lend money, many of which were in neighborhoods occupied predominantly by African Americans (Shapiro, 1993). Color-coded maps were created for every metropolitan area in United States, with neighborhoods being colored red if they were thought to be high-risk loan areas because houses in these areas would likely lose value and have a higher rate of loan default. Reflecting the prevailing residential racial segregation practices at the time, if the neighborhood was black, racially mixed, or even if there were white neighborhoods nearby that might become integrated in the near future, these red-lined areas were deemed to be too great a risk to offer buyers low-interest, government-backed loans. Lenders claimed that these red-lining practices were justified because it was too great an economic risk to issue loans in poorer neighborhoods since there would be a much higher rate of default. However, lenders also red-lined neighborhoods occupied by middle-class black families and denied loans to well-off blacks who wanted to move into all-white neighborhoods, as well as to developers who wanted to build new homes for blacks that would be located near white neighborhoods (Sugrue, 2005). These practices strongly suggest that redlining was based more on racial discrimination than economic considerations.

> "The federal government played a direct and deliberate role in creating segregated spaces: refusing to back mortgage loans in racially mixed neighborhoods, subsidizing private development of all-white suburbs, and restricting GI Bill housing benefits so that black military veterans could buy homed only in minority communities. Discrimination—not income or choice or convenience—dictated where black people could live."
>
> —DR. JENNIFER EBERHARDT, PROFESSOR OF PSYCHOLOGY, STANFORD UNIVERSITY

Redlining real-estate practices were also encouraged by a manual issued by the U.S. government's Federal Housing Administration (FHA)—an agency responsible for disseminating low-interest loans to homeowners. The manual instructed real estate appraisers to give higher eligibility ratings to neighborhoods where there was "protection against some adverse influences [and] among adverse influences . . . are infiltration of inharmonious racial or nationality groups." The handbook also warned real estate brokers to guard against "a colored man of means who was giving his children a college education and thought they were entitled to live among whites" (Rothstein, 2016, pp. 65 & 228). Government-backed loans were also denied to black homebuilders that were granted to white homebuilders of similar socioeconomic status who were planning to build homes in white neighborhoods (Sugrue, 2005). Rothstein (2017) notes that government policies which helped support racial segregation in San Francisco were "particularly striking because, in contrast to metropolitan areas like Chicago, Detroit, Cleveland or Baltimore, northern California had few African Americans . . . . The government was not just following preexisting racial patterns; it was imposing segregation where it hadn't previously taken root" (p. 14).

The practice of redlining continued until it was made illegal by passage of the Community Reinvestment Act in 1977 (Perry, 2020). However, by that time, New Deal-era reforms had al-

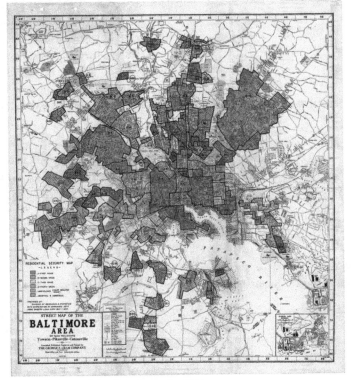

Source: Federal Home Owners' Loan Corporation, 1937

ready created large disparities in homeownership by backing mortgage loans for millions of whites while tacitly reusing to insure mortgages for black Americans and explicitly discouraging housing loans in integrated neighborhoods.

Although redlining is technically illegal today, real estate agents still use racially coded terms to steer white homebuyers away from "sketchy" neighborhoods and toward "good" neighborhoods" or "gated communities" (Benjamin, 2009; DiAngelo, 2018). Studies conducted by the Department of Housing and Urban Development have shown that real estate agents are more likely to steer blacks to specific neighborhoods, show blacks fewer residential options, quote them higher rents, and offer them less favorable financing packages (Turner et al., 2002, 2013).

Government-Sanctioned Housing Discrimination during World War II and the Postwar Years

When the United States was preparting for the Second World War, Congress passed the Lanham Act in 1940 to finance needed housing for workers in the defense industries. These housing facilities were typically built in suburban areas and were reserved for white workers, which left blacks with no residential option other than living in already-congested urban slums where their geographic access to war-industry jobs was limited. In some cities, housing was provided for black workers, but only in segregated settings. Even in rare cases where the government attempted to build integrated housing, these attempts were resisted by white members in the local community and white military leaders. For instance, one massive governmental-funded project was once planned to house 14,000 workers and their families near a naval shipbuilding yard outside of San Francisco, awarding apartments not on the basis of race but on a first-come-first-serve basis. However, navy officials strongly resisted the idea, claiming that it would cause racial conflict among the workers and interfere with ship construction and efficiency of ship repair. Local officials then changed their plans and housed blacks in separate, segregated quarters.

By the end of WW II, these wartime policies along with the previous discriminatory housing policies associated with the New Deal combined to create or exacerbate racial segregation in metropolitan areas throughout the United States (Rothstein, 2017). After the great Northern migration of blacks had been completed in 1970, sociologists were using the term "hypersegregation" to describe how residential segregation had become so extreme and extensive that blacks and whites rarely had contact with one another other than their place of work. By 1980, the most segregated areas in the United States were the ten cities where most blacks had settled after migrating north: Chicago, Detroit, Cleveland, Milwaukee, Newark, Gary (Indiana), Philadelphia, Los Angeles, Baltimore, and St. Louis (Wilkerson, 2010).

Another negative consequence of racial segregation policies for blacks was their having to pay rental costs for apartments up to 50% higher than whites because of the higher demand and lower supply of black housing (Wilkerson, 2010). Landlords often demanded weekly or biweekly payments; if those payments were not met, the landlords quickly found other housing-desperate black tenants to take their place (Sugrue, 2005). In 1946, one national magazine article described a Chicago building where the landlord divided two stories of a storefront building into six cubicles, each of which housed a black family. The total monthly rent collected by the landlord was equal to what he would have received for renting a luxury department on Chicago's "Gold Coast" along Lake Michigan. In a

1947 Supreme Court case involving racial discrimination in housing, justices reviewed multiple studies submitted by the plaintiff and concluded that blacks were being "forced to pay higher rents and housing costs by the semi-monopoly which segregation fosters" (Rothstein, 2017, p. 173).

The GI Bill and the Development of Racially Segregated Suburbs

After World War II ended, the federal government passed the GI Bill to provide returning veterans with financial assistance to attend college and obtain low-interest home loans. The bill was designed to be "color blind" so that its benefits could be experienced by veterans of all races who served America during the war. However, politicians from southern states insisted that the implementation of the Bill not be administered by the federal government, but by local political officials. These local officials then proceeded to implement the Bill in a way that denied black GIs (veterans) access to state universities and allowed local bank executives to deny black and Latino GIs access to low-interest home loans. Daryl Smith (2015) notes that "implementation of the housing policies of the GI Bill is a perfect example of institutional racism under cover of state's rights" (p. 38). However, systemic racism triggered by the GI Bill was not restricted to the South; it occurred in northern states as well. One black World War II veteran in New York owned a trucking company that transported building material for homes being developed in Levittown, a suburb of New York City. The veteran and his family members were denied the opportunity to buy a home in the very area where his company had helped build numerous homes—despite the fact that he had the same socioeconomic status as returning white veterans who were able to buy homes in Levittown. The refusal of white developers to sell suburban homes to blacks was not just a matter of personal prejudice. If they chose to build homes for blacks in suburban areas, the federal government would have refused to subsidize them.

Racially segregated suburbs were designed in this way across the country for almost two decades after World War II. In effect, the U.S. government's Federal Housing Administration (FHA) implemented a nationwide policy that solidified segregation in all metropolitan areas by not insuring mortgages for homes in black neighborhoods and by subsidizing builders for mass-production of homes built and sold only to whites. This practice continued until 1962, at which time President Kennedy issued an executive order that prohibited the use of federal funds for practices that contributed to racial discrimination in housing (Rothstein, 2017). However, by that time, the federal government had invested $120 billion in housing development and insured the mortgages of nearly one-third of all new housing in America, less than 2% of which went to people of color (Benjamin, 2009).

With the help of the GI Bill, millions of white Americans bought homes, attended colleges, found gainful employment, started business ventures, and accumulated wealth to pass on to their children. Thirty years after the passage of the GI Bill, almost 7 of 10 whites owned homes and had a net household worth of over $39,000; in contrast, black households had a net worth of less than $4,000. The GI Bill is widely considered to be the most generous social program that the U.S. government has ever provided its citizens. However, because of the way in which the Bill was organized and administered, it was also a governmental program that did the most to further widen the racial gap in wealth by denying blacks equal opportunity to purchase and own homes and accrue wealth through home equity (Katznelson, 2005). The GI Bill's failure to give blacks equal opportunity for home ownership led one researcher to make the following observation about the long-term societal consequences of the GI Bill: "There is far less resilience in a family that does not own property than in a family that can leverage assets to get through hard times. It is difficult not to speculate whether, if the GI Bill had provided as many African Americans with opportunities for home ownership and higher education as it did Whites, there would be more resiliency, stability, and equity within American society today" (Smith, 2015, p. 15).

Similarly, Andrew Khouri points out the important and enduring consequences associated with the GI Bill's discriminatory housing practices: "Black citizens were denied the same opportunity to build wealth as white citizens during the country's unprecedented post-war expansion, restricting their ability to invest in education, start businesses or pass along inheritances to their children" (Khouri, 2020a, p. A11). White children are now twice as likely to receive an inheritance from a family member than the children of blacks, and the amount white children receive through inheritance is three times that received by black children (Thompson & Suarez, 2015). What makes this racial inequity in inheritance even more disturbing is that the average black citizen today is likely to have more generations of relatives who've lived in the United States than the average white American (Feagin, 2005).

Reflection 7.6

Will you receive (or have you received) an inheritance from your parents? Do you think that your family's race will have any impact on the likelihood of your receiving an inheritance, or the amount of the inheritance you receive? If yes, why? If no, why not?

Racially Segregated Public Housing Projects

Currently, the U.S. government attempts to alleviate the cost of housing costs and expenses for people with low to moderate incomes with "public housing" programs or "subsidized housing" projects. However, the original purpose of these forms of governmental assistance was not to build affordable housing for people who were too poor; it was to build housing for people who could already afford it but not enough was available. The first federally developed housing project took place during World War I when the government built residences for defense workers near ship-building yards and ammunition plants. Blacks were excluded from these residences, including those built outside the Jim Crow South. In some cases, the federal government used public housing projects to impose racial segregation in areas where there already was racial integration. For instance, in Cleveland, the central city was once a racially integrated community where blacks lived along with Italian and Eastern European immigrants. In his autobiography, the famous black poet and playwright, Langston Hughes, recalled that when he attended high school in central Cleveland, his best friend was Polish and he dated a Jewish girl. Despite the city's racially integrated history, government-sponsored public housing projects proceeded to build separate housing facilities for whites and blacks. The quality of housing built for blacks was of poorer quality and packed into smaller areas that concentrated them into more crowded, slum-like dwellings (Rothstein, 2017).

During the Great Depression of the 1930s, only affluent Americans could afford to purchase homes or rent new apartments. To alleviate matters, as part of President Roosevelt New Deal, the government funded housing projects for the American people. Once again, the funds were used to build separate housing for blacks, or no funds were used to build black housing. In Tennessee, one government-developed village with comfortable homes was built for white workers on a government-funded construction project, while blacks were forced to occupy barren barracks at a greater distance from the construction site. When a government official was asked why this was being done, he said the town was being reserved for whites because "Negroes do not fit into the program." In New Jersey, the state governor cited "local resentment" as his reason for refusing to allow building of work residences for blacks who were participating in a government-sponsored program for unemployed youth and young adults. In Gettsyburg, Pennsylvania, when blacks were working on a government-sponsored work project to restore its historic battleground, the local government built lower-quality black quarters about 20 miles from the work site because the town's residents objected to having blacks living in the vicinity (Rothstein, 2017).

On top of these federally sanctioned segregated housing projects, local government officials often refused to permit any construction of racially integrated public housing in suburban areas within their jurisdictions, fearing that it would alienate their white constituents who believed that mixing of races in their neighborhood would result in a dramatic increase in crime. As previously mentioned, research has shown there is little or no link between the availability of subsidized housing in neighborhoods and increased criminal activity in those neighborhoods (Khouri, 2020b).

Today, federally funded housing for low-income families is used mainly to help low-income families to rent apartments in racially segregated inner cities where economic and employment opportunities are scarce (Rothstein, 2017). Whites have come to view these federally funded public housing as "Negro housing" and the financial help they give to black families as "government interference" (Sugrue, 2005)—even though it was governmental interference (public housing policies) that helped create urban ghettos in the first place.

"Identification of African Americans with slum conditions, and the resulting white flight to escape the possibility of those conditions, all had their bases in federal government policy."

—RICHARD ROTHSTEIN, AUTHOR, *THE COLOR OF LAW: A FORGOTTEN HISTORY OF HOW OUR GOVERNMENT SEGREGATED AMERICA*

Policies and Practices Leading to the Development of Urban Slums and Black Ghettos

Urban ghettos in America date back to the late 1700s when free blacks could only live legaly live in segregated sections of northern cities typically comprised of shacks and cellars, such as "Nigger Hill" in Boston, "Five Points" in New York, and "Little Africa" in Cincinnati." These race-based housing policies helped to solidify racist ideas among white citizens that they should not live with or near blacks, which further depresses the value of property in areas where blacks lived (Litwack, 1961).

During the Great Migration of the 1920s, blacks traveled to the North in hopes of escaping the South's harsh Jim Crow laws and high rates of unemployment resulting from the mechanization of agriculture, which led to poverty rates as high as 80% among black agricultural workers. Over the course of the next 50 years, roughly six million blacks left the South, transforming America's black population from one that was originally southern and rural to one that was more northern and urban. Once the first wave of black migration from the South took place, Jim Crow-like segregation policies began to spread to other parts of the country where they had not previously existed (Kendi, 2016). For instance, for decades following the Civil War, blacks lived and thrived in the state of Montana where they typically lived in integrated middle-class communities. However, in the early 1900s, blacks began to be systematically excluded from predominantly white communities in Montana by the adoption of public policies prohibiting blacks from living in white sections of town and barring blacks from being in white sections of town after dark (known as "sundown towns"). It was also not uncommon for white mobs to forcibly drive blacks out of the town's population. Similar to Montana, other smaller towns in Western and Midwestern states adopted exclusionary racial policies or drove blacks out of smaller towns, forcing blacks to move to larger cities (Rothstein, 2017).

At the same time that blacks were voluntarily moving from the South to the North to find better employment and other blacks were being involuntarily forced out of smaller towns to the cities, those cities were losing manufacturing jobs. Consequently, blacks had a difficult time finding steady jobs and stable wages. They also experienced substantially higher rates of unemployment than workers who were already living and working in Northern cities because they had no seniority. They were placed at the very back of the line for employment opportunities, and if they did find employment, they were the first to be fired when there were layoffs ("last hired, first fired"). Thus, black migrants soon became the very poorest citizens of American cities, many of whom were unable to buy a home or even to rent in desirable areas beyond the inner city. Even if they had fiscal resources to do so, discriminatory real-estate practices kept blacks out of most of the city's single-family housing market.

The combination of these factors resulted in the vast majority of black migrants ending up confined to the poorest and most densely populated parts of the city where they inhabited old, often dilapidated buildings subdivided into tiny apartments and rooming houses that were hastily and cheaply built to accommodate the large incoming black migration (Rothstein, 2017). These housing properties were typically owned and operated by absentee landlords or "slumlords" who maximized their profits by charging overpriced rents while providing minimal maintenance of their rental properties (Wilkerson, 2010). Black tenants living in the Harlem district of New York City were packed in so densely that they sometimes had to sleep in shifts—when one person woke up and left, the bed was taken over by someone else (Osofsky, 1963). These densely crowded and decaying neighborhoods contributed to white perceptions that blacks would ruin any white neighborhood they moved into and stoked bankers' fears of investing in black neighborhoods (Sugrue, 2005).

Urban Renewal and Slum Clearance Projects

From the 1950s through the 1970s, the government funded "slum clearance" projects nationwide that resulted in the demolition of thousands of inner-city black homes, apartments, and businesses. A common major slum-clearance practice was to build federally funded interstate highways and expressways through areas of the city where low-income blacks lived. For instance, when the I-10 highway was built in New Orleans during the 1960s, it cut through the city's largest black communities. One of those communities was Tremé, which at the time was the oldest free black community in the United States; it included as many as 200 black-owned businesses and a large public park used for recreation, cultural events, and family gatherings. By the time construction of the I-10 highway was completed, the park was destroyed along with hundreds of homes and businesses in what was once America's most prosperous black business district (Wise, 2011).

First enacted in 1956, these government-funded highway programs often required families to vacate within 30 days, and the families forced to vacate received no compensation or assistance for doing so. Not only were renters displaced, but so were homeowners and shopkeepers who were unable to sell their property because it would soon be demolished, they had to move without earning any revenue from property sales (Sugrue, 2005).

City officials also used urban renewal funds to revitalize their city's economy by funding businesses and developing middle- and upper-class housing projects, driving blacks from their existing urban neighborhoods deeper into inner-city ghettos and farther away from city business districts where white commuters and shoppers would feel more comfortable spending their time and money (Rothstein, 2017).

Slum conditions were further worsened by industrial and toxic wasted zoning policies that prohibited industrial plants from being built and operated in the suburbs. Thus, pollution-promoting plants were located in the inner cities, resulting in a high concentration of commercial waste treatment facilities, incinerators, and uncontrolled waste dumps in black neighborhoods across the country. Rothstein (2017) explains how these zoning policies contributed to systemic racism in housing and furthered racist beliefs about blacks:

> The frequent existence of polluting industry and toxic waste plants in African American communities, along with subdivided homes and rooming houses, contributed to giving African Americans the image of slum dwellers in the eyes of whites who lived in neighborhoods where integration might be a possibility. This, in turn, contributed to white flight when African Americans attempted to move to suburbs. Zoning thus had two faces. One face . . . attempted to keep African Americans out of white neighborhoods by making it difficult for lower-income families, large numbers of whom were African Americans, to live in expensive white neighborhoods. The other attempted to protect white neighborhoods from deterioration by ensuring that few industrial or environmentally unsafe businesses could locate in them. The first contributed to creation of exclusive white suburbs, the second to creation of urban African American slums (pp. 56–57).

> "The instruments of government-sanctioned bias—zoning restrictions, racial covenants, mortgage refusals, and a building boom in suburbs open only to whites—forced black families to crowd into undesirable areas where amenities were few, the housing stock was often decrepit or cheaply built, and the streets were lined with factories spewing industrial pollution."
> —DR. JENNIFER EBERHARDT, PROFESSOR OF PSYCHOLOGY, STANFORD UNIVERSITY

It is noteworthy that, prior to the Great Migration of blacks to Northern cities took place from the 1920s through the 1950s, there were many areas of the city where blacks and white immigrants lived together in the same neighborhoods. It was only after white backlash to the growing black population and segregationist governmental policies were enacted in Northern cities did racial integration decline and black slums and ghettos emerge (Sugrue, 2005). Gunnar Myrdal, Nobel Prize-winning urban economist and sociologist, called this the "Northern Paradox": Northerners say they are against discrimination generally but practice discrimination personally by not allowing blacks into their neighborhoods, schools, unions, and social interactions. Based on his research on Northern metropolitan areas conducted in the 1940s, Myrdal concluded that "it is the culmination of all these personal discriminations which creates the color bar in the North . . . and causes unusually severe unemployment, crowded housing conditions, crime and vice" (Myrdal, 1944).

These deteriorating urban conditions spawned black riots in Northern cities during the late 1960s. Following these riots, an 11-member Presidential Commission known as the Kerner Commission (aka, The National Advisory Commission on Civil Disorders) investigated the race riots to gain an understanding of why they occurred and how they could be prevented from happening again. The Commission reached the following conclusion: "What white Americans have never fully understood—but what the Negro can never forget—is that white society is deeply implicated in the ghetto. White institutions created it, white institutions maintain it and white society condones it" (Report on the National Advisory Commission on Civil Disorders, 1968, p. 1). Among the Commission's top recommendations offered was for the U.S. government to allocate funds to construct, new, affordable spaced-out housing units for black residents who had been forced to live in deteriorating, segregated houses and high-rise projects (Kendi, 2016).

The racially segregated, poverty-stricken ghettos that exist in inner cities throughout America today would not exist if it were not for the adoption of governmental policies that gave birth to them (Masserly & Denton, 1993; Sugrue, 2005). A summary of these key policies and practices is provided in **Box 7.1**.

Box 7.1   Governmental Policies and Practices That Supported Systemic Racism in Housing

The federal government built racially segregated public housing in cities where segregation had not previously existed, thus contributing to the creation of black city ghettos and white suburbs.

The federal government stimulated white flight from integrated cities to segregated suburbs by providing fiscal support for the development of white suburbs, then allowing these suburban areas to adopt exclusionary zoning laws that blocked black residents.

The government spent billions of dollars in tax breaks for single-family suburban homeowners, while not providing guaranteed loans for building homes in black working-class neighborhoods.

State governments endorsed and enforced racial segregation through discriminatory neighborhood association rules and restrictive covenants that barred middle-class blacks from living in previously all-white communities—even if they had the financial means to do so.

Local police agencies ignored, and often encouraged, white violence against black families that attempted to move into white neighborhoods.

Real estate agents were allowed to impose and maintain racial segregation by only showing and selling them homes to blacks in black-majority neighborhoods.

The government authorized the building of federal and state highways only through urban areas, which led to the demolition of black neighborhoods occupied by blacks—without compensation to black families and business owners for their their housing and financial losses—displacing black residents into more concentrated and impoverished sections of the inner city.

Government programs that have, and still continue to, reinforce racial segregation by only providing housing assistance to low-income blacks in already-segregated neighborhoods—the very neighborhoods that had become segregated as a result of earlier governmental policies.

Sources: Rothstein (2017); Sugrue (2005)

Furthermore, systemic racism in housing policies that helped create residential segregation have also fostered other forms of systemic racism that combine to fortify one another. As Feagin (2005) notes: "Residential segregation reinforces, even creates, segregated schools, religious, organizations, recreational facilities, and workplaces. All such segregated organizations in turn reinforce residential segregation—and thus reinforce white isolation and stereotyping of people of color" (p. 247).

"In modern America, where you live determines to a great extent the quality of your schools, your roads, [and] your access to employment."

—THOMAS SUGRUE, PROFESSOR OF HISTORY & SOCIOLOGY, UNIVERSITY OF PENNSYLVANIA

Reflection 7.7

Do your family members live in an area that would be best described as suburban, urban, or inner city? Would they prefer to live somewhere else? If yes, why? If no, why not?

Relationship between Past Governmental Housing Polices and Current Gaps in Racial Wealth

In 2014, 71% of white families lived in homes they owned compared to 41% of black families (Kendi, 2019). As Rich Benjamin (2009) notes: "Home ownership through a thirty-year mortgage has long been the primary mechanism by which most American families created wealth. So deferred home ownership opportunities have compounded economic disadvantages for racial minorities. Residential segregation furthers unacceptable disparities in wealth between the races, and it creates a geography of opportunity, determining who has access to the valuable resources that improve one's life" (pp. 187–188).

A dramatic example of how racial discrimination in home and property ownership interferes with opportunity for blacks to build wealth took place during the 1920s in Manhattan Beach, California, where a black married couple by the names of Charles and Willa Bruce owned a beachfront lodge, café, and dance hall that served as a popular site for blacks to gather socially and experience the "California dream." The area eventually became known as "Bruce's Beach" and other black families migrated there, building cottages by the ocean. However, white neighbors grew resentful of the resort's popularity and began slashing the tires of visitors, setting fires to the resort property and to nearby black-owned homes. When the harassment failed to drive the back community out of town, city officials condemned the neighborhood and seized more than two dozen properties under the false pretense of an urgent need for the city to build a public park. The Bruces were forced to sell their beachfront properties at one-fifth the going price they asked for and had to vacate the area. After the Bruce family left, no park was built on their vacated property and the area remained vacant for decades. Had they been allowed to keep the beachfront property, descendents of the Bruce family would be millionaires today because the property is now worth an estimated $75 million (Bradford, 2021; Xia, 2021).

"Individual private acts of prejudice and discrimination count for less than more pervasive institutional ones. When government is directly involved, claims for systemic compensation to match systemic harm become most compelling."

—IRA KATZNELSON, PROFESSOR OF POLITICAL SCIENCE & HISTORY, AND AUTHOR OF *WHEN AFFIRMATIVE ACTION WAS WHITE*

The racial wealth gap remains as wide today as it was in 1968, when the Fair Housing Act was first passed to make housing discrimination illegal. The economic strides black

Americans made in the decades since 1968—largely through homeownership, the traditional cornerstone of wealth-building in the United States—have almost all been wiped out by the Great Recession of 2008. According to the Pew Research Center, from 2005 to 2009 the median net worth of black households dropped 53 percent, while white household net worth dropped 16 percent (Serwer, 2020). In a national study that controlled for such factors as housing quality, access to amenities, school ranking, and crime, homes in majority black neighborhoods are priced at about one-half the price of homes in neighborhoods with no black residents. Homes owned by blacks have an average worth of $48,000 less than similar homes in white neighborhoods, resulting in a cumulative loss of $156 billion nationwide for black families (Perry et al., 2018). Lower home values also generate lower property taxes, resulting in less local funding for schools, infrastructure, public safety, and recreational facilities in black neighborhoods. Andre Perry, lead researcher of the study, drew the following conclusion from the study's findings:

> Many will say lower school quality, crime, poor housing stock, and other problems with either the home or the neighborhood are the reasons for the lower prices [of black homes]. We controlled statistically for many of those variables. We found that differences in home and neighborhood quality do not fully explain the lower prices of homes in Black neighborhoods. Black-majority neighborhoods do exhibit features associated with lower property values, including higher crime rates, longer commute times, and less access to high-scoring schools and well-rated restaurants. Yet these factors explain only roughly half of the undervaluation of homes in Black neighborhoods (Perry, 2020, pp. 55–56).

As a result of racial disparities in family income and home equity, the median net worth of black families today is less than $20,000 compared with more than $170,000 for white families. These disparities in wealth persist in both middle- and low-income families as well and reflect the historical by product of many years of government-sanctioned racially discriminatory, governmental housing policies that have had cumulative cross-generational impact (Darity & Mullen, 2020). As Rothstein (2017) notes:

"The federal government must reckon with and acknowledge the role that it has played in stripping wealth and opportunity from Black communities."

—JOE BIDEN, 46TH PRESIDENT OF THE UNITED STATES

"The housing industry, aided and abetted by Government, must bear the primary responsibility for the legacy of segregated housing . . . . Government and private industry came together to create a system of residential segregation."

—U.S. COMMISSION ON CIVIL RIGHTS, 1973

> By the time the federal government decided finally to allow African Americans into the suburbs [by passing the Fair Housing Act in 1968], the window of opportunity for an integrated nation had mostly closed. Seventy years ago, many working- and lower-middle-class African American families could have afforded suburban single-family homes that cost about $75,000 (in today's currency) with no down payment. Millions of whites did so. But working- and lower-middle-class African American families cannot now buy homes for $350,000 and more with down payments of 20 percent. The right that was unconstitutionally denied to African Americans in the late 1940s cannot be restored by passing a Fair Housing law that tells their descendants they can now buy homes in the suburbs, if only they can afford it. The advantage that FHA and VA loans gave the white lower-middle class in the 1940s and '50s has become permanent. (pp. 182–183)

Discriminatory Private Real Estate Practices

Governmental policies that denied black families the opportunity to obtain affordable home mortgages created money-making opportunities for real estate investors. They took advantage of these opportunities to engage in two profit-making practices that further disadvantaged blacks: blockbusting and predatory lending.

Blockbusting

This real-estate practice was used by investors to buy property from whites in borderline black–white neighborhoods and then sell or rent those properties to black families at above-market prices. Investors would first tell white families residing in borderline neighborhoods and nearby neighborhoods that their home values was going to soon drop sharply because blacks were about to move into their area. This was done intentionally to create panic among white homeowners so they could be persuaded to sell their homes at below-market value. Once homeowners were persuaded to sell their property, the investors then turned around and sold the homes to blacks at above-market values, thus making themselves a hefty profit (Sugrue, 2005). For instance, in 1954, a homeowner in a whites-only area in East Palo Alto (California), just across a highway from the Stanford University campus, sold his house to a black family. Upon hearing about the sale, the president of the California Real Estate Association set up an office in the neighborhood to inform white families that a "Negro invasion" was starting which would collapse the property value of their homes. Soon thereafter, panicked white homeowners sold their homes to the real estate agency at discounted prices. The agency then began running ads in San Francisco newspapers with a "Colored Buyers!" banner headline. Investors and real estate agents went so far as to place advertisements in black newspapers for homes in white areas—even if they were not up for sale—to encourage blacks to visit white areas that they hoped to target for blockbusting (Sugrue, 2005). When white home owners got the idea that the property value of their homes would soon be declining because blacks would be moving in, the owners had little incentive to invest further in home upkeep or home improvement. So, by the time black families eventually moved in, they ended up paying above-market prices for homes that were in below-average condition (Wilkerson, 2010).

Blockbusting was accompanied by another real-estate practice called "contract sales"—a form of loan sharking in which the home purchaser does not accumulate equity from the down payment and monthly payments, while the real-estate firm is allowed to evict a black homeowner for any late monthly payment and resell the home to another black family (Rothstein, 2017). The combination of having to pay higher housing costs and higher loan-interest rates meant that blacks had to make large payments to meet their debt obligation and had higher risk for loan default and eviction. To meet their monthly payments, blacks often doubled up with other families, took in boarders, and deferred property maintenance on houses that were old and poorly maintained when they bought them in the first place (Sugrue, 2005). Even blacks owning homes in the inner city who wanted to move out when the quality of housing in their neighborhood began to decline were unable to do so because if they sold their property before the mortgage was paid in full, they would lose everything they had invested in it (Rothstein, 2017).

"The arrival of colored home buyers was often the final verdict on a neighborhood's falling property value rather than the cause of it."
—ISABEL WILKERSON, PULITZER-PRIZE WINNING AUTHOR

"The costs to blacks of residential segregation are high: they are likely to pay more for housing in a limited market, likely to have lower-quality housing, less likely to own their housing, likely to live in an area where employment is difficult to find, and likely to have to contend with prematurely depreciated housing."
—EDUARDO BONILLA SILVA, PROFESSOR OF SOCIOLOGY, AND AUTHOR OF *RACISM WITHOUT RACISTS*

Predatory Lending

When the once government-sanctioned practice of redlining was declared illegal, the practice of denying low-interest home loans to blacks continued in a form called "predatory lending"—a practice in which the lender provides *subprime loans* (also known as subpar or second-chance loans) with much higher interest rates and less favorable repayment terms to applicants who are likely to have difficulty maintaining the repayment schedule. Since blacks could not obtain government-backed, low-interest loans from conventional lenders, subprime loan agents flooded black communities (without competition from lenders offering standard loan agreements) and steered blacks toward accepting higher-priced subprime loans they often were never able to repay. This practice is one of the major reasons why the higher the percentage of people of color that lives in a particular metropolitan area, the higher is the number of foreclosures in that area (Rothstein, 2017; Rugh & Massey, 2010).

Among homeowners who refinanced their homes in 2000, lower-income blacks were more than twice as likely as lower-income whites to have subprime loans; this disparity was not based on the borrowers' economic status, but on their race—as evidenced by the fact that higher-income blacks were three times more likely than higher-income whites to receive subprime loans. During the Great Recession of 2008, a disproportionate number of subprime loans led to higher numbers of foreclosures, which played an important role in the national financial collapse because it led to multiple defaults (Rugh & Massey, 2010). Mortgage brokers received bonuses or kickbacks if they made loans with interest rates higher than those recommended by their banks. This practice provided brokers with a strong incentive to pressure borrowers into accepting subprime mortgages—often without disclosing the risks and consequences to the borrower. These developments led the Justice Department to conclude in a 2010 report that the "more segregated a community of color is, the more likely it is that homeowners will face foreclosure because the lenders who peddled the most toxic loans targeted those communities" (Rothstein, 2017, pp. 111–112). These foreclosures often resulted in the evicted homeowners being forced to double up with relatives, renting apartments in poorer and more congested neighborhoods, or ending up homeless. Because home-ownership is critical to the future economic growth of families and the neighborhoods in which families live, home foreclosures experienced by people of color are likely to have negative cross-generational impact on people of color (Schwartztol, 2011).

White Flight

In addition to whites opposing racial integration through sheer force, adoption of segregationist governmental policies and private real estate practices, they resisted integration by simply moving away from blacks—a phenomenon called "white flight" or "white exodus" (Kweit, 2015). Most of the segregated neighborhoods that whites once vigorously and violently defended have now become majority black neighborhoods because whites finally upped and left. One observer put it this way: "Whites hold on 'til the dam bursts, then they run like hell" (Sugrue, 2005, pp. 256–257).

Among the largest migrations in twentieth-century America was the migration of whites from its central cities to its suburbs. After World War II, with the help of financial incentives from the federal government, large numbers of whites from multiple ethnic groups (Italians, Irish, Jews, etc.) were able to purchase homes in the suburbs, enabling them to move out of cities and move away from blacks who lived there. For example, by the mid-1950s, Dearborn, Michigan—a suburb just outside of Detroit—experienced a surged of white migrants from the city. Dearborn's mayor, told a Montgomery, Alabama advertising publication that he was happy to welcome these new white residents, saying that they are "so anti-colored, much more than you in Alabama . . . and negroes can't get in here." In 2000, almost fifty years after this white migration to Dearborn, whites now make up 99% of Dearborn's population andblacks make up 80% of Detroit's urban population (Wilkerson, 2010).

Studies show that white flight starts to take place when a formerly white neighborhood reaches about 7% black. If more than just a few black families move into a white neighborhood, the demand for new white homeowners virtually disappears (Bonilla-Silva, 2018). The only exception to this general rule is when no affordable homes are available to whites in other neighborhoods, in which case wealthier whites start to move into lower-income black neighborhoods, upgrade the residences, and drive up housing costs, which forces lower-income blacks to move somewhere else (Rothstein, 2017)—a process known as "gentrification." For example, in New York City, once black-majority areas in Brooklyn and Harlem have become gentrified, as have once black-majority neighborhoods in Oakland and Seattle (DiAngelo, 2018).

More recently, white flight is taking place from suburbs to areas even farther away from cities that are now called *exurbs*—residential communities that lie beyond the outer suburbs of cities and are crop up in small-town or rural communities. These "suburbs of the suburbs" are growing faster in population and have higher concentrations of white people than either cities or suburbs; in fact, the rate of whites moving from integrated suburbs to segregated exurbs now exceeds the rate of the original white flight from inner cities to suburbs (Benjamin, 2009).

The bottom line: Systemic racism in residential segregation still persists in American society. Four of every five of America's major cities are more segregated now than they were 30 years earlier (Mendenian et al., 2021). Systemic racism in housing has limited blacks' residential options, employment opportunities, the wages they earn, and the amount of wealth they accumulate. It also limits the quality of education they receive—which will be discussed next.

Reflection 7.8

Could your family sell or rent the house or apartment in which they live to a member of any race? If no, why not?

Could your family easily buy or rent a house or apartment in a neighborhood where they would be the racial minority? If no, why not?

The Education System: Quality of Schools and Equality of Learning Opportunities

Blacks have been systematically discriminated against with respect to equal access to education from America's inception. Starting with slavery, plantation owners feared that educated slaves would overturn the system and upset the economy, so enslaved blacks were forbidden from learning to read and write. During the almost 100 years of Jim Crow that followed slavery, educational discrimination continued in the form of racially segregated and poorly funded black schools. Despite the heralded 1954 Supreme Court ruling that declared segregated schools to be inherently unequal, and despite increasing racial diversity in our country, America's schools today remain highly segregated. Students of color are more likely to attend schools where other students of color comprise the majority of the school's population. Studies show that about 75% of black students attend schools in which they are the majority group on campus. In contrast, white students attend schools where 75% of their schoolmates are white (Mervosh, 2019; Orfield et al., 2012). The number of extremely segregated schools—defined as schools whose enrollment consists of more than 90% students of color—has more than tripled during the past 30 years; a large majority students enrolled in these highly schools are from low-income families (Eberhardt, 2019). Not only are these schools segregated, they are unequal. Compared with white suburban schools, inner-city schools attended by racial minorities are more crowded, have older and less well-maintained buildings, poorer equipment, less experienced and qualified teachers, fewer college preparatory courses, and more limited educational resources and learning support services (Bonilla-Silva, 2018; Hsieh, 2014; Orfield & Eaton, 1996).

> "Many of the schools that our nation's most vulnerable children attend, especially those in economically strapped urban areas, are dilapidated and segregated."
>
> —C. TALBERT-JOHNSON, "STRUCTURAL INEQUALITIES AND THE ACHIEVEMENT GAP IN URBAN SCHOOLS"

> "Of all the civil rights for which the world has struggled and fought for 5,000 years, the right to learn is undoubtedly the most fundamental."
>
> —W. E. B. DUBOIS, AFRICAN AMERICAN SOCIOLOGIST, HISTORIAN, AND CIVIL RIGHTS ACTIVIST

Roots of Systemic Racism in Education

The roots of unequal educational conditions and opportunities can be traced to previously discussed governmental housing policies adopted after World War II, including those of the Federal Housing Authority (FHA), which intentionally blocked racial integration of schools by not providing federally funded loans for homes to be built in integrated neighborhoods. The racial prejudice underlying this policy was patently clear in the FHA's manual, which stated that if children "attend school where the majority or a considerable number of the pupils represent a far lower level of society or an incompatible racial element, the neighborhood under consideration will prove far less stable and desirable than if this condition did not exist" (Rothstein, 2017, pp. 65–66). Consequently, in many U.S. states, students of color were educated in racially segregated schools with unequal educational facilities and programs. It was legal to do so until the groundbreaking Supreme Court case in

© APN Photography/Shutterstock.com

1954 (*Brown v. Board of Education*) when the court's justices ruled that "separate educational facilities are inherently unequal." That judicial decision made it illegal for Kansas and 20 other states to deliver education to African Americans in segregated classrooms. Nonetheless, as previously mentioned, America's schools continue to remain segregated because Americans continue to live in racially segregated communities.

Inequitable School Funding Policies

Unlike most other major democratic countries whose central government funds its education system (Diamond, 2019), America has a large, highly decentralized educational system that includes more than 15,000 separately funded school districts. The advantage of decentralization is that it allows different schools the freedom to be responsive to the unique needs of their local community. Its disadvantage is that it creates wide disparities across schools in terms of how well they are resourced because they are funded by local property taxes. Consequently, the higher the value of the residential property where the school is located, the higher is its property taxes and the more funds are available to support its schools. As discussed previously, the value of property in black neighborhoods is substantially lower as a result of government-sanctioned residential segregation policies, racially discriminatory real estate practices, and public policy decisions about where industrial factories could be built. Thus, urban schools, particularly those in the inner city, have substantially fewer fiscal resources to support the education of its children. Some states reduce funding gaps between their school districts by providing additional funding to schools in very high-poverty districts; however, unequal school-funding gaps continue to exist in all states. Nationally, the highest poverty districts have been found to average about $1,200 less in per-student funding than the lowest poverty districts (The Education Trust, 2015). Because a disproportionate number of students of color have low-income families and attend racially segregated schools (Arum & Roska, 2011), inequities relating to school-funding formulas disproportionately impact the quality of education received by students from minority racial and ethnic groups. Almost one-half of the nation's school-age population are students of color and about 27% of these students live below the poverty line (U.S. Department of Education, 2013).

These educational inequities become even more disturbing when viewed in light of the fact that a disproportionate share of the federal government's tax income comes from urbanized states that educate large numbers of students of color (e.g., New Jersey, Illinois, California, and New York). These states are sometimes referred to as "donor states" because they pay more in federal taxes than they receive in federal funding in return; in contrast, non-donor states (called "burden states") receive more federal funding per dollar than they pay in federal taxes. For instance, New Jersey receives 55 cents for every dollar paid to the federal government; Illinois receives 72 cents; California receives 79 cents; and New York receives 79 cents. One award-winning journalist calls this the "reverse Robin Hood syndrome"—tax revenue from more densely populated urbanized states with higher percentages of people of color (including students of color) goes to less-populated suburbanized and rural states that have a higher percentages of whites and less urban-based poverty (Benjamin, 2009). Among students attending extreme-poverty schools (defined as having more than 90% of their student body living in poverty), only 1% of its students are white compared to 12% of Black and Hispanic students (Orfield & Lee, 2005).

Thus, the inequitable irony is that the poverty rates among students of color in major U.S. cities are appreciably higher than it is among white students, yet schools educating low-income students of color in urban areas receive less fiscal support to educate their students than schools educating higher-income white students living in non-urban areas (Sugrue, 2005).

Reflection 7.9

How would you rate the K-12 schools you have attended in terms of the quality of the buildings, the curriculum, and the educational support services? Do you think the neighborhood in which you lived affected the quality of education you received? If yes, in what way(s)?

Racial Gaps in Educational Achievement

Educational inequities exacerbate gaps in academic achievement between white students and students of color (Ladson-Billings, 2006; The Education Trust, 2008). Research conducted by the National Assessment of Educational Progress (NAEP) (2019) reveals significant racial gaps in reading and math achievement scores at the fourth-grade, eighth-grade, and twelfth-grade levels. These gaps have remained stubbornly in place since 1992 (NAEP, 2015a, 2015b). Furthermore, such gaps raise the risk that students of color will drop out of school altogether. About 12% of America's public high schools account for one-half of the nation's high-school student dropouts; in these "dropout factories," only 40% of ninth graders are enrolled as twelfth graders four years later (compared to 90% of students enrolled in other high schools around the country). Disturbingly, these dropout factories are high schools that enroll very high percentages of low-income, students of color (Balfanz & Legters, 2004)—the very students for whom education is the only ticket to upward socioeconomic mobility for themselves and their future families. Well-paying jobs in the new knowledge-based economy will go to those who have had the opportunity to attend good schools that prepare them well for college; those schools are not usually found in segregated, poorly funded inner-city neighborhoods where attended by black children and other students of color reside (Irons, 2002).

"Education … is the great equalizer. It does better than to disarm the poor of their hostility towards the rich: it prevents being poor."

—HORACE MANN, ABOLITIONIST, EDUCATIONAL REFORMER, AND "FATHER OF THE COMMON (PUBLIC) SCHOOL"

"Education can be transformative. It reshapes the healthy outcomes of a people; it breaks the cycle of poverty; it improves housing conditions; it raises the standard of living [and] increases voter participation. In short, education strengthens democracy."

—CAROL ANDERSON, CHAIR OF AFRICAN AMERICAN STUDIES, EMORY UNIVERSITY

America's democratic principles stress the importance of equal opportunity for all citizens. Originating with the work of Horace Mann in the mid-1800s, the primary purpose of America's public school system was to provide all citizens with equal educational opportunity to attain upward social mobility and improve their quality of life (Groen, 2008). Our educational system is still viewed as the primary vehicle for reducing socioeconomic inequality, promoting social justice and transforming society, but our schools still mirror the inequalities that exist in our larger society (Gorski, 1995–2019). Instead of serving as a social engine to lift poor students to higher levels of socioeconomic status, America's inequitable school-funding formulas work to do just the opposite: reduce the likelihood of upward social mobility by perpetuatinge existing societal inequalities (Kozol, 1991). Unless longstanding school-funding formulas are changed to ensure that all students are given equal educational opportunities and resources to achieve academic success, expressions such as "no child left behind" and "every student succeeds" are likely to be nothing more than political platitudes and demoralize educators and schools that serve socioeconomically disadvantaged communities (Mintrop & Sunderman, 2009).

The Role of Racially Integrated Schools in Closing the Educational Achievement Gap

Research strongly suggests that the ultimate solution to reducing the racial gap in educational achievement is by reducing racial segregation in America's schools. Studies consistently show that compared to students who attend racially segregated schools, black students who attend integrated schools demonstrate higher levels of educational achievement and go on to attain higher occupational positions and earn higher levels of income as adults; and so do their children (Eberhardt, 2019). In fact, the advantages that blacks gain by attending integrated schools were observed as far back as the early 1930s when many black families moved from the South—where schools were segregated and moved North—where schools were more racially integrated. The more time Southern-born black children spent in more integrated schools after they moved North, the higher was their level of academic achievement. These findings later provided the basis for the 1954 "*Brown v. the Board of Education*" Supreme Court ruling that made intentional school segregation illegal (Wilkerson, 2010).

Despite that historic ruling, schools are now more segregated today than they were in 1970 because they are located in neighborhoods that have become more racially segregated (Benjamin, 2009). To combat school segregation, some school districts have adopted polices to increase racial integration by changing how students are assigned to particular schools within the district (Clotfelter, 2004). Unfortunately, these efforts have often failed to improve racial integration because most racial segregation in K-12 schools does not exist *within* school districts but *between* school districts that are farther apart geographically (Wells & Associates, 2014). Since so few children of color live close enough to white school districts, busing has become the only viable strategy for reducing some of the extensive school segregation that exists today (Rothstein, 2017), but strategy also has limitation because it requires black children to take long bus rides from their homes to attend better-funded schools located in predominantly white school districts (DiAngelo, 2018).

Ultimately, the most effective and efficient way to decrease systemic racism in America's K-12 educational system is to increase racial integration in America's residential communities. A promising example of how this could be done has taken place in Montgomery County (Maryland) where the county implemented a home-building policy that requires developers in more affluent communities to set aside a percentage of housing units for moderate-income families. The county then uses public housing funds to purchase one-third of these set-aside units for rental to lower-income families. As a result of this practice, children from lower-income black families have been able to live these integrated communities, attend integrated schools, and reach higher levels of academic achievement than comparable black children living in segregated areas of the county (Rothstein, 2017).

"School districts with the greatest needs often receive the least funding. In too many communities, students who are poor, minority, or English learners do not get their fair share of education funds. With the right leadership, inequitable funding patterns can be changed. We can unstack the deck."

—THE EDUCATION TRUST

Reflection 7.10

Would you describe the K-12 schools you attended as racially segregated or racially integrated?

What do you think accounted for their degree of racial integration (or lack thereof)?

Conclusion

Evidence reviewed in this chapter demonstrates that there has been a history of systemic racism in employment, housing, and education that has affected and continues to affect blacks at all socioeconomic levels (Collins, 1997; Cose, 1995). In many ways, the conclusion reached by the Kerner Commission following the 1967 riots in Northern inner cities is still relevant today:

> Racial prejudice has shaped our history decisively; it now threatens to affect our future. White racism is essentially responsible for the explosive mixture which has been accumulating in our cities since the end of World War II. Among the ingredients of this mixture are: Pervasive discrimination and segregation in employment, education and housing, which have resulted in the continuing exclusion of great numbers of Negroes from the benefits of economic progress. (Report on the National Advisory Commission on Civil Disorders, 1968, p. 9)

The different forms of systemic racism identified in this chapter (economic, housing, and education) were discussed separately for organizational purposes; in reality, they do not operate separately but a joint and symbiotic fashion, in which they reinforce one another to magnify their separate effects. It is estimated that the combined and cumulative effects of systemic, mutigenerational racism in employment, housing, and education have resulted in an estimated loss of 24 trillion dollars to African Americans families (Feagin, 2004).

Chapter Summary and Highlights

Racism can take place at different levels, ranging from individuals who exhibit it on a personal basis to *institutional* racism that takes place within a particular institution or organization—such as a school or corporate organization, and *systemic* racism that cuts across entire societal systems—such as housing, health care, and criminal justice systems. Even if people do not engage in discrimination on an individual basis, racism can still be practiced and perpetuated by policies and practices implanted in organizational and societal structures that operate automatically to exert a collective discriminatory impact on different racial groups.

Social systems in the United States have been shaped by historical events and political decisions that put policies into practice that continue to maintain racial inequities and injustices today. These historically rooted and still lingering forms of systemic racism need to be understood and acknowledged before they can be effectively uprooted. This requires knowledge not only of the psychology of personal racism, but the politics, economics, and sociology of systemic racism. These historical roots are the underlying and often unacknowledged causes of current systemic racism. Gaining knowledge and understanding of these roots is the key first step to weeding out systemic racism that exists in society today.

Currently, systemic racism exists in the following social systems:

- *Economic* System: Employment, Wages, and Wealth
- *Housing* System: Residential Choice and Home Ownership Opportunities
- *Education* System: Quality of Schools and Equality of Learning Opportunities
- *Health Care* System: Access to Quality Medical Care and Equal Medical Treatment
- *Electoral* System: Voting Rights and Political Representation
- *Criminal Justice* System: Policing Practices, Legal Representation, and Sentencing Policies

Economic inequality gaps exist between blacks and whites in terms of wages earned, family income, and *wealth*—the value of all assets owned, such as savings, stocks, and home equity. Blacks have considerably less wealth than whites; much of this disparity has to do with gaps in home equity that have resulted from many decades of racially discriminatory governmental policies and private real-estate practices. Less wealthy black families are particularly vulnerable to downturns in the national economy; they were disproportionately affected by the 2008 Great Recession and the COVID-19 pandemic.

Unemployment rates among low-income blacks have continued to increase since the early 1970s. This increase can be traced to increased racial segregation of blacks in inner cities areas that took place at the same time that city-located business and job opportunities shifted to the suburbs. These developments compounded decades of previous discriminatory labor practices that tracked black males into low-paid machinery jobs— many of which have now been eliminated by automation, restructuring, or relocating manufacturing jobs in other countries. The COVID-19 pandemic is expected to further widen the black–white employment gap because more blacks and other people of color lost their jobs during the COVID crisis than did whites. In addition to these factors, research indicates that racial bias in hiring practices also contribute to higher black unemployment rates.

Even if job applicants are not intentionally discriminated against in the hiring process, research reveals that people of color do not have equal access to jobs, particularly higher-paying jobs, because many of these jobs are obtained through word of mouth. This networking opportunity (sometimes referred to as "social capital") advantages job applicants who live and socialize with people holding similar positions and with people who make hiring decisions— most of who are white, not people of color.

A number of governmental policies and economic practices have contributed to systemic racism in housing and promoted racial segregation, namely:

- The federal government building racially segregated public housing in cities where segregation had not previously existed, thus contributing to the creation of black city ghettos and white suburbs.
- The federal government stimulating white flight from integrated cities to segregated suburbs by providing fiscal support for the development of white suburbs and allowing these suburban areas to adopt exclusionary zoning laws that blocked black residents.
- The government spending billions of dollars in tax breaks for single-family suburban homeowners, while not providing guaranteed loans for building homes in black working-class neighborhoods.
- State governments endorsing and enforcing racial segregation of blacks through discriminatory neighborhood association rules and restrictive covenants that barred middle-class blacks from living in previously all-white communities—even if they had the financial means to do so.
- Local police agencies ignoring, and often encouraging, white violence against black families that attempted to move into white neighborhoods.
- Real estate agents being allowed to impose and maintain racial segregation by only showing and selling them homes to blacks in black-majority neighborhoods.
- The government authorizing federal and state highways to be built only through urban areas, which led to the demolition of neighborhoods occupied by blacks—without compensating black families and business owners for their housing and financial losses forcing displaced residents into more concentrated and impoverished sections of the inner city.
- Government programs that have, and still do, reinforce racial segregation by only providing housing assistance to low-income blacks in already-segregated neighborhoods—the very neighborhoods that had become segregated as a result of earlier governmental policies.

Systemic racism in housing not only limited blacks' residential options, it also limited their employment opportunities, the wages they earned, the amount of wealth they accumulated, and the quality of education they received. Students of color are more likely to be educated in schools where other students of color comprise the majority of the school's population. These schools are not only segregated, they're also unequal. Compared to white suburban schools, inner-city schools attended by racial minorities are more crowded, have older and less well-maintained buildings, poorer equipment, less experienced and qualified teachers, fewer college preparatory courses, and more limited educational resources and learning support services. Since schools are funded by local property taxes, the higher the value of the residential property where schools are located, the higher are the property taxes and the more funds are available to support its neighborhood schools. Urban schools, particularly those in the inner-cities, are located in areas that generate substantially less property tax revenue, thus these schools receive substantially fewer fiscal resources to educate their students. These educational inequities have created persistent gaps in academic achievement between white students living in wealthier suburbs and poorer students of color living in inner cities.

Research strongly suggests that the ultimate solution to reducing the racial gap in educational achievement is by reducing racial segregation in America's schools. Studies consistently show that compared to students attending racially segregated schools, black students attending integrated schools demonstrate higher levels of educational achievement, attain higher occupational positions, and earn higher levels of income as adults; so do their children.

The three forms of systemic racism identified in this chapter (economic, housing, and education) do not operate separately but in a combined and symbiotic fashion, reinforcing one another in ways that fortify and magnify their separate effects. It is estimated that the combined and cumulative effects of systemic, mutigenerational racism in employment, housing, and education have resulted in an estimated loss of 24 trillion dollars to African American families.

Internet Resources

Systemic Racism Explained: https://www.youtube.com/watch?v=YrHIQIO_bdQ

Systemic Racism in Employment: https://www.americanprogress.org/issues/economy/reports/2019/12/05/478150//african-amricans-face-obstacles-getting-good-jobs/

Systemic Racism in Housing: https://www.bing.com/videos/search?q=systemic+racism+housing&qpvt=systemic+racism+housing&FORM=VDRE

Systemic Racism in Education: https://www.benjerry.com/whats-new/2017/11/systemic-racism-education

References

Alexander, M. (2020). *The new Jim Crow: Mass incarceration in the age of colorblindness.* The New Press.

Allen, T. (1997). *The invention of the white race: The origin of racial oppression in Anglo-America, vol. II.* Verso.

Anderson, M. W. (2008). Cities inside out: Race, poverty, and exclusion at the urban fringe. *UCLA Law Review, 55,* 1095–1160.

Anderson, C. (2016). *White rage: The unspoken truth of our racial divide.* Bloomsbury.

Arum, R., & Roska, J. (2011). *Academically adrift: Limited learning on college campuses.* University of Chicago Press.

Balfanz, R., & Legters, N. (2004). *Locating the dropout crisis.* Johns Hopkins University Center for Social Organization of Schools.

Bates, B. T. (2012). *The making of black Detroit in the age of Henry Ford.* The University of North Carolina Press.

Benjamin, R. (2009). *Searching for whitopia: An improbable journey to the heart of white America.* HarperCollins.

Bertrand, M., & Mullainathan, S. (2004). Are Emily and Greg more employable than Lakisha and Jamal? A field experiment on labor market discrimination. *American Economic Review, 94*(4), 991–1013.

Bonilla-Silva, E. (2018). *Racism without racists: Color-blind racism and the persistence of racial inequality in America.* Rowman & Littlefield.

Bowman, P. J., Muhammad, R., & Ifatunji, M. (2004). Skin tone, class, and racial attitudes among African Americans. In C. Herring, V. M. Keith, & H. D. Horton (Eds.), Skin/deep: How race and complexion matter in the "color blind" era (pp. 128–158). Institute on Race and Public Policy, University of Illinois at Chicago. University of Illinois Press.

Bradford, S. (2021, April 13). Californians must face hard truths: If you can inherit wealth from your ancestors, you can also inherit their debts. *Los Angeles Times*, A11.

Clotfelter, C. T. (2014). *After Brown: The rise and retreat of school desegregation*. Princeton University Press.

Collins, S, (1997). *Black corporate executives: The making and breaking of a black middle class*. Temple University Press.

Cose, E. (1995). *The rage of a privileged class*. HarperCollins.

Darity, W., & Mullen, A. K. (2020). *From here to equality: Reparations for black Americans in the twenty-first century*. University of North Carolina Press.

Davis, (2010). D. B. The rocky road to freedom: Crucial barriers to abolition in the antebellum years. In A. Tsesis (Ed.), *The promises of liberty: The history and contemporary relevance of the thirteenth amendment* (pp. i–xvi). Columbia Press.

DiAngelo, R. (2018). *White fragility: Why it's so hard for white people to talk about racism*. Beacon Press.

Duster, T. (1997). Pattern, purpose, and race in the drug war: The crisis of credibility in criminal justice. In C. Reinarman & H. G. Levine (Eds.), *Race in America: Demon drugs and social justice* (pp. 260–287). University of California Press.

Eberhardt, J. L. (2019). *Biased: Uncovering the hidden prejudice that shapes what we see, think, and do*. Viking.

Edelman, B., Luca, M., & Svirsky, D. (2017). Racial discrimination in the sharing economy: Evidence from a field experiment. *American Economic Journal: Applied Economics, 9*(2), 1–22.

Elliott, J. R., & Smith, R. A. (2004). Race, gender, and workplace power. *American Sociological Review, 69*(3), 365–386.

Espinosa, L. L., & Mitchell, T. (2020). The state of race and ethnicity in higher education. *Change, 52(2), 27–31.*

Feagin, J. R. (2004). Documenting the costs of slavery, segregation, and contemporary racism: Why reparations are in order for African Americans. *Harvard BlackLetter Law Journal, 20*, 53–55.

Feagin, J. (2005). *Systemic racism: A theory of oppression*. Routledge.

Flipen, C. (2004). Unequal returns to housing investments? A study of real housing appreciation among Black, White, and Hispanic households. *Social Forces, 82*(4), 1523–1551.

Foner, E. (2014). Reconstruction*: America's unfinished revolution, 1863-1877*. HarperCollins.

Gilbert, J., Wood, S. G., & Sharp, D. (2002). Who owns the land? Agricultural land ownership by race/ethnicity. *Rural America, 17*(4), 55–62.

Gorski, P. C. (1995–2019). *EdChange, Multicultural Pavilion*. http://www.edchange.org/multicultural/index.html

Grodsky, E., & Pager, D. (2001). The structure of disadvantage: Individual and occupational determinants of the Black-White wage gap. *American Sociological Review, 66*(4), 542–567.

Groen, M. (2008). The Whig party and the rise of common schools, 1837–1854. *American Educational History Journal, 35*(1/2), 251–260.

Harper, S. R. (2012). Race without racism: How higher education researchers minimize racist institutional norms. *Review of Higher Education, 36*(1), 9–30.

Holzer, H. J. (1991). The spatial mismatch hypothesis: What has the evidence shown? *Urban Studies, 28*(1), 105–122.

Hsieh, S. (2014, March 21). 14 disturbing stats about racial inequality in American public schools. *The Nation*. https://www.thenation.com/article/archive/14-disturbing-stats-about-racial-inequality-in-American-public-schools/

Irons, P. H. (2002). *Jim Crow's children: The broken promise of the Brown decision.* Penguin.

Kasarda, J. (1990). Urban industrial transition and the underclass. *Annals of the American Academic of Political and Social Science, 501*(1), 26–47.

Katznelson, I. (2005). *When affirmative action was white: An untold history of racial inequality in twentieth-century America.* W. W. Norton & Company.

Kendi, I. X. (2016). *Stamped from the beginning: The definitive history of racist ideas in America.* Bold Type Books.

Kendi, I. X. (2019). *How to be an antiracist.* One World.

Khouri, A. (2020a, July 19). Racism and the Black housing crisis. *Los Angeles Times,* A11.

Khouri, A. (2020b, August 26). State bill seeks to end single-family zoning. *Los Angeles Times,* A10.

Kochlar, R., Fry, R., & Taylor, P. (2011, July 26). *Wealth gaps rise to record highs between Whites, Blacks and Hispanics.* Pew Research Center. https://www.pewresearchorg/social-trends/2011/07/26/wealth-gaps-rise-to-record-highs-between-whites-blacks-hispanics/

Kozol, J. (1991). *Savage inequalities: Children in America's schools.* Harper Collins.

Kweit, R. W. (2015). *People and politics in urban America* (2nd ed.). Routledge

LaBounty. (2000, August). "Willie Mays on Miraloma Drive." https//outsidelands.org/sw5.php

Ladson-Billings, G. (2006). From the achievement gap to the education debt: Understanding achievement in U.S. schools. *Educational Researcher, 35*(7), 3–12.

Lazarus, D. (2021, April 9). A disturbing racial pattern in financial ads: People of color are disproportionately targeted by payday lenders, ignored by banks, study says. *Los Angeles Times,* A8.

Levey, N .N. (2020, December 27). Racial disparities on health agenda. *Los Angeles Times,* A1, A10.

Litwack, L. F. (1961). *North of slavery: The Negro in the free states, 1790-1860.* The University of Chicago Press.

Logan, E. B. (2021, May 20). Inclusive zoning for American dream. *Los Angeles Times,* A2.

López, I. H. (2014). *Dog whistle politics: How coded racial appeals have reinvented racism & wrecked the middle class.* Oxford University Press.

Masserly, D., & Denton, N. (1993). *American apartheid: Segregation and the making of the underclass.* Harvard University.

Meizhu, L., Robles, B. J., Leondar-Wright, B., Brewer, R. M., Admanson, R. (2006). *The color of wealth: The story behind the U.S. racial wealth divide.* The New Press.

Mervosh, S. (2019, February 27). How much wealthier are white school districts than nonwhite ones? $23 billion, report says. *The New York Times.* https://www.nytimes.com/2019/02/27/education/school-districts-funding-white-minorities.html?module=inline

Milkman, R. (1997). *Farewell to the factory: Auto workers in the late twentieth century.* University of California Press.

Mintrop, H., & Sunderman, G. L. (2009). Predictable failure of federal sanctions-driven accountability for school improvement—and why we may retain it anyway. *Educational Researcher, 38*(5), 353–364.

Myrdal, G. (1944). *An American dilemma: The negro problem and modern democracy.* Routledge.

National Assessment of Educational Progress. (2015a). *2015 Reading Grade 12 Assessment Report Card: Summary Data Tables for National and Pilot State Sample Sizes, Participation Rates, Proportions of SD and ELL Students Identified, Demographics, and Performance Results.* https://www.nationsreportcard.gov/reading_math_g12_2015/files/Appendix_20

National Assessment of Educational Progress. (2015b). *2015 Mathematics Grade 12 Assessment Report Card: Summary Data Average scores and achievement-level results in NAEP mathematics for twelfth-grade students, by selected characteristics: Various years, 2005–2015.* https://www.nationsreportcard.gov/reading_math_g12_2015/files/Appendix_20

National Assessment of Educational Progress. (2019). *Results from the 2019 mathematics and reading assessments. The National Report Card.* National Center for Education Statistics. https://www.nationsreportcard.gov/mathematics/supportive_files/2019_infogra

Northrup, A. J. (2012). *Slavery in New York: A historical sketch.* State Library Bulletin History. University of the State New York.

Orfield, G., & Eaton, S. E. (1996). *Dismantling desegregation: The quiet reversal of Brown v. Board of Education.* The New Press.

Orfield, G., & Lee, C. (2005). *Why segregation matters: Poverty and educational inequality.* The Civil Rights Project at Harvard University.

Orfield, G., Kucsera, J., & Siegel-Hawley, G. (2012). *E pluribus . . . separation: Deepening double segregation for more students.* The Civil Rights Project/Proyecto Derechos Civiles, University of California, Los Angeles. http://civil-rightsproject.ucla.edu/research/k-12-eduction/integration-and-diversity/mlk-national/e-pluribus . . . separation-deepening-double-segregation-for-more-students

O'Rourke. (2016, November 14). "Chronicle covers: When Willie Mays was denied housing because he was black." *San Francisco Chronicle.* https:www.sfchronicle.com/chronicle_vault/article/Chronicle-Covers-When-Willie-Mays-was-denied-10518685.php

Osofsky, G. (1963). *Harlem: The making of a ghetto: Negro New York, 1890-1963.* Harper and Row.

Pager, D. (2007). *Marked: Race, crime, and finding work in an era of mass incarceration.* The University of Chicago Press.

Perry, A. M. (2020). *Know your price: Valuing black lives and property in America's cities.* Brookings Institution Press.

Perry, A. M., Rothwell, J., & Harshbarger, D. (2018). *The devaluation of assets in black neighborhoods.* Brookings. www.brookings.edu/edu/research/devaluation-of-assets-in-black-neighborhoods/

Peter G. Peterson Foundation. (2019, October 4). *Income and wealth in America: An overview of recent data.* https://www.pgpf.org/blog/2019/10/income-and-wealth-in-the-united-states-an-overview-of-data

Quillian, L., Pager, D., Hexel, O., & Midtbøen, A. H. (2017). Meta-analysis of field experiments shows no change in racial discrimination in hiring over time. *Proceedings of the National Academy of Sciences, 114*(41), 10870–10875.

Report on the National Advisory Commission on Civil Disorders. (1968). *Summary of Report.* Bantom Books. http://www.eisenhowerfoundation.org/docs/kerner.pdf

Rothstein, R. (2017). *The color of law.* Liveright Publishing.

Royster, D. A. (2003). *Race and the invisible hand: How white networks exclude men from blue-collar jobs.* University of California Press.

Rugh, J. S., & Massey, D. S. (2010). Racial segregation and the American foreclosure crisis. *American Sociological Review, 75(5), 629–651.*

Schwartztol, L. (2011, September 16). *Predatory lending: Wall Street profited, minority families paid the price.* https://www.aclu.org/blog/racial-justice/race-and-economic-justice/predatory-lending-wall-street-profited-minority

Serwer, A. (2020, October). The new reconstruction. *The Atlantic.* https://www.the-atlantic.com/magazine/archive/2020/10/the-next-reconstruction/615475/

Shapiro, S. R. (1993). *Human rights violations in the United States: A report on U.S. compliance.* Human Rights Watch, American Civil Liberties Union.

Smith, D. (2015). *Diversity's promise for higher education: Making it work* (2nd ed.). Johns Hopkins University Press.

Sugrue, T. J. (2005). *The origins of the urban crisis: Race and inequity in postwar Detroit.* Princeton University Press.

The Education Trust. (2008). *Funding gaps 2008.* Author.

The Education Trust. (2015). *Funding gaps 2015.* Author.

Thomas, A. J., Witherspoon, K. M., & Speight, S. L. (2008). Gendered racism, psychological distress, and coping styles of African American women. *Cultural Diversity and Ethnic Minority Psychology, 14*(4), 307–314.

Thompson, J. P., & Suarez, G. A. (2015). *Exploring the racial wealth gap using the survey of consumer finances.* Finance and Economics Discussion Series 2015-076. Board of Governors of the Federal Reserve System, http://dx.doi.org/10.17016/FEDS.2015.076. https://www.federalreserve.gov/econresdata/feds/2015/files/2015076pap.pdf

Turner, M. A., Ross, S. L., Galster, G. C., & Yinger, J. (2002). *Discrimination in metropolitan housing markets: National results from phase 1 HDS.* The Urban Institute.

Turner, M. A., Santos, R., Levy, D. K., Wissoker, D., Aranda, C., & Pitingolo, R. (2013). *Housing discrimination against racial and ethnic minorities 2012.* U.S. Department of Housing and Urban Development, Office of Policy Development and Research.

Wells, A. S. & Associates (2014, May). *Divided we fall: The story of separate and unequal schools 60 years after Brown v. Board of Education.* Center for Understanding Race and Education (CURE). http://bit.ly/PXy3HQ

Widick, B. J. (1976). *Auto works and its discontents.* Johns Hopkins University Press.

Wilkerson, I. (2010). *The warmth of other suns: The epic story of America's great migration.* Vintage Books.

Wilkerson, I. (2020). *Caste: The origins of our discontents.* Random House.

Wilson, W. J. (1996). *When work disappears: The world of the new urban poor.* Knopf.

Wilson, V. (2015). *Black unemployment is significantly higher than white unemployment regardless of educational attainment.* Economic Policy Institute. https:www.epi.org/publication/black-unemployment-educational-attainment/

Wise, T. (2011). *White like me: Reflection on race from a privileged son* (3rd ed.). Soft Skull Press.

Xia, R. (2021, March 29). Apology? Restitution? City split on rectifying racist past. *Los Angeles Times*, A1, A6.

Reflections and Applications

Name

_____

Date

_____

7.1 Review the sidebar quotes contained in this chapter and select two that you think are particularly meaningful or inspirational. For each quote you selected, provide an explanation why you chose it.

7.2 Compared to whites, people of color have experienced systemic racism in employment, housing, and education; however, these forms of systemic racism have been experienced more intensely and extensively by blacks. Why do you think this is so?

7.3 Interview three students on campus and ask them the following questions.
   a) Have you heard of the term "systemic racism?"
   b) What do you think the term means?
   c) Can systematic racism take place without personal racism?
   d) Do you think systemic racism still exists in society today?

Based on the answers you received to these questions, would you say that the students had a good understanding of what systemic racism is and are aware of its current relevance?

7.4 When people are asked about whether school policies should be created to insure that there is more racial integration in America's schools, they often say things like: "I support integration, but I do not believe in forcing people to do anything they don't want to do" or, "People have the right to make their own personal choices and no one should interfere with a person's right to choose."

Would you agree or disagree with these arguments? Why?

7.5 Someone offered the following explanation for why many neighborhoods are racially segregated: "Blacks like living with blacks, and whites like living with whites . . . it's a natural thing."

Do you agree with this explanation? If yes, why? If no, why not?

7.6 "The past is the past; people just have to get over it and move on" is a common objection to examining the history of system racism in America. In what way do you think this statement is true? In what way do you think it's false?

Understanding Systemic Racism, Part II: Health Care, Voting Rights, and Criminal Justice

Chapter Purpose and Preview

This chapter examines systemic racism in America's health care system, providing evidence of how people of color compared to whites of equivalent socioeconomic status, receive lower-quality health care. The chapter also examines how America's electoral system has often restricted or denied the right of people of color to vote through the use of voter suppression tactics and policies. The chapter concludes with an analysis of historical and current racial inequities in the criminal justice system with respect to monitoring and arrest, pretrial detention, conviction and sentencing, incarceration rates, and post-incarceration punishment.

Health Care System: Access to Quality Medical Care and Equal Medical Treatment

In his 1944 State of the Union address, Franklin D. Roosevelt urged America to adopt a "Second Bill of Rights," which included the "right to adequate medical care and the opportunity to achieve and enjoy good health" (Roosevelt, 1944). Studies show that America has more work to do to ensure that right because systemic racism has existed, and continues to exist, in its health care industry. For instance, compared to expecting white mothers, black mothers with similar levels of income and socioeconomic status are less likely to receive quality medical care during childbirth, experience infant mortality at rates twice as high as white women (Effion et al., 2020), and have a 3–4 times higher risk of maternal death due to pregnancy-related complications (CDC, 2019; Perry, 2020). These racial disparities exist at all levels of income and education (James et al., 2007; Smedley et al., 2003).

Blacks are also less likely to receive: (a) breast cancer screenings, (b) follow-up visits after hospitalization for mental illness, and (c) maximum-strength pain medication when reporting to physicians that they're experiencing high levels of pain (Chabria, 2019; Friedman et al., 2019; Schneider et al., 2002). The last may be accounted for by research which indicates that medical students and residents are more likely to believe that blacks have higher pain thresholds than whites (Hoffman, 2016). It may also explain why doctors have been more liberal in their pain-killing prescription of opioids to whites, which has led to higher rates of opioid addiction among whites compared to people of color (Wilkerson, 2020). Other examples of systemic racism in medicine and health care include: (a) medical school students being trained on skin diseases that appear on white skin, not black and brown skin, which has led to misdiagnoses of skin disorders experienced by people of color, and (b) diagnosing white children with attention disorder when they display impulsive or unruly behavior in the classroom and providing them with medical treatment or educational accommodations, while identical behavior in black children is more often diagnosed as a conduct disorder for which they receive detention rather than treatment or accommodation (Tanner, 2021).

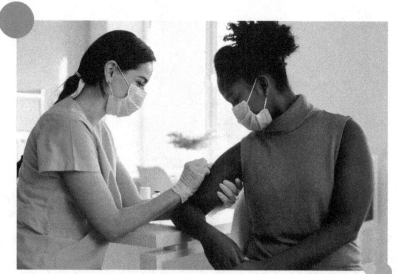

A history of racism in health care and medical experimentation has left blacks leery of government-sponsored health care programs, such as the recently developed COVID-19 vaccine. © Studio Romantic/Shutterstock.com

Blacks have also been subjected to inequitable and unethical medical experiments, starting during slavery when blacks who were disabled or too ill to work were often bought by white medical institutions and used in experiments or operations designed to advance "medical science" and "medical education" (Feagin, 2005). Some of those medical experiments included operating on blacks without anesthesia to determine their level of pain tolerance (Kendi, 2016) and letting diseases go untreated in their bodies for the purpose of tracking their course and discover vaccines to prevent or cure them for example, this is how the vaccine for typhoid fever was discovered (Wilkerson, 2020). One consequence of this history of discriminatory medical treatments is that blacks today are distrustful of governmental health programs, which may account for why blacks have been more reluctant to participate in the governmental rollout of vaccines for treating COVID-19 (Stoler et al., 2020).

 Consider This…

Between 1932 and 1972, the infamous "Tuskegee Experiment" on black males with syphilis was conducted in Alabama. Despite the fact that syphilis treatments were available at the time, almost 400 black Americans with the disease were not given medical treatment so that researchers could determine the course of the disease and its impact on the body's neurological and cardiovascular systems. The subjects chosen for the experiment were poor black sharecroppers from rural Tuskegee, Alabama who were deceitfully told that they were going to be receiving treatments for "bad blood." The "treatments" were just medical tests that measured how severe their syphilitic condition had progressed and no actual treatment was given to them. During this multi-decade study of black men with syphilis, 40 of their wives became infected with the disease, and 19 children were born with congenital syphilis. Many of the untreated men went on to experience painful and prolonged deaths.

The study finally attracted national attention in 1972 when a Washington newspaper reporter learned about the experiment and published an article about it. The article triggered public outrage, leading to the termination of the study and the passage of several medical ethics laws to regulate future health-related research. A year after the study was stopped, the NAACP won a nine million dollar lawsuit against the federal researchers and used the money to fund medical care for the experiment's subjects. Later, the U.S. government agreed to provide lifetime free medical care to the infected men along with their wives and surviving children, and in 1997, President Bill Clinton delivered a formal, public apology for the federal government's role in the Tuskegee Experiment.

Source: (McMahon, 2020)

Public health professionals today use the term "social determinants of health" to refer to the fact that American citizens' residential area, race, and income strongly influence and can often determine their overall level of health and life expectancy by affecting their access to quality health care, quality nutrition, and other health-promoting environmental conditions (Belk, 2020). For example, the residential environments of poor black children who grow up in urban slums often contain old, deteriorating buildings with lead paint peeling from walls and from lead pipes that deliver water to neighborhood homes and schools. As a result, black children have been found to have higher levels of lead in their bloodstream than any other racial group. High blood-lead levels increase their risk of death from lead poisoning, and low lead-blood levels have been found to impair children's mental ability, reduce attention span, and lower impulse self-control—which increases their tendency to engage in high-risk behavior that can jeopardize their physical well-being and lower their life expectancy (Packtor, 2018).

The COVID-19 pandemic has further widened racial gaps in health and longevity by disproportionately affecting people of color. Black Americans, for example, have experienced higher COVID infection rates (Lee, 2020) and account for more than 33% of COVID-related deaths—despite representing only about 12% of the population (Levey, 2020). Studies involving more than 10,000 patients reveal that these black–white differences in COVID infection and death rates are not related to biological differences between the two races (Healy, 2021) but to differences in their social roles and environmental conditions. For instance, people of color are more likely to have lower-paying jobs in the service sector that requires them working in public spaces rather than from their own home, and when people of color live at home, they are more likely to live in smaller, more crowded residences because they cannot afford larger, more spacious housing (Lin et al., 2021). Despite these racial disparities in health outcomes, a national poll during the COVID-19 pandemic showed that only 38% of Americans believed that systemic racism played a major role in people of color experiencing poorer health and having lower life expectancies (Southern Poverty Law Center, 2021).

Reflection 8.1

Do you think that your racial characteristics have affected the quality of health care or medical treatment you have received in life thus far? If yes, in what way(s)?

The Electoral System: Voting Rights and Political Representation

System racism has taken place with respect to the right of people of color to vote (suffrage), serve on juries, and hold political office. Slaves, of course, had none of these civic rights. Attempts to deny blacks the right of political representation can be traced back to the infamous "three-fifths" clause included in the original Constitution of the United States, which stipulated that three-fifths of all slaves be counted as citizens in Southern slave-holding states to determine how many state representatives would be included in Congress, even though no blacks had the right to vote as American citizens (Wills, 2003). This clause gave whites in the South's slave-holding states extra political representatives and more votes in the U.S. House of Representatives and Electoral College, which they could use to ensure that the system of slavery was maintained (Feagin, 2005). After the Civil War was fought and slavery was finally abolished, Abraham Lincoln planned to grant voting rights to educated black men but was assassinated before he could do so. In fact, the motive of his assassin, John Wilkes Booth, had less to do with the South's loss of the war and more to do with Lincoln's plans to give voting rights to blacks, which Booth decried as "nigger citizenship." Lincoln's successor as president, Andrew Johnson, was a politician from Tennessee who opposed black voting rights, having gone on record as saying that "negroes have shown less capacity for government than any other race of people" and that granting them the right to vote would lead to "such a tyranny as this continent has never yet witnessed" (Serwer, 2020). Congress did eventually pass the 15th Amendment in 1869, which prohibited denying citizens the right to vote based on their skin color. However, the amendment failed to ensure that voting practices would be implemented uniformly (and fairly) across all individual states and counties (Foner, 2014).

Emboldened by President Johnson's views of black voting rights and the freedom to exert local control of their own voting practices, whites in the South began implementing a

"Here [in America], where universal suffrage is the fundamental idea of the Government, to rule us [blacks] out is to make us an exception, to brand us with the stigma of inferiority."
—FREDERICK DOUGLASS, ABOLITIONIST, STATESMAN, AUTHOR, AND FORMER SLAVE

number of practices designed to suppress black votes and remove elected black politicians. In some parts of the South, armed whites, including members of the Ku Klux Klan (first formed in 1866) blocked blacks from attempting to vote or prevented black polls from opening on Election Day, often using violence to do so. The Klan functioned basically as a military force that served to ensure that the politicians elected represented white plantation owners, which at the time, were Democrats. The Klan even blocked blacks from publishing statements of support for Republican candidates. For instance, in 1868, white gangs broke into Republican meetings in a New Orleans parish, demolished a Republican newspaper office and drove its editor out of the parish. Similarly, in an Alabama country, a gang of armed whites broke up a Republican campaign rally, killing four blacks and wounding 54 in the process (Foner, 2014). In Wilmington, North Carolina, after black political leaders had been legitimately elected to local government positions in 1868, a mob of 2,000 white men overthrew the elected local government, expelled them from the city, destroyed the only black newspaper in the city, and demolished properties and businesses that blacks developed after being freed by the Civil War; at least 60 people were killed in the process. The event came to be known as the "Wilmington Massacre"—the first coup in U.S. history in which Americans overthrew, removed, and replaced duly and democratically elected officials (Zinn Education Project, 2021).

Violent voter-suppression tactics continued into the twentieth century, such as the one that took place in Ocoee, Florida on Election Day, 1920. After a black man attempted to vote, 60 black homes and businesses were burnt to the ground, men were castrated and lynched, and the remaining blacks in town were driven out of town in what one historian called the "single bloodiest election day in modern American history" (Wilkerson, 2020, pp. 228–229). Such aggressive, often violent voter intimidation tactics served to sharply reduce black vote tallies; in some counties, it resulted in no blacks registering to vote at all.

Southern Democrats also used their economic power to control the voting process by cutting off financial credit to blacks who attended Republican meetings and by threatening to evict blacks from their employment on plantations if they attempted to vote Republican. Northern politicians turned a blind eye to these voter-interference maneuvers because they worried that empowering blacks with voting rights would disrupt the South's agricultural labor force and have a negative economic impact on Northern cotton manufacturers, merchants, and financiers (Foner, 2014).

In addition to suppressing black voting rights by physical force and economic sanctions, Southern states took advantage of the fact that the 15th amendment allowed them to conduct local voting practices as they saw fit. Consequently, they adopted voting laws and policies to suppress black votes that did not technically qualify as racial discrimination, such as imposing: (a) poll taxes that blacks couldn't afford to pay, (b) literacy tests that blacks couldn't pass because they were denied the opportunity to attend school, and (c) felon laws that barred blacks from voting if they violated "Jim Crow" laws that didn't apply to whites (e.g., curfew violations) (Alexander, 2020).

It was to protest these voter restriction and suppression laws that on March 7, 1965, 600 civil rights activists marched from Selma to Montgomery, Alabama. They were driven back by state troopers, sheriff deputies, and a horse-mounted posse that clubbed and gassed the unarmed marchers as they crossed the Edmund Pettus Bridge. Media coverage of the event, which came to be known as "Bloody Sunday," shocked the nation and ultimately led to the passage of the Voting Rights Act of 1965, which banned racially discriminatory voting policies. The Act required voting laws in the South be approved by a federal official to ensure they would not have discriminatory impact on people of color. After the Voting Rights Act

"The right to vote freely for the candidate of one's choice is of the essence of a democratic society, and any restrictions on that right strike at the heart of representative government."

—EARL WARREN, CHIEF JUSTICE OF THE UNITED STATES, 1953-1969

On March 1, 2020, people from across the country gathered to commemorate the anniversary of the famous "Bloody Sunday" march for voting rights that took place in 1965. © Michael Scott Milner/Shutterstock.com

was passed, the turnout among black voters increased dramatically. In Mississippi, for example, black voter turnout increased from 6% in 1964 to 59% in 1969 (Kendi, 2016).

In 2008, when Barack Obama won the presidential election, for the first time in U.S. history the rate of voter turnout for blacks almost equaled that of whites (Roberts, 2009). In 2012, another large black voter turnout helped elect Obama again. In 2013, the U.S. Supreme Court then ruled that the Voting Rights Act law was no longer needed and states with histories of racial discrimination were no longer required to have their voting laws approved by the federal government. States were again allowed to establish their own election rules and procedures, and those rules and procedures could be controlled by the political party in power at the state and local level. Soon thereafter, over 20 states proceeded to adopt voting policies that state legislators claim were designed to protect the integrity of the election process but also were likely to restrict black participation in the voting process (Anderson, 2016). For instance, in some states, voter ID laws were adopted that required a driver-license photo as proof of identification to vote. Since people of color are disproportionately represented among low-income groups, they are less likely to have a driver's license photo ID because they are less likely to own a car. And lower-income people of color who do have licenses are more likely to have their license temporarily suspended because of yet-to-be paid driver registration fees or traffic fines. Other states required voters to register within a very short period of time before Election Day or opened election offices only during work hours or weekdays, which reduces turnout among low-income voters of color because they cannot afford to miss work. Other states eliminated voting precincts in areas with large minority populations, forcing voters to travel long distances and wait in long lines; at the same time, precincts in highly white-populated areas were expanded (Kent, 2020). In 2021, some states attempted to adopt policies that would block early voting on Sundays, but their attempt was blocked by critics who called it out as a direct attempt to suppress black votes by interfering with the traditional "Souls to the Polls" practice used by black churches to organize trips to the voting polls after Sunday church services (Izaguirre, 2021).

Reflection 8.2

Did your family members vote in the last presidential election? Was their decision to vote or not to vote influenced by how easy it was for them to vote?

Disinformation has also been used to suppress or intimidate voters. In 2020, tens of thousands of minority voters in several Midwestern and Northern states received robocalls falsely claiming that voting by mail could be dangerous. Authorities eventually traced the calls to two white supremacists who were charged with felony voter intimidation (SPLC, 2021). Also during the 2020 election year, members of white supremacist group "deputized" themselves as enforcers of election laws and threatened to show up at the polls to "fight voter fraud" (SPLC, 2020).

Recently, some states have adopted voting laws that are likely to suppress voter turnout among people of color. © Orlowski Designs LLC/Shutterstock.com

Vote-suppression policies have contributed to the fact that the voter turnout is typically over 80% for Americans with incomes exceeding $150,000 but less than 50% for Americans with incomes less than $20,000—a disproportionate number of whom are people of color (Peter G. Peterson Foundation, 2019). UCLA professor Richard Diamond (2019) points out that voter-suppressing policies and practices are inconsistent with the "fundamental advantages of American democracy . . . citizens knowing that they are being heard and that they have peaceful outlets for expression; reduction of the risk of civil violence; [and] incentives to the government to invest in all citizens (ultimately, because they vote), rather than just in an elite fraction of citizens" (p. 362).

The United States is also one of the few democratic countries in the world that prohibit incarcerated citizens from voting, and in so doing, it suppresses the vote of low-income blacks who are disproportionately incarcerated for crimes than more affluent whites—due in large part to systemic racism in the criminal justice system (see pp. 250-269 for details and documentation)—and no other country disqualifies citizens of their right to vote after being released from prison as extensively as does the United States (Alexander, 2020). A small number of European nations will disqualify released prisoners from voting, but the disqualification is limited to certain crimes and disqualifies only a fraction of former prisoners. In the United States, voting disqualification can be automatically applied to all former prisoners, regardless of the nature or circumstances of their crime (Ispahani, 2006). To win back their right to vote, former felons must pay fines and court costs, and submit extensive paperwork to multiple agencies. According to Michelle Alexander, highly acclaimed legal scholar and civil rights attorney: "These bureaucratic minefields are the modern-day equivalent of poll taxes and literacy tests—'colorblind' rules designed to make voting a practical impossibility for a group defined largely by race" (Alexander, 2020, p. 198).

Some states have gone as far as to block voting access for any citizen who have ever had a felony conviction, even after all conditions of the sentence have been successfully completed. For instance, Florida adopted this policy and in so doing, disenfranchised 1.7 million of its residents, the majority of whom were people of color (Anderson, 2016).

The Criminal Justice System: Policing Practices, Legal Representation, and Sentencing Policies

Formally defined, criminal justice is a society's system of law enforcement that involves apprehension and legal defense of criminal suspects, and the prosecution and sentencing of suspects convicted of criminal offenses. Evidence of systemic racism has been found to occur at each of the following stages in the criminal justice system:

- Monitoring and Arrest
- Pretrial Detention
- Conviction and Sentencing
- Incarceration
- Post-Incarceration Punishment

Evidence for racial bias at each of these stages will be discussed next.

Monitoring and Arrest

Compared to whites, blacks are subjected to more police stops and searches (Harris, 2002), in part because police more closely monitor the behavior of people living in densely populated "high crime" areas such as inner-city ghettos, where a disproportionate number of blacks live. Nonetheless, the closer observation and surveillance of inner-city residents still qualifies as a form of racial bias and racial profiling because ghettos are segregated by race. A good example of the extent of such bias is a report form used in 2016 by one inner-city Baltimore police precinct that included a space next to trespassing misdemeanors for the suspect's race and gender which was pre-printed: "Black Male" (Natapoff, 2018).

Research also shows that in geographical areas beyond the ghetto that are occupied by both blacks and white, blacks are more likely to be subjected to police stops and searches. For instance, a study conducted in New Jersey revealed that 15% of all drivers on the New Jersey Turnpike were people of color, yet 42% of all traffic stops and 73% of all arrests were for black motorists—despite the fact that blacks and whites violated traffic laws at almost exactly the same rate. Similar results were reported in studies conducted on a stretch of the I-95 highway outside of Baltimore, where blacks comprised about 17% of the drivers but accounted for 70% of those who were stopped and searched. The vast majority of these stops and searches were conducted to catch motorists suspected of carrying illegal drugs, but in both studies, results showed that the percentage of stops that led to the discovery of illegal drugs was higher for white drivers than black drivers (Harris, 2002).

Alexander (2020) suggests that the disproportionate rate at which people of color are arrested is as much a *product* of racial profiling as it is a justification for racial profiling. She suggests there are two key reasons why blacks are more often the targets of stops, searches, and arrests: (a) they are more likely to live in overcrowded housing neighborhoods that lack private spaces so all their activities, including illegal activity, tend to take place outdoors where they can be more easily detected and (b) police would be subjected to more public outrage and political backlash if they conducted stop-and-search practices in white middle-class neighborhoods. Supporting these arguments is research showing that whites use and sell illegal drugs at similar or higher rates than poorer blacks (Schwartztol, 2011), but whites are less likely to be monitored and caught for doing so because they have the privilege of living in less-policed neighborhoods that allows them to engage in illegal drug activities within the privacy of their own homes. Author and anti-racist activist, Tim Wise (2011), relates a personal story that captures his drug-using privileges as a white teenager living in a place where there was little police surveillance and interference:

I can't even remember, because there are simply too many to recall, the number of parties I attended in high school at which hundreds of underaged kids, including myself, were drinking and taking various types of drugs. Guys were taking cover charges at the end of the driveway and stamping people's hands, right on the road, in plain view of everyone, including the police cars that would occasionally cruise by to make sure the noise wasn't getting too loud. On more than a few occasions the cops would even come onto the property in response to a noise complaint and tell us to cut the music down. There is simply no chance that the officers didn't know alcohol was being served; likewise, they had to have been able to detect the smell of marijuana in the air. Yet not once did they arrest anyone or warn us that next time we wouldn't be so lucky. There would always be a few people of color around, but for the most part these were white spaces, which immediately gave law enforcement officials reasons to cut us slack. Had these house parties been in black neighborhoods they would never have been allowed to go on at all. Our illegality was looked at with a wink and a nod. (p. 73)

Reflection 8.3

Would you say the neighborhood in which you grew up was over-policed or under-policed compared with some other neighborhoods? Why?

Pretrial Detention

The criminal justice system requires that people arrested for a crime must pay bail—a fee determined by the court to ensure they will show up for trial. Wealthier arrestees can avoid pretrial jail time by paying bail fee to the court or a bond company; those who lack the financial resources to pay bail are detained in jail. Since blacks have lower levels of income and higher rates of poverty than whites, they are less able to the pay bail fee and, therefore, are more likely to be jailed as they await trial. Furthermore, the average bail fee for blacks charged with a crime is 35% than it is for whites because the two major factors are used to determine the bail amount are employment stability and family resources, which has a disproportionate impact on blacks because they have higher rates of unemployment and less family income. As a result, pretrial detention rates for blacks are four times higher than whites charged with the same crimes (Alexander, 2020). The time spent in pre-trial detention can last for months, penalizing the person detained in multiple ways that have long-term consequences. Eberhardt (2019) effectively summarizes the enduring consequences of lengthy pretrial detention:

> Being behind bars for months awaiting trial can unravel a life: the accused can be fired from a job, be subject to eviction, incur debt from being unable to pay bills, [and] lose custody of children. Many defendants are so desperate to be free that they bargain for short sentences or immediate release by pleading guilty to whatever lesser charge the prosecutor presents. That can saddle them with a criminal conviction that has lifelong consequences, limiting where they can live, what jobs they can perform, their ability to vote, and their eligibility for college student loans (p. 108).

Legal Representation

The majority of black defendants do not have the fiscal resources to hire a private, personal attorney. The minority of black defendants who have those fiscal resources are almost twice as likely to have the charge against them reduced than the majority of less-affluent blacks assigned court-appointed public defenders—who are poorly paid and saddled with outrageously high caseloads totaling 100 or more clients at a time (Eberhardt, 2019). Often pressured by long, mandatory sentences, blacks with public defendants often agree to plea bargains in which they enter a guilty plea before going to trial—even for crimes they didn't commit (Alexander, 2020). One report issued by the American Bar Association (2004) reached the following conclusion about the inequities in America's legal defense system: "All too often, defendants plead guilty, even if they are innocent, without really understanding their legal rights or what is occurring. The fundamental right to a lawyer that Americans assume applies to everyone accused of criminal conduct effectively does not exist in practice for countless of people across the United States" (p. iv).

Conviction and Sentencing

"The lighter the skin, the lighter the sentence."

—POPULAR EXPRESSION USED TO DESCRIBE RACIAL BIAS IN THE CRIMINAL JUSTICE SYSTEM

Once convicted, America's harsh sentencing policies—particularly for drug-related offenses—require inmates to spend more time in jail or prison than any other country in the world (Alexander, 2020). Research shows that the length of the assigned sentence is influenced by the racial features of the person convicted. African Americans with darker skin, wider noses, and thicker lips are more likely to receive harsher sentences than lighter-skinned blacks (Eberhardt, 2019). Simply put, skin lightness mitigates the judged severity of the crime; skin darkness magnifies it.

Studies also show that prosecutors exhibit racial bias by more aggressively pursuing and prosecuting crimes committed by black youths than crimes committed by white youths (Graham & Lowery, 2004). Contributing to this racial bias was the popularization of a criminology theory that began circulating during the 1990s, called "superpredator" theory, which characterized black juvenile delinquents as impulsive and remorseless criminals. The theory predicted there would be a large increase in youth crime and violence due to the growing population of black youth and that white Americans were in danger of being victimized. Politicians picked up on this theory and used it to pass get-tough-on-crime laws aimed at juvenile offenders. The superpredator prediction never materialized; juvenile crime rates actually dropped after the theory was circulated (Vitale,

2018). Nonetheless, the theory went viral and politicians continued to pass harsh "adult time for adult crime" sentencing laws for juvenile offenders (Taylor-Thompson, 2020).

Studies also show that racial bias takes place with respect to death penalty sentences. In one Southern state, 70% of the cases that involved a black offender and white victim, prosecutors sought the death sentence; in contrast, the death penalty was sought in only 19% of the cases where the offender was white and the victim black. Also, black offenders convicted of killing a white victim are more than four times likely to receive a death sentence than those charged with killing a black victim (Alexander, 2020). In a 20-year review of black males convicted of homicide, it was found that black men with more "stereotypically black" facial features (e.g., darker skin color, broader noses, thicker lips, and kinkier hair) who were convicted of murdering a white victim were more than twice as likely to receive the death sentence; however, if their victim was black, they were sentenced to death at exactly the same rate as those with less stereotypically black features (Eberhardt, 2019).

Incarceration

Blacks make up 13% of America's total population but 45% of its total prison population (Anderson, 2016). The incarceration rate for black male youth (age 16–25) is more than five times higher than white youth (Plaut, 2010); among first-time youth offenders, blacks are six times more likely than whites to be sentenced to prison for exactly the same crime (Hoyt et al., 2002).

Incarcerated inmates are housed in prisons supported by private-sector investments and these prisons operate like any other profit-making business or industry. Entrepreneurs in the prison-construction industry obtain federal contracts to build prisons; in

Research shows that compared with white youth, black youth are 5 times more likely to be incarcerated and 6 times more likely to be sentenced to prison for committing the same crimes. © Motortion Films/Shutterstock.com

2020 alone, the prison-construction industry spent over a million dollars on political lobbying. In many rural areas across the country, prisons are the main source of local employment (Alexander, 2020). Thus, efforts to reduce the number of prisons and the prison population often encounter resistance because it's likely to result in lost jobs, lost investments, and other collateral economic benefits generated by the current penal system. Michele Alexander argues that such resistance, based on economic self-interest, is often shrewdly repackaged and sold as being good crime-prevention criminal justice policy: "Few would openly argue that we should lock up millions of people just so that other people can have jobs or get a good return on their private investments. Instead, familiar arguments resurface about the need to be tough on 'criminals,' not coddle them or give 'free passes'" (Alexander, 2020, p. 298). This "tough on crime" rationale (or rationalization) requires the American government to spend lots of money to jail lots of low-income people of color for low-level crimes, most of which are related to drug use and mental illness (Cosgrove, 2020). This is a major reason why America's incarceration rate is the highest in world, exceeding the rate of all European democracies by 500 percent; the United States holds only 5% of the world's population yet accounts for 25% of the world's prison population (López, 2014).

The 1960s marked the passage of the Civil Rights Act, the Voting Rights Act, and the Fair Housing Act—all part of President Johnson's "Great Society" initiative or what historians have called the "Second Reconstruction." However, similar to how America's first attempt at Reconstruction after the Civil War was obliterated by Jim Crow policies, its second Reconstruction attempt to promote racial equality and economic justice was drowned out by anti-crime laws (Serwer, 2020). Politicians from both parties proceeded to reduce funding for the Great Society's social and economic equity programs while redirecting vast amounts of funding into law enforcement programs, most of which targeted drug-related offenses committed by low-income racial minorities. Thus, law enforcement agencies, jails, and prisons became the primary government-funded programs in many low-income communities across America (Hinton, 2016). The loads of money divested from programs designed to provided systemic, large-scale crime prevention and invested in programs aimed at criminal detection and prosecution of individual low-level street infractions did more to exacerbate racial inequitiesin the criminal justice system than it did to alleviate crime (Alexander, 2020; Pager, 2007).

Reflection 8.4

Do you think more governmental resources now need to be devoted to crime-prevention programs or crime detection-and-arrest programs? Why?

Post-Incarceration Punishment

After prisoners are released from the penal system, they encounter what sociologists and criminologists refer to as the "period of invisible punishment"—a post-incarceration type of penalty that goes beyond the criminal justice system and is imposed as a form of "legal" societal discrimination in access to employment, housing, education, and public benefits. For instance, ex-offenders have restrictions placed on their access to federal loans for education, employment in many public sector jobs, public housing, and food stamps (Travis et al., 2001). López (2014) provides summarizes the consequences of post-incarceration punishment as follows:

> When you come out [of prison], you find your life chances vastly diminished, your right to vote gone, no right to welfare to help you back to your feet or to catch you if you falter, locked out of government-supported housing and discriminated against when seeking a place to rent, disqualified for a student loan, and every time you apply for a job they ask about your criminal record and that provides a perfect legal reason not to hire you (p. 53).

The first year after prison, in particular, represents a critical transition period for ex-cons trying to make a successful reentry into society. "Get tough on crime" political policies have made this transition difficult by underfunding the parole system, leaving it poorly equipped to help parolees make a successful post-incarceration transition. Budgets for parole departments have been cut substantially and the average caseload for parole officers has grown exponentially—from 25 to 70—twice the recommended load for adequate parolee supervision and support (Pager, 2007). Thus, the vast majority of parolees receive little or no personalized assistance for transitioning back to their communities (Petersilia, 1999). Instead, a parole system that was originally designed to focus on the rehabilitation and societal integration of former inmates has been shifted to becoming a surveillance-and-detection system, in which parolees are routinely and randomly checked for drug use, failure to locate or hold a job, missing meetings, not making curfews, and a host of other minor (often petty) behaviors or technical violations of parole stipulations (Irwin & Austin, 2012). Police are also free to stop and search a parolee at any time, even without probable cause or reasonable suspicion (Eberhardt, 2019). In addition, a standard condition for parole is that the parolee not associate with anyone who has had a felony conviction. For someone returning from prison to inner-city ghettos, this can be a very difficult condition to meet (Alexander, 2020).

Not surprisingly, the move away from a parole system that once focused on rehabilitation to a system that now focuses more on detection, apprehension, and reincarceration has resulted in a sharp reduction in the percentage of parolees who successfully complete the terms of their probation without being rearrested. One study revealed that the percentage of parolee recidivism rates increased by over 25% after the parole system purpose moved from an emphasis on parolee rehabilitation to a greater focus on parolee monitoring and parole-violation detection (Petersilia, 1999). The shift to a detect-and-catch parole system has led to what criminologists and sociologist call a "revolving door of prison" (Pager, 2007) that returns two of three former prisoners back to prison within a few years after their release—mostly not for committing further crimes, but for not meeting a condition stipulated by their parole (Eberhardt, 2019).

> "No one could claim that our prisons, which emphasize punishment and deterrence rather than rehabilitation and retraining, constitute investments in our future."
>
> —JARED DIAMOND, GEOGRAPHER, HISTORIAN, ANTHROPOLOGIST, AND PULITZER-PRIZE-WINNING AUTHOR

Long-Term Impact of Incarceration on Employment and Income

Racially discriminatory incarceration practices can and do have major, long-term negative consequences, particularly on the lives of black youth, because being incarcerated as a juvenile sharply reduces future prospects for finding stable adult employment, even if the juvenile never engages in criminal activity as an adult (Sampson & Laub, 1993). Since nearly 80% of parole boards require "gainful employment" as a condition for parole, this condition is rarely met because parolees return to inner-city neighborhoods where unemployment rates are very high; consequently, about 75% of ex-offenders remain unemployed up to a year after their release (Petersilia, 2003).

Inmates who are given the opportunity to participate in educational and vocational training programs while in prison are over 40% less likely to become repeat offenders after being released and much more likely to secure employment; however, less than one-third of American prisons offer such training programs (Eberhardt, 2017). Thus, the majority of inmates have no opportunity to build employability skills while they're imprisoned; at the same time, they're not able to make contacts with potential employers outside of prison (Pager, 2007).

After being released, when former inmates apply for job openings, they face major discrimination in the hiring process because potential employers often use their criminal record as a screening device to immediately reject them without even the opportunity to engage in a personal interview. In one series of studies, bright and articulate college students, black and white, were well coached on how to present themselves to potential employers that had advertised position openings. When applying for these positions, the students also supplied with fictitious resumes that showed their level of education and work experiences matched up well with the position's qualifications and responsibilities. One-half of the students were also assigned a fictitious criminal record as an ex-offender that was submitted along with their resume. The researchers found that when white and black applicants with fictitious criminal records applied for the same position, the rejection rate of black applicants was twice as high—despite their having the same level of education and prior work experiences. In fact, any mention of a criminal offense on the black student's application form almost tripled their rejection rate; 95% of them never received callbacks from the employers for an in-person interview. Amazingly, white applicants with a criminal record were found to receive slightly higher rates of callbacks from employers (17%) than black applicants without a criminal record (14%). This finding which suggests that even black job applicants with no criminal record encounter race-based employment discrimination because they belong to a racial group or category that employers view as associated with criminal behavior (Pager, 2007). Furthermore, when blacks have an arrest record for a crime that they were judged not to be guilty of, white employers still are reluctant to hire them, even if their job application is accompanied by a judge's letter certifying that the black applicant was found innocent. Thus, any contact at all with the criminal justice system is often enough to remove a black job applicant from further consideration (Cohen & Nisbett, 1997; Schwartz & Skolnick, 1962).

It is noteworthy that unlike other democratic nations, America allows employers virtually unlimited and ongoing access to information about people's criminal background and arrest record, thus leaving arrestees subject to subsequent "legal" employment discrimination for the remainder of their lives. In the United States, if a person is not convicted of a criminal charge, a criminal record for that person is still added to the state database and the record is visible not only to law enforcement agencies but to prospective employers (Agan et al., 2021). Even when state records have been officially sealed or erased, online criminal background-check services often allow employers to gain access to a job applicant's criminal history (Pager, 2007).

Employers' willingness to hire people with criminal records tends to be highest in fields that require little customer contact, such as construction or manufacturing; however, those jobs have virtually disappeared from inner cities due to relocation of industries and manufacturing work to suburbs (Alexander, 2020). When black men with criminal records apply for jobs in suburban areas where there is a much higher demand for workers than inner cities, studies show that they encounter particularly high rates of rejection (Holzer & Lalonde, 2000; Pager, 2007).

Summarizing research on the the employment prospects of blacks who have any criminal record, Devah Prager, Harvard professor of sociology and public policy, reached the following conclusion:

> These results are suggestive of a "two strikes and you're out" mentality among employers, who appear to view the combination of blackness and criminal re-

cord as an indicator of serious trouble. Black men already appear to be risky prospects for employment; those with known criminal pasts, however, are officially certified bad news. Where for whites a criminal background represents one serious strike against them, for blacks it appears to represent almost total disqualification . . . . Employers continue to use race as an easy way to screen out applicants at the first stage of review (Prager, 2007, pp. 146–147 & 158).

Adding insult to injury, when parolees leave prison, they leave with substantial debt that is owed to a number of agencies, including fees they need to pay to probation departments, court systems, and child-support enforcement offices for debts they accumulated while they were incarcerated and unemployed. Released prisoners are even required to pay for drug testing services and drug treatment programs that they received as a condition of their parole. In addition, many states impose "poverty penalties" by tacking on fines for late payment of fees and by charging interest to parolees who are unable to pay off all their monthly debts at once (thus adding to profits made by private debt collectors). As a result, even for those ex-offenders who manage to find employment after being released from prison, many of them have their paychecks garnished to pay off debts. Thus, former prisoners often end up without a wage-earning job, a decent place to live, and difficulty paying back parole-related debt and child support. Thus, blacks who get caught up in the criminal justice system end up getting punished twice: first they are locked up in prison and then they are locked out of mainstream society (Alexander, 2020).

An in-depth, four-year study of families of black men who were incarcerated, it was found that they were stigmatized. Not only did the man experience the stigma of being put in prison, but the consequences his imprisonment stigmatized his family—by leaving the family fatherless, more dependent on welfare, and lost social respect among members of the community (Braman, 2007). Michelle Alexander (2020) points out that another major consequence of imprisonment on black families is that black youth are stigmatized by being left with a weaker family support structure and a stronger tendency to turn to their peers to provide them with compensatory social support. They are also more likely to internalize and embrace their stigma to regain some measure of self-esteem. As she notes: "It is helpful to step back and put the behavior of young black men who appear to embrace 'gangsta culture' in the proper perspective. There is absolutely nothing abnormal or surprising about a severely stigmatized group embracing their stigma. Psychologists have long observed that when people feel hopelessly stigmatized, a powerful coping strategy—often the only apparent route to self-esteem—is embracing one's stigmatized identity" (p. 213).

"Economic and racial inequality constrain individual and family choices. They set the limits of human agency. Within the bounds of the possible, individuals and families resist, adapt, or succumb."

—THOMAS J. SUGRUE, PROFESSOR OF HISTORY & SOCIOLOGY, UNIVERSITY OF PENNSYLVANIA

Reflection 8.5

Visualize a person incarcerated in a state penitentiary, what image comes to mind? What thought comes to mind about why that person is in prison?

How the "War on Drugs" Has Contributed to Systemic Racism in Criminal Arrests and Incarceration Rates

A national survey once included a question that asked respondents to "close your eyes for a second, envision a drug user, and describe that person to me." The survey results showed that 95% of the respondents reported an image of someone black—despite the fact that at the time of the survey, only 15% of America's drug users were black. The survey responders also reported picturing the typical drug trafficker as black, even though the majority of those selling drugs at the time were white (Burston et al., 1995). Blacks do not commit drug-related offenses (e.g., possession and sale) at higher rates than whites, yet they are almost three times more likely to be arrested for drug-related crimes (Schwartztol, 2011), are incarcerated at a rate six times higher than whites accused of similar offenses (Wilkerson, 2020), and serve longer sentences for their drug offenses (Alexander, 2020). Yet, when compared with white youth, black youth are less likely to use and sell illegal drugs (Johnson et al., 2007; Snyder & Sickman, 2006) and the rate at which white youth are admitted to hospitals for drug-related emergencies is about three times higher than it is for black youth (Western, 2006). Summarizing data gathered by the Centers for Disease Control, and the Department of Health and Human Services, Wise (2001) reports the following:

> White high school students are seven times more likely than blacks to have used cocaine; eight times more likely to have smoked crack; ten times more likely to have used LSD and seven times more likely to have used heroin . . . . What's more, white youth ages 12–17 are more likely to sell drugs: 34 percent more likely, in fact, than their black counterparts. And it is white youth who are twice as likely to binge drink, and nearly twice as likely as blacks to drive drunk (p. 1).

The bottom line: Young black men are *less* likely to use or sell drugs than white young men but are more likely to be arrested for drug use or sale. Once arrested, they are more likely to be sentenced, and once sentenced, they are likely to receive longer jail terms.

The roots of these racial disparities can be traced back to 1986, when the U.S. government declared a "war on drugs" and passed the Anti-Drug Abuse Act that established long, mandatory minimum prison terms for low-level drug dealing or drug using (possession) of just five grams of crack cocaine. The typical mandatory sentence for a first-time offender was set at 5–10 years. In other developed countries, a first-time drug offenders may not be jailed at all, and even if incarcerated, they would not spend more than a few months in jail. In fact, the U.S. criminal justice system imposes sentences for drug crimes that are often longer than those imposed for violent crimes in many other countries (Mauer, 1999).

Once the severe sentencing policies proposed by the Anti-Drug Abuse Act put in place, America's prison population quadrupled over the course of the next 15 years; drug offenders accounted for two-thirds of this rapid growth in prison inmates (Mauer, 2006). Between 1981 and 1991, Department of Defense antidrug expenditures grew from $86 million to $1,042 million and FBI antidrug budgets swelled from $38 million to $181. At the same time, no extra federal funds were targeted for other crimes (including violent crimes) and funding for drug treatment, prevention, and education were slashed sharply. In addition, the U.S. Justice Department cut in half the number of specialists assigned to identify and prosecute white-collar crimes (Beckett, 1997)—crimes that inflict much greater economic harm on the public—such as the 2008 financial crisis—during which blacks lost more than half their wealth due to white-collar banking crimes (Karakatsanis, 2019).

Along with the increased federal funding for anti-drug law enforcement, more aggressive tools and tactics were approved to "fight" the war on drugs. SWAT teams that were originally created and used only for emergency situations, such as rescuing hostages and combat hijackers, began to be used by local police for drug raids. Law enforcement agencies were also given access to military bases, intelligence and weaponry for use in the "war" on drugs, thus moving community policing toward military policing (Alexander, 2020). Later, after the September 2001 terrorist attack on the United States, the Patriot Act was passed to root out potential terrorist, empowering law enforcement agents to search homes and apartments without notifying the resident. This practice ended up being used mainly to gain forceful entry into residences of suspected drug users. Such aggressive search and arrest tactics resulted in larger numbers of publicized drug-related arrests which, in turn, led the public to conclude that what they were seeing was a sudden and massive surge of drug use in America (particularly among inner-city people of color); instead, what they were seeing had more to do with the massive infusion of money to support and reward police departments to seek and make drug-related arrests (Russell, 1988).

Law enforcement agencies were also empowered with the rights "no knock" entries and break into private property for the purpose of catching suspected drug users or dealers. This practice was used in 2020 to break into the apartment of a 26-year-old black woman named Breonna Taylor, an emergency room technician. She was asleep with her boyfriend when police broke into her apartment. Suspecting criminal intruders, her boyfriend fired his licensed gun to fend them off. The entering police officers fired six shots in return, one of which killed Ms. Taylor. No drugs were found in the apartment (Wilber, 2021).

Many state and local law enforcement officials did not approve of the federal government's involvement with, and fiscal support for aggressive tactics targeting drug use, often viewing the war on drugs as a diversion that took away funds needed to deal with more serious crimes. To overcome this local resistance, the federal government offered large cash grants to local law-enforcement agencies as incentives for making federal drug-law enforcement a top priority. In addition, Congress passed a law in 1984 that allowed local police agencies to gain and retain 80% of all assets confiscated from people arrested for drug-related crimes (e.g., cash, car, and property). This law also empowered law enforcement to confiscate assets of family members of the drug offender whose property may have been involved in the commitment of a drug crime. For instance, if a young man was arrested for marijuana possession while driving his mother's car and his mother knew that he was using marijuana (even if just occasionally for recreational purposes), she could have her car confiscated. Similar to how the prison industry has profited from building and housing convicts arrested for drug-related offenses, so too has law enforcement agencies. Law enforcement agencies were allowed not only to seize but keep property confiscated when making arrests for associated with illegal activity, thus providing additional incentives to make drug raids and drug busts (Alexander, 2020).

In a comprehensive review of police traffic stops nationwide, it was found that many of these stops often had less to enforcing traffic laws and keeping road safe and more to do with using the stops as a pretext to search for and arrest motorists for drug possession. As previously noted, black drivers are more likely to be stopped for traffic violations under this pretext (Baumgartner et al., 2018). In a federal investigation of the Ferguson,

Missouri police department in 2015, the Department of Justice discovered that police officers were instructed to increase city revenue by filling ticket-writing quotas, which led the authors of the Justice report to conclude that the police were encouraged to "see residents, especially those who live in Ferguson's predominantly African American community less as constituents to be protected than as potential offenders and sources of revenue." The investigation also showed that black drivers were twice as likely to be stopped and have their cars searched for drugs, even though they were 26% less likely to be in possession of illegal drugs than white drivers. The federal investigators concluded that "this disproportionate burden on African Americans cannot be explained by any difference in the rate at which they violate the law. Rather . . . these disparities occur, at least in part, because of unlawful bias against and stereotypes about African Americans" (Eberhardt, 2019, p. 101).

Supporting and extending the conclusion drawn by the federal investigation in Ferguson are findings of a large-scale national study that examined 95 million traffic stop records of 56 city agencies between 2011 and 2018. The analysis included 113,000 stops made around 7 PM that, depending on the season of the year, would be a time when it would either be dark or light outside. The analysis revealed that black drivers were less likely to be pulled over by police less at night than during the day—when the color of their skin was more clearly visible and subject to racial bias (Pierson et al., 2020). The analysis also revealed that law-enforcement agents participated in a federally funded training on how to make traffic stops for minor driving violations, how to extend their length, and how to use them for drug searches, including how to use drug-sniffing dogs (Bascuas, 2007). One law enforcement agency in a Wisconsin county used this federal funding policy to quadruple its federal funding in just one year by quadrupling the number of drug arrests made during that year (Elbow, 2001). These financial incentives were so attractive that even local law enforcement officials who originally opposed the War on Drugs as unnecessary meddling by the federal government were persuaded to vigorously engage in the war. As Michelle Alexander notes, the next question became:

> Where should this war be fought and who should be taken prisoner? From the outset, the drug war could have been waged primarily in overwhelmingly white suburbs or on college campuses. SWAT teams could have rappelled from helicopters in gated suburban communities and raided the homes of high school lacrosse players known for hosting coke and ecstasy parties after their games. Suburban homemakers could have been placed under surveillance and subjected to undercover operations designed to catch them violating laws regulating use and sale of prescription "uppers" . . . but it did not. Instead, when police go looking for drugs, they look in the 'hood. [Such] tactics that would be political suicide in upscale white suburbs. So long as mass drug arrests are concentrated in impoverished urban areas, police chiefs have little reason to fear a political backlash (2020, p. 155).

Alexander (2020) notes further that "once blackness and crime, especially drug crime, became conflated in the public consciousness, the 'criminal black man' would inevitably become the primary target for law enforcement [and] many honestly and consciously would believe that black men deserve extra scrutiny and harsher treatment" (p. 135). One way in which harsher treatment was meted out came in the form of *mandatory* sentencing for drug-related crimes. Mandatory sentencing removes any opportunity for judges to consider a lighter sentence in light a defendant's background and extenuating circumstances—a particularly important consideration in drug cases because the offender's motivation for engaging in criminal activity often stems from drug addiction (Mumola & Karberg, 2006). Long-term minimum mandatory sentences also pressure those charged with drug offenses to enter a guilty plea and plea bargain (whether guilty or not) to avoid the risk of spending multiple years in prison. Such inequitable drug laws and sentencing policies led a number of federal judges to resign in protest, including judges with conservative political viewpoints (Alexander, 2020).

Many of those arrested and sentenced for drug-related crimes involved rack cocaine, a cheaper form of cocaine used by poorer, inner-city blacks. In contrast, wealthier suburban whites were using more expensive powder cocaine, which carried a much lighter sentence. A white cocaine dealer or user would have to be caught with 500 grams of powder cocaine to receive the same sentence as a black user of crack cocaine, even though both forms of the drug have the same pharmacological properties (Drug Policy Alliance, 2020). If a person were caught selling cocaine, the infamous "100-to-1" rule was applied, which meant that a person would have to be selling 100 times the amount of powder cocaine to get the same 10-year mandatory minimum prison sentence as a person selling crack cocaine (Savage, 2021). These vastly different sentencing policies were justified by claiming that crack cocaine was much more addictive and females who used it were likely to give birth to "crack babies." The former argument has not been consistently supported by research (Morgan & Zimmer, 1997; Reinarman et al., 1997) and the latter argument has been definitively disproved by scientific studies (Ackerman et al., 2010).

Contrary to the common belief that blacks are arrested for using and trafficking more "dangerous" drugs, marijuana accounted for almost 80% of the increased growth in drug arrests of blacks during the 1990s (King & Mauer, 2006). Even though the use of marijuana is essentially the same across all racial groups, blacks are three times more likely to be arrested for marijuana possession than whites, and despite increased legalization of the drug in many states, 545,000 people were arrested for marijuana-related offenses in 2019 alone (Abcarian, 2020). Many people of color are in jail for possession of marijuana—a drug that is now being grown and sold legally in many parts of the country by white entrepreneurs as part of the expanding marijuana and CBD production industry (Wilkerson, 2020).

Reflection 8.6

In the neighborhood where you grew up, what illegal drug do you think was most commonly used?

Were you aware anyone in your neighborhood who was arrested for using that drug or any other illegal drug?

Do you think that your race had anything to do with how you answered the two previous questions?

Carefully conducted research indicates that the increased incarceration of blacks for drug offenses fueled by the War on Drugs has played a major role in creating long-term unemployment, urban poverty, and broken families. Prison sentences for drug-related crimes reached such a high level that many criminologists and sociologists have concluded that the consequences of imprisonment are now more of a threat to the stability and safety of blacks in inner-city communities than crime itself (Clear, 2007). The fact is that most blacks now in prison are in prison for non-violent, drug-related crimes, and despite the common belief that increased incarceration rates reduce the rate of violent crimes committed in the context of drug trafficking, research consistently shows little relationship between the two (Mauer, 1999). For instance, during the 1980s, official crime rates in the United States remained steady while incarceration rates doubled; during the 1990s, crime rates fell by 30%, yet incarceration rates climbed by 60%. Comparing America with other countries, between 1960 and 1990, crime rates in Finland, Germany, and the United States were almost identical; however, during the same 30-year period, incarceration rates in the United States quadrupled, while the German rate remained stable and the Finnish rate fell (Pager, 2007).

> "The lie that most people sent to prison are 'violent offenders' is dangerous because it perpetuates the false notion that our system of mass incarceration is primarily concerned with violence and that it is well designed to keep communities safe."
> —MICHELLE ALEXANDER, AUTHOR, *THE NEW JIM CROW: MASS INCARCERATION IN THE AGE OF COLORBLINDNESS*

This massive increase in the size of the American prison population was not due to increase in crime but to changes in laws and policies, particularly those that redefined certain forms of drug use as felonious crimes and imposed sentences for these drug-related offenses that drug offenders to long prison terms. Today, America has an incarceration rate that is between 6 and 10 times higher than other industrialized nations. This difference can be traced directly to the war on drugs; there are more people locked up today just for drug offenses alone than were for *all* criminal offenses in 1980 (Alexander, 2020). Most of these drug offenders have no history of drug-related violence or major drug trafficking activity (Mauer & King, 2007), yet every year from 1993 and 2009, more Americans were incarcerated for drug crimes than violent crimes; and during this time period, blacks convicted of nonviolent drug offenses spent about the same amount of time in prison as whites convicted of violent crimes (Kendi, 2019).

It should be noted that "war on drug" laws were originally passed at a time when illegal drug use was not rising but actually declining. Politicians declared this war primarily to seek voter support for being seen as "tough on crime." Ironically, the political administration that declared the War on Drugs made a foreign policy decision that actually served to increase illegal drug use in America by allowing a foreign military group to fund a war against a totalitarian regime in their home country by using profits it made on sales of cocaine to the United States (Constantine Report, 2013). This foreign policy decision took place at the very time that the United States was experiencing an economic downturn and unemployment rates were rising, particularly in the inner cities. Thus, crack cocaine became more available to blacks in inner-city ghettos at the very time they were more likely to be unemployed and tempted vulnerable to use and sell it—providing one way to earn income at a time of rampant unemployment. The disproportionate number of arrests of blacks for such drug selling and using during this period created the erroneous belief among many Americans that most illegal drug using and drug selling took place in urban ghettos. The truth is that it was taking place in suburbia as well; blacks sold to blacks in the inner city while whites sell to whites elsewhere (Riley, 1997). The only difference was that suburban whites were selling drugs to friends and acquaintances to earn some extra cash and without close police surveillance, whereas inner-city blacks were selling them to make a living and with close police surveillance (Alexander, 2020).

Harsh laws passed during the drug war have largely remained in place because no aspiring politician wants to risk being viewed as "soft on crime" (Anderson, 2020). However, more than half of American citizens believe that drug abuse should be treated as a health issue rather than not a crime, and a considerable body of research supports their belief by showing that drug-treatment programs are more effective in reducing recidivism than incarceration, and are more cost-effective as well (Travis et al., 2001). Treatment programs would not only help those arrested from repeating their drug use, it would increase their prospects for employment by sending a message to potential employers that their drug use is under control and, therefore, less likely to interfere with their job performance.

It is noteworthy that the opioid abuse crisis—a crisis that largely involves whites—has not been viewed by the government as a criminal issue but as a public health problem. This different governmental response to drug use by whites and people of color reflects a repeated pattern discovered by historians and social scientists: When drug use is associated with people of color, the severity of punishment hardens; when it's associated with whites, it softens (Musto, 1997; Provine, 2007). For instance, whites have a long history of disproportionately higher rates of binge-drinking and drunk-driving (Mauer, 2006; Wise, 2011), but penalties for these forms of substance abuse are much less severe than for blacks arrested for possession of a small amount of crack cocaine. As Michelle Alexander (2020) notes:

> White people are generally allowed to *have* problems, and they've historically been granted the power to define and respond to them. But people of color . . . are regularly viewed and treated as the problem. This war [on drugs] did not merely increase the number of people in prisons and jails. It radically altered the life course of millions, especially black men who were the primary targets in the early decades of the war. Their lives and families were destroyed for drug crimes that were largely ignored on the other side of town (pp. xxxiv, xxviii).

 Consider This...

On election night in November 2020, the state of Oregon made history by decriminalizing "hard drugs" for personal use (e.g., cocaine, methamphetamine, and heroin), making it the first state to end participation in America's long "war on drugs" and the first state to begin treating substance use as a health issue rather than a criminal offense. Any person caught using these drugs will be cited for a civil violation similar to that of a traffic ticket and receive a fine that can be waived by participating in a free health assessment conducted by an addiction counselor. Oregon based its new approach on a model adopted in Portugal, a country which decriminalized drug use in 2001 as part of a national strategy to treat drug use as a public health issue. In the years following adoption of Portugal's new national policy, drug-related infections and overdose dropped sharply, as did its overall national rate of drug use. Portugal now has one of the lowest rates of drug use in Europe.

Source: Los Angeles Times (2020, November 25)

Implicit Racial Bias in the Perception, Detection, and Reaction to Crime

Racial bias in the perception of violent criminal activity has been documented by studies conducted with citizens of all ages and with police officers as well. In one study, college students were exposed to a series of black and white faces followed by objects that started out as grainy and became progressively clearer in successive frames. Some of the objects were related to crime (e.g., guns or knives) and others were not (e.g., staplers or cameras). Students were told to press a button the moment they could detect what each object was. Results showed that when students saw a black and white face, it had no impact on how long (how many frames) it took for them to then recognize an ambiguous picture of an object unrelated to crime after viewing the face. However, if the object was related to crime (e.g., a gun), students detected the picture sooner (in fewer frames) when it followed exposure to a black face. The quicker detection of crime-related objects after seeing a black face suggests an implicit (subconscious) bias toward perceiving blacks as more associated with crime than whites (Eberhardt, 2019). A follow-up study of implicit bias was conducted with police officers as the study's participants. Half the officers were exposed to words related to crime (e.g., "apprehend," "arrest," "capture," and "shoot") that were flashed for 75 milliseconds—too quickly to be consciously detected but long enough for the officer to report seeing "something." The other half of officers were flashed a series of jumbled letters instead of crime-related words. Both groups of officers were then shown two faces simultaneously—one white and one black. Compared with officers who were exposed to the jumbled letters, officers who were exposed to the crime-related words prior seeing the black and white faces were more likely to look at the black face, suggesting an implicit bias toward associating arrest and shooting with blacks (Eberhardt, 2019).

Similar results were found in an experimental study with police officers and juvenile probation officers who were asked to first read a short scenario about an adolescent that allegedly committed a crime; the scenario did not mention the race of the alleged criminal. After reading the crime scenario, half of the study's participants were asked to focus their attention on an asterisk in the middle of a screen while a word was flashed in a corner of the screen—so rapidly that the participants could see something but were not able to say for sure what they saw was, thus leaving open the possibility they may still have perceived it subliminally (subconsciously). Half the police officers and probation officers were exposed to rapidly flashed words associated with blacks (e.g., Harlem, homeboy, dreadlocks, basketball); the other half were exposed to rapidly flashed race-neutral words (e.g., heaven, kindness, devil, loneliness). Results of the study showed that the police and probation officers who were exposed to the briefly flashed words associated with blacks were more likely to rate the juvenile offender in the story they just read as being more responsible or blameworthy for the crime committed and deserving of a harsher sentence (Graham & Lowery, 2004). Again, these results again suggest an implicit (subconscious) bias toward perceiving blacks as connected to crime as well as being more culpable for their criminal offense.

Alexander (2020) notes that implicit racial bias can affect the everyday experiences of blacks that extend beyond the criminal justice system: "One need not be formally convicted in a court of law to be subject to this shame and stigma. As long as you 'look like' or 'seem like' a criminal, you are treated with the same suspicion and contempt, not just by police [but] by security guards, or hall monitors at your school,. . . the woman who crosses the street to avoid you and by the store employees who follow you through the aisles" (p. 202).

Racial Bias in Police Arrest Practices

In recent years, there have been a number of incidents in which blacks have been killed while in the process of being arrested by police officers. Some of the more high-profile incidents are summarized in **Box 8.1**

Box 8.1 **High-Profile Incidents of Blacks Dying during Police Arrests**

2020: During an arrest for allegedly passing a counterfeit $20 bill, George Floyd, a 46-year-old man, died in Minneapolis while a police officer knelt on Floyd's neck for nine minutes and 29 seconds while he was handcuffed and lying face down. Floyd's death sparked worldwide protests.

2020: Breonna Taylor, a 26-year-old black woman was shot while in bed in her apartment in Louisville when police broke into her apartment looking for a drug dealer who they mistakenly thought was living there. In commemoration of Ms. Taylor's death, a ceramic bust was constructed in Oakland, California. (The bust was smashed and eventually stolen.)

2018: In Sacramento, California, Stephon Clark was shot and killed in his grandmother's backyard while using his cell phone that the police mistakenly thought was a gun.

2015: After being arrested for carrying a knife, Freddie Gray died after being shot in the back while being loaded into the back of a Baltimore police van.

2015: After being stopped for a broken break light in North Charleston, South Carolina, Walter Scott was shot in the back when attempting to run away.

2014: After being accused of selling cigarettes from packs that didn't have tax stamps, Eric Garner died on a New York City sidewalk when a police officer applied an illegal choke hold.

2014: 17-year old Laquan McDonald was shot 16 times by a Chicago police officer who saw him carrying a knife and behaving erratically; the officer kept firing after McDonald was lying motionlessly on the ground.

2014: In Cleveland, Ohio (an open-carry state), Tamir Rice, a 12-year-old boy, was shot and killed by police officers within moments of their arrival. The boy was playing with a toy gun that the officers mistook as a real gun.

Sources: Seidman (2020); Serwer (2020); Wilkerson (2020)

Reflection 8.7

Why do you think there are so few news reports of whites dying while being arrested or apprehended by police?

Research suggests that some of the police incidents described in **Box 8.1** may stem from the type of implicit racial bias previously discussed. For instance, in one research study, white college students were exposed to a series of photographs rapidly flashed on a screen that contained images of white and black males holding something in their hand that was either a gun or harmless object (e.g. a wallet, soda can, or cell phone). The students were instructed to press the "shoot" button on a device they were holding if they thought the man was holding a gun, or press the "don't shoot" button if they thought the man was not. They had to make this decision in a very short period of time (a little less than a second). Results showed that white students were more likely to shoot unarmed black men than unarmed white men and vice versa. Also, their reaction times differed: they shot at black men holding guns quicker than white men holding guns, and they were slower to press the "don't shoot" button when the unarmed was black rather than white (Correll et al., 2002). In a follow-up study using the same procedure, members of the Denver Police Department and other Denver residents served as the participants. Similar to the earlier study, both police officers and community members were quicker to shoot at blacks they thought were carrying guns than they did whites (Correll et al., 2007). These results suggest that the brain is wired to respond quickly to possible threats and that both average citizens and police officers are implicitly biased toward seeing black males as being more threatening (Dixon, 2010).

Experimental research in social psychology also show that people are more likely to interpret ambiguous actions as threatening when those actions are exhibited by blacks than by whites. In a classic study, 96 white college students viewed an altercation between two people, one black and one white, which they thought was real but was actually staged. When the person doing the shoving in the altercation was black and the person being shoved was white, 75% of the participants rated the behavior as "violent." When the person doing the shoving was white and the person being shoved was black, only 17% of the students rated that behavior as "violent" (Duncan, 1976). Taken together, these findings suggest there are two key conditions that increase the likelihood of unconscious racial bias: making decisions *rapidly* and making them in *ambiguous* situations (Eberhardt, 2019; Pager, 2007). Thus, cases in which police prematurely killed blacks in the process of arresting them may have not reflected intentional anti-black malice or hostility toward blacks, but resulted from having to make quick decisions in uncertain situations. Research suggests that the likelihood of these incidents could be minimized through more systematic and comprehensive police training on how to reduce implicit racial bias (Eberhardt, 2019).

Social justice advocates also argue that these incidents may lso reflect racist remnants of a police culture that has had a long history of serving the political interests of whites are more interested in containing or controlling blacks than protecting them. Police reform advocates remind us that the police force originated with slave patrols whose primary responsibility was to catch fugitive black slaves and return them to their masters; in fact, America's distinctive gun culture has its roots in the enforcement of slavery by armed whites (Feagin, 2005). In his book, *Reconstruction: America's Unfinished Revolution*, Eric Foner (2014) notes during the Reconstruction period that immediately followed the Civil War and the abolition of slavery, blacks in the South faced a "wave of counter-revolutionary terror" unlike anything seen in America or in any other country in the Western Hemisphere. For instance, between 1865 and 1866, 500 white men were indicted for the murder of blacks in Texas, but not one was convicted, prompting a visiting Northern observer to say that in Texas, "Murder is considered one of their inalienable state rights."

Laws were also put in place to contain and control recently freed blacks by arresting them for "black only" offenses and incarcerated them for petty crimes that were not applied to whites, ranging from carrying a firearm to simply making an insulting gesture. These laws were often enforced by Confederate veterans who still wore their gray uniforms. When blacks were arrested for violating black-only laws, their sentence required they work for no wages and they were leased to white plantation owners and industrialists to provide them with a source of free labor (Foner, 2014). In the first decade following the Civil War, the black convict population in the South grew at a rate that was ten times faster than the general population (Oshinsky, 1996). According to Alexander (2016), during this period: "The criminal justice system was strategically employed to force African Americans back into a system of extreme repression and control, a practice that would continue to prove successful for generations to come" (p. 4).

When the convict leasing system was eventually abolished, Jim Crow laws soon followed that were violently enforced by a Southern police force which often included members of the Ku Klux Klan (Oluo, 2019). Klan members continued to make up members of the police well into the 20th century. For instance, in 1985, a black couple (Robert and Martha Marshall) purchased a home in Sylvania, Kentucky, an exclusively white suburb of Louisville. On the night they moved in, their house was firebombed; a month later, a second arson attack destroyed their house. A few hours later, a Ku Klux Klan meeting was held during which a speaker bragged about how no blacks would ever be permitted to live in Sylvania. The black couple sued a police officer who had been identified as the speaker. When the case was brought to court, the officer testified that about half of the forty Klan members he knew were also in the police department and his superiors condoned police officers' Klan membership, as long as they didn't make it public (Rothstein, 2017).

Police reform advocates argue that remnants of this racially discriminatory history still exists in the police culture and needs to be addressed. Reform advocates also point out that systemic racism in housing, education, and employment have created poverty, addiction, and homelessness in urban settings that are root causes of crime and are beyond the scope of the police and that more governmental resources should be devoted to addressing these systemic issues in low-income, inner-city communities (Serwer, 2020).

However, the views of and police reform advocates and activists are not shared by many American citizens. In one national survey, only 36% of them felt that "racism in our police department is widespread and requires fundamental institutional change" and when asked about police killings of unarmed black men, 42% of the respondents thought "this rarely occurs and attracts more media attention than it should" (SPLC Report, 2021). Defenders of the current policing system also argue that blacks living in inner cities want the same or more police presence in their communities. Surveys of blacks in inner-city communities show that this is generally true, but also show that the police presence they favor is not harsh policing practices and severe, get-tough-on-crime sentencing policies that result in offenders serving lengthy prison time. In fact, research shows that such practices and policies have been found to increase crime rates by decreasing community stability, increasing community distrust of law enforcement, and reducing the likelihood that community members will cooperate with police to report crimes (van Rooij & Fine, 2021).

Interestingly, the vast majority of whites who support "get tough on crime" measures have never been victims of black crime (Peffley et al., 1997) and whites living in rural areas are more likely to favor aggressive anti-crime practices and policies aimed at fighting crime in the inner cities, despite the fact that they live nowhere near inner cities (Cohn et al., 1991). In contrast, blacks in inner-city communities, although being more often the victims of black crime than whites, are more supportive of crime-prevention practices—

such as increasing the quality of inner-city schools, local job opportunities, and urban economic development (Meares, 1997). Their views are supported by an analysis of data from 63 counties that revealed a clear link between poverty and homicide and that improved educational outcomes in low-income neighborhoods reduced murder and assault by 30 percent (van Rooij & Fine, 2021).

Conclusion

To sum up, the systemic racism in the criminal justice system is manifested by discriminatory treatment of people of color—particularly those living in low-income urban areas—who, compared with whites, are:

- more closely monitored to detect criminal activity,
- more frequently apprehended for alleged crimes,
- more likely to experience excessive force while being apprehended,
- more poorly defended,
- more frequently convicted,
- more likely to be incarcerated once they are convicted, and
- more likely to experience substantial long-term losses of privileges and opportunities after being released from incarceration.

Reflection 8.8

Which of the racial disparities listed above were you most and least aware of prior to reading this chapter?

"Individuals are forced to make choices in an environment they did not choose. They would surely prefer to have a broader array of good opportunities. The question we should be asking—not instead of but in addition to questions about penal policy—is whether the denizens of the ghetto are entitled to a better set of options, and if so, whose responsibility it is to provide them."

–TOMMIE SHELBY, PROFESSOR OF AFRICAN AND AFRICAN AMERICAN STUDIES AT HARVARD UNIVERSITY

Research reviewed in this chapter on the relationship between race and crime strongly points to the conclusion that the higher conviction and incarceration rates of people of color are the result of an accumulation of political decisions and criminal justice policies implemented across many decades that first created environmental conditions conducive to crime in inner-city communities segregated by race, and then created racially discriminatory policing and judicial system to arrest, prosecute, convict, and imprison people of color for crimes committed in crime-conducive environments that past political decisions and criminal justice policies helped create in the first place.

Legal scholar and civil rights activist, Michelle Alexander, provides a fitting summary and historical perspective on systemic racism in America's criminal justice system:

Historians will undoubtedly look back and marvel that such an extraordinarily comprehensive system of racialized social control existed in the United States. How fascinating, they will likely say, that a drug war was waged almost exclusively against poor people of color—people already trapped in ghettos that lacked jobs and decent schools. They were rounded up by the millions packed away in prisons, and when released, they were stigmatized for life, denied the right to vote, and ushered into a world of discrimination. Legally barred from employment, housing, and welfare benefits—and saddled with thousands of dollars of debt—these people were shamed and condemned for failing to hold together their families. They were chastised for succumbing to depression and anger, and blamed for landing back in prison. Historians will likely wonder how we could describe the new caste system as a system of crime control, when it is difficult to imagine a system better designed to create—rather than prevent—crime (Alexander, 2020, p. 219)

In his 1944 State of the Union Address, President Franklin D. Roosevelt called for a "second Bill of Rights" that included: "The right to a useful and remunerative job . . .; the right to earn enough to provide adequate food and clothing and recreation; . . . the right of every family to a decent home; the right to adequate medical care and the opportunity to achieve and enjoy good health . . . [and] the right to a good education" (Roosevelt, 1944). Access to these rights still remains unequal across racial groups in America today. Despite rhetoric about racial equality being achieved after the Jim Crow ending in the South and the passage of civil rights legislation in the 1960s, racial divisions along the lines of income, wealth, education, employment, and political power have remained deeply entrenched in American society (Sugrue, 2005). Multiple decades of racial discrimination in multiple sectors of society are still baked into America's social structures and continue to contribute to systemic racism in six societal systems that have been discussed in the previous and current chapter:

> "When the COLORED ONLY signs went down, inequality didn't suddenly disappear, nor did the "twenty-four trillion dollars in multigenerational devastation that African Americans had suffered in lost wages, stolen land, educational impoverishment, and housing inequalities."
> —CAROL ANDERSON, PROFESSOR OF AFRICAN AMERICAN STUDIES, EMORY UNIVERSITY

- *economic* system,
- *housing* system,
- *education* system,
- *health care* system,
- *electoral* system, and
- *criminal justice* system

Anti-racist strategies that citizens can use to help address and redress these systemic inequities will be discussed in the next chapter.

Chapter Summary and Highlights

Studies show that systemic racism has existed, and continues to exist, in America's health care industry. For instance, compared to expecting white mothers, black mothers with similar levels of income and socioeconomic status are less likely to receive quality medical care during childbirth, experience infant mortality rates twice as high as white women, and have a 3–4 times higher risk of maternal death due to pregnancy-related complications. Blacks are also less likely to receive breast cancer screenings, follow-up visits after hospitalization for mental illness, and maximum-strength pain medication reporting to physicians that they're experiencing high levels of pain. These racial disparities in health-care exist at all levels of income and education.

Blacks have also been subjected to inequitable an unethical medical experiments throughout U.S. history, starting during slavery when blacks who were disabled or too ill to work were often bought by white medical institutions and used in experiments or operations designed to advance "medical science" and "medical education." One consequence of this history of discriminatory medical treatment is that blacks today are distrustful of governmental health programs, which may account of why they have been reluctant to participate in the governmental rollout of vaccines for treating COVID-19.

Historically, system racism in the electoral system has taken place with respect to blacks' right to vote (suffrage), serve on juries, and hold political office. Originally, some states tried to suppress the black vote through sheer force or violence and by adopting voting laws that intentionally prevented blacks from casting votes, such as imposing poll taxes that blacks could not afford to pay, literacy tests they were unable to pass because they were denied the opportunity to attend school, and felon laws that prevented them from voting if they violated Jim Crow laws that did not apply to whites (e.g., curfew violations). Recently, more than 20 states have adopted voting policies that their legislators claimed are designed to protect the integrity of the election process, but at the same time, are likely to restrict black participation in the voting process.

The United States is one of the few democratic countries in the world that prohibits its incarcerated citizens from voting, and in so doing, suppresses the vote of low-income blacks who are disproportionately incarcerated for crimes than whites—due in large part to systemic racism in the criminal justice system—where there's evidence of racial bias at each of the following stages in the criminal justice process:

- Monitoring and Arrest,
- Pretrial Detention,
- Conviction and Sentencing,
- Incarceration, and
- Post-Incarceration Punishment

Compared to whites, blacks are subjected to more police stops and searches. If charged with a crime, blacks are more likely to be jailed as they await trial because they are disproportionately represented in lower-income brackets and less able to the pay bail. For the same financial reason, the majority of black defendants cannot afford a private attorney and are defended by court-appointed public defenders who are poorly paid and saddled with outrageously high caseloads that often total more than 100 clients at a time. If convicted, the length of the sentence assigned to blacks is influenced by their racial features. African Americans with darker skin, wider noses, and thicker lips are more likely to receive harsher sentences than lighter-skinned blacks. Simply put, skin lightness mitigates the judged severity of the crime; skin darkness magnifies it.

Racial bias has also been found with respect to death penalty sentence. Prosecutors are more likely to seek and secure a death-penalty sentence for black defendants—if the victim is white; black offenders convicted of killing a white victim are more than four times likely to receive a death sentence than those charged with killing a black victim. Black men with more "stereotypically black" facial features (e.g., darker skin color, broader noses, thicker lists, and kinkier hair) who are convicted of murdering a white victim are more than twice as likely to receive the death sentence.

Incarceration rates also reflect racial disparities. Blacks make up 13% of America's total population yet constitute 45% of its total prison population. The incarceration rate for black male youth (age 16–25) is more than five times higher than it is for white youth, and among first-time youth offenders, blacks are six times more likely than whites to be sentenced to prison for committing exactly the same crime.

Once released from the penal system, black parolees encounter a "period of invisible punishment"—a post-incarceration penalty that goes beyond the criminal justice system and takes the form of "legal" societal discrimination in access to employment, housing, education, and public benefits. Racially discriminatory incarceration practices have major, long-term negative consequences on the lives of black youth by sharply reducing their prospects of finding stable adult employment, even if they never commit another crime. When former inmates apply for jobs after being released, they face significant discrimination in the hiring process because their employers use criminal record as a screening device. Unlike other democratic nations, the United States allows employers virtually unlimited and ongoing access to information about people's criminal background and arrest record, thus leaving them subject to subsequent "legal" employment discrimination for the remainder of their lives.

The majority of blacks in prison have been incarcerated for drug convictions related to "war on drugs" policies first established in the 1980s. Blacks have been the primary targets of that war. Although young black men are *less* likely to use or sell drugs than young white men, they are more likely to be arrested for drug use or sale. Many blacks now in prison were arrested and sentenced for drug-related crimes involving crack cocaine, a cheaper form of cocaine used by poorer, inner-city residents. In contrast, whites living in wealthier suburbs were using more expensive powder cocaine that carried a much lighter sentence. Similarly, even though the use of marijuana is essentially the same across all racial groups, blacks are three times more likely to be arrested for marijuana possession than whites; and despite increased legalization of the drug in many states, 545,000 people were arrested for marijuana-related offenses in 2019 alone. Many people of color have been incarcerated for possession of marijuana—a drug that is now being grown and sold legally in many parts of the country by white entrepreneurs as part of the expanding marijuana and CBD production industry.

Offenders convicted for drug-related crimes receive long jail terms; the U.S. criminal justice system imposes sentences for drug crimes that are often longer than those imposed for violent crimes in many other countries. Blacks convicted of nonviolent drug offenses have been found to spend about the same amount of time in prison as whites convicted of violent crimes.

Implicit racial bias in the perception of violent criminal activity has been documented by multiple studies conducted with citizens of all ages as well as police officers. The results of these studies point to people holding an implicit (subconscious) bias toward perceiving blacks as connected to criminality and as being blameworthy for their criminal behavior. This research suggests that implicit racial bias likely played a role in news-making incidents of blacks being killed while being apprehended by police officers. Social justice advocates argue that these incidents also reflect racist remnants of a police culture with a long history of serving the prejudicial and political interests of whites to contain or control blacks rather than protect them.

In addition, police reform advocates point out that systemic racism in housing, education and employment have created poverty, addiction and homelessness in urban settings that are beyond the scope of the police and that more governmental resources need to be devoted to addressing these systemic issues and are often the root causes of crime.

In short, the systemic racism in the criminal justice system is manifested by discriminatory treatment of people of color—particularly those living in low-income urban areas—who are:

- more closely monitored to detect criminal activity,
- more frequently apprehended for alleged crimes,
- more likely to experience excessive force while being apprehended,
- more poorly defended,
- more frequently convicted,
- more likely to be incarcerated once they are convicted, and
- more likely to experience substantial long-term losses of privileges and opportunities after being released from incarceration.

Internet Resources

History of Systemic Racism in America: https://www.smithsonianmag./history/158-resources-understanding-systemic-racism-america-180975029/

Systemic Racism in Health Care: https://www.healtcareline.com/health/healthcare-provider/system-racism-in-american-healthcare#Building-discrimination-into-algorithms-and-medical-devices

Voter Suppression: https://ballotpedia.org/Voter_suppression

Systemic Racism in Criminal Justice: https://mercatornet.com/systemic-racial-bias-in-the-us-criminal-justice-system-is-not-a-myth/64497/

References

Abcarian, R. (2020, December 9). Pot, the perfect issue to unite a divided nation. *Los Angeles Times*, A13

Ackerman, J. P., Riggins, T., & Black, M. M. (2010). A review of the effects of prenatal cocaine exposure among school-aged children. *Pediatrics, 125*(3), 554–565.

Agan, A. Y., Doleac, J. A., & Harvey, A. (2021). *Misdemeanor prosecution*. Working Paper 28600. National Bureau of Economic Research. https://cdpsdocs.state.co.us/ccjj/Committees/SRTF/Materials/2021-04-02_Misd-Prosecution_NBER-W28600_2021-03.pdf

Alexander, M. (2020). *The new Jim Crow: Mass incarceration in the age of colorblindness.* The New Press.

American Bar Association. (2004). *Gideon's broken promise: America's continuing quest for equal justice.* A Report on the American Bar Association's Hearings on the Right to Counsel on Criminal Proceedings. American Bar Association.

Anderson, C. (2016). *White rage: The unspoken truth of our racial divide*. Bloomsbury.

Bascuas, R. J. (2007). Fourth amendment lessons from the highway and the subway: A principled approach to suspicionless crimes. *Rutgers Law Journal, 38*, 719.

Baumgartner, F. R., Epp, D., & Shoub, K. (2018). *Suspect citizens: What 20 million traffic stops tell us about policing and race.* Cambridge University Press.

Beckett, K. (1997). *Making crime pay: Law and order in contemporary American politics.* Oxford University Press.

Belk, J. (2020, April 26). A stacked deck on health. *Los Angeles Times, 17.*

Braman, (2007). *Doing time on the outside: Incarceration and family life in urban America.* The University of Michigan Press.

Burston, B. W., Jones, D., & Robertson-Saunders, P. (1995). Drug use and African Americans: Myth versus reality. *Journal of Alcohol and Drug Abuse, 40*(2), 19–39.

Centers for Disease Control and Prevention. (2019, January 16). *Pregnancy mortality surveillance system.* www.cdc.gov/prproductivehealth/maternalinfanthealth/pregnancvy-mortality-surveillance-system.htm

Chabria, A. (2019, September 14). 3 bills on bias are sent to Governor. *Los Angeles Times,* B1, B4.

Clear, T. R. (2007). *Imprisoning communities: How mass incarceration makes disadvantaged communities worse.* Oxford University Press.

Cohen, D., & Nisbett, R. E. (1997). Field experiments examining the culture of honor: The role of institutions in perpetuating norms about violence. *Personality and Social Psychology Bulletin, 23(11), 1188–1199.*

Cohn, S. G., Barkan, S. E., & Halteman, W. A. (1991). Punitive attitudes toward criminals: Racial consensus or racial conflict? *Social Problems, 38*(2), 286–296.

Constantine Report. (2013). *Iran contra, cocaine & the war on drugs in the 'hood.'* https://constantinereport.com/iran-contra-cocaine-the-war-on-drugs-in-the-hood

Correll, J., Park, B., Judd, C. M., & Wittenbrink, B. (2002). The police officer's dilemma: A decade of research on racial bias in the decision to shoot. *Social and Personality Psychology, 83*(6), 1314–1329.

Correll, J., Park, B., Judd, C. M., Wittenbrink, B., Sadler, M. S., & Keesee, T. (2007). Across the thin blue line: Police officers and racial bias in the decision to shoot. *Journal of Personality and Social Psychology, 92*(6), 1006–1023.

Cosgrove, J. (2020). Momentum for criminal justice reforms. *Los Angeles Times, B3.*

Diamond, H. (2019). *Upheaval: Turning point for nations in crisis.* Little, Brown and Company.

Dixon, A. (2010). Policing bias. In J. Marsh, R. Mendoza-Denton, & J. A. S. Smith (Eds.), *Are we born racist? New insights from neurosciences and positive psychology* (pp. 80–87). Beacon Press.

Drug Policy Alliance. (2020). *10 facts about cocaine.* Drug Policy Alliance. https://drug-policy.org/drug-facts/cocaine

Duncan, B. L. (1976). Differential social perception and attribution of intergroup violence: Testing the lower limits of stereotyping of blacks. *Journal of Personality and Social Psychology, 34*(4), 590–598.

Eberhardt, J. L. (2019). *Biased: Uncovering the hidden prejudice that shapes what we see, think, and do.* Viking.

Effion, U., Hogan, E., & Okorie, O. (2020). *Infant mortality among black babies.* University of Michigan School of Public Health. https://sph.umich.edu/pursuit/2020posts/infant-mortality-among-black-babies.html

Elbow, S. (2001, August 18). Hooked on SWAT: Fueled with drug enforcement money, military style-police teams are exploding in the backwoods of Wisconsin. *Madison Capitol Times.* https://madison.com/ct/news/local/writers/steven_elbow/hooked-on-swat/article_f1bc13e6-b29b-5ab0-ac7cf-ba46b1b3860c.html

Feagin, J. (2005). *Systemic racism: A theory of oppression.* Routledge.

Foner, E. (2014). Reconstruction: *America's unfinished revolution, 1863-1877.* HarperCollins.

Friedman, J., Kim, D., & Schneberk, T. (2019). Assessment of racial/ethnic and income disparities in the prescription of opioids and other controlled medications in California. *JAMA Internal Medicine, 179*(4), 469–476. https://jamanetwork.com/journals/jamainternalmedicine/fullarticle/2723625

Graham, S., & Lowery, B. S. (2004). Priming unconscious racial stereotypes about adolescent offenders. *Law and Human Behavior, 28,* 483–504.

Harper, S. R. (2012). Race without racism: How higher education researchers minimize racist institutional norms. *Review of Higher Education, 36*(1), 9–30.

Harris, D. (2002). *Profiles in injustice: Why racial profiling cannot work*. The New Press.

Healy, M. (2021, January 1). Injecting race into plans to dispense vaccines. *Los Angeles Times,* A1, A-9.

Hinton, E. (2016). *From the war on poverty to the war on crime: The making of mass incarceration in America*. Harvard University Press.

Hoffman, K. M. (2016). Racial bias in pain assessment and treatment recommendations, and false beliefs about biological differences between blacks and whites. *Proceedings of the National Academy of Science, 113(16), 4296–4301.*

Holzer, H. J., & Lalonde, R. J. (2000). Job change and job stability among less-skilled young workers. In D. Card and R. Blank (Eds.), *Finding jobs: Work and welfare reform. Russell Sage Foundation.*

Hoyt, E. H., Schiraldi, V., Smith, B. V., & Ziedenberg, J. (2002). *Reducing racial disparities in juvenile detention.* Annie E. Casey Foundation.

Ispahani, L. (2006). *Out of step with the world: An analysis of felony disenfranchisement in the U.S. and other democracies.* American Civil Liberties Union.

Izaguirre, A. (2021, April 22). Earl-voting trend faces GOP wall. *Los Angeles Times,* A2.

James, C., Lille-Blanton, M., & Garfield, R. (2007). *Key facts: Race, ethnicity and medical care.* The Kaiser Family Foundation.

Johnson, L. D., O'Malley, P. M., Bachman, J. G., & Schulenberg, J. E. (2007). *Monitoring the future, national survey results on drug use, 1975-2006, volume 1, secondary school students.* National Institute of Health and Human Services, National Institute on Drug Abuse.

Karakatsanis, A. (2019). *Usual cruelty: The complicity of lawyers in the criminal injustice system.* The New Press.

Kendi, I. X. (2016). *Stamped from the beginning: The definitive history of racist ideas in America.* Bold Type Books.

Kendi, I. X. (2019). *How to be an antiracist.* One World.

Kent, D. J. (2020). *A brief history of systemic racism in America.* http://www.davidjkent-writer.com/2020/06/08/a-brief-history-systemic-racism-in-america/

King, R. S., & Mauer, M. (2006). The war on marijuana: The transformation of the war on drugs in the 1990s. *Harm Reduction Journal, 3*(1), 6. https://doi.org/10.1186/1477-7517-3-6

Lee, D. (2020, December 5). A tale of two families, and a growing divide. *Los Angeles Times,* A1, A10.

Levey, N .N. (2020, December 27). Racial disparities on health agenda. *Los Angeles Times,* A1, A10.

Lin, R.-G., II, Wigglesworth, A., Karlamangla, S., & Lee, W. (2021, January 4). Outbreaks worsen at job sites. *Los Angeles Times,* A1, A11.

López, I. H. (2014). *Dog whistle politics: How coded racial appeals have reinvented racism & wrecked the middle class.* Oxford University Press.

Los Angeles Times. (2020, November 25). "Oregon experiments with drugs." A10.

Mauer, M. (1999). *Race to incarcerate.* The New Press.

Mauer, M. (2006). *Race to incarcerate* (rev. ed.). The New Press.

Mauer, M., & King, R. (2007). *A 25-year quagmire: The "war on drugs" and its impact on American society.* Sentencing Project.

McMahon, M. (2020). *What was the Tuskegee experiment?* https://www.wisegeek.com/what-was-the-tuskegee-experiment.htm

Meares, T. (1997). *Charting race and class differences in attitudes toward drug legalization and law enforcement: Less for federal criminal law.* Faculty Scholarship Series., Paper 474. http://digitalcommons.law.yale.edu/fss_papers474

Morgan, J. P., & Zimmer, L. (1997). Social pharmacology of smokeable cocaine. In C. Reinarman & H. G. Levine (Eds.), *Crack in America: Demon drugs and social justice* (pp. 131–170). University of California Press.

Mumola, C. J., & Karberg, J. C. (2006). *Drug use and dependence, state and federal prisoners, 2004*. U.S. Department of Justice, Bureau of Justice Statistics.

Musto, D. (1997). *The American disease: Origins of narcotics control* (3rd ed.). Oxford University Press.

Natapoff, A. (2018). *Punishment without crime: How our massive misdemeanor system traps the innocent and makes America more unequal*. Hachette Book Group.

Oluo, I. (2019). *So you want to talk about race*. Seal Press.

Oshinksy, D. M. (1996). *Worse than slavery: Parchman farm and the ordeal of Jim Crow justice*. Free Press.

Packtor, C. (2018). *Racial gaps in children's lead levels*. Public Health Post, Boston University School of Health. https://www.publichealthpost.org/databyte/racial-gaps-in-childrens-lead-levels/

Pager, D. (2007). *Marked: Race, crime, and finding work in an era of mass incarceration*. The University of Chicago Press.

Payne, K. (2001). Prejudice and perception: The role of automatic and controlled processes in misperceiving a weapon. *Journal of Personality and Social Psychology, 81*(2), 181–192.

Peffley, M., Hurwitz, H., & Sniderman, P. (1997). Racial stereotypes and whites' political views of blacks in the context of welfare and crime. *American Journal of Political Science, 41*(1), 30–60.

Perry, A. M. (2020). *Know your price: Valuing black lives and property in America's cities*. Brookings Institution Press.

Peter G. Peterson Foundation. (2019, October 4). *Income and wealth in America: An overview of recent data*. https://www.pgpf.org/blog/2019/10/income-and-wealth-in-the-united-states-an-overview-of-data

Petersilia, J. (1999). Parole and prisoner reentry in the United States. In M. Tonry & J. Petersilla (Eds.), *Crime: Public policies for crime control* (pp. 483–508). Institute for Contemporary Studies Press.

Petersilia, J. (2003). *When prisoners come home: Parole and prisoner reentry*. Oxford University Press.

Pierson, E., Simoui, C., Overgoor, J., Corbett-Davies, S., Jenson, D., Shoemaker, A., Ramachandran, V., Barghouty, P., Phillips, C., Shroff, R., & Goel, S. (2020). A large-scale analysis of racial disparities in police stops across the United States. *Nature Human Behaviour, 4*, 736–745.

Plaut, V. C. (2010). Diversity science: Why and how difference makes a difference. *Psychological Inquiry, 21*, 77–90.

Provine, D. M. (2007). *Unequal under law: Race in the war on drugs*. University of Chicago Press.

Reinarman, C. Waldorf, D. Murphy, S. B., & Levine, H. G. (1997). The contingent call of the pipe: Bingeing and addiction among heavy cocaine smokers. In C. Reinarman & H. G. Levine (Eds.), *Crack in America: Demon drugs and social justice* (pp. 77–97). University of California Press.

Riley, K. J. (1997). *Crack, powder cocaine and heroin: Drug purchase and use patterns in six U.S. cities*. National Institute of Justice.

Roberts, S. (2009, July 21). "2008 surge in black voters nearly erased racial gap." *New York Times*. https://www.nytimes.com/2009/07/21/us/politics/21vote.html

Roosevelt, F. D. (1944, January 11). *State of the union message to Congress*. FDR Library National Archives. https://www.fdrlibrary.org/address-text

Rothstein, R. (2017). *The color of law*. Liveright Publishing.

Russell, K. (1988). *The color of crime*. New York University Press.

Sampson, R., & Laub, J. H. (1993). *Crime in the making: Pathways and turning points through life*. Harvard University Press.

Savage, D. G. (2021, June 15). High court upholds crack cocaine prison sentence. *Los Angeles Times*, A6.

Schneider, E. C., Zaslavsky, A. M., & Epstein, A. M. (2002). Racial disparities in the quality of care for enrollees in Medicare managed care. *Journal of the American Medical Association, 287*, 1288–1294.

Schwartz, R., & Skolnick, J. (1962). Two studies of legal stigma. *Social Problems, 10(2)*, 133–142.

Seidman, L. (2020, December 30). Breonna Taylor bust first was mashed; now it's been stolen. *Los Angeles Times*, B3.

Serwer, A. (2020, October). The new reconstruction. *The Atlantic*. https://www.theatlantic.com/magazine/archive/2020/10/the-next-reconstruction/615475/

Smedley, B., Stith, A. Y., & Nelson, A. R. (2003). *Unequal treatment: Confronting racial and ethnic disparities in health care*. National Academics Press.

Snyder, H. N., & Sickman, M. (2006). *Juvenile offenders and victims: 2006 national report*. U.S. Office of Juvenile Justice and Delinquency Prevention. U.S. Department of Justice.

Southern Poverty Law Center. (2020). *Antigovernment movement*. https://www.splcenter.org/fighting-hate/extremist-files/ideology/antigovernment

Southern Poverty Law Center. (2021). *Overcoming the unprecedented: Southern voters' battle against voter suppression, intimidation, and a virus*. https://www.splcenter.org/news/2021/03/16/overcoming-unprecedented-voters-deep-south-battled-voter-suppression- intimidation-and-virus

Southern Poverty Law Center Report. (2021). SPLC poll shows divide in how Americans see racism. *Intelligence Report, 51*(1), 3.

Stoler, J., Klofstad, C., & Uscinsky, J. (2020, July 8). *Will black Americans fear a vaccine more than COVID-19?* https://www.mewsweek.com/will-black-americans-fear-vaccine-more-covid19-opinion-1516087

Street, P. (2002). *The vicious circle: Race, prison, jobs, and community in Chicago, Illinois, and the nation*. Chicago Urban League, Department of Research and Planning.

Sugrue, T. J. (2005). *The origins of the urban crisis: Race and inequity in postwar Detroit*. Princeton University Press.

Tanner, L. (2021, June 3). Twin doctors battle racism in medical world. *Los Angeles Times,* A2.

Taylor-Thompson, K. (2020, November 27). The lie that killed Black boys. *Los Angeles Times*, A11.

Travis, J., Solomon, A., & Waul, M. (2001). *From prison to home: The dimensions and consequences of prisoner reentry*. Urban Institute Press.

van Rooij, B., & Fine, A. (2021). *The behavioral code: The hidden ways the law makes us better or worse*. Beacon Press.

Vitale, A. A. (2018, March 28). The new 'superpredator' myth. *The New York Times*. https://www.nytimes.com/2018/03/23/opinion/superpredator-myth.html

Western, B. (2006). *Punishment and inequality in America*. Russell Sage.

Wilber, (2021, April 27). U.S. launches investigation of police practices in Louisville. *Los Angeles Times*, A7.

Wilkerson, I. (2020). *Caste: The origins of our discontents*. Random House.

Wills, G. (2003). *Negro president: Jefferson and the slave power*. Houghton Mifflin.

Wise, T. (2001). School shootings and white denial. *Alter Net*. www.timwise.org/2001/03/school-shootings-and-white-denial

Wise, T. (2011). *White like me: Reflection on race from a privileged son* (3rd ed.). Soft Skull Press.

Zinn Education Project. (2021). *November 10, 1868: Wilmington Massacre*. https://www.zinnedproject.org/news/tdih/wilmington-massacare-2/

Reflections and Applications

Name

_____

Date

_____

8.1 Review the sidebar quotes contained in this chapter and select two that you think are particularly enlightening, meaningful, or inspirational. For each quote you selected, provide an explanation why you chose it.

8.2 In 2021, more than 20 states proposed or adopted voting policies that legislators say are designed to protect the integrity of the election process, but civil rights advocates say are designed to lower voter turnout among low-income people of color. Some of the voting laws proposed include: requiring a driver-license photo as proof of identification to vote, no early voting, restricting mail-in voting, early closing of voting polls, and reducing the number of polling locations. Do you these measures as well-intended efforts to ensure election integrity or as veiled attempts to suppress the vote of low-income minority groups? What arguments or evidence would you offer to support your position?

8.3 Joblessness, poverty, and lack of educational and vocational opportunities are frequently cited as the root causes of crime? Would you agree or disagree with this assessment? Why?

8.4 The "War on Drugs" has been criticized for creating criminal justice polices that have resulted in excessively high incarceration rates in the United States and the destabilization of black families and communities in America's inner cities. Critics argue that more attention and funding should be directed at drug prevention-and-treatment programs that treat drug abuse as an illness rather than punish it as a crime. Would you agree with this argument? If yes, why? If no, why not?

8.5 The United States has the highest incarceration rate and largest percentage of imprisoned citizens than any other democratic nation in the world, and unlike most other democratic nations, America disqualifies all its incarcerated citizens from voting. Do you agree or disagree with this policy of denying prisoners the right to vote? Why?

8.6 Americans disagree about whether use of excessive police force and police brutality represent the behavior of a "few bad apples" or reflect something more pervasive and embedded in America's "police culture." Which of these viewpoints do you favor? What evidence or arguments would you cite to support the viewpoint you favor?

Engaging in Anti-Racism and Advocating for Social Justice

Chapter Purpose and Preview

This chapter describes the difference between being "non-racist"—someone who does not personally profess or practice racism, and "anti-racist"—someone who takes an active role in opposing racism displayed by other individuals and existing societal systems. The chapter identifies specific strategies for countering common racist beliefs with anti-racist arguments supported by sound logic and hard evidence, as well as strategies for taking collective action to change societal systems and political policies that serve to preserve or perpetuate racial injustice.

What Is Anti-Racism?

Making a conscious attempt to overcome implicit personal biases and interact with members of all racial groups in an open and appreciative manner are behaviors that characterize a non-racist; an anti-racist goes beyond that to take counteract racism exhibited by other individuals and social systems (Bonilla-Silva, 2018). A non-racist does nothing harmful *to* discriminate against members of another race but also does nothing *for* members of other races who are experiencing racial prejudice and discrimination. As Kendi (2019) puts it: "What's the problem with being 'not racist'? It is a claim that signals neutrality: 'I am not a racist, but neither am I aggressively against racism.' But there is no neutrality in the racism struggle. The opposite of 'racist' isn't 'not racist.' It is 'anti-racist.'" (p. 9).

© Maria Symchych/Shutterstock.com

Anti-racism is demonstrated by: (a) challenging racist remarks and microaggressions, (b) countering racist arguments with evidence-based counterarguments, and (c) taking collective action with others to combat systemic racism.

Challenging Racist Remarks and Microaggressions

One way to engage in anti-racism is by confronting racism displayed by other individuals. Here are some specific strategies for doing so.

Challenge those who make racist remarks and engage in racial microaggressions. Studies show that people are more likely to believe negative stereotypes about racial groups when they think those stereotypes are widely held by other members of society (Crandall et al., 2002). By saying or doing nothing when others make negative remarks about a certain race, including friends and family, it is tempting to remain silent and avoid conflict, but our silence may send the message that we tacitly agree with the a prejudicial remark.

"In the end, we will remember not the words of our enemies, but the silence of our friends."
—MARTIN LUTHER KING, JR.

The need to take an active role in combating racist remarks is supported by a study of more than 6,000 white college students at 28 campuses across the country. These students were asked to note any racist comments and microaggressions they observed during the upcoming two months and record them in a personal journal. Later analysis of the students' journals revealed that they had recorded numerous instances of racist comments or microaggressions displayed by others, ranging from friends and family members to strangers and acquaintances. In most of these instances, after the person made a racist comment, it was followed by agreement or laughter by others who were present, while others remained silent; only rarely did anyone object, and if they did, they were often told it was just a joke or they should "lighten up" (Picca & Feagin, 2007).

Studies also show that when members of the same peer group hear one of their group make a prejudicial remark about another race, it elevates the level of prejudice held by other members of the peer group who overhear the remark—probably due to peer pressure and group conformity (Stangor et al., 2001). However, if the prejudicial remark is challenged by another peer, particularly a peer who is liked and respected, it reduces the level of prejudice of both the person making the remark and other members of the group who hear it (Baron et al., 2008). Even if the person challenged gets defensive and denies being a racist, anti-racist progress is made because instead of the comment being followed by positive social reinforcement (e.g., agreement or laughter from others), it receives negative social feedback—which reduces the person's confidence and willingness to make such comments again. Negative social feedback can still be provided to someone who claims their comment wasn't intended to be racist by offering a response like: "You say you didn't mean to offend anybody, but you offended me, so you did offend somebody" (Oluo, 2019).

"Take some of the burden of racism off of people of color. Bring it into your life so that you can dismantle racism in the white spaces of your life that people of color can't even reach."
—IJEOMA OLUO, AUTHOR, *SO YOU WANT TO TALK ABOUT RACE*

Reflection 9.1

If you were to challenge a friend or family member who made a racist remark, how do you think that person would react?

 ## Consider This…

By actively opposing prejudice on campus, you demonstrate leadership and character. You send a clear message to other members of the campus community that opposing racism is not just the "politically correct" thing to do; it is the *right* thing to do.

Use strategic interpersonal communication and human relations skills to reduce the risk that others will react emotionally and defensively when you challenge their racist views. Scholars have noted that when the topic of racism is raised with whites, particularly their role in promoting it either intentionally or unintentionally, they often become uncomfortable and react with denial or anger (Anderson, 2016; DiAngelo, 2018). The risk of this happening may be reduced by using socially intelligent and socially sensitive communication and human relations strategies. This is not to say that those espousing racist views should be "treated with kid gloves" or that arguments used to counter their racist views should be "sugar coated." What is to say is that anti-racist arguments should be coated in a communication capsule that's less likely to be immediately and defensively rejected and more likely to be receptively ingested and digested by the recipient in a way that leads to attitudinal change.

"White fragility is a state in which a minimum amount of racial stress becomes intolerable, triggering a range of defensive moves."
—ROBIN DIANGELO, AUTHOR, *WHITE FRAGILITY: WHY IT'S SO HARD FOR WHITE PEOPLE TO TALK ABOUT RACISM*

Express anti-racist arguments *assertively*—not aggressively. When we're *aggressive*, we make our point forcefully or angrily in a way that denigrates the person being called out by labeling them and demeaning their character (e.g., "You're a bigot"). We make our point, but so offensively that the person reacts so defensively that they don't even process the point we're making. When we make our point *assertively*, we make it not in an angry or agitated manner but in a firm yet even-tempered fashion. Instead of trying to get our point across by "getting in the face" of the other person, we get it across in a less-threatening way that focuses less on criticizing the person and more on criticizing the person's action (e.g., "You may not be a racist, but what you just said qualifies as a racist comment.") Remember that the end goal is not to search for and separate out people into racist and non-racist categories, but to change actions and ideologies that preserve or perpetuate racial inequalities (Bonilla-Silva, 2018).

Use "I" messages when challenging others for making racist remarks. Instead of calling out a person by saying, "*You* are a racist" an "I message" would be to say something like: "*I* consider what you just said to be a racist remark." "I" messages are less aggressive because they're not aimed at a person; instead they focus on our perception of the person's behavior (McKay et al., 2009). This sends a less-threatening message that reduces the likelihood the person will respond defensively and deny the validity of our objection. An "I" message focuses on *us*—what we perceive and feel. A person can easily resent or quickly deny making a racist comment, but it's much harder for that person to resent or deny our perception of their comment and how we feel about it.

Give the person a chance to respond. You may have a clearly justifiable reason to call the person out, but it doesn't mean that they must forfeit all rights to free speech and self-defense. You might even give the person an opportunity to respond before fully challenging them by first asking questions like, "Why did you say that?" "Would you have said that if a person of that race were present?" (Oluo, 2019). After thoughtfully listening to their response, check your understanding of it summarizing it in your own words (e.g., "What I hear you saying is . . .").

After you've allowed the person a chance to respond and checked to with them to show you understand the reasoning behind what they said, even if you strongly disagree with their explanation, don't dismiss or discount it with flippant statements made with a tone of superiority, such as: "That's ridiculous!" or "That's so ignorant!" Instead, acknowledge you heard and processed their response; for instance, say something like: "I understand what you were thinking" or "I see how you might have come to think that way." After making this acknowledgment, you can then explain why your complaint or concern is still justified.

Countering Common Racist Arguments with Evidence-Based Counterarguments

Another way to be an anti-racist is by equipping yourself with an arsenal of knowledge that you can deploy to refute racist arguments with historical truths, statistical evidence, and scientific research. Changing the attitudes of those who hold racial biases or deny the existence of systemic racism often starts by exposing them to information that they were not be aware of and that clearly contradicts their point of view (Zinn, 2005). Described next are common viewpoints held by those who hold racial biases and deny the existence of systemic racism, accompanied by evidence-based counterarguments that can be used to refute their viewpoints.

Slavery and racism are is over; there are constitutional amendments and civil rights laws now in place that ensure blacks are not discriminated against. People making this argument should be reminded that after the Civil War ended slavery in the 1860s and after the Civil Rights Movement of the 1960s instituted Jim Crow laws, racial inequities didn't suddenly disappear and get immediately replaced by a colorblind society and colorblind practices that ensured with equal opportunity for those who experienced more than 100 years of racial discrimination (Anderson, 2016). Passing constitutional amendments and civil rights laws is one thing, how those amendments and laws are *interpreted*, *implemented*, and *enforced* is quite another thing. There have been numerous instances throughout American history when equality was espoused in principle but not enacted in practice. In fact, there have been so many instances of principle versus practice contradictions that historians and social scientists refer to it as the "principle-implementation gap" (Dixon et al., 2017).

For instance, when the 13th amendment was passed in 1865, it authorized Congress to "pass all laws necessary and proper for abolishing all badges and incidences of slavery in the United States." However, the Supreme Court, which decides on whether or not specific societal practices violate the constitution, ruled that excluding blacks from housing markets was not a "badge or incident of slavery," thus it allowed racial discrimination in housing to remain legal for the next 100 years (Rothstein, 2017). (See Chapter 7 for detailed documentation.)

Similarly, the 15th amendment adopted in 1870 stated that "the right of citizens of the United States to vote shall not be denied or abridged by the United States or by any State on account of race, color, or previous condition of servitude." However, states were still allowed to impose their own voting "qualifications" rules and did so in ways that prevented many blacks from exercising their constitutional right to vote—such as imposing poll taxes on freed slaves that they could not afford to pay and literacy tests that they could not pass, and allowing white citizens to engage in voter intimidation tactics. Practices such as these, which were intentionally designed to prevent blacks from exercising their right to vote, and they continued for more than 45 years until the Voting Rights Act was passed in 1965 (Jardina, 2019).

Thus, prejudicial attitudes and discriminatory and practices continued to take place well after slavery was abolished that have shaped our current societal systems and continue to perpetuate systemic racism in housing, employment, education, health care, voting rights, and criminal justice (detailed documentation for which is provided in Chapters 7 and 8) So, when some whites ask questions like: "why is it always about race?" or "why are we still talking about race?", the answer is: For people of color, it's always been about race and it still continues to be about race.

"You do not take a person who, for years, has been hobbled by chains and liberate him, bring him up to the starting line of a race and then say, 'You are free to compete with all the others,' and still justly believe that you have been completely fair."
—LYNDON B. JOHNSON, 37TH PRESIDENT OF THE UNITED STATES

I went to an all-Black school until the fourth grade. Integration then took place in 1965. I did not have a Black teacher again until I started working on my Ph.D. I didn't see my mother and father vote for the first time until 1967 because Blacks were denied that basic constitutional right granted was passed two years earlier until the Voting Rights Act. I had my house set on fire three times when I was a child because someone in the White community felt that the Civil Rights movement was encouraging Blacks to "get out their place." I have been denied jobs, faced unfair accusations, stereotyped, stopped by law enforcement while driving because I was Black, and have a family history of inferior inadequate health care and education. Structural and systematic racism is a sickness that does exist! We must continue to educate and advocate for the cure!

—Aaron Thompson

Personal Experience

I haven't discriminated against any member of any other racial group, so why should I feel guilty about, or take responsibility for, past discrimination by others and current

social systems. Research cited throughout this book points to two major loopholes in this argument, which assumes that racism refers only to individuals who consciously and intentionally engage in racial discrimination: (a) evidence that people who are non-racist still experience of implicit bias—racial bias exhibited without deliberate intent or conscious awareness, and (b) evidence that racial discrimination is not just something engaged in by racist individuals but also takes place at a broader, systemic level that involves multiple societal institutions.

So, yes, individuals who have not discriminated against members of other racial groups should not feel guilty about being personally and intentionally responsible for racism, but they should acknowledge the reality of implicit bias and be concerned about systemic racism that continues to take place at the societal level. They should also gently reminded that being a non-racist is not the same as being anti-racist; the former is about avoiding racial bigotry personally; the latter is about countering racial bigotry in others and remedying racial injustice societally (López, 2014). Systemic racism is sustained not by individual intent but by the collective impact of racist systems and the complacency (and complicity) of individuals who allow those systems to maintain the racial status quo (Oluo, 2019). As Eberhardt (2019) points out, "When something is regarded as a norm, people cease to judge it harshly. They are not only inclined to believe that the norm is 'just the way things are'; they are inclined to believe that [it] is 'the way things should be', p. 281).

I'm tired of hearing about "white privilege." I am white and not privileged; I've had to work hard to get where I am. "White privilege" refers to group advantages that whites take for granted that members of minority racial groups haven't been granted (McIntosh, 2012). For instance, more whites than people of color are privileged legacies—individuals who experience advantages because of their relationship to a family member—such as inheriting money from a wealthy parent or being admitted to a college because a family relative previously attended the college. These advantages are less available to younger people of color whose family members grew up during times of civil rights violations that denied them equal opportunity for housing, education, employment, and the accumulation of family wealth (Minnich, 2005).

White privilege does not mean that whites haven't experienced struggles of their own and have never had to overcome obstacles to get where they are. What white privilege does means that people of color face distinctive and disproportionate struggles related to their race that whites have not had to face, and that whites should honestly acknowledge the advantages they have had because they are not people of color (DiAngelo, 2018). Wilkerson (2020) puts it this way: "We are responsible for recognizing that what happened in previous generations at the hands of or to people who look like us set the stage for the world we now live in and that what has gone before us grants us advantages or burdens . . . gains or deficits that others who do not look like us often do not share" (p. 388). For example, as detailed in Chapter 7, blacks were routinely and systematically discriminated against when they sought home mortgage loans throughout the 20th century. Many blacks renting apartments today would likely be living in homes of their own if their parents and grandparents were given the same home loan-procuring opportunities as whites. As Ben Mathis-Lilley notes: "If you are not black and if your parents were alive in the 1960s and got a mortgage, you benefitted directly and materially from discrimination" (Wilkerson, 2020, p. 185).

Again, this is not to say that whites who have acquired wealth as a result of their parents' racial privilege haven't worked hard to maintain that wealth or built on it to acquire wealth of their own, but neither of these outcomes would have been possible if their racial group was denied the opportunity to attain wealth in the first place, as it has been for multiple generations of black families.

Any right or privilege of a racial group that has been obtained at the expense of a wrong done to another group is simply wrong. Anti-racists acknowledge that wrong and support polices or practices that attempt to right the wrong.

© Alexander Oganezov/Shutterstock.com

It's been my experience that the language used to challenge and combat racist views really matters. Certain anti-racist terms, words, or phrases almost immediately trigger defensive reactions, causing the conversation to get emotional or shut down altogether. For instance, the term "white privilege" is one of those terms that seems to put whites back on their heels and then dig in their heels to deny it. I think that people who react to this defensively is because is due in part to the word "privilege"—which simply means "advantage" but is interpreted as "entitlement"—which which suggests that the benefits they enjoy were simply granted or handed to them because they belong to a group that white and had nothing to do with their individual effort.

Because of this defensive reaction, I've decided to change the language whenever I discuss the concept of white privilege by rephrasing it as "white advantage." Then I ask questions : "Do you think you've experienced any advantages growing up white rather than a member of a minority race?" If they say "no," I ask: "Do you think would have experienced more advantages if you grew up black or brown?" I've found that this strategy allows me to make the same point about racial privilege, without triggering as much immediate defensiveness and push back.

Conversations involving racism, whether personal or systemic, should produce at least some discomfort in people whose attitudes you're trying to change; however, the degree of discomfort shouldn't be so high that they respond at an emotional or visceral level. The discomfort caused by the conversation should take place at the mental level—causing the person to experience what psychologists call *cognitive dissonance*—discomfort in the thought process that takes place when the mind encounters ideas that conflict with or contradict preexisting ideas (Eagly & Chaiken, 1995). Research supports the effectiveness of producing change in attitude and behavior by creating cognitive dissonance than research supporting the effectiveness of producing attitude change, rather than attempting to produce attitude change by triggering emotions like guilt, shame, or anger (Cialdini, 2001). When these feelings are triggered, a lower part of the human brain (the amygdala) responsible for the fight-and-flight response reacts first and overwhelms the higher brain center responsible for rational thinking (the frontal lobe), interering with the person's ability to respond logically. This phenomenon is so well-documented that has come to be called the "amygdala hijack" (Goleman, 2005).

Similar to the term "white fragility," there has been intense resistance to anti-racist activists, use of the phrase "defund the police." Activists used this term to argue for redirecting

> "When we become Americans, we accept not only citizenship's privileges that we did not earn but also its responsibilities to correct wrongs that we did not commit."
>
> —RICHARD ROTHSTEIN, AUTHOR, *THE COLOR OF LAW: A FORGOTTEN HISTORY OF OUR GOVERNMENT SEGREGATED AMERICA*

Personal Experience

or reallocating funds spent on crime detection and apprehension toward funding programs that improve the poor living conditions and lack of community services in inner-city neighborhoods that give rise to crime in the first place. The word "defunding" immediately triggered a vehement backlash among whites who interpreted it (understandably) to mean eliminating police enforcement altogether, thus threatening their public safety. My guess is that police reform would have triggered less intense emotional and more rational consideration if the language used "reform the police" or "reallocate police funds" instead of "defund the police."

I have come to the conclusion that although it is important to be honest and direct when discussing matters of race and racism, it's also important to be tactful and strategic. Otherwise, anti-racists may win the battle (induce emotional discomfort) but lose the war (fail to produce change in racist attitudes and racist systems).

—Joe Cuseo

Reflection 9.2

Have you found any particular anti-racist or social-justice terms that tend to put you or others on the defensive? If yes, what are those terms and why do you think they trigger defensiveness?

Racism would not be such an issue if people of color would stop being so "race conscious" and if whites would just be "color blind" and treat everyone the same. Sociologists point out that since whites have so long been the dominant, majority race in America, whiteness has become synonymous with "mainstream" culture. Thus, it's easy for whites not to be as race conscious of or focused on their racial group identity (or the advantages associated with it). As one sociologist put it, "To be white in America is not to have to think about it" (Terry, 1981, p. 120). When people don't have to think about their race because they're members of the racial majority and cultural mainstream, it reduces their awareness of the importance of race to less dominant, minority racial groups (Lipsitz, 1998), particularly racial groups that have been marginalized by "legal" systemic racism (Doane, 1997). According to Oluo (2019), the process works like this: "We like to filter new information through our own experience to see if it computes. If it matches up with what we have experienced, it's valid. If it doesn't match up, it's not. But race is not a universal experience. So when a person of color says, 'this is different for me because I'm not white,' it often won't compute. This is usually where the desire to dismiss claims of racial oppression come from" (pp. 21—22).

Even if blacks were to become less "race conscious" because whites treat them in a "race blind" or "color blind" manner on a person-to-person basis, it would not eliminate racism that takes place on institutional and systemic levels. So, for someone to say the problem of racism would go away if everyone would not see or care about color would be the same as saying they don't see or care about the consequences of color, including the consequences of systemic color-based discrimination on people of color (Wise, 2011). This can be just as problematic as overt personal racism because color-blindness can be (and has been) used as an ideological and political tool to deny the existence of systemic racism and not take legal or legislative action to address it (Bonilla-Silva, 2018). In fact, being "color blind" can lead to the adoption of policies that that appear on the surface to be "race neutral" but actually have inequitable impact on people of color (Garces, 2020). For instance, recent state proposals to change voting laws is a seemingly race-neutral policy designed to increase election security or election integrity but will likely have inequitable impact on citizens of color by making it more difficult for them to vote (Izaguirre, 2021). Scholars have coined a number of different terms to describe such seemingly race-neutral practices that actually have racially discriminatory impact or intent, referring to them as "color-blind racism" (Bonilla-Silva, 2019), "the new racism" (Ebert, 2004), "laissez-faire racism" (Bobo et al., 1997), and "smiling discrimination" (Brooks, 1990).

DiAngelo (2018) argues further that those who claim to be "color blind" are also more likely to conclude that people who talk about race and racism are the ones who are being racist; in other words, to bring up the topic of race is to be racist because you're not being colorblind. This tactic has been called "strategic colorblindness"—intentionally avoiding talk about race, or even to acknowledge racial difference—to avoid being seen as racially biased. Kendi (2019) suggests claiming to be "color blind" also allows white supremacists to claim they are "not racist" even as they argue that the inequities experienced by non-white racial groups are not the result of personal or systemic racism, but reflect their inferior culture or deficient character.

There is now more "reverse discrimination" against whites than discrimination against people of color. A significant number of whites believe there is "reverse racism" currently taking place in the United States that discriminates against whites (Norton & Sommers, 2011).This belief became more prevalent after the Civil Rights Movement of the 1960s when the government took action to reduce racial inequities due to generations of systemic discrimination. White politicians who opposed these equity-promoting policies re-branded them as "unfair attempts to acquire unearned privileges" (Feldman & Huddy, 2005). Such claims of reverse racism made by white politicians have a long history in the United States. When Congress passed the first Civil Rights Act in 1866, it was an Act designed to finally give blacks the full rights of American citizenship, stating that no state law could be created that deprived a person of citizenship based on race. President Andrew Johnson, who had recently replaced the assassinated Abraham Lincoln, denigrated it as a "bill made to operate in favor of the colored against the white race" (Kendi, 2019, p. 130).

"To avoid dealing with the legacy of white supremacy, we will change the subject, blame the victim, [and] play the victim"
—TIME WISE, AUTHOR, *WHITE LIKE ME: REFLECTIONS ON RACE FROM A PRIVILEGED SON*

Johnson's argument is similar to one used today by those who vehemently oppose affirmative action as an equity practice for redressing generations of discrimination experienced by people of color. Those who strongly oppose affirmative action may need to be reminded that whites have been the recipients of preferential race-based governmental programs throughout U.S. history that were denied to blacks (e.g., low-interest housing loans, unemployment insurance, and social security benefits). After a comprehensively reviewing of history of these governmental programs, Katznelson (2005) firmly concluded: "Affirmative action then was white." (p. 23). Sociologist George Lipsitz notes that a major source of current-day wealth in America was accumulated through the appreciation of housing assets secured by federally insured loans between 1932 and 1962 that were given to whites and not blacks, "yet they [blacks] find themselves portrayed as privileged beneficiaries of special preferences by the very people who profited from their exploitation" (Wilkerson, 2020, p. 186).

"When you're accustomed to privilege, equality feels like oppression."
—FRANKLIN LEONARD, AFRICAN AMERICAN FILM EXECUTIVE

Whites still continue to receive privileged treatment in college admissions policies that grant preference to children whose parents attended the college or whose parents have been generous donors to the college—the vast majority of whom are white (Hu, 2020). Studies show that compared with students of color admitted to college with the help of affirmative action considerations, twice as many white college applicants who failed to meet normal college-admissions standards were admitted under the category of "connection preferences" — applicants whose relatives graduated from the college or donated to the college). Yet critics of affirmative action rarely object to this form of preferential treatment (Wise, 2011). In the classic 1978 case that first ignited white backlash to affirmative action in college admissions, the white male (Allan Bakke) who was not accepted to a University of California medical school sued the university for admitting blacks and Latino students who had lower medical admissions test scores than him. However, he also could have sued the university for admitting white students with lower test scores than him, many of whom got in because they had political connections to the university or were children of alumni and donors (Bowen & Bok, 1998).

College-admissions practices that favor privileged whites practice still continues, as evidenced by the results of a study of more than 30 very selective colleges in the United States, that revealed "legacy applicants"—children of alumni—received a 23 percentage-point increase in their likelihood of admission. Children whose parents attended the college received an even larger boost of 45.1 percentage points (Hurwitz, 2011). These policies are so widespread that they are sometimes referred to as "affirmative action for whites" (Zagorin, 2014).

Also inconsistent with the argument that affirmative action for racial minorities is causing whites to experience "reverse discrimination" are research findings indicating that the majority of whites who hold this belief have not themselves ever experienced discrimination on the basis of their race (Gonyea, 2017). Furthermore, the number of reverse discrimination suits that have been formally filed by whites is very small (Wicker, 1996), and the vast majority of them that were filed were dismissed for lack of evidence (Bonilla-Silva, 2018). Despite beliefs to the contrary, affirmative action is not a policy that requires a company or organization to meet a quota by admitting or hiring a certain number of black applicants, regardless of their qualifications; it is a policy designed to ensure that *qualified* members of minority groups are given equal consideration as whites.

Reflection 9.3

Do you know anyone who claimed to be unfairly penalized because of affirmative action, or who thought that someone else gained an unfair advantage because of affirmative action? If yes, what were the circumstances? If no, why do you think you have never encountered anyone who made this claim?

Those who argue that affirmative action is reverse discrimination are also confusing the concepts of equality and equity. *Equality* refers to treating everyone the *same*, whereas *equity* refers to treating everyone *fairly* so that they have equal opportunity to compete (e.g., starting the race at the same starting line). Treating everyone equally after the race has begun doesn't ensure they're being treated equitably if some have already begun the race with an unearned advantage (e.g., starting the race on steroids or starting closer to the finish line). As Banks (2016) explains it: "A significant problem . . . is the assumption that treating groups the same will result in equity, even though some groups have been historic victims of racism and discrimination. Some groups must be treated differently in order for them to attain equity" (p. 26).

Current racial inequities may be viewed as a byproduct of past racial injustices and attempts to redress these inequities as a form of restorative or "corrective justice"—a way of dealing with previously committed social injustices and taking collective responsibility for correcting them by restoring justice to the their descendants (McPherson, 2015). It may also be viewed as being akin to paying back "debt" or "back wages" to family members whose forbearers were not able to pass on wealth to their children because they were denied equal employment, equal pay (or any pay at all), or equal educational opportunity (Ladson-Billings, 2006). In contrast, not taking action to right a past wrong by allowing current systemic injustices to perpetuate that wrong adds on a second wrong; and two wrongs don't make a right.

> "In order to get beyond racism, we must first take account of race. And in order to treat persons equally, we must treat them differently."
> —JUSTICE HARRY BLACKMUN, FORMER ASSOCIATE JUSTICE OF THE UNITED STATES SUPREME COURT

Personal Experience

In professional sports, one reason for the salary cap is to ensure that all teams have equal opportunity to compete and to help maintain competitive balance among all teams by restricting wealthier clubs from using their wealth to dominate by signing all the best players. For a similar reason, teams that previously finished lower in the standings are given higher draft picks so they can access the best upcoming players, enabling them to pull themselves up in the standings and compete with already-winning teams. Thus, the American professional sports system has been intentionally designed to promote equity and equal opportunity for all teams to succeed. I wonder if other social systems could or should take a similar compensatory approach to ensure that all racial groups have equal opportunity to compete for socioeconomic success rather than allowing one already economically-advantaged group to use their advantage to maintain or further their dominance.

—Joe Cuseo

Blacks are more violent and criminally prone than whites. It is true that black males make up a disproportionate percentage of the incarcerated population. However, as documented in chapter 8, the vast majority of black arrests are for drug-related offenses (Alexander, 2020). Even among blacks living in "high-crime" inner-city ghettos, only about 3% are arrested for violent crimes (Eberhardt, 2019). Not only are more blacks are incarcerated for drug-related crimes than violent crimes—despite the fact that blacks are no more likely to use drugs as whites and are less likely to sell drugs than whites—and blacks convicted of drug offenses are sentenced to prison for almost the same amount of time (58.5 months) as whites sent to prison for violent offenses (61.7%)(Kendi, 2019).

It's important to keep in mind that someone can be convicted and labeled a felon for non-violent crimes, such as a property-related or drug-related crime. Among blacks charged with felonies, only one-quarter of them were charged with a felony that involved any kind of violence. It's true that 52% of those in prison today are incarcerated for violent offenses, but that statistic is misleading because prisoners jailed for violent crimes get longer prison sentences than nonviolent offenders. The fact is that the majority of America's

> "The general public seems to imagine that our prisons are filled with 'rapists' and 'murderers,' but they actually account for a small minority of our nation's prison population."
> —MICHELLE ALEXANDER, AUTHOR, *THE NEW JIM CROW: MASS INCARCERATION IN THE AGE OF COLORBLINDNESS*

prison population consists of different nonviolent offenders who rotate in and out for shorter periods of time (Alexander, 2020).

Furthermore, when violent black crimes are committed, they are more likely to be concentrated in low-income, inner-city ghettos where unemployment rates are extremely high. Studies have repeatedly shown that joblessness, not black genetic make-up or black culture, is the key factor associated with crime in these communities. In fact, when researchers account for racial differences in employment status, no difference is found between the violent crime rates between young black and white males (Wilson, 1997). As for the higher proportion of blacks incarcerated for drug-related crimes, much of this has to do with racial bias in policing, legal defense, and sentencing practices (see Chapter 8 for supporting research), and some of it has to do with research showing that when legal earning job opportunities are eliminated from overcrowded and racially segregated inner cities, illegitimate (illegal) income-earning opportunities emerge to replace them. One report on inner cities with high unemployment rates described it this way: "Under conditions where a gap in legitimate opportunity exists in the world, deviant occupations grow up to fill the void. The motif is one of survival; it is not based on thrill seeking" (Sugrue, 2005, p. 261). It should also be noted that about 33% of middle- and upper-income black families live in areas that border on severely disadvantaged neighborhoods—compared to 6% of whites in middle- and upper-income levels. Thus, even middle-class black youth live close to inner-city ghettos where there are more opportunities to get caught up in illegal activities (Rothstein, 2017).

> "We don't call crime that happens in white communities 'white-on-white' crime, even though the majority of crimes against white people are perpetrated by other white people. Communities with high poverty, fewer jobs, and less infrastructure are going to have higher crime, regardless of race."
> —IJEOMA OLUO, AUTHOR, *SO YOU WANT TO TALK ABOUT RACE*

Another way to look at and respond to the argument that blacks are more violent than whites is to look at racial violence from a historical perspective. After being forcefully transported to America and enslaved, blacks resisted the oppressive but "legal" system of slavery with revolts. Rather than viewing these black revolts as an understandable and justifiable reaction to the loss of liberty and brutality associated with slavery, blacks were depicted as violent criminals (Greene, 2016). After slavery was abolished, large numbers of former slaves were released without any property or employment opportunities in rural areas of the South and began migrating to Southern cities in search of employment. Rumors and fear then began to spread about a massive invasion of formerly enslaved and now-rebellious black males who were ready to rise up, attack white men, and rape their women (Alexander, 2020). The irony about these unfounded fears of black sexual violence is that it was whites who raped and sexually abused black women with regularity and impunity during the slavery period (Andrews, 2019). Even after slavery was abolished, sexual abuse of black females by white males continued into the Jim Crow era; in fact, black women's bodies were used as an acceptable sexual "training ground" for young white men (Wood, 1968).

White-on-black violence continued throughout the first-half of the 20th century when blacks attempted to live in white neighborhoods (Gilbert, 1985). White youth physically assaulted blacks and these assaults not only went unpunished, they were actually sanctioned by older members of the white community (Hirsch, 1998). White adults who forcefully resisted black integration typically did so by burning and vandalizing black homes and business properties (Sugrue, 2005).

Thus, a close look at history doesn't support the argument that blacks are a more violent race than whites; in fact, it could argued that the opposite is closer to the truth.

Too many blacks are on welfare; they need to take personal responsibility for self-improvement rather than depending on government handouts. The truth is that the majority of welfare recipients in the United States today are low-income whites. Low-income blacks are more visible because their poverty is concentrated in racially segregated, densely populated, and under-resourced ghettos. In contrast, white poverty tends to be spread out across different geographical areas that include better-resourced neighborhoods in where poor whites live among or nearby non-impoverished whites (Badger, 2015). For instance, in the New York metropolitan area, one study showed that 70% of the city's poor black and Hispanic residents were concentrated in high-poverty neighborhoods, whereas 70% of the city's poor white lived in non-poverty neighborhoods that are resourced with better job opportunities, schools, banks, and grocery stores (Beckett & Sasson, 2004). Research also consistently shows that welfare benefits do not encourage poor people to stay unemployed and unmotivated to seek work. In a 2020 study published by the Federal Reserve Bank of Chicago, it was found that recipients of unemployment benefits actually search for jobs at a higher rate than those who did not receive benefits (Faberman & Ismael, 2020).

It is true that unemployment rates among blacks are higher than they are for whites, but that difference cannot be simply and solely attributed to black dependency on welfare or poor work ethic; it has much to do with decades of systemic racism in employment opportunities and residential segregation practices. (See Chapter 7 for evidence.) These discriminatory practices have led to today's inner-city ghettos where poor black families live side-by-side with other poor black families and without resources available to poor white families living in neighborhoods that are better resourced because they are located closer to more affluent white families living in nearby neighborhoods. Sociologists refer to this additional aspect of black poverty associated with living in poorly resourced neighborhoods is referred to as the "double burden of poverty" (McNair et al., 2020).

The assumption is often made that the superior socioeconomic status whites hold today is entirely the result of what they have done for themselves (and by themselves), and black's lower socioeconomic status is the result of what they have failed to do for themselves (or have done to themselves)—that is to say, their higher rate of poverty and unemployment are due to their lack of initiative and effort. This assumption can be traced back to old racist arguments made by black slaveholders who justified the slavery system by claiming that blacks were lazier and more dependent than whites (Kendi, 2016). The truth is that the higher rate of poverty among people of color today is largely the result of a long history of racially discriminatory governmental income-support policies that favored whites, starting with the "headright" system that gave 50 acres of free land (confiscated from Native Americans) to all white males who were willing to leave England and come to Virginia to farm it (Wise, 2011). Similarly, after the Civil War, the U.S. government provided millions of dollars to white-owned railroad companies as part of a national effort to reconstruct the South; at the same time, the government declined to award just-freed blacks small plots of land on the large plantations they worked on and cultivated for decades as unpaid slaves (Foner, 2014).

Historically, first formal "welfare" program for low-income Americans began in the 1930s and was made available only to white women so they could stay home and raise children. In fact, this was the sole purpose of the program. When women of color began to access the same benefits, politicians then decided that the program would encourage laziness and out-of-wedlock childbirths—a belief contradicted by research that shows no such relationship; in fact, states with the most generous income-support programs actually have lower rates of out of-wedlock childbirth than states offering the lowest income support (Wise, 2011). Later came the New Deal, the GI Bill and federal subsidization of

"Americans have long been trained to see the deficiencies of people rather than policy. It's a pretty easy mistake to make: People are in our faces. Polices are distant. We are particularly poor at seeing the policies lurking behind the struggles of people."
—IBRAM X KENDI, AUTHOR, *HOW TO BE AN ANTIRACIST*

the suburbs, all of which were forms of government-sponsored welfare or "handouts" provided to white Americans that were denied to blacks. (See Chapter 7 for details.) Describing the scope and racial consequences of the 1944 GI Bill alone, Kendi (2016) notes:

> It was the most wide-ranging set of welfare benefits ever offered by the federal government in a single bill. More than 200,000 war veterans used the bill's benefits to buy a farm or start a business; 5 million purchased new homes; and almost 10 million went to college. Between 1944 and 1971, federal spending for former soldiers in this "model welfare system" totaled over $95 billion. As with the New Deal welfare programs, however, Black veterans faced discrimination that reduced or denied them the benefits. . . . The GI Bill gave birth to the White middle class and widened the economic gap between the races, a growing disparity racist blamed on poor Black fiscal habits (p. 358).

Because of these past forms of governmental programs that provided major fiscal support for whites to help advance their socioeconomic status, but were denied to blacks, Perry (2020) argues: "Policy must now work for Black people in the same way it has supported White people's efforts to lift themselves up. Bootstrapping, financial literacy, and other things we wrongly attribute to White success didn't save them from urban plight and rabid unemployment during and after the Great Depression. Federal housing, transportation, and employment policies did, and the U.S. government largely excluded Black people from those efforts" (pp. 21–22).

The fact that there are many successful black people proves that systemic racism is not an issue; unsuccessful blacks are just "playing the race card" and using racism as an excuse or crutch. Yes, there are successful blacks who have broken through racial barriers to become successful, but blacks who achieved success typically had to have more talent, exert more effort, and overcome more obstacles to achieve their success than successful whites. There's as an old saying that goes: "Blacks have to be twice as good and work twice hard to get half as far." Kendi (2019) describes the process as working this way: "It makes success attainable for even unexceptional Whites, while success, even moderate success, is usually reserved for extraordinary Black people" (p. 93). Thus, it cannot be automatically concluded that because individual blacks have not achieved the same level of socioeconomic success as whites, it's because blacks (as a group) are less hard-working than whites. That conclusion assumes that both groups had equal opportunities to succeed and equally high mountains to climb on the road to success. Extensive evidence of systemic racism across different societal systems (housing, education, employment, etc.) indicates that the opportunities and mountains experienced by blacks and whites have been, and still remain, unequal.

Surveys show that many white Americans acknowledge that blacks face longer odds and often have "two strikes against them," yet still believe that blacks use racism as a crutch or excuse for not being successful. Whites holding these somewhat contradictory views have been called the "ambivalent majority" because they seem to be saying two opposite things at the same time: the game has been rigged to favor whites, but that shouldn't stop blacks from winning (Entman & Rojecki, 2000). Some anti-racist scholars argue that this ambivalence may stem from highly publicized black achievements in America (e.g., recent elections of a black president and black vice president). While these exceptional

"The election of black man in the United States hardly speaks to the issue of racism facing 85 million people of color here. Individual success and accomplishment says little about larger institutional truth."

—TIM WISE, ANTI-RACIST ACTIVIST AND AUTHOR

and historic achievements are noteworthy and be celebrated, they are often used to reinforce the belief that it's lack of black initiative, not systemic racism, which is responsible for gaps in black–white success rates (Kendi, 2016). This argument was once used in a Supreme Court case by legislators in a Southern state who tried to prove that it wasn't necessary to provide more equal state funding to under-resourced black school districts by parading stories before the Court of black children who had excelled despite living in under-resourced school districts. Thurgood Marshall, the first black Supreme Court Justice, a member of the Court that heard the case, responded with the counterargument that if a child is "forced to attend an underfunded school with poorer physical facilities, less experienced teachers, larger classes" [compared to] "a school with substantially more funds, it is to the credit of the child not the State" (Anderson, 2016, p. 114). As Oluo (2019) reminds us: "The racial exceptionalism of people of color does not detract from, but instead adds to, the argument of racial inequality" (p. 17).

Colleges and universities are using education as a "political correctness" tool to advance their liberal agenda. A significant number of Americans believe that college professors impose their liberal political and social views on students rather than allowing students to think for themselves (Brewer, 2018; Parker, 2019). Yes, there are college professors with liberal leanings, as there are professors with conservative leanings, but professors are not advancing a liberal agenda as much as a factual agenda by providing college students with a more accurate and complete base of knowledge than that they were exposed to in high school. This includes knowledge of America's racial history that includes the minority perspectives and experience of people of color. As documented in Chapters 6–8, American history includes the history of racist policies and practices that spanned 250 years of enslavement, followed by sharecropping (indentured servitude), Jim Crow laws mandating residential and educational segregation, anti-black riots and lynchings, banning blacks from voting, jury service, and due process, and denying blacks equal wages or access to unions. These events have been typically under-reported or not reported at all in elementary and high school textbooks. At one time, colleges and universities failed to cover these events in the curriculum, didn't accept students from racial minority groups who were part of this history, and sponsored research by professors that aimed to prove the inferiority of minority racial groups (Karabel, 2005; Kendi, 2016; Zuberi, 2001).

Including this missing history is referred to as *historical revisionism*—revision of traditional depictions of history in light of additional, alternative, or missing evidence (Krasner, 2019). The need for historical revisionism is illustrated by Rothstein (2017), who reviewed a widely used high school textbook on American history (*United States History: Reconstruction to the Present*) that praises America's New Deal programs for helping Americans recover from the Great Depression, but fails to make any mention that black Americans were excluded from these very same programs. The high school history textbook also states that there was racial segregation in the North, but unlike the South, it wasn't by law but by "unwritten custom or tradition." The truth is that Northern segregation did not happen simply by "custom or tradition," it was officially written into official federal government policies that intentionally funded construction of racially segregated housing. Following his review of other textbooks widely used in the schools, Rothstein (2017) reached the following conclusion about how about they contribute to the denial of systemic racism that people exhibit today:

With very rare exceptions, textbook after textbook adopts the same mythology. If middle and high school students are being taught a false history, is it any wonder that they come to believe that African Americans are segregated only because they don't want to marry or because they prefer to live only among themselves? Is it any wonder that they grow up inclined think that programs to ameliorate ghetto conditions are simply undeserved handouts? (p. 200)

This is not to say that history traditionally taught in high school was totally inaccurate, but that it was certainly incomplete, particularly with respect to covering the cultural perspectives and experiences of minority groups. Shocking evidence of how incomplete this coverage has been is provided by the results of a 2021 national survey, which revealed 31% of Americans knew "nothing" about the infamous 1921 "*Tulsa Race* Massacre"—a momentous and horrendous event in which white mobs burnt down at least 1,250 black residences, churches, schools, and businesses in a 40-block area of Greenwood, Oklahoma, leaving 300 blacks killed and dumping their bodies into unmarked mass graves. It was not until 2020 that the massacre was finally added to the Oklahoma history school curriculum (Kaleem, 2021).

Reflection 9.4

In high school, did the topics of slavery and Jim Crow receive much coverage in your history textbooks or discussed in your history classes? If no, why do you think they weren't? If yes, what impact do you think their coverage had (if any) on students' understanding of, or empathy for African Americans?

The expression, "History is written by the victors" reflects the reality that the voices and perspectives of dominant or dominating are featured predominantly in history books while the voices and perspectives of the conquered or oppressed are left out. Revisionist history detects and corrects this discrepancy. This is not a form of "cancel culture"; it is an inclusion of cultures were cancelled. Nonetheless, critics claim that calling students' attention to racial oppression encourages them to be "unpatriotic." In fact, in 2020, a presidential commission was created for the explicit purpose of promoting "patriotic" education and downplaying America's involvement in slavery. Although the commission was disbanded because the president who formed it wasn't reelected, politicians in a variety of states have continued to pursue the issue. For example, one state governor proposed a three-million Patriotic Education Fund to combat what he criticizes as politicized "revisionist history" (DeMillo, 2021).

"Until lions have their historians, tales of the hunt shall always glorify the hunters."
—AN OLD AFRICAN PROVERB

If anti-racists who call out systemic racism caused by U.S. government policies can be accused of being unpatriotic and making excuses for blacks, systemic-racism deniers can be rightly accused of "blind patriotism" and making excuses for America's racist policies. And those who criticize revisionist history as an attempt by "woke" liberal professor to indoctrinate students with politically correct multiculturalism can equally be accused of continuing to allow students to be indoctrinated with conservative, politically correct (and blindly patriotic) monoculturalism. Similarly, those who label history lessons that include minority cultural perspectives as "PC" could equally be labeled "PC" for excluding honest discussion of the flaws in the policies and practices of national heroes covered in traditional American history textbooks. As Wise (2011) argues,

> The old fairy tale about George Washington cutting down the cherry tree and telling his dad because 'he couldn't tell a lie,' exists because no fabrications too extreme in the service of national self-love. Anything that makes us feel proud can be said, fact notwithstanding. Anything that reminds us of the not-so-noble pursuits of our forefathers or national heroes, on the other hand, gets dumped down the memory hole. And if you bring those kinds of things up, you'll be accused of hating America (p. 31).

Critics of historical revisionism may need to be reminded that being factually correct isn't being politically correct and that being patriotic doesn't mean romanticizing or sugar-coating our country's history, but truthfully acknowledging both its exceptional success stories and egregious mistakes. True patriots don't whitewash their nation's history; they reflect deeply on both "the bitter and the sweet" and strive to make the bitter better—to make it "a more perfect union" as suggested in a speech given by former U.S. President Barack Obama (National Constitution Center, 2008).

> "We can't just learn what we want to know, but what we should know . . . the good, the bad . . . everything. That's what great nations do. They come to terms with their dark sides."
> —JOE BIDEN, 46TH PRESIDENT OF THE UNITED STATES

Taking Collective Action to Combat Systemic Racism

Historically rooted and still lingering forms of racism in America's social institutions suggest that even if individuals do their best to be "race blind" and treat people in a non-discriminatory way on a person-by-person basis, it will not eliminate racial discrimination in American society because much of it takes place at institutional and systemic levels. Thus, for racism to be fully addressed, anti-racists not only need to change the racist thinking of racist individuals, they need to change policies that perpetuate racism on a societal level—that is to say, they need to take collective action to combat systemic racism (Perry, 2020). As Jardina (2019) notes, "Equality is achieved not merely by changing the negative attitudes whites direct at racial and ethnic minorities; instead, equality is realized by dismantling a system of racial stratification" (p. 180).

> "I was taught to recognize racism only in individual acts of meanness by members of my group, never as invisible systems. I was taught to think that racism could end if White individuals change their attitude. Individual acts can palliate but cannot end these problems."
> —PEGGY MCINTOSH, AUTHOR, *WHITE PRIVILEGE: UNPACKING THE INVISIBLE KNAPSACK*

Comprehensive anti-racism involves combating racism at multiple levels by using strategies that do not include personal persuasion (e.g., providing compelling arguments against persons who espouse racist ideas), but also support anti-racist litigation and legislation (e.g., supporting enactment of laws that promote racial equity) that dismantle systemic racism (Sugrue, 2005). As Oluo (2019) puts it: "When we look at racism simply as 'any racial prejudice,' we are entering into a battle to win over the hearts and minds of everyone—fighting only the symptoms of the cancerous system, not the cancer itself." (p. 39). Similarly, Kendi (2019) argues that when blacks combat white racism by concentrating "their hatred on everyday White people, as I did freshman year in college, they are not fighting racist power or racist policymakers, which means those policies are more likely to flourish" (p. 131).

> "Justice for black people cannot be achieved without radical changes in the structure of our society. The comfortable, the entrenched, the privileged cannot continue to tremble at the prospect of change in the status quo."
> —MARTIN LUTHER KING, JR.

American citizens who have benefited from a system of past and present governmental policies provided inequitable privileges to members of their own racial group, but denied those same privileges to members of other racial groups, have an obligation to use their privileged status to help redress these inequities (Wise, 2011). Research shows that anti-racist efforts which focus on combating racial prejudices held by individuals on a personal level are insufficient; they need to be augmented by efforts that focus on addressing racism on structural or institutional levels (Adams et al., 2008).

Described next are specific practices and action strategies combating systemic racism and advancing anti-racist policies. Many of these strategies and practices are political in nature but they should not be viewed and dismissed as simply "playing politics." The fact is that racist policies are in place because of politics—a long history of political actions and decisions; thus, changing racist political policies requires anti-racist political actions and decisions. In fact, history tells us that racist policies often have to be changed before racist attitudes are changed. For instance, greater white support for desegregated schools came after school-desegregation laws were adopted in the 1950s and 1960s; white support for interracial marriage began to rise after a policy change in 1967 that dismantled all state laws prohibiting interracial marriage; and overwhelming support for affordable health care emerged after passage of the 2010 Affordable Care Act—which reduced socio-economic inequities in health care across all racial groups (Goodnough et al., 2020).

Using the Electoral Process to Combat Systemic Racism

One of the most effective ways to exert collective action against system racism is by going to the ballot box and voting for political candidates at the local, state, and national levels who endorse policies that promote racial equity and voting against candidates whose proposed policies would serve to preserve or prolong racial inequities (Perry, 2020). Naturally, racial equity shouldn't be the only factor considered when voting for public officials, but any citizen who believes in upholding America's democratic principles and egalitarian ideals should give this factor considerable weight.

Give strong consideration to candidates and policies that:

- Increase the minimum wage and reduce the income gap between whites and people of color working in low-wage jobs
- Provide support for development of a transportation infrastructure that makes it possible for people of color living in the inner-city to access jobs in the suburbs
- Develop inclusionary housing practices that ensure affordable housing is available to people of color in new residential developments, and prohibit development of more single-family zoning housing that would result in further racial segregation
- Establish tax systems that discontinue to advantage already-wealthy Americans and further the gap in wealth between different racial groups
- Create school-funding formulas that increase fiscal support for inner-city schools, and bring it to a level comparable to the fiscal support supplied to schools in wealthier suburban communities
- Support a school curriculum infused with critical thinking about racism and how to combat it (e.g., critical race theory).
- Improve health care benefits in ways that would reduce racial gaps in access to health insurance and high-quality health care
- Reform law enforcement and incarceration practices to reduce racial inequities in the criminal justice system

- Establish social media guidelines and practices that minimize hate speech and hold hate groups accountable for disseminating race-based hate on the Internet

Electing Diverse Political Representatives

Voting for candidates based on their racial identity has been criticized by some as a form of "identity politics" that divides rather than unites different racial groups (O'Neill, 2015). However, if divisiveness already exists between different groups in terms of racial equity, one way to reduce it may be to elect candidates from racial groups that have experienced inequities because these candidates are likely to have a deeper appreciation of the nature and extent of these inequities, and may be better equipped to serve communities where their racial group is heavily represented (Oluo, 2019). As DiAngelo (2018) explains:

> The identities of those sitting at the table of power in this country have remained remarkably similar: white, male, middle- and upper-middle class. Acknowledging this fact may be dismissed as political correctness, but it is still a fact. The decisions made at those tables affect the lives of those not at the tables . . . Inequity can occur simply through homogeneity: if I am not aware of the barriers you face, then I won't see them, much less be motivated to remove them (p. xiii).

Reflection 9.5

If you were elected president of the United States, what executive action you would take first to reduce racial inequalities and racial tension in this country?

Joining, Donating to, or Volunteering for Anti-Racist Organizations

Albert Einstein, who was Jewish, came to America to escape anti-Semitism in Nazi Germany. He soon joined the NAACP and gave the following explanation for his decision to join: "The more I feel an American, the more this situation [racism] pains me. I can escape the feelings of my complicity in it only by speaking out" (Wilkerson, 2020, p. 379).

In addition to the NAACP (https://naacp.org), other major anti-racist and social justice organizations that can be joined or financially supported include: the Southern Poverty Law Center (SPLC) (https://www.splcenter.org), The Center for Community Change (https:communitychange.org), and the National Council for La Raza (express.nclr.org).

Engaging in Anti-Racist Allyship, Activism, or Protest

In a 2020 national survey, 76 percent of Americans reported that they considered racism and discrimination a "big problem"—up from 51 percent in 2015 (Serwer, 2020). This suggests that there is a growing pool of Americans who share common views on the existence of racism and can potentially join forces to do something about it. America has a long history of whites standing in solidarity with people of color to oppose racism, dating as far back as the late 1600s when the Mennonites—a religious group that moved to America to escape persecution in Europe—first engaged in anti-racist activism by circulating antislavery petitions, including one that stated: "There is a saying that we shall do to all men as we will be done ourselves, making no difference of what generation, descent or colour they are. In Europe there are many oppressed for their religion, and here those are oppressed for their black colour . . . [they have] 'the right to fight for their freedom'" (Kendi, 2016, p. 52). In 1776, both whites and blacks (both free an slaved) joined forces to fight in the American Revolution against Great Britain (Lindebaugh & Rediker, 2000), and in 1833, white and black abolitionists formed the American Anti-Slavery Society to activate and agitate for black emancipation, creating an "Underground Railroad" of secret routes through which blacks in slave states could travel to free states (Cross, 2010). These early abolitionists raised national awareness of the injustices of slavery that later supplied Union forces with a moral rationale for fighting the Civil War and a rationale supporting the passage of the first civil rights amendments to the U.S. Constitution after the war (Feagin, 2005).

"Congress shall make no law . . . abridging the freedom of speech, or of the press; or the right of the people peaceably to assemble, and to petition the Government for a redress of grievances."
—FIRST AMENDMENT OF THE UNITED STATES CONSTITUTION

In the 1960s, Martin Luther King Jr. organized series of peaceful protests and demonstrations that were joined by both blacks and whites alike. Just before his assassination in 1968, King organized a multiracial alliance, known as the Poor People's Campaign, to gain economic justice for all poor Americans. This interracial effort united blacks, whites, Asian Americans, Hispanic Americans, and Native Americans. A month after King's death, 3,000 people of different races and ethnicities set up a protest camp outside of Washington D.C., where they remained for six weeks.

Reflection 9.6

Would you be willing to engage in anti-racism protests? Do have friends who would willing to join you? If yes, why? If no, why not?

After the 2014 shooting death of Trayvon Martin, a black teenager who was mistakenly suspected of committing a crime, three black women started the "Black Lives Matter (BLM)" movement—a non-violent movement to protest racially biased law-enforcement practices. In 2016, BLN expanded into a national network of 30 chapters across the United States. In 2020, the movement gained national and international attention following protests over the death of Georg Floyd, a black man who expired under the knee of a Minneapolis police officer. People from all racial groups joined together in protests in all parts of the nation and around the world to protest the event and call attention to systemic racism in America's criminal justice system. Their protests led to changes in police accountability, policing policies, and reallocation of police funding in a number of cities. Contrary to the belief of some critics, 93% of these protests were peaceful (ACLED, 2021).

The historical record shows that deep, long-last changes in social justice have often often resulted from movements and protests (Bonilla-Silva et al., 2003; Piven, 2006); there are limits to what can be done through public debate and electoral politics alone (Feagin, 2000). Even social movements

In June, 2020, thousands of people of all races participated in a Black Lives Matter protest held in Washington, D.C. © Eli Wilson/Shutterstock.com

and protests that do not produce immediate change have been found to heighten national awareness of social justice issues that often sow the seeds for change that germinate at a later point in time (Haiven & Khasnabish, 2013). See **Box 9.1** for a summary of civil rights protests that have led to immediate and eventual changes in social justice.

"Critiquing racism is not activism. Changing minds is not activism. An activist produces power and policy change."

—IBRAM X. KENDI, *NEW YORK TIMES* BESTSELLING AUTHOR AND FOUNDING DIRECTOR OF THE ANTIRACIST RESEARCH & POLICY CENTER AT AMERICAN UNIVERSITY

Box 9.1   Civil Rights Protests That Led to Systemic Changes in Social Justice

1955: In Montgomery, Alabama, Rosa Parks was arrested for resisting racial segregation laws by refusing to yield her bus seat to a white passenger. Her resistance sparked civil rights leaders to organize a bus boycott in Montgomery, Alabama, where blacks—who made up 75% of the city's bus riders—boycotted the bus system by collaborating to use a variety of other forms of transportation to get to and from work. A year later, the U.S. Supreme Court ruled that segregated busing practices were unconstitutional.

1960: In Greensboro, North Carolina, "the Greensboro Four"—four black first-year college students at North Carolina A&T University—protested against racial segregation by taking seats at a "white only" Woolworth lunch counter. They were denied service, but remained seated and continued to come back for several more days and were eventually joined by hundreds of other blacks, including students from another local college and high school. As the sit-ins continued, other students began a broader boycott of stores with segregated lunch counters, causing sales at the boycotted stores to drop sharply that lead multiple stores in the city to eliminate their segregation policies. Their protest efforts also led to a series of similar sit-ins in other states that produced similar results.

"Those who profess to favor freedom, and yet deprecate agitation, are men who want crops without plowing up the ground. Power concedes nothing without a demand; it never has and it never will."

—FREDERICK DOUGLASS, ABOLITIONIST, STATESMAN, AUTHOR, AND FORMER SLAVE

1963: In Washington, D.C., more than 250,000 people gathered to participate in the "March on Washington for Jobs and Freedom." One year later, the Civil Rights Act was passed, which ended segregation in public places and prohibiting employment discrimination on the basis of race, color, religion, sex, or national origin.

1965: Martin Luther King, along with other civil rights activists, organized three marches from Selma, Alabama, to the state capital in Montgomery to protest governmental practices that blocked blacks from voting. In the first march, which came to be known as "Bloody Sunday," the peaceful protesters were attacked by police with tear gas and clubs as they attempted to cross the bridge to Montgomery.

A week later, President Lyndon B. Johnson offered protection from the National Guard for the protesters' next march to the state capital and promised to enact laws that would ensure black voting rights. Several months later, the Voting Rights Act was passed, which prohibited state and local government from implementing practices that blocked or interfered with black voting rights guaranteed by the 14th and 15th amendments of the U.S. Constitution.

2020: "Black Lives Matter (BLM)" protests against police brutality took place across the country and around the world. These interracial protests led to changes in policies relating to police accountability and use of excessive force.

The protests and movements summarized in **Box 9.1** illustrate how anti-racist activism is often a necessary and powerful tool for promoting ethical and enduring change in social systems. Anti-racist action taken collectively serves to multiply and magnify actions taken individually in a way that make systemic change more possible.

Chapter Summary and Highlights

Overcoming implicit personal biases and interacting with members of all racial groups in an open and appreciative manner are behaviors that characterize a non-racist; an anti-racist goes further by taking action against racism displayed by other individuals and social systems. Anti-racism is demonstrated by challenging racist remarks and microaggressions, countering common racist arguments with evidence-based counterarguments, and taking collective action with others to combat systemic racism.

Anti-racism can be implemented on a person-to-person basis by challenging racism displayed by other individuals. Here are some specific strategies for doing so.

Challenge others who deliver racist remarks and racial microaggressions. By saying or doing nothing when others make negative remarks about a certain race, particularly if they are made by friends or family members, we can avoid conflict by remaining silent, but our silence also sends the message that we agree with the person making the racist remark.

Use strategic interpersonal communication and human relations skills to reduce the risk that others react emotionally and defensively when you challenge their racist views. When the topic of white racism is raised with whites, they can get uncomfortable and react with denial or anger. The risk of this happening may be reduced by using effective communication and human relations strategies, such as the following.

Express anti-racist arguments *assertively*—not aggressively. When we're *assertive*, we make our point not in an angry or agitated manner but in a firm, even-tempered fashion. We get across our point in a less-threatening way by focusing less on calling out the person as a racist and more on calling attention to the person's racist action (e.g., "You may not be a racist, but what you just said qualifies as a racist comment.") Remember that the end goal is not to seek and separate people into racist and non-racist categories, but to change racist actions and ideologies that preserve and perpetuate racial inequalities.

Use "I" messages when challenging others' racist remarks. Instead of calling out a person by stating, "*You* are a racist" an "I message" would involve saying something like: "*I* consider what you just said to be a racist remark." An "I" messages is assertive but not aggressive because it's not aimed at the person, but focuses on your perception of the person's behavior. Someone can resent or deny making a racist comment, but it's much harder for that person to resent or deny your perception of their comment and how you felt about it.

Give the challenged person a chance to respond. You can give the person an opportunity to respond before fully challenging them by first asking questions like: "Why did you say that?" "Would have said that if a person of that race were present?" After acknowledging you heard their response, you can then explain why your complaint or concern is still justified.

Anti-racism can also be practiced by equipping yourself with an arsenal of knowledge that can deploy to counter racist arguments with historical truths, statistical evidence, and research findings. Here are common viewpoints held by people who hold racial biases and deny systemic racism, accompanied by evidence-based counterarguments that can be used to refute these viewpoints.

Slavery is over and constitutional amendments and civil rights laws are not in place that ensure blacks are not discriminated against. People making this argument should be reminded that after the Civil War ended slavery in the 1860s and after the Civil Rights Movement ended Jim Crow laws in the 1960s, hundreds of years of racial prejudice and discrimination weren't suddenly replaced by a colorblind society that provided with equal opportunity for all. Historical events and practices that took place well after slavery served to shape our current societal systems and continue to perpetuate systemic racism in housing, employment, education, health care, voting rights, and criminal justice.

I haven't discriminated against any member of another racial group, so why should I feel guilty about, or take responsibility for, past discrimination committed by others and that exist in current social systems. This argument assumes that racism refers only to individuals who consciously and intentionally engage in racial discrimination. This assumption is refuted by: (a) evidence of implicit bias—racial bias exhibited without deliberate intent or conscious awareness and (b) evidence that racial discrimination is not just something that takes place on a person-to-person basis, but takes place at a broader, systemic level involving societal institutions. Systemic racism is sustained not by individual intent but by the collective impact of racist systems and the complacency (and complicity) of individuals who allow those systems to remain in place.

I'm tired of hearing about "white privilege." I am white and not privileged; I've had to work hard to get where I am. "White privilege" refers to group advantages which whites take for granted that members of minority racial groups haven't been granted. It doesn't mean that whites have not experienced personal struggles and have had to overcome obstacles to get where they are; it means that that people of color have faced distinctive and disproportionate struggles related to their race that whites have not. Any right or privilege a racial group has obtained at the expense of a wrong done to another group is wrong. Anti-racists acknowledge that wrong and support polices or practices that attempt to right the wrong.

Racism would not be such an issue if people of color would stop being so "color conscious" and if whites would just be "color blind" and treat everyone the same. Even if blacks were to become less "race conscious" and whites would treat them in a "color blind" manner on a person-to-person basis, it would not eliminate racism that takes place on institutional and systemic levels. So, to say the problem of racism would go away if everyone would not see or care about color would be the equivalent of saying that they don't see or care about the consequences of color, including the consequences of systemic color-based discrimination on people of color.

There is now more "reverse discrimination" against whites than discrimination against people of color. This belief became to emerge after the Civil Rights movement of the 1960s when the government took action to reduce racial inequities in American society due to generations of systemic racial discrimination. These governmental efforts were were reframed by opposing white politicians as "unfair attempts to acquire unearned privileges." A similar argument is used today by those who vehemently oppose affirmative action. Opponents of affirmative action should be reminded that whites have been recipients of race-based governmental support programs throughout U.S. history that were denied to blacks (e.g., low-interest housing loans, unemployment insurance, and social security benefits). When those programs were in place, it would be accurate to say that affirmative action was for whites. Not taking action to right those past wrong and allowing current systemic injustices to perpetuate that past wrong adds another wrong and two wrongs don't make a right.

Blacks are more violent and criminally prone than whites. It is true that black males make up a disproportionate percentage of the incarcerated population; however, the vast majority of blacks in prison are there were for nonviolent drug-related offenses—despite the fact that blacks are no more likely to use drugs as whites and are less likely to sell drugs than whites. This speaks more to racial bias in the criminal justice system than it does to black proneness to criminality. When crimes are committed by blacks, they are more likely to be concentrated in low-income, inner-city ghettos where unemployment rates are extremely high. Studies have repeatedly shown that joblessness, not black genetic make-up or black culture, is the key factor associated with crime in these communities. In fact, when researchers account for black-white differences in employment status, no differences are found in violent crime rates between black and white males.

Too many blacks are on welfare; they need to take personal responsibility for improving themselves rather than depending on government handouts. The truth is that the majority of welfare recipients in the United States today are low-income whites. Low-income blacks are more visible because their poverty is concentrated in racially segregated, densely populated, and under-resourced ghettos. In contrast, white poverty tends to be spread out across different geographical areas that include better-resourced neighborhoods where poor whites live among or nearby non-impoverished whites. It is true that unemployment rates among blacks are higher than they are for whites, but that difference cannot be simply and solely attributed to blacks' dependency on welfare or their poor work ethic; it has much to do with decades of systemic racism in employment residential and residential segregation practices.

The fact that there are many successful black people proves that systemic racism is not an issue; unsuccessful blacks are just "playing the race card" and using racism as an excuse or crutch. Yes, there are successful blacks who have broken through racial barriers to become successful, but blacks who achieve typically need to exert more effort, have more talent, and overcome more obstacles to achieve success than do whites. There's as an old saying that goes: "Blacks have to be twice as good and work twice hard to get half as far." The fact remains that systemic racism across different societal systems (housing, education, employment, etc.) results in an uneven playing field where blacks experience fewer opportunities and more obstacles than whites in the race to achieve socioeconomic success.

Colleges and universities are using education as a "political correctness" tool to advance their liberal agenda. Professors accused of advancing a liberal agenda are actually advancing a factual agenda by providing college students with a more accurate and complete base of knowledge. This includes knowledge of America's racial history and the perspectives and experience of people of color that was likely missing from the curriculum covered during their earlier years in school. Covering this missing history is referred to as *historical revisionism*—revision of traditional depictions of history in light of additional, alternative, or missing evidence. The expression, "History is written by the victors" reflects the reality that the voices and perspectives of those who dominate and are dominant are the ones predominately are featured in history books, while the voices and perspectives of the conquered or oppressed are left out. Revisionist history is an attempt to call out and correct this discrepancy.

Historically rooted and still lingering forms of racism in America's social institutions suggest that even if individuals do their best to be "race blind" and treat people in a non-discriminatory way on a person-by-person basis, it will not eliminate racial discrimination because much of it takes place at institutional and systemic levels. Research shows that anti-racist efforts that focus on combating racial prejudices held by individuals on a personal level are insufficient; they need to be augmented by efforts that focus on addressing racism on structural or institutional levels, such as the following.

Use the Electoral Process to Combat Systemic Racism. One way to take collective action against system racism is by going to the ballot box and voting for political candidates at the local, state, and national levels who endorse policies that promote racial equity and by voting against candidates whose proposed policies serve to preserve or prolong existing racial inequities.

Electing Diverse Political Representatives. Voting for candidates based on their racial identity has been criticized by some as a form of "identity politics" that divides rather than unites different racial groups. However, if divisiveness already exists between different groups in terms of racial equity, one way to reduce it may be to elect candidates from racial groups that experience those inequities because these candidates are likely to have a deeper appreciation of them and may be better equipped to serve communities where their racial group is heavily represented.

Joining, Donating to, or Volunteering for Anti-Racist Organizations. Major anti-racist and social justice organizations that can be joined or financially supported include: the NAACP (https://naacp.org), the Southern Poverty Law Center (SPLC) (https://www.splcenter.org), the Center for Community Change (https:communitychange.org), and the National Council for La Raza (express.nclr.org).

Engaging in Anti-Racist Allyship, Activism, or Protest. There are limits to what can be done through public debate and electoral politics alone. History shows that deep, long-lasting changes in social justice are often made through movements and protests. Even social movements and protest that do not produce immediate change have been found to heighten national awareness of social justice issues that sow seeds for change that germinate at a later point in time.

Internet Resources

Anti-Racism Resources: https://www.ochumanrelations.org/anti-racism-resources/

Color of Change: https://colorofchange.org (the nation's largest online racial justice organization).

Fair Fight: https://fairfight.com/ (sign up at this site to join others in a concerted effort to fight voter suppression)

Fighting Racism in Education: https://www.americanprogress.org/issues/education-k-12/news/2020/07/08/487386/fighting-systemic-racism-k-12-education-helping-allies-move-keyboard-school-board/

Anti-Racist Parenting: https://www.peps.org/ParentResources/by-topic/anti-racist-resources-parents

References

Armed Conflict Location & Event Data Project. (2021). *A year of racial justice protests: Key trends in demonstrations supporting the BLM movement.* https://acledata.com/2021/05/25/a-year-of-racial-justice-protests-key-trends-in-demonstrations-supporting-the-BLM-movement/

Adams, G., Edkins, V., Lacka, D., Pickett, K., & Cheryan, S. (2008). Teaching about racism: Perniciaous implications of the standard portrayal. *Basic and Applied Social Psychology, 30,* 349–361.

Alexander, M. (2020). *The new Jim Crow: Mass incarceration in the age of colorblindness.* The New Press.

Anderson, C. (2016). *White rage: The unspoken truth about our racial divide.* Bloomsbury.

Andrews, W. L. (2019). *Slavery and class in the American South: A generation of slave narrative testimony 1840-1865.* Oxford University Press.

Badger, E. (2015, August 12). "Black poverty differs from white poverty." *Washington Post.* https://www.washingtonpost.com/news/wonk/wp/2015/08/12/black-poverty-differs-from-white-poverty

Banks, J. A. (2016). *Cultural diversity and education: Foundations, curriculum, and teaching* (6th ed.). Routledge.

Baron, R. A., Branscombe, N. R., & Byrne, D. R. (2008). *Social psychology* (12th ed.). Pearson.

Beckett, K., & Sasson, T. (2004). *The politics of injustice: Crime and punishment in America*. SAGE.

Benjaimin, R. (2009). *Searching for whitopia: An improbable journey to the heart of white America*. HarperCollins.

Bobo, L., Kluegel, H., & Smity, R. (1997). Laissez-faire racism: The crystallization of a kinder, gentler, antiblack ideology. In S. A. Tuch & J. Martin (Ed.), *Racial attitudes in the 1990s: Continuity and change* (pp. 15–42). Praeger.

Bonilla-Silva, E. (2018). *Racism without racists: Color-blind racism and the persistence of racial inequality in America* (5th ed.). Rowman & Littlefield.

Bonilla-Silva, E., Forman, T. A., Lewis, A. E., & Embrick, D. G. (2003). "It wasn't me!": How will race and racism work in the 21st century America. *Research in Political Sociology, 12*, 111–134.

Bowen, W. G., & Bok, D. (1998). *The shape of the river: Long-term consequence of considering race in college and university admissions*. Princeton University Press.

Brewer, S. (2018, September 17). *WGBH news national poll uncovers America's sentiments about higher education including perceptions about impact on society, race and college admissions and the value of a college degree*. https://www.wgbh.org/foundation/press/wgbs-news-national-poll-uncoversamerican-sentiments-about-higher-education-including-perceptions-about-impace-on-society-race-and-college-admissions-and-the-value-of-a-college-degree

Brooks, R. L. (1990). *Rethinking the American race problem*. University of California Press.

Cialdini, R. (2001). *Influence: Science and practice* (4th ed.). Allyn & Bacon.

Crandall, C. S., Eshleman, A., & O'Brien, L. (2002). Social norms and the expression and suppression of prejudice: The struggle for internalization. *Journal of Personality and Social Psychology, 82*(3), 359–378.

Cross, L.D. (2010). *The Underground Railroad: The long journey to freedom in Canada*. James Lorimer Limited Publishers.

DeMillo, A. (2021, February 9). GOP states weigh teaching race, slavery. *Los Angeles Times*, A5.

DiAngelo, R. (2018). *White fragility: Why it's so hard for white people to talk about racism*. Beacon Press.

Dixon, J., Durrheim, K., & Thomae, M. (2017). The principle-implementation gap in racial equality (and how to close it). *Advances in Political Psychology, 38*(1), 91–126.

Doane, A. W. (1997). Dominant group ethnic identify in the United States: The role of 'hidden' ethnicity in intergroup relations. *The Sociological Quarterly, 38*(3), 375–397.

Eagly, A., & Chaiken, S. (1995). Attitude strength, attitude structure and resistance to change. In R. Petty and J. Kosnik (Eds.), *Attitude strength* (pp. 413–432). Erlbaum.

East, P. D. (1960). *The Magnolia jungle: The life, times, and education of a Southern editor*. Simon and Schuster.

Eberhardt, J. L. (2019). *Biased: Uncovering the hidden prejudice that shapes what we see, think, and do*. Viking

Ebert, K. L. (2004). Demistifying color-blind ideology: Denying race, ignoring racial inequalities. In C. Herring, V. M. Keith, & H. D. Horton (Eds.), *Skin/deep: How race and complexion matter in the "color blind" era* (pp. 174–196). Institute on Race and Public Policy, University of Illinois at Chicago. University of Illinois Press.

Entman, R. M., & Rojecki, A. (2000). *The Black image in the White mind media and race in America*. University of Chicago Press.

Epstein, R. (2015, March 5). *"White history month" sign stirs up Flemington*. https://www.ameren.com/news/2015/03/white-history-month-sign-stirs-up-flemington/

Faberman, J., & Ismael, A. H. (2020). How do unemployment benefits relate to job search behavior? *Chicago Fed Letter*, No. 444. Federal Reserve Bank of Chicago. https://www.chicagofed.org/publications/Chicago-fed-letter/2020/441

Feagin, J. R. (2000). *Racist America: Roots, realities, and future reparations*. Routledge.

Feagin, J. (2005). *Systemic racism: A theory of oppression*. Routledge.

Feldman, S., & Huddy, L. (2005). Racial resentment and white opposition to race-conscious programs: Principles or prejudice? *American Journal of Political Science, 49*(1), 168–183.

Foner, E. (2014). *Reconstruction: America's unfinished revolution, 1863-1877*. HarperCollins.

Garces, L. M. (2020). The false notion of "race-neutrality": How legal battles in higher education undermine racial equity. *Change, 52*(2), 51–55.

Gilbert, J. (1985). *The cycle of outrage: America's reaction to the juvenile delinquent of the 1950s*. Oxford University Press.

Goleman, D. (2005). *Emotional intelligence: Why it can matter more than IQ*. Random House.

Gonyea, D. (2017, October 24). "Majority of white Americans say they believe whites face discrimination." *NPR*. https://www.npr.org/2017/10/24/559064836/majority-of-white-americans-think-theyre-discriminated-against

Goodnough, A., Abelson, R., Sanger-Katz, M., & Kliff, S. (2020, March 23). "Obamacare turns 10. Here's a look at what works and doesn't." *The New York Times*. https://we.archive.org/web/20200230105840/https:www.nytimes.com/2020/03/23/health/obamacare-aca-coverage-cost-history.html

Greene, L. G. (2016). *The negro in colonial New England*. Martino Fine Books.

Haiven, M., & Khasnabish, A. (2013). Between success and failure: Dwelling with social movements in the hiatus. *Interface: A Journal for and About Social Movements, 5*(2), 472–498.

Hirsch, A. R. (1998). *Making the second ghetto: Race and housing in Chicago 1940-1960*. The University of Chicago Press.

Hu, K. (2020, August 27). Affirmative action for rich white students. *Los Angeles Times*, 13.

Hurwitz, M. (2011). The impact of legacy status on undergraduate admissions at elite colleges and universities. *Economics of Education Review, 30*(3), 480–492.

Izaguirre, A. (2021, April 19). As America embrace early voting, GOP hurries to restrict it. *Los Angeles Times*. https://www.latimes.com/world-nation/story/2021-14-16/as-america-embraces-early-voting-gop-hurries-torestrict-it

Jardina, A. (2019). *White identity politics*. Cambridge University Press.

Kaleem, J. (2021, June 19). For many, 156th Juneteenth Is a first. *Los Angeles Times*, A-1.

Karabel, J. (2005). *The chosen: The hidden history of admission and exclusion at Harvard, Yale, and Princeton*. Houghton Mifflin.

Katznelson, I. (2005). *When affirmative action was white: An untold history of racial inequality in twentieth-century America*. W.W. Norton & Company.

Kendi, I. X. (2016). *Stamped from the beginning: The definitive history of racist ideas in America*. Bold Type Books.

Kendi, I. X. (2019). *How to be an antiracist*. One World.

Krasner, B. (Ed.). (2019). *Historical revisionism*. Current Controversies. Greenhaven Publishing.

Ladson-Billings, G. (2006). From the achievement gap to the education debt: Understanding achievement in U.S. schools. *Educational Researcher, 35*(7), 3–12.

Lindebaugh, P., & Rediker, M. (2000). *The many-headed hydra: Sailors, slaves, commoners, and the hidden history of the revolutionary Atlantic*. Beacon Press.

Lipsitz, G. (1998). *The possessive investment in whiteness: How white people profit from identity politics*. Temple Universe Press.

López, I. H. (2014). *Dog whistle politics: How coded racial appeals have reinvented racism & wrecked the middle class*. Oxford University Press.

McIntosh, P. (2012). White privilege and male privilege: A personal account of coming to see correspondence through work in women's studies. In M. Anderson & P. Hill (Eds.), *Race, class, and gender: An anthology* (pp. 94–105). Wadsworth.

McKay, M., Davis, M., & Fanning, P. (2009). *Messages: The communication skills book* (2nd ed.). New Harbinbger.

McNair, T. B., Bensimon, E. M., & Malcom-Piiquex, L. (2020). *From equity talk to equity walk: Expanding practitioner knowledge for racial justice in higher education*. John Wiley & Sons.

McPherson, L. K. (2015). Righting historical injustice in higher education. In H. Brighouse & M. McPherson (Eds.), *The aims of higher education: Problems of morality and justice* (pp. 113–134). University of Chicago Press.

Minnich, E. K. (2005). *Transforming knowledge* (2nd ed.) Temple University Press.

National Constitution Center. (2008). "A more perfect union: A virtual exhibit of Barack Obama's race speech at the Constitution Center on March 18, 2008." https://constitutioncenter.org/amore perfectunion/

Norton, M. I., & Sommers, S. R. (2011). Whites see racism as a zero-sum game that they are now losing. *Perspectives on Psychological Science, 6*(3), 215–218.

Oluo, I. (2019). *So you want to talk about race*. Seal Press.

O'Neill, B. (2015, February 15). Identity politics has created an army of vicious, narcissistic cowards. *The Spectator*. https://spectator.co.uk/article/identity-politics-has-created-an-army-of-vicious-cowards

Parker, K. (2019). *The growing partisan divide in views of higher education*. Pew Research Center. https://www.pewsocialtrends.org/essay/the-growing-partisan-divide-in-views-of- higher-education

Perry, A. M. (2020). *Know your price: Valuing black lives and property in America's cities*. Brookings Institution Press.

Picca, L. H., & Feagin, J. R. (2007). *Two-faced racism: Whites in the backstage and frontstage*. Routledge/Taylor & Francis Group.

Piven, F. F. (2006). *Challenging authority: How ordinary people change America*. Rowman & Littlefield.

Rothstein, R. (2017). *The color of law*. Liveright Publishing.

Serwer, A. (2020, October). The new reconstruction. *The Atlantic*. https://www.theatlantic.com/magazine/archive/2020/10/the-next-reconstruction/615475/

Stangor, C., Sechrist, G. B., & Jost, J. T. (2001). Changing racial beliefs by providing consensus information. *Personality and Social Psychology Bulletin, 27*, 484–494.

Sugrue, T. J. (2005). *The origins of the urban crisis: Race and inequity in postwar Detroit*. Princeton University Press.

Terry, R. W. (1981). The negative impact on white values. In B. P. Bowser & R. G. Hunt (Eds.), *Impacts of racism on white Americans* (pp. 119–151). SAGE.

Wicker, T. (1996). *Tragic failure*. Morrow.

Wilkerson, I. (2020). *Caste: The origins of our discontents*. Random House.

Wilson, W. J. (1997). *When work disappears: The world of the new urban poor*. Vintage Books.

Wise, T. (2011). *White like me: Reflection on race from a privileged son* (3rd ed.). Soft Skull Press.

Wood, F. G. (1968). *Black scare: The racist response to emancipation and reconstruction.* University of California Press.

Zagorin, E. (2014). Race-blind admissions are affirmative action for whites. *The American Prospect.* http://propspect.org/article/race-blind-admissions-are-affirmative-action-whites

Zinn, H. (2005, March 1). Changing minds, one at a time: What does it take to bring a turnaround in social consciousness. *The Progressive.* https://progressive.org/magazine/changing-minds-one-time-Zinn/

Zuberi, T. (2001). *Thicker than blood: How racial statistics lie.* University of Minnesota Press.

Reflections and Applications

Name

Date

9.1 Review the sidebar quotes contained in this chapter and select two that you think are particularly enlightening, meaningful, or inspirational. For each quote you selected, provide an explanation why you chose it.

9.2 Identify one action you could take to combat systemic racism in your:

(a) local community

(b) neighborhood schools

(c) place of work.

9.3 Do you think it is possible to dismantle systemic racism without also dismantling racial inequalities in income and wealth. If yes, how? If no, why not?

9.4 How do you think whites and people of color can most effectively team up as allies to combat:
    (a) racist attitudes and behaviors expressed by individuals?

    (b) systemic racism practiced by institutions and organizations?

9.5 In 2015, a white man taped a sign to the window of his business in New Jersey that read: "Celebrate Your White Heritage in March: White History Month." His sign generated controversy and criticism in the community. When asked about the sign by a local newspaper, the man offered the following explanation: "No matter what you are—Muslim, Jewish, black, white, gay, straight—you should be proud of what you are. I shouldn't have to feel bad about being white. If there's any racial discrimination going on, it's by the people who are objecting to the sign because I'm white. I just want to be included. Why is this such a big deal? I don't get it."

Sources: Epstein (2015); Jardina (2019)

Reflection Questions

   (a) Some residents in the community thought that this man's sign was racist. Would you agree or disagree? Why?

   (b) The man who hung the sign suggests that if there is any racism being displayed by the sign, it's anti-white discrimination displayed by the people who objected to his sign? Do you think his claim about being a victim of "reverse racism" has any merit? If yes, why? If no, why not?

9.6 When college students were asked about what they thought of affirmative action, one of them gave the following answer:

"I have a problem with it. You're gonna discriminate against a group and what happened in the past is horrible and it should never happen again, but I also think that to move forward you have to let go of the past and let go of what happened, you know? And it should really start equaling out 'cause I feel that some of it is going too far and it'll swing the other way. One group is going to be discriminated against. I don't believe in that. I don't think one group should have an advantage over another regardless of what happened in the past."

Source: Bonilla-Silva (2018)

Reflection Questions

    (a) Do you agree or disagree with this student's general position on affirmative action?

    (b) What arguments or evidence would you provide to justify your agreement or disagreement with the student's position?

Glossary of Diversity and Anti-Racism Terminology

AAPI: Asian and Pacific Islanders.

Ableism: prejudice displayed toward people who are disabled or handicapped (physically, mentally, or emotionally).

Achievement Gap: disparity in academic achievement levels between different ethnic and racial groups.

Affirmative Action: laws enacted to ensure equal opportunity for employment, education, and athletic participation among groups whose opportunities have been limited by past or current discrimination.

Ageism: prejudice or discrimination toward certain age groups, particularly the elderly.

Allyship: when a person of privilege works in solidarity and partnership with a less-privileged, marginalized group of people to help reform social systems that interfere with the marginalized group's basic rights, access to equal opportunities, and ability to thrive in society.

Alt-Right: racist group that supports white nationalism and actions taken to protect the white race.

American Indian or Alaska Native: people whose lineage may be traced to the original inhabitants of North and South America (including Central America) and who continue to maintain their tribal affiliation or attachment.

Anti-bias Curriculum: an educational process designed to promote understanding and fair treatment of different social groups (e.g., groups of different race, ethnicity, or gender).

Anti-racist: a person who takes an active role in opposing racism displayed by other individuals and societal systems.

Anti-racist Curriculum: a form of education that engages both educators and students in the process of detecting and dismantling racial discrimination in the classroom, school, and community.

Anti-Semitism: prejudice or discrimination directed at Jews and other people who practice the religion of Judaism.

Apartheid: an institutionalized system of "legal racism" supported by a nation's government. (Apartheid derives from a word in the Afrikaan language that "apartness.")

Asian: people whose lineage may be traced to the original inhabitants of the Far East, Southeast Asia, or the Indian subcontinent, which includes such countries as Cambodia, China, India, Japan, Korea, Malaysia, Pakistan, the Philippines, Thailand, and Vietnam.

Bias: a leaning toward viewing a social group either positively or negatively, based on inaccurate or incomplete information and which often takes place without conscious awareness.

Bisexual: a person who is sexually attracted to males and females.

Black (African American): Americans whose heritage can be traced to any of the black racial groups that occupied the continent of Africa.

Black Lives Matter (BLM): a movement formed to protest racially biased law-enforcement practices.

Blockbusting: a real-estate practice that involved buying property from whites in borderline black–white neighborhoods and then selling or renting those properties to black families at above-market prices.

Chauvinism: irrational belief in the superiority or dominance of one's own group, which is viewed as strong and virtuous and viewing other groups as weak or inferior.

Cisgender: persons whose gender identity matches the biological sex they were assigned at birth (as opposed to transgender persons).

Civil Rights: the rights to full legal, economic, and social equality, regardless of race, nationality, color, gender, age, religion, or disability.

Classism: prejudice or discrimination based on social class, particularly toward people of lower socioeconomic status.

Color-blind Racism: "race-neutral" policies that appear on the surface to be color-blind but have inequitable impact on people of color.

Colorism: a form or subset of racism that ascribes positive attributes and privileges to lighter-skinned people of color with more Anglo-like facial features.

Comparative Cultural Perspective: a reference point that positions people to see more clearly how their particular culture shaped who they are by comparing it to other cultures.

Critical Multiculturalism: an educational process in which students analyze power relationships and inequalities between different cultural groups.

Critical Race Theory (CRT): an academic field of study that examines how race and racism have been and continue to be embedded in institutional and systemic inequities; it focuses on critical thinking about race, not criticism of specific races or particular people based on their race.

Cross-cultural: experiences that take place in different cultures or between people from different cultures.

Cultural Appropriation: a process in which a dominant group incorporates into its culture something taken from the culture of people who have been systematically oppressed by the dominant group.

Cultural Competence: ability to effectively relate to, learn from, and collaborate with people of diverse cultural backgrounds.

Cultural Pluralism: a society in which the unique cultural identities, customs, and practices of smaller cultural groups are maintained and accepted by the larger, dominant culture.

Culturally Relevant Teaching (a.k.a. Culturally Responsive Pedagogy): instruction that is relevant and responsive to students from different cultural backgrounds.

Culture: a distinctive pattern of behaviors, beliefs, and values learned by a group of people who share the same social heritage, traditions and ways of living (e.g., their shared language, fashion, food, art, music, and spiritual beliefs).

Demagoguery: use of political arguments or practices to seek voter support by appealing to voters' emotions and prejudices rather than through rational arguments and viable policies.

Discrimination: unequal and unfair treatment of a person or group of people motivated by bias or prejudice.

Diversity: the variety of differences among people that comprise humanity (the human species).

Diversity Education: an educational process that empowers students to evaluate ideas in terms of their cultural validity and potential bias, and actively engages students in learning experiences that foster interaction among students from different cultural groups.

Domestic Diversity: cultural differences that exist within the same nation.

Domestic Terrorism: a form of terrorism in which terrorists target citizens of their own nation.

Empathy: sensitivity to the emotions and feelings of others.

Equality: treating people the same.

Equity: treating people fairly.

Essentializing: tendency to automatically assume that a specific member of a group possesses the same characteristics stereotypically associated with other members of that cultural group.

Ethnic Group (Ethnicity): a group with the same cultural characteristics, which have been learned through their shared social experiences.

Ethnocentrism: viewing one's own culture or ethnic group as "normal" or "superior" and viewing others as "deficient" or "inferior."

Familiarity Principle: tendency for people to view what's familiar to them as being "good" or better than what's unfamiliar.

Gay: a male sexually attracted to males.

Gender Dysphoria: a condition in which a person experiences discomfort or distress (e.g., depression) because of a mismatch between the person's gender identity and the biological sex assigned to that person at birth.

Gender Expression: how person's gender identity is expressed through behavior, clothing, haircut, or voice, which may or may not conform to behaviors and characteristics typically associated with being either masculine or feminine.

Gender-fluid: persons who do not identify themselves as having one particular gender identity, or whose gender identity fluctuates between male and female.

Gender Identity: a person's innermost concept of self as male, female, a blend of both, or neither.

Genderqueer (a.k.a. Non-binary): persons who do not identify as completely male or completely female; instead, they identify with both genders or neither gender.

Gendered Racism: when gender and race combine or intersect to create discrimination (e.g., black women with some college education make less than white women with only a high school degree).

Generation: a group or cohort of individuals born during the same historical period who, as a result of experiencing the same historical events, develop similar personal interests, values, and attitudes.

Generation 1.5: children of immigrants who have received part of their education in another country and another part in the United States.

Genocide: mass murdering of a particular ethnic or racial group motivated by prejudice.

Glass Ceiling: traditional, invisible discriminatory barriers that block women and racial or ethnic minorities from advancing in careers, regardless of their qualifications or prior achievements.

Group Polarization: tendency for an individual holding a particular point of view to become more extreme in that point of view after discussing it with a group of people holding similar views.

Groupthink: tendency for like-minded members of the same group not to challenge each other's ideas, which results in the group overlooking flaws or biases in their own thinking and making decisions that are inaccurate or incomplete.

Hate Crime: a criminal offense against a person or property motivated in whole or in part by the offender's bias against a race, religion, disability, sexual orientation, ethnicity, gender, or gender identity.

Hate Group: a social group or organization [whose] primary purpose is to promote animosity, hostility, and malice toward people belonging to a race, religion, disability, sexual orientation, or ethnicity/national origin that differs from their own.

Heterosexism: belief that heterosexuality is the only acceptable sexual orientation.

Historical Revisionism: revision of traditional presentations of history in light of additional, alternative, or missing evidence.

Homophobia: extreme fear or hatred of homosexuals.

Homophily: tendency for people to associate with others who are similar to themselves.

Homosocial Reproduction: tendency for employees who depart an organization to be replaced by hiring replacements whose characteristics (e.g., race and gender) are similar to the departing person or the person doing the hiring.

Humanity: universal aspects of the human experience shared by all people from all cultures.

Identity Politics: making political decisions based primarily or exclusively on how they impact a particular group (e.g., a racial group or gender group).

Illegal Immigrant: an alien (non-citizen) who has entered the United States without government permission or stayed beyond the termination date of a visa.

Implicit Bias: an unconscious (subconscious) bias held about a particular social group.

Inclusion: a process in which all social groups are recognized and included, ensuring that they feel included and their voices are heard—particularly members of groups that have been previously excluded or marginalized as "out groups."

Inclusive Pedagogy: a student-centered teaching process that motivates and engages learners from all cultural backgrounds by giving them a voice and equal opportunity to participate in the learning process.

Income Inequality Gap: gap between the amount of money earned by the richest and poorest members of a society.

Institutional Racism: racial discrimination rooted in organizational policies and practices that disadvantage certain racial groups (e.g., race-based discrimination in real estate and bank loans).

Intercultural Communication: communication between individuals from different cultures.

Intercultural Competence: ability to appreciate and learn from cultural differences and to interact effectively with people from diverse cultural backgrounds.

International Diversity: cultural differences that exist between different nations.

Intersectionality: when membership in two or more disadvantaged social groups (e.g., race and social class) intersect to exert a combined effect that further disadvantages people who hold joint membership in the intersecting groups.

Intersex: a term referring to a variety of conditions characterizing a person born with features of sexual anatomy that are not typically male or female (e.g., having the anatomy of one sex externally but a different sex internally, or having genitals that appear to be in-between male and female—such as a female with an enlarged clitoris or a male with an usually small penis).

Islamophobia: fear, hatred of, or prejudice against people who practice the religion of Islam, or Muslims in general, often because they are viewed as potential terrorists.

"Jim Crow" Laws: formal and informal laws to segregate blacks from whites following the abolition of slavery.

Jingoism: an extreme form of nationalism characterized by excessive interest and belief in the superiority of one's own nation (while failing to acknowledge its mistakes or weaknesses), often accompanied by an aggressive, self-serving foreign policy that ignores the needs of other nations or the common needs of all nations.

John Henryism: a term referring to the added effort that people of color must exert to overcome race-based obstacles to to compete equally with whites, which can often have negative impact on their physical and mental health. (Named after John Henry Martin, a steel-driving African American folk hero who worked hard enough to complete with a steam-powered machine, but died prematurely as result.)

Juneteenth: a term referring to June 19th, 1865, the date on which black Americans were emancipated from slavery; in 2021, June 19th was declared a national holiday to commemorate this historic event.

Latina: Hispanic female.

Latino: Hispanic male.

Latinx: a person of Latin American origin or descent as well as a gender-neutral way to refer to someone who is either Latina or Latino.

Lesbian: a female sexually attracted to females.

LGBTQ: an acronym for Lesbian, Gay, Bisexual, Transgender, and Queer or Questioning.

Mainstream Curriculum: the traditional, Eurocentric, male-centered curriculum that gives little or no attention to the perspectives and contributions of non-dominant, minority social and cultural groups.

Majority Group: a group whose membership accounts for more than one-half of the population.

Marginalization: viewing or treating a group as an insignificant or unimportant "out group."

Melting Pot: a metaphor for a society in which different cultures (such as the cultures brought to America by different immigrant groups) are expected to "melt away" or eliminate their separate cultural identities as they assimilate into the dominant culture.

Microaggression: indirect or subtle hostile messages aimed intentionally or unintentionally at a member of a marginalized group (e.g., asking someone a Hispanic American: "Where are you really from?").

Minority Group: a group whose membership accounts for less than one-half of the population.

Miscegenation Laws: laws that prohibit marriage, or even sexual relations, between members of different racial groups.

Misgender: referring to a transgender person with a pronoun that does not correctly represent the gender the person identifies with.

Multicultural: cultural differences that exist within the same society or nation (e.g., cultures associated with different racial and ethnic groups that co-exist in the United States).

Multicultural Curriculum: a curriculum that integrates diverse cultural perspectives into the traditional, mainstream curriculum.

Multiculturalism: a perspective that views cultural differences in a society as something that should be preserved and appreciated.

Multiracial Family: a family comprised of members from more than one race.

Native Citizen: a citizen of one's country by birth.

Native Hawaiian or Pacific Islander: people whose lineage may be traced to the original inhabitants of Hawaii, Guam, Samoa, and other Pacific Islands.

Nationalism: excessive interest and belief in the strengths of one's own nation without acknowledging its shortcomings.

Nativism: a political policy of preserving or advancing the interests of native citizens against those of immigrants, and opposing immigration based on fears that foreigners (particularly from non-European nations) will dilute or displace America's existing cultural norms and values.

Naturalized Citizen: a person born in another country who has lawfully become a citizen of the United States.

Non-Western Cultures: non-European cultures, such as Asian, African, Indian, Latin American, and Middle Eastern cultures.

Overrepresented Group: a group whose percentage (proportion) in a particular social category is higher than its percentage of the overall population. For example, the percentage of people of color in America that falls that into the social category of "low-income" is much higher than their percentage of the overall American population.

Own-race Bias: tendency for people to more accurately detect differences between the faces of individuals from their own race than individuals from other races.

Pluralistic Ignorance: tendency for members of different social groups to make incorrect assumptions about one another (e.g., two groups that incorrectly assume that members of another racial group do not want to interact with members of their own racial group).

Positionality: the idea that peoples' particular cultural background or position influences the knowledge they construct, create, and disseminate.

Political Correctness (a.k.a. "PC"): a term used to describe words and actions that a person intentionally uses to avoid offending disadvantaged social groups; the term is generally used in a sarcastic or derogatory way to imply that these words and actions are unnecessary or overindulgent.

Post-racial Society: belief that America has overcome has moved beyond racism to the point where racial discrimination no longer exists or is no longer a problem in society today.

Prejudice: negative bias (pre-judgment) about another group of people.

Privilege: an unearned advantage experienced by a group that is not experienced by another group.

Privileged Legacy: an unearned advantage handed down across generations, such as inheriting money or gaining admission to a college because a family member previously attended the college or donated to the college.

Queer: a general term that includes all members of a sexual-orientation or gender-identity group that is not heterosexual or cisgender.

Questioning: the process engaged in by people who may be unsure of, or uncomfortable about, identifying themselves as having a particular sexual orientation or gender identity.

Race: people who have been categorized into a social group on the basis of their physical characteristics, such as their skin color or facial features.

Racial Dog Whistles: coded racial language used by politicians to appeal to racist voters and block civil rights policies without appearing to be racist themselves.

Racial Profiling: using race as a basis for targeting someone as a crime suspect.

Racial Zoning Ordinances: laws prohibiting blacks from buying homes on blocks where whites are a majority.

Racism: belief that one's own racial group is superior to another racial group and expressing that belief in attitude (prejudice) or action (discrimination).

Redlining: the practice of marking red lines on a map to indicate neighborhoods where banks are not willing to invest or lend money, many of which are neighborhoods inhabited predominantly by African Americans and other people of color.

Regional Bias: prejudice or discrimination toward people based on the geographical region in which they are born and raised (e.g., Northerners who hold biased views of Southerners and vice versa).

Religious Bigotry (a.k.a. Religious Intolerance): denying the right of people to hold religious beliefs or to hold religious beliefs that differ from one's own.

Restrictive Covenants: written agreements among white homeowners in a neighborhood designed to maintain residential segregation by prohibiting sale or rental of property to blacks.

Reverse Racism (a.k.a. Reverse Discrimination): the idea that affirmative action and similar equity-promoting programs designed to redress racial inequality are forms of anti-white racism that disadvantage white people.

Scapegoating: blaming another person or social group for one's personal failures without evidence or justification.

Scientific Racism: attempts to support racist beliefs and justify racist political policies with alleged scientific evidence.

Segregation: the intentional decision made by a group to separate itself (socially or physically) from another group.

Selective Memory: the tendency for biased and prejudiced people to remember information that reinforces their point of view and forget information that contradicts it.

Selective Perception: tendency for biased and prejudiced people to see what supports their point of view while failing to see what contradicts it.

Self-Similarity Principle: tendency for people to associate and develop relationships with others whose backgrounds, beliefs, and interests are similar to their own.

Sexism: prejudice or discrimination toward others based on their sex or gender.

Slavery: a system of forced labor in which people are viewed as property, held against their will, and deprived of the right to earn income.

Social Capital: advantages and privileges afforded to people by virtue of who they know— for example, personal contacts with employers, college admissions officials, lawyers and politicians.

Social Identity: the social groups an individual identifies with, which shape or influence that person's identity.

Social Identity Theory: a psychological process in which people gain status by comparing their group with other groups and concluding that they belong to an "in group" that is superior to other "out groups."

Social Justice: the principle that opportunities for pursuing health, wealth, and well-being should be distributed equally to people from all social groups.

Socioeconomic Mobility: ability to move up the socioeconomic ladder (e.g., from poverty to the middle class).

Socioeconomic Status: the status of social groups based stratification of groups of people into social classes based on their level of education, income level, and occupational prestige of the jobs they hold.

Social Stratification: divisions of society into higher and lower layers (strata) or sub-groups based on their level of income, education, and occupational status.

Stereotype Threat: tendency for members of a group to perform more poorly on a task when others hold negative stereotypes about their group's ability to perform the task.

Stereotyping: viewing all (or virtually all) members of the same social group as having the same personal traits or characteristics.

Stigmatizing: ascribing inferior or unfavorable traits to members of a particular group.

Strategic Colorblindness: avoiding talking about race, or even acknowledging racial difference, to avoid being viewed as racist.

Strategic Racism: purposeful efforts to use racial animus as leverage to gain material wealth, political power, or heightened social standing.

Subordinate Group: a group with less power in society than the majority or dominant group.

Systemic Racism (a.k.a. Structural Racism): racial discrimination that pervades multiple institutions and societal systems.

Terrorism: unlawful use of violence and intimidation, especially against civilians, which is driven by political ideology.

Tokenism: a superficial or token attempt to appear being inclusive and committed to equity by including a very small number of people from an underrepresented group.

Transgender (a.k.a. Trans or Gender-Nonconforming): persons whose gender identity differs from the biological sex they were assigned at birth.

Transphobia: negative attitudes and feelings (e.g., fear, discomfort, or hostility) toward people who are transgender.

Uncle Tom: a derogatory term used to refer to a black man who is excessively subservient or submissive to whites. (The term was taken from a novel titled *Uncle Tom's Cabin* that included a character named Tom, a black man who displayed great deference and obedience to whites.

Underrepresented Group: a group represented in a social category at a percentage lower than their representation in the general (overall) population. For example, the percentage of women engineers is far less than the percentage of women in the general population.

Western Culture (Western Civilization): culture that originated in, or is associated with Europe.

White: people whose lineage may be traced to the original inhabitants of Europe, the Middle East, or North Africa.

White Flight (a.k.a. White Exodus): departure of large numbers of whites from neighborhoods that are becoming more racially integrated.

White Fragility: a state in which even a minimum amount of racial stress becomes intolerable to whites and triggers an assortment of defensive reactions.

White Genocide (a.k.a. "Replacement Theory"): a racist conspiracy theory that white people are being displaced by immigrants and people of color, with the secret assistance of prominent Jews.

White Identity Politics: people who support political officials and political policies that advance the self-interests and social status of whites.

White Privilege: group advantages that whites take for granted that members of minority racial groups are not granted.

White Supremacy: the view that whites are a genetically superior group and should maintain dominance over other racial groups or live in a whites-only society.

Woke: awareness of racial and social inequalities.

Working Poor: people who spend half the year or more working or looking for work but whose income level falls below the poverty line.

Xenophobia: extreme fear or hatred of foreigners, outsiders, or strangers.

Index

action, 133–134
awareness, 128–130
hiring, 205–206
model for overcoming, 128
Black Americans, 198, 245
Black defendants
majority of, 252
minority of, 252
Black History Month, 70
"Black Lives Matter (BLM)" movement, 300
Black migrants, 202–203, 218
majority of, 218
Blacks, 267, 291
arrest for vagrancy, 201
athletes, 173
codes, 201
constitutional rights, 210
convict population, 267
crimes, 292
culture, deficiencies of, 168
dying during police arrests, 265
employment, 203, 256
equality for, 206
ghettos, development of, 217–218
incarceration of, 262
inequitable and unethical medical experiments, 244
initiative, 295
minority of, 203
owned businesses, 200
pain tolerance, 244
pretrial detention rates for, 251
racial segregation of, 204
riots in Northern cities, 219–220
sexual violence, 292
slaveholders, 293
surveys of, 267
Tuskegee Experiment on, 245
unemployment rates of, 204, 293
Black voting rights, 246–247
suppressing, 247
Black–white differences in COVID infection, 245–246
Black–white employment gap, 204–205
Black–white wage gap, 199
Blind patriotism, 105, 296
BLM movement. *See* Black Lives Matter (BLM) movement
Blockbusting, 223
Block voting access, 249
Bloody Sunday, 247
Boas, Franz, 166
Body language, 139

Boogaloo Boys, 101
Burnett, Peter, 32

C

Career preparation, 77–78
"Caucasian" race, 210
Chicago Race Riot, 171
Chinese Americans, 40
Chinese Exclusion Act, 105
Civil rights, 177
convention, 46
Civil Rights Act, 32, 254, 289
Civil Rights Movement of the 1960s, 285, 289
Civil rights protests, 301–302
Classism, 104
Climate theory, 165
Co-curricular programs, 145
Cognitive bias, 109
Cognitive dissonance, 75, 287
Collaborative learning, 143
Color-based discrimination, 288–289
Color-blind racism, 288, 289
Color/colorism, 104, 178–181
consequences of, 288–289
Combat systemic racism
collective action to, 297–298
electoral process to, 298–299
Community Reinvestment Act in 1977, 213–214
Comparative perspective, 71
Complacency, collective impact of, 286
Comprehensive anti-racism, 297
Conviction, 252–253
Cooley, George, 130
Creative thinking, 75–76
Criminal aliens, 36
Criminal conduct, 252
Criminal justice system, 250, 285, 301
conviction and sentencing, 252–253
implicit racial bias, 264
incarceration, 253–254
on employment and income, 255–257
legal representation, 252
monitoring and arrest, 250–251
post-incarceration punishment, 254–255
pretrial detention, 251–252
racial inequities, 254
war on drugs, 258–263
Cross-cultural differences, 6
Cross-race facial identification errors, 110

Cross-stimulation effect, 75
Cultural/culture, 5, 30
    appropriation, 7
    competence, 133
        developing and demonstrating, 135–140
        stairway to, 134
    components of, 4
    diversity and, 3–4
    groups, 128–129, 143
    mainstream, 288
    perspectives, 75
    racism, 168–169
    sensitivity, 133

D

Daley, Richard, 209
Darker-skinned blacks, 179
Darwin, Charles, 166
Decision-making, 73–74
Defunding, 288
Deindustrialization, 203–204
Desirable residential characteristics, 210
Diamond, Jared, 44
Diamond, Richard, 249
DiAngelo, R., 164, 289
Discrimination, 94, 97–98, 104, 173, 201, 203
    causes of, 106
    forms of, 94
    group prejudice and, 78–79
    historic victims of, 291
    prejudice and, 32
    racial prejudice and, 282
    rationalizing, 111
Discriminatory covenants, 211
Discriminatory private real estate practices, 223
    blockbusting, 223
    predatory lending, 224
Divergent thinking, 75
Diverse groups, personal contact and interpersonal
    interaction with, 140–145
Diversity
    African Americans (Blacks), 37–39
    appreciating, 128, 130
    Asian Americans, 39–41
    cognitive benefits of, 74–75
    in college, 11
    and college experience, 13–14
    and culture, 3–4

definition and description, 2
    discussions of, 144
    educational benefits of, 70
        career preparation, 77–78
        creative thinking and problem-solving, 75–76
        group prejudice and discrimination, 78–79
        learning, 71–73
        preserves democracy, 79–80
        self-awareness and self-knowledge, 70–71
        social networks and builds emotional intelligence, 76
        think critically from multiple perspectives, 73–75
    ethnic diversity, 30–32
    gender diversity, women, 45–48
    generational diversity, 52–53
    Hispanic Americans (Latinos and Latinas or Latinx),
        34–36
    and humanity, 2, 7–10
    of immigrants, 41
    and individuality, 10–11
    Native Americans (American Indians), 32–33
    racial diversity, 26–29
    religious diversity, 51–52
    sexual-orientation and gender-identity diversity, 48–51
    socioeconomic diversity, 42–43
        socioeconomic mobility, 44–45
        widening income gap, 43–44
"Divide-and-conquer" belief, 164
Dog whistle, 165
Domestic diversity, 77
Double burden of poverty, 293
Douglass, Frederick, 179
Drug possession, 259–260
Drug-related crimes, 258, 291
    arrested and sentenced for, 261
    blacks incarcerated for, 292
    mandatory sentencing for, 260–261
    prison sentences for, 262
Drug trafficking, 262
Drug-using privileges, 251
Du Bois, W.E.B., 170

E

Eberhardt, J. L., 252, 286
Economic capital, 42
Economic disparity, 39
Economic exploitation, 159–161
Economic inequality, 231
Education/educational

forms of, 94
frequency of negative behavior, 110–111
"in" groups and "out" groups, 109
level of, 282–283
perceiving members of unfamiliar groups, 109–110
rationalizing, 111
selective perception and memory, 108
targets of, 96
Prejudicial attitudes, 285
Pretrial detention, 251–252, 252
Principle-implementation gap, 285
Privileged legacies, 98, 286
Privileged slave labor, 178
Problem-solving, 75–76
Property-related crimes, 291
Protests, 300–302, 301
Proud boys, 101
Public housing projects, 216–217
Public school system, 228

Q

Quality medical care, 244–246
Quilt metaphor, 9

R

Race/racial/racism, 105, 284, 288
  based employment discrimination, 256
  blind, 297
  classifications, 166
  conscious, 288
  conversations involving, 287
  current forms and varieties of, 173
    colorism, 178–181
    miscegenation laws, 176–178
    racial segregation, 173–176
  current racial gaps in employment, 204–205
  definition of, 158
  deindustrialization, 203–204
  demographics, 100
  differences, 289
    explanation for, 26
  disparities, 222, 244
  dog whistles, 165
  economic roots of, 159–160
  equity, policies that promote, 298
  gaps
    in health and longevity, 245
    in income and wealth, 200–202

"The Great Migration," 202–203
group, 245, 285–286, 287, 299
hiring bias, 205–206
historic victims of, 291
inequities, 291, 298
injustice, 286
integration, resistance to, 209
minorities, 41, 221, 226, 295
neutral, 289
oppression, 296
origins and root causes of, 158
  cultural racism, 168–169
  economic exploitation, 159–161
  political racism, 162
  religious racism, 168
  scientific racism, 165–167
  strategic racism, 163–165
origins of, 158
privilege, 286–287
specific forms of, 198
underlying psychological causes of, 169
  group bias, 169–170
  implicit racial bias, 170–171
  role of media in promoting racial bias, 171–173
violence, 292
wealth, 221–222
zoning ordinances, 209–210
Racial bias, 252, 253, 284, 292
  in police arrest practices, 265–268
  role of media in, 171–173
Racial discrimination, 98, 269, 286
  in housing, 214–215
Racial diversity, 13, 26–29
  growth of, 41–42
Racial groups, 31, 77, 297–298
  category, 27
  discriminated against members of, 286
Racially segregated suburbs, 215–216
Racial prejudice, 230
  and discrimination, 282
Racial profiling, 32, 105
  justification for, 250
  product of, 250
Racial segregation, 110, 173–176, 231
  in America's schools, 232–233
  federal government's role in promoting, 212
  policies for blacks, 214
Racist arguments, with evidence-based
  counterarguments, 284–297
Racist beliefs, 158, 164–165
Racist remarks, 282–284, 284

decades of, 293
denial of, 295
employment and income, 199
evidence of, 250
existence of, 284, 289
extensive evidence of, 294
forms of, 198, 230, 233
historical roots of, 198
K-12 educational system, 229
legal, 288
in residential segregation, 225
wealth, 199–200
System racism, 246

T

Taylor, Breonna, 259
Teeter-totter belief, 164
Terrorism, 106
"Tough on crime" rationale, 253–254
Traffic violations, 259–260
Tulsa Race Massacre, 160–161

U

Uncivilized non-Christian savages, 32
Unconscious biases, 129
Unemployment rates, 231
Urban employment, 204
Urban renewal projects, 218–221
Urban slums, development of, 217–218

V

Violent crimes, 291
Violent criminals, 292
Violent voter-suppression tactics, 247
Vocational training programs, 255
Voter-interference maneuvers, 247
Voter intimidation, 249
Vote-suppression policies, 249
Voting rights, 246–249, 285
Voting Rights Act, 247–248, 248, 254

W

Wages, 203
shared, 201
War on drugs, 165, 258–263
Washington, George, 159
Wave of counter-revolutionary terror, 266
Wealth
racial gaps in, 200–202
systemic racism, 199–200
"Welfare" program for low-income Americans, 293
White, 26
affirmative action for, 290
communities, black homes in, 208
flight, 224–225
fragility, 287–288
genocide, 106
neighborhoods, 208
non-impoverished, 293
privilege, 286, 290
race, 29
rates of poverty, 251
resistance to residential integration, 207–209
reverse discrimination against, 289
supremacy, 106
unemployment rates of, 204
victim, 253
Whitecapping, 201
White-collar crimes, 258–259
White Nationalists, 101
White-on-black violence, 292
White resistance, 207–209
to black integration, 207–208
Wilkerson, Isabel, 27, 29, 169, 202, 286
Wise, Tim, 169, 251, 297
Wlodkowski, R. J., 45, 71
Women's Civil Rights Movement, 45
Women's rights movement, 46

X

Xenophobia, 106

CPSIA information can be obtained
at www.ICGtesting.com
Printed in the USA
LVHW051319010422
714770LV00001B/1

9 781792 465765